Cambridge Middle East Library

The making of contemporary Algeria, 1830–1987

Cambridge Middle East Library

General Editor
ROGER OWEN

Editorial Board
EDMUND BURKE, SERIF MARDIN, WALID KAZZIHA, AVI SHLAIM, BASIM MUSALLAM

Medicine and power in Tunisia, 1780–1900
NANCY ELIZABETH GALLAGHER

Urban notables and Arab nationalism: the politics of Damascus, 1860–1920
PHILIP S. KHOURY

The Palestinian Liberation Organisation: people, power and politics
HELENA COBBAN

Egypt in the reign of Muhammad Alī
AFAF LUTFI AL-SAYYID MARSOT

Women in nineteenth-century Egypt
JUDITH E. TUCKER

Egyptian politics under Sadat
RAYMOND A. HINNEBUSCH

Nomads and settlers in Syria and Jordan, 1800–1980
NORMAN N. LEWIS

Islam and resistance in Afghanistan
OLIVIER ROY

The Imamate tradition of Oman
JOHN C. WILKINSON

King Abdullah, Britain and the making of Jordan
MARY C. WILSON

The Ottoman Empire and European capitalism, 1820–1913
ŞEVKET PAMUK

Merchants of Essaouira: urban society and imperialism in southwestern Morocco, 1844–1886
DANIEL J. SCHROETER

The birth of the Palestinian refugee problem, 1947–1949
BENNY MORRIS

Jordan in the 1967 war
SAMIR A. MUTAWI

War's other voices: women writers in the Lebanese civil war
MIRIAM COOKE

Colonising Egypt
TIMOTHY MITCHELL

Womanpower: the Arab debate on women at work
NADIA HIJAB

The making of contemporary Algeria, 1830–1987

Colonial upheavals and post-independence development

MAHFOUD BENNOUNE
UNIVERSITY OF ALGIERS

CAMBRIDGE UNIVERSITY PRESS
CAMBRIDGE
NEW YORK   NEW ROCHELLE   MELBOURNE   SYDNEY

PUBLISHED BY THE PRESS SYNDICATE OF THE UNIVERSITY OF CAMBRIDGE
The Pitt Building, Trumpington Street, Cambridge, United Kingdom

CAMBRIDGE UNIVERSITY PRESS
The Edinburgh Building, Cambridge CB2 2RU, UK
40 West 20th Street, New York NY 10011-4211, USA
477 Williamstown Road, Port Melbourne, VIC 3207, Australia
Ruiz de Alarcón 13, 28014 Madrid, Spain
Dock House, The Waterfront, Cape Town 8001, South Africa

http://www.cambridge.org

© Cambridge University Press 1988

This book is in copyright. Subject to statutory exception
and to the provisions of relevant collective licensing agreements,
no reproduction of any part may take place without
the written permission of Cambridge University Press.

First published 1988
Reprinted 1990
First paperback edition 2002

A catalogue record for this book is available from the British Library

Library of Congress Cataloguing in Publication data
Bennoune, Mahfound.
The making of contemporary Algeria, 1830–1987.
(Cambridge Middle East Library)
Includes index.
1. Algeria – Economic conditions – 1962–
2. Algeria – Economic policy.
3. Algeria – History – 1830–1962.
4. Algeria – History – 1962–
I. Title. II. Series.
HC815.B48   1988   338.965   87-33814

ISBN 0 521 30150 5 hardback
ISBN 0 521 52432 6 paperback

Contents

List of tables	*page* vi
Preface	x
List of abbreviations	xi
Introduction	1

PART I THE ALGERIAN PRE-COLONIAL SOCIO-ECONOMIC SYSTEM

1	Algerian society and economy before 1830	15

PART II THE UNEVEN DEVELOPMENT GENERATED BY COLONIALISM

2	The nature of colonialism	35
3	Colonial development, population and manpower	52
4	Socio-economic consequences of colonial development	60

PART III POST-INDEPENDENCE DEVELOPMENT

5	The aftermath of the war of national liberation	89
6	Industrialisation as the motor of development	114
7	The development of the private industrial sector	162
8	Agriculture: the stagnation of production and its consequences	176
9	Education and development	218
10	Post-independence urbanisation and the housing crisis	237
11	Public health since 1962	245
12	The growth of employment, income and consumption	252
13	The new economic policy and its implications	262
	Conclusion	303
	Notes	312
	Index	320

Tables

1.1	Political units in pre-colonial Algeria	page 18
2.1	French casualties in Algeria, 1830–51	42
2.2	The development of colonialism	48
2.3	Land transactions between the settlers and the Algerians	49
2.4	Transfer of land to the settlers, 1830–1951	50
3.1	Growth of the Algerian population	53
4.1	The process of pauperisation and proletarianisation of the rural population, 1901–60	61
4.2	Distribution of land between Algerians and settlers and among each national grouping, 1954	62
4.3	Distribution of agricultural income within Algerian rural society, 1955	62
4.4	The pattern of colonial agricultural production, 1910	64
4.5	Daily pay: a comparison between Algerian and European agricultural wages, 1913–30	65
4.6	The use of farm machinery by settlers and Algerians, 1930	66
4.7	The rate of economic growth contrasted with the rate of population growth, 1880–1950	70
4.8	The contribution of agricultural exports to total production, 1960	72
4.9	Urban daily wages, 1929	75
4.10	The structure of non-agricultural employment, 1954	75
4.11	Migratory movement between Algeria and France, 1947–55	78
5.1	The structure of the GDP, 1950–62	92
5.2	The structure of the GDP, 1963–5	103
5.3	Production of cereals and wine, 1956–65	108
6.1	Industrial investment under the second four-year plan (1974–7)	132
6.2	Industrial investment under the 1978 annual plan	135
6.3	The hydrocarbons development plan (1976–2005)	136
6.4	Annual added value produced by industry	142
6.5	Employment in the industrial public sector, 1967–78	143

List of tables

6.6	The increase in the production of certain basic Algerian industrial products, 1962–81	144
6.7	Production and growth of demand for categories of Algerian industrial products, 1967–78	146
6.8	Industrial units and numbers of workers under the control of the Ministries of Heavy and Light Industries and the Ministry of Energy and Petrochemical Industries	148
6.9	SONAREM's production, 1966–77	149
6.10	Hydrocarbons production, 1967–78	152
6.11	Petrochemicals production, 1973–6	154
6.12	SNS production, 1969–78	155
6.13	SONACOME's production, 1967–78 (some products)	158
7.1	The size, number and turnover of the private non-agricultural sectors in 1954	164
7.2	The concentration of wholesale trade, 1969	165
7.3	The geographical distribution of wholesale traders and their annual turnover, 1969	167
7.4	The number of private enterprises and the origins of the new industrial capital, 1954–71	168
7.5	The legal forms of private industrial firms, 1954–71	169
7.6	The total number of private industrial enterprises, 1969–77	170
7.7	The private sector in industrial employment, 1966–77	170
7.8	The private sector in construction and public works, 1969–77	171
7.9	The contribution of the private sector to the GDP, 1969–77 (excluding customs taxes on imports)	173
7.10	The contribution of the private sector in the formation of gross fixed capital, 1965–77	174
8.1	The structure of Algerian agriculture, 1978	177
8.2	The contribution of the three sectors to agricultural production, 1978–9	177
8.3	Agricultural potentialities and limits of Algeria, 1976	180
8.4	Man–land ratio, 1962–90	181
8.5	Principal characteristics of farming units in Algeria, 1968	186
8.6	Land ownership, 1965 and 1973	192
8.7	Agricultural investment during the three successive plans of development, 1967–77	194
8.8	Net agricultural investment within the national economy, 1967–79	195
8.9	Acquisition of farm equipment by the private sector, 1967–77	196

8.10	Acquisition of farm machinery and equipment, 1973–7	196
8.11	Consumption of insecticides, fungicides and herbicides by the self-managed sector, 1970–7	197
8.12	Utilisation of chemical fertiliser by the private sector, 1969–78	198
8.13	Distribution of fertiliser by the state to the three sectors of agriculture	199
8.14	The number of tractors owned by the three sectors, 1969–77	199
8.15	Imports of cattle, 1967–77	201
8.16	The growth of livestock breeding on self-managed farms, 1967–77	201
8.17	Livestock in the private sector, 1967–79	202
8.18	Irrigated crops in the private agricultural sector, 1966–79	203
8.19	Sectoral distribution of irrigated areas, 1976	204
8.20	Basic irrigated crops of Algeria, 1976	205
8.21	Objectives and fulfilled targets of the second four-year plan in the protection and restoration of soil by sector, 1974–7	207
8.22	Areas reforested, 1963–8	207
8.23	Minimum wages, 1963–78	209
8.24	The number of agronomists and technicians qualifying, 1967–77	210
8.25	The structure of agricultural employment, 1966–77	211
8.26	Vegetable production, 1967–78	213
8.27	Annual average production of fruits, dates and olives, 1967–77	215
8.28	Annual average imports and exports of foodstuffs, 1966–77	216
8.29	Growth of household income, 1969–79	217
9.1	Geographical distribution of illiteracy, 1966	220
9.2	Pupil enrolment in primary education, 1966–78	225
9.3	Secondary school pupils, 1966–78	225
9.4	Algerian teachers in middle and high schools, 1967–78	226
9.5	Pass rates in various examinations, 1978–9	227
9.6	The growing shortage of manpower, 1970–7	233
10.1	Classification of migrants according to date of arrival in Algiers and type of family	240
10.2	Types of housing and family structure	241
11.1	Medical infrastructure, 1962–79	247
11.2	The number of doctors, pharmacists and dentists, 1962–79	248

List of tables

11.3	The concentration of doctors in the major cities during the mid 1970s	250
12.1	Non-agricultural employment, 1967–77	253
12.2	Income patterns, 1967–78	253
12.3	The growth of total wages and salaries, employment and the wage rate, 1977/67	255
12.4	The growth of disposable income, 1967–77	256
12.5	The distribution of annual income in the major cities, 1968–76	257
12.6	Income distribution, 1977	257
12.7	Comparison of average annual urban and rural income, 1973 and 1977	258
12.8	The consumption of basic foodstuffs, 1938–79	259
12.9	Women in employment, 1966–82	260
13.1	The new structure of national enterprises, 1984–5	264
13.2	The number of new public enterprises at the *wilayate* level, August 1985	265
13.3	The projected investment structure of the first five-year plan (1980–4)	277
13.4	The structure of the GDP, 1979–84	280
13.5	The sectoral growth of the GDP, 1979–84	280
13.6	The production of hydrocarbons, 1979–84	282
13.7	Imports, 1979–84	285
13.8	The creation of jobs in the non-agricultural sectors, 1980–4	286
13.9	The employment structure, 1979–84	287
13.10	The programme of national investment during the second five-year plan (1985–9)	292
13.11	Manpower balance sheet: 1986–99	296
13.12	Total value of the annual consumption of households, 1987–99	297
13.13	Sectoral allocation of investment, 1988–99	299

Preface

The book I present here to English readers expresses not only an insider's but also a participant's views, interpretations and perceptions of the historical events and processes that came to shape the development of contemporary Algeria.

I am very grateful to Albert Hourani, whose idea this book was, for his stimulating remarks and questions; his support and encouragement have sustained my efforts throughout its preparation. I should also like to thank Dr Roger Owen for his valuable suggestions and editorial assistance and Elizabeth Wetton for her help and understanding over technical matters. I also thank many Algerian friends and colleagues, too numerous to mention here, for their moral support and intellectual stimulation. Finally, I would like to express my deepest gratitude and appreciation to my wife, Dorothy, to my mother-in-law, Elizabeth Sutton, to my daughter, Karima and my son, Kamal; without their patience, moral support and material assistance this study would not have been completed.

However, I alone am responsible for all errors and shortcomings in this work.

Algiers
September 1987

Abbreviations

AD	Algerian dinar (created in 1964 and defined as one French franc)
ALN	National Liberation Army
ANP	National popular army
APC	Assemblées Populaires Communales
APW	Assemblées Populaires des Wilayates
BCA	Central Bank of Algeria
BNA	Banque Nationale d'Algérie
BNBV	Bureau Nationale des Biens Vacants
CAD	Algerian Bank of Development
CAEC	Coopératives d'Exploitation en Commun
CAPCS	Coopérative Agricole Polyvalent de Commercialisation et de Service
CAPER	Caisse d'Accession à la propriété et à l'Exploitation Rurale
CAPRA	Agricultural co-operatives of the agrarian revolution
CNRA	National Council of the Agrarian Revolution
COFEL	Coopératives des Fruits et Légumes
CORA	Coopérative de l'Office de la Réforme Agraire
CORE	Coopérative d'Ecoulement
ENA	North African Star
FLN	National Liberation Front
FNRA	National Funds of the Algerian Revolution
GEP	Groupements d'Entraide Paysanne
GI	Groupements d'Indivisaires
GMV	Groupings of land reclamation
GPMV	Groupements Pré-coopératifs de Mise en Valeur
GPRA	Provisional government of the Algerian Republic
MARA	Ministry of Agriculture and Agrarian Reform
MTLD	Movement for the Triumph of Democratic Liberties
OAIC	Office Algérien Interprofessionel des Céréales
OFLA	Marketing board for Algerian fruit and vegetables
ONAC	Office National Algérien de Commercialisation des Céréales

List of abbreviations

ONAMA	Office National d'Approvisionnement en Matériel Agricole
ONCV	Office National de Commercialisation du Vin
ONRA	Office National de la Réforme Agraire
PPA	Algerian Popular Party
SAP	Société Agricole de Prévoyance
SNS	National steel company
SONACOME	Société Nationale de Constructions Mécaniques
SONATRACH	National oil company
UGTA	Union Générale des Travailleurs Algériens
UNFA	National Union of Algerian Women
UNJA	National Union of Algerian Youth
UNPA	National Union of Algerian Peasants

Introduction

This is a study of Algerian development and underdevelopment, and particularly of socio-economic change under both colonial and post-independence conditions. In order to comprehend the nature and extent of the transformations during these two periods, I have studied the pre-1830 socio-political and economic institutions and patterns. Indeed, since such consecutive historical phenomena are structurally and causally interconnected, I could not analyse them in isolation from one another. To do so would have risked providing only partial explanations to a highly complex and multi-layered socio-economic and political reality in constant movement and change. To quote Albion Small: 'conditions are what they are, events occur as they do, because, a long chain of antecedent conditions and occurrences has set the stage and furnished the motives'.[1] Indeed, contrary to erroneous leftist voluntarism, it is a well-established fact that 'men make their own history, but they do not make it under circumstances chosen by themselves, but under circumstances directly encountered, given and transmitted from the past'.[2]

A study of the making of contemporary Algeria therefore requires a diachronic analysis. In the words of André Gunder-Frank, 'the essence of concrete and real history is a diachronical interaction between the structure of change and the change of structure'.[3] Again, according to Anthony Smith

> change consists in temporal, event-referring, motion of spatial patterns resulting in clear difference from the preceding pattern (or state of patterns), (socioeconomic) change is pre-eminently historical in nature, . . . it is essentially concerned with sequence of events and movement in space and time; and hence . . . change cannot be studied apart from the historical record, which indeed must form the starting point of every investigation in this field.[4]

In attempting to reconstruct analytically the three consecutive socio-economic systems which prevailed in pre-conquest, colonial and post-independence Algeria, I came to realise that, despite disruptive upheavals and apparent historical discontinuities, these superimposed structures not only preconditioned and shaped one another to a certain degree, but also

Introduction

continued to influence the course of contemporary Algerian political, social and economic history. In other words, the nature of French colonialism cannot be comprehended without an analysis of pre-1830 Algerian society and economy.

Several scholars had tried to explain the nature of the pre-1830 socio-economic system. For Samir Amin Maghrebi society was characterised by a dominant 'tributary mode of production'.[5] But, according to René Gallissot, it was a semi-feudal mode of production (*féodalité de commandement*) that prevailed in pre-colonial Algeria.[6] However, these two authors failed to identify the specific features characterising this socio-economic organisation.

Abdelatif Benachenhou[7] attempted to demonstrate the co-existence of a statist tributary system and a communal socio-economic organisation. The latter appeared to him to be more important than the former. According to him the relationship between these two systems mediated by the capacity of the state to levy tribute from the producers was weak and instable. They were articulated by a dominant–dependent relation which was very fragile, as was demonstrated on the one hand by the 'slow development of colonialism' and on the other by 'the capacity of resistance of the communal system'.

This analysis highlighted the mode of production prevalent before 1830. It accorded more importance to the understanding of the working of the communal economic system, which constituted the essential object of colonisation to which it owed its advances as well as its limits. In this communal system the acquisition of the main means of production (land) was almost impossible through the medium of money, because its 'reproduction' excluded the individual or collective sale. In other words, land was not considered to be a mere commodity that could be bought and sold in the market place. The system of land tenure determined the inalienable nature of land. 'This economic system was subjected only temporarily and in a very unstable fashion to the statist tributary economic system.' This unstable domination was, according to Benachenhou, responsible for the fact that the dominant ruling class, which consisted mainly of a small Turkish and Turkified group, was unable to exercise a total and efficient control over the means of production. Nevertheless, this situation did not mean that the ruling group did not have an economic basis. However, its subjection and elimination as a political class by the French invading army did not, in fact, open the way to the colonisation of the means of production of the communal system.

My approach to the study of the pre-1830 socio-economic structures and patterns and their connections and articulations with the central state system differs from the reductionist 'economism' of these three authors.[8]

Introduction

Since the economic system was inextricably embedded in the socio-political organisation, we should give them equal importance by analysing them in terms of the theory of segmentarity. Indeed, pre-colonial Algerian society was made up of various autonomous and semi-independent socio-economic segments that were loosely and differentially integrated into a central segmentary state system. In order to comprehend the functioning and inter-relationships of what Benachenhou had dichotomised into a statist tributary system and a communal system we must undertake a concrete empirical analysis of the multi-various structural units making up a highly segmentary socio-political and economic order.

However, despite their segmentary nature, the capacity of the Algerian rural collectivities to resist foreign military encroachments is a well-established historical fact. Although efficiency and military discipline had distinguished the French army since the revolution of 1789, which 'discovered or invented total war: the total mobilisation of a nation's resources through conscription, rationing, and a rigidly controlled war economy, and virtual abolition . . . of the distinction between soldiers and civilians',[9] the Algerian rural population transformed the colonial conquest into a protracted and devastating war. In the words of the Egyptian economist S. Amin,

The collapse of the regency government and the war of extermination undertaken by the French army gave this early period (1830–1884) certain special characteristics, which are not found elsewhere . . . faced with military power, the urban ruling class was thrown into thorough disarray and could think of no other alternative but flight . . . As for the peasants, flight was out of the question. Faced with the threat of extermination, they turned the Algerian countryside into the terrain for a fifty-years war which claimed millions of victims.[10]

Besides the military and political ramifications of this conquest, the introduction of capitalism, in its colonial form, involved the destruction of the pre-1830 socio-economic structures and patterns. This destruction was accompanied by a coercive restructuring of Algerian society along capitalist lines, resulting in the pauperisation and proletarianisation of the rural population and the development of a colonial agrarian capitalism.

The process of capital accumulation in colonial Algeria was marked by three successive stages. The 1830–80 period saw the emergence and slow development of a colonial capitalism which was seriously thwarted by the resistive and elastic nature of the endogenous socio-political organisation; it was also hampered by the inadequacy and incoherence of French agrarian, commercial and financial policies. The primitive accumulation of capital took place during this period, which coincided with the consolidation of industrial capitalism in France. The second stage extended from 1881 to

Introduction

1930. Basic economic indicators reveal that the social process of capital accumulation associated with mature capitalism has become dominant. Indeed, despite recurring crises, the growth of exports, the employment of the labour force and the expansion of commercial transactions become important features of the Algerian colonial economy.

The last stage of capital accumulation under colonial conditions, which covered the 1931–54 period, was characterised by the stagnation of agricultural production and slow industrial growth. During the Second World War and the occupation of France by the German army, an industrial policy of import-substitution resulted in the installation of a few factories, specialising in the production of consumer goods. However, as soon as the war was over, most of them either went bankrupt or were shut down by their metropolitan owners. Thus, the unwillingness of the French to industrialise their colony, coupled with the conservative nature of colonial agrarian capitalism, had caused the decline of capital accumulation.

In sum, colonisation ushered in a double-contradictory process of uneven and 'extraverted' development. In other words, not only was the development of the colonial sectors made possible by the underdevelopment of the autochthonous traditional sectors, but that development was also geared to the extraction and/or cultivation of mineral and vegetal raw materials for export to the French metropolis. Thus, capital accumulation under colonial conditions stimulated the growth of the latter and the decay and disintegration of the former. This state of affairs resulted in the pauperisation and proletarianisation of a growing number of the Algerian population. The logic and exigencies of the colonial system were thus bound to generate a severe socio-economic crisis which accentuated the political antagonism between the colonised and the colonisers. Indeed, the crisis of capital accumulation and its consequences coincided with the ascendancy of Algerian populist nationalism. In other words, the nature and degree of French colonisation had conditioned and even moulded the form, intensity and consequences of the struggle for independence carried out by the most radical nationalist movement. This movement was known between 1926 and 1937 as the North African Star (ENA); between 1937 and 1946 as the Algerian People's Party (PPA); and between 1946 and 1954 as the Movement for the Triumph of Democratic Liberties (MTLD), whose consequent militants established the FLN and the ALN, which waged the war against the colonial power between 1954 and 1962.

By 1962 Algeria had wrested its independence from France after an eight-year war of national liberation. Most of the countryside had been devastated; the French settlers, who had controlled the public administration and managed the economy, fled to Europe. The basic activities of the new nation were almost at a standstill.

The situation was worsened by a severe political crisis within the National Liberation Front (FLN) and the National Liberation Army (ALN). Upon the proclamation of the cease-fire on 19 March 1962, which followed the signing of the Evian agreements concluded between the provisional government of the Algerian Republic (GPRA) and the French government, a struggle for power broke out between the leaders of the FLN and the ALN.

The tragic events of the summer of 1962 were precipitated by what amounted to a coup d'état perpetrated by Ahmed Ben Bella, one of the Vice-Presidents of the GPRA, at the instigation of the putschist officers of the external ALN headed by Houari Boumedienne, against a historically legitimate provisional government. This legitimacy resulted from the fact that the principal leaders of the GPRA had just led the country to independence under extremely difficult wartime conditions. This *coup d'état* had not only discouraged the majority of the people, particularly the hard-core militants of the interior who supported all the weight of the war, but had also paved the way for the ascendancy and consolidation of a conglomerate of anti-national, anti-popular and anti-socialist class forces. Their narrow economic interests and ideological archaism made them in the long run insuperable obstacles to the construction of an independent socialist society and economy, geared to the satisfaction of the needs of the popular strata.

However, in the short run, confronted with a vacuum, the Algerian workers, with the assistance of the trade unions, set up self-management committees in the agricultural, industrial and even service sectors, in order to keep production going. Thus, the first regime of independent Algeria (1962–5) came to be associated with the so-called movement of self-management. However, workers' self-management involved only agricultural estates, industrial firms and commerical companies left idle by the departed settlers; national private interests and the local subsidiaries of multinational companies remained untouched. The lack of a coherent economic policy and the absence of experienced skilled manpower resulted in a serious economic and social crisis whose immediate consequence was the second *coup d'état* of 1965, perpetuated by Boumedienne, Ben Bella's Vice-President and Minister of National Defence, and his group, which consisted of the officers of the ALN stationed in Tunisia and Morocco during the war.

The economic and political disorder created by the departure of the settlers and accentuated by the incapacity of the first regime to formulate an adequate policy of development made this second *coup d'état* inevitable. The immediate task of the second regime (1965–78) was to construct a strong state, capable of developing the country and hence creating the conditions for the restructuring of Algerian society.

Introduction

At this time there were at least three political forces representing conflicting interests. The majority of the so-called revolutionary council advocated what may be called a *comprador* development; that is, they were willing to let a new breed of middlemen (*compradors*) – who were anxious to become the local representatives of multinational companies – play an important role in the development of the country. A small nationalist-populist group pushed for a so-called non-capitalist path, which implied the nationalisation of foreign interests and the establishment of public companies. A left-wing minority, represented mostly by the Algerian Communist Party, preferred a socialist development. President Boumedienne arbitrated in favour of the nationalist-populist approach and instructed his Minister of Industry and Energy to prepare for the gradual nationalisation of all foreign interests in the country, and to formulate a strategy of development based on industrialisation.

The problematics of this economic development can be stated as follows: given the limits of Algerian agriculture, the high rates of redundancy and underemployment in the rural areas, accentuated by one of the highest rates of demographic growth in the world, and the increasing number of the jobless in the urban centres, industrialisation was and continues to be the only feasible option. In the modern world no nation can develop an efficient economy without the establishment of basic national industry, which alone is capable of stimulating the growth of all other sectors. According to this strategy, industrialisation constitutes a *sine qua non* for the construction of a viable economy, without which no society can resolve its fundamental problems or create a modern state strong enough to resist external pressures and encroachments, and to avoid internal stagnation and decay. It was also considered the basis for the revolutionisation of the mode of production.

The post-independence strategy of development was predetermined by specific historical, social, economic and political factors. The colonial situation and the conditions under which the country had wrested its independence were bound to induce the nationalist leadership to nationalise all foreign interests and to hand them over to public companies. This strategy of development appeared to be primarily a strategy of economic growth because the emphasis was put on the development of productive forces as a guarantee of the realisation of national independence through industrialisation.

The major direction of this strategy was derived from the conception of development apprehended in relation to the nature of underdevelopment, considered as a by-product of colonisation. The colonial situation had transformed the Algerian economy into an 'extraverted' and 'disarticulated' economy. This conception of development was, in the words of

Boumedienne, based upon 'the fundamental idea that development as well as its social and political finality . . . is inseparable from our conception of socialism as defined in the national charter' adopted by the nation in 1976. This charter presents socialism in Algeria as 'a process underlying the national movement of liberation and provides a coherent answer to the problems of our time'.[11] This strategy of development aimed at the realisation of three main objectives:

1 The consolidation of national independence
2 The construction of a society free from the exploitation of man by man
3 The promotion of man and his fulfilment.[12]

The fulfilment of these objectives entailed, first of all, that the state must not only nationalise the country's resources, but also undertake their processing in order to increase their utilisation by the national economy instead of exporting them as raw materials to advanced capitalist countries. This would progressively put an end to the 'extraversion' of the Algerian economy engendered by the colonial situation, and so stimulate the construction of a complete productive apparatus, capable of providing full employment, inputs required by various production units and sectors and hence the satisfaction of the basic needs of the popular strata of Algerian society.

The populist socialist option which was proclaimed successively by the programme of Tripoli of 1962, the charter of Algiers of 1964, and the national charter of 1976 as the most fundamental, irreversible option, appeared to the leadership and the people to be the only possibility. Such a course was dictated by the disastrous results of colonial capitalism. Therefore, development was viewed as a desperately needed basis for the economic independence and social progress of the nation. Its ideological foundation – which was derived from the political programmes of the first nationalist movement, the North African Star (1926), the People's Party (1937), the Movement for the Triumph of Democratic Liberties (1946) and the wartime National Liberation Front – was economic nationalism. According to Benaouda Hamel, 'what was sought was first of all the realisation of national independence through the realisation of economic independence as a complement and consolidation of political independence'.[13] As the national charter put it, 'a genuine independence postulates economic independence, which is essentially based on the acquisition of national resources, the appropriation by the community of the basic means of production, a balanced external trade, the financial independence of the state and the creation of a national market as well as the mastery of technology'.[14]

This strategy of development, whose ideological foundation was economic nationalism, fostered and cemented politically by a pervasive

Introduction

social populism, derived from a sort of traditional gentile democratism, reinforced by a revolutionary egalitarianism of the period of the popular war of independence, was supposed to be the political expression of the national union of diverse social or class forces. In the course of the implementation of this strategy of development, which implied constant conflict with the former colonial power, Boumedienne attempted to elaborate a corresponding political strategy favouring the emergence and consolidation of an alliance between the anti-imperialist social forces of the revolution: workers, peasants, and young people, whose mobilisation was deemed necessary for the fulfilment of the nationally planned objectives of development, geared to the satisfaction of their needs. Indeed, the Algerian strategy of development of the 1967–78 period, which discarded the theories of development propagated by the economists of the advanced capitalist countries, defied the control of the imperialist and neo-colonial powers over the resources of the third world countries. The national charter denounced these theories and strategies advocated by 'the proponents of the world imperialist system, which continued to exploit the resources' of the underdeveloped regions. These theories and strategies intended to 'influence the policies of development of the third world and to reorientate them in such a way as to preserve the interests of the imperialist countries'. The underdeveloped countries should try to undermine 'the foundations of the [old] economic order, which has been at the service of the interests of the imperialists'[15] and to replace it by a new equitable world economic order, based on mutual respect and fair shares.

In sum, the strategy of development adopted by Boumedienne called for national austerity in order to establish an efficient and modern productive apparatus and to train sufficient engineers, managers, technicians and skilled workers capable of mastering the newly imported industrial technology. The planners projected that by the 1980s Algeria would become an industrialised, economically independent society where full employment and the repatriation of emigrant workers in Europe would be achieved.

By 1965, before even formulating a perspective of development, the second regime set aside all political institutions inherited from the previous regime, thereby undermining any chance for the establishment of a genuinely representative government in the country. Thenceforth, acting on behalf of society but without consulting it, the state exercised all powers: executive, legislative and judiciary. Furthermore, as the process of nationalisation of economic assets progressed, the state became the principal agent of industrialisation and development, which reinforced its political, social and cultural omnipresence within society. In the absence of democracy, the state apparatus came to be run by an awkward bureaucracy unaccountable to its citizens. This state of affairs stifled the population,

Introduction

especially in the political and cultural spheres, despite the substantial progress which had been made in industry and in some social services.

Despite a high rate of demographic growth and a rapid rate of urbanisation, agricultural production stagnated. The development of social and cultural services kept pace neither with the rhythm of industrialisation nor with the population increase and the increasing demand generated by the growth of the gross domestic product and the improvement of the standard of living of a large segment of the population. This unbalanced sectoral growth generated intractable problems, which compounded and magnified the political and social contradictions caused by the process of development. These imbalances were caused primarily by the striking lack of dynamism exhibited by the non-industrial sectors, which was brought about by the maintenance within the regime of class forces hostile to socialism. Their political reluctance to have a genuine national and popular development of the economy under the aegis of the state and the mediocrity and incompetence of the overwhelming majority of their leaders, whose limitations prevented them from even attracting efficient advisers, experienced administrators and managers, have been chiefly responsible for the uneven development of the various sectors of the national economy. This unwillingness can be explained by the fact that almost all of the members of the so-called revolutionary council, a self-appointed executive committee that supposedly formulated the policy of the state from 1965 to 1979, privately favoured an economic development geared to the aspirations of a growing number of Algerian *affairistes* (businessmen) specialised in *comprador* parasitic activities (for example, import–export).

Indeed, despite the predominance of the public sector, private enterprises benefited greatly from the 1967–78 period of development. The emergence of private entrepreneurs, speculators and middlemen associated with the private sector reinforced the position of the pro-*comprador* elements within the power structure. These elements, although they had managed to accumulate significant amounts of capital in the shadow of the public sector, had always preferred a non-planned and non-regulated development that would allow them to become local representatives of multinationals rather than nationally orientated dynamic entrepreneurs. Their political influence was so great that, upon the death of Boumedienne in December 1978, economic policy was changed in favour of the private sector, accompanied by a shift in the development priorities and the destructuring of the industrial public corporations, which amounted to a debilitating atomisation.

In addition, the recent so-called 'liberalisation' of the economy has not been accompanied by the institutionalisation of democracy in the political field. On the contrary, the exercise of power is more authoritarian than

Introduction

ever. If this trend continues the progress of development itself may be thwarted. Social pressures, magnified by a high rate of population growth, are being opposed by the growing influence of right-wing political forces, a fact that may transform Algeria, in the forseeable future, into a Latin-American style authoritarian republic dominated by local oligarchies, closely tied to a foreign power. Since 1979 the dominant political forces have been pushing Algeria into a process of underdevelopment despite two decades of rapid economic growth. This is why the success or failure of development is determined by political rather than technical factors. Therefore, an analysis of development at the macro-economic level has to take into account the social forces underlying Algerian politics. The social forces underlying Algerian politics had in the past, and continue to have, differing views regarding the purpose and nature of development. These social and political aspects, which constitute, in my opinion, a determinant factor in the success or failure of industrialisation, have been overlooked by the theorists of development.

Indeed, in the case under study, the major problems encountered in the process of development were caused primarily by the lack of democracy. Therefore, any genuine development which aims at the general well-being of the population necessitates the institutionalisation of democracy at every level of decision-making. The democratisation of political, economic and social institutions would have transformed the citizens into free individuals, conscious of their prerogatives, duties and responsibilities, a fact that makes the office-holders accountable to the population through its freely chosen and elected representatives. This could be done even within the framework of the single party. In other words, democracy is not just a philosophical abstraction or political slogan, but a highly efficient and practical way of managing society, if applied without any restriction or mystification. Only a political system based upon clearly defined principles of social justice and guaranteeing to the citizens freedom of expression, freedom to choose and elect their representatives and freedom to determine their own individual lives and collective future can mobilise the people for the construction of their society. In short, there is a dialectical relationship between development and democracy. Development must aim, among other things, at the realisation of democracy, which promotes and consolidates the process of development. The two are as inextricably intertwined as the processes of development and underdevelopment were during the colonial period.

Consequently, since the making of contemporary Algeria has been determined and moulded by the unfolding of historical processes, events and upheavals, this work has to begin by delineating and comparing the essential features characterising both the French and the Algerian societies and economies on the eve of 1830. Such an historical reconstruction and comparison should enable us to comprehend and highlight the major changes, disruptions, disintegrations and transformations that occurred during the subsequent periods: colonial (1830–1962) and post-independence (1962–87).

I

The Algerian pre-colonial socio-economic system

Chapter 1

Algerian society and economy before 1830

One of the aims of this chapter is to compare the two different techno-economic levels of development attained by the French and Algerian societies just before 1830, when France invaded Algeria. This may enable us to comprehend from the outset the striking dissimilarities between the basic institutions of the two countries at this crucial historical juncture as well as to underline the different socio-economic and political dynamics underlying respectively the nature and functioning of French capitalism and the Algerian pre-capitalist orders.[1]

By the 1820s the French economy had become primarily capitalist in nature, that is, based on commercial agriculture, industry and trade. Although the development of capitalism in France started during the end of the Middle Ages, it had to undergo a bourgeois democratic revolution before it finally institutionalised a liberal democracy devoted to the free market, the separation of powers, industrialisation and colonial expansion.

French society and economy between 1789 and 1830

The French Revolution is the archetype of a bourgeois, violent revolution directed against the feudal nobility, who not only hampered but threatened the irresistible drive towards the development of a capitalist economy and its political corollary, liberal or parliamentary democracy. The institutionalisation of capitalism as a full socio-cultural system was bound to condition and propel, in France as elsewhere, the modern *homo economicus*. In a word, in the case of France, the *ancien régime* became an obstacle to basic societal change; it had to be eliminated. Barrington Moore stated the significance of this liberal capitalist revolution thus:

> The central message that I have been able to discern in the origins, course, and consequences of the revolution is that the violent destruction of the *ancien régime* was a crucial step for France on the long road toward democracy. It is necessary to underscore the point that the step was crucial for France, where the obstacles democracy faced were different from those in England. French society did not, and probably could not generate a parliament of landlords with bourgeois overtones, in

The pre-colonial economic system

the English manner. Previous trends in France had made the upper classes into the enemy of liberal democracy . . . Hence, if democracy were to triumph in France, certain institutions would have to be gotten out of the way.[2]

The underlying ideology of the French Revolution is revealed in the Declaration of the Rights of Man, whose concrete principles were translated in the constitution. The *ancien régime*, based on the privileged orders, was abolished, the equality of all before the law was affirmed and the recognition of the sovereignty of the people was proclaimed. Men are born and remain free with equal rights; private property is an inviolable and sacred right; no one can be deprived of it.

The French Revolution was the final adoption by France of integral capitalist socio-economic institutions. As Barber put it, 'the substance of the revolution which consisted of the substitution, as the dominant ethos of French society, of universalistic and rational values for the particularistic and traditional values of the old regime made the bourgeois way of life the strategic one from then on.'[3] The outcome of the French Revolution of 1789, in spite of its complex historical vicissitudes, led to the triumph of large-scale capitalist enterprises, especially under the continental system. During this period the capitalists succeeded in constituting a monopoly by imposing their finished products on the European markets. This fostered a rapid accumulation of capital and technological expertise that was destined to play a determinant role in the industrial revolution of France.[4] The Napoleonic period was marked by the setting up of a rational social organisation of French society as a whole. The famous and still functioning Napoleonic civil code was institutionalised. The basic social rules and regulations concerning the family, justice, administration, education, the army, commerce, the system of inheritance, inter- and intra-family relations and structures and so on were defined. Most of the scientific and cultural institutions of modern France, such as the five Institutes of France, the Ecole Normale Supérieure and the Ecole Polytechnique, which became one of the best scientific institutions in the world, were founded. In short, the basic institutional prerequisites and many other things that form the basic requirements of a modern capitalist society came into being during the Napoleonic era.

An efficient army and bureaucratic machinery were also established and broken in during the Napoleonic Wars. This highly disciplined and organised army developed a modern system of 'logistics' and planning techniques in engineering, transportation and communication which was made possible by the modernisation of the economy.

The following examples may more adequately illustrate the rise of the dynamism of French capitalistic economy, in contrast to the relative stagnation exhibited by the Algerian pre-capitalist economy at the turn of

Society and economy before 1830

the nineteenth century. In 1822, the United States General Consul in Algiers, William Shaller, evaluated Algerian external commerce at only 8 million francs, while at the same time the total volume of French trade reached 950 million francs. During the period 1818 to 1828, French production of cast iron doubled; that of processed cotton tripled between 1812 and 1827; in less than fifteen years the silk industry of Lyon grew by 400 per cent. Between 1825 and 1830 the quantity of money minted by France increased by 82 per cent and that of gold by 156 per cent.[5]

The Algerian state remained basically a military-theocratic pre-capitalist state whose organisational and institutional features were characterised by certain 'archaic' traits, which appear to have prevented the further development of the productive forces of the civil society.

The political organisation of the pre-1830 Algerian state

The political organisation of pre-colonial Algeria was articulated by inexpugnable segmentary structures. This state organisation was founded upon a multiplicity of rural tribal or lineage regional sub-systems. The country was divided into four provinces. The province of Algiers, the capital city of the state, which became also the capital province, was considered to be *Dar-es-Sultan* (the house of the Sultan) because it was administered directly by the head of state, or *dey*. The remaining three provinces were ruled by regional governors or *beys*, appointed by the *dey*. The latter was chosen by the *divan* or council of the state. Upon his ascension to power, he designated five ministers to form a cabinet. Every minister assumed the direction of a department. The *dey* was always seconded by a lieutenant or Khalifa.

These four sub-divisions varied in size of population and in resources. For instance, the Beylik of Constantine possessed a budget that was estimated to be three times that of the central state and the two other provinces, Titri and Wihran.[6] Nonetheless, despite the excessive decentralisation of power, which resulted partly from the segmentary social organisation, this pre-colonial state had with a bureaucratic and military apparatus managed to govern the population and hence to hold the entire society together for more than three centuries.[7]

On the regional level, every province was further divided into local districts administered by *qaids* appointed by the *beys*, *shaykhs* and *amins*.[8] In the case of the *awatan*, or principalities, a relative autonomy was maintained. Indeed, the number of politically independent principalities and of semi-independent chiefdoms was, according to Louis Rinn, very important. His survey, which summarised the bulk of information gathered by French officers and civil servants pertaining to the Algerian

The pre-colonial economic system

Table 1.1 *Political units in pre-colonial Algeria*

Units	Algiers	Titri	Oran	Constantine	Total
Makhzen	19	14	46	47	126
Subject tribes	11	23	56	14	104
Semi-independent	20	12	29	25	86
Independent tribes	23	13	26	138	200
Total	73	62	157	224	516

territorial appropriation, provided some evidence of power distribution during the pre-colonial period. Table 1.1 summarises Rinn's findings.

Thus, the 126 *makhzen* tribes and the 104 subject groups controlled only 16 per cent of Algeria. The 86 semi-autonomous chiefdoms and their confederations extended over 15 per cent. The principalities, which were located mostly in the high plateaus, the steppes and in the Sahara, covered the remaining 69 per cent of the known territory. This table gains in classificatory coherence as we proceed from top to bottom, that is, from the areas submitted to direct control to the periphery. A total of 200 units are considered as autonomous. As such, they refused to be taxed by the central authority and hence were politically dissident. During the early period of the regency the distinction between the centre of power and the autonomous and semi-independent units situated in the periphery was referred to as *Bled el-Turk* and *Bled el-Baroud* or 'land of the Turks' and 'land of gunpowder'.

However, Rinn, like most early colonial historians, tended to exaggerate the political fragmentation of pre-colonial Algeria in order to prove that the country had 'never formed a nation'. Even these rural principalities were loosely linked to the national political and economic organisation of the country through the pre-capitalist marketing networks, religious institutions and pilgrimage. As a whole, this state apparatus was 'characterised by a great local variation in administrative usage, and by a semi-autonomy for the professional, religious or ethnic groups'.[9]

However, at the national level, the power structure was articulated in accordance with a hierarchical principle, that is, political authority was distributed from the centre both *de jure* and *de facto*. It was at the provincial level that the *loci* of power lay and the central administrative apparatus was replicated. The nature of power relations in the peripheries was based on a sort of pyramidal principle, in the sense that the regional segmentary structures entailed the dependence of the exercise of political power on

Society and economy before 1830

the consensual allegiance expressed by a series of interconnected segmentary units, without any permanent acknowledgement of the right to enforce or impose this by coercive means. This is in contradistinction to the political practice which prevailed both at the national and provincial politico-administrative centres and their controllable hinterlands. At the regional and local levels, this actual diffusion of political authority had been predetermined by complex socio-political mechanisms that generated and propelled a systematic dialectic governing the balance, opposition and allocation of power at all the structurally interlinking units and sub-units making up such a peculiar segmentary state system of government. Hermassi explained this state of affairs differently. He noted that:

> If for heuristic reasons, one were to construct a model of the traditional Maghrebi state, it would be useful to present three concentric circles. The first circle would represent the locus of central power, which was based in the cities and which had a threefold vocation: military, commercial and religious. In these urban zones, dynasties of a patrimonial kind were established. To defend themselves and to control the rest of the country, they relied upon tax exempt tribes whose members gradually began to assume military responsibilities. Surrounding this circle of protected cities and privileged tribes, there existed an intermediary zone composed of subject tribes, which were administered either by local notables or by agents from the center and which were submitted to the heaviest system of taxation . . . Finally, there was a third, peripheral circle with varying boundaries. Within these circles were regularly dissident and semidissident tribes. These marginal units not only constituted a challenge to the central authority through their dissidence but also constantly invaded the state and established dynasties, of which there are historical records. Such dynasties were, however, replaced by dynasties established by other tribes having equal ambition. The model of the Maghrebi state is, then, composed of three elements: people who raise taxes, those who submit to exploitation, and those who refuse it. One may justifiably perceive in this a symbol of the human condition.[10]

Thus, the basic unit of this socio-political system of rural Algeria was the tribe – in Arabic, *gabyla*, and in Berber, *taqbilt*. The concept of tribe has been deliberately confused and ossified, first by the French colonial officials for the purpose of assigning themselves a 'civilising mission' in a 'tribal-stateless' society. Later the concept was beclouded by colonial ethnologists, who, accepting the theoretical premises of the colonial administrators, have analysed 'tribal systems as final political units, more or less islands unto themselves'.[11]

In the case under study, every so-called tribal segment was socially and economically linked to other neighbouring tribes, towns and cities through a series of market networks. They were all loosely tied politically, economically and, in varying degrees, administratively, to some organic

The pre-colonial economic system

governmental regional structure. Despite some linguistic differences between the Arabised and Berber-speaking groups, the entire population of the country shared a more or less common culture. As Muslims, they maintained continual contact with other Islamic states both in sub-Saharan Africa and in the Orient, where caravans of pilgrims and traders maintained a steady flow of ideas and goods. Indeed, in Hermassi's words:

> the social units . . . whatever their degree of segmentation and marginality, are part of a larger Arab-Moslem civilisation. They participate in a universalistic system of values and norms, and they perceive themselves as an integral part of a vast community. Even the tribe's decision to declare dissidence attests to the fundamental reference of the larger community, regardless of the particular regime.

And Hermassi went on to stress the organic relations cementing together the various regions and social units as follows:

> The links between the Maghrebi cities and the rural tribal areas, both in terms of defense and of markets, were deeply organic. The point is that if political bifurcation was indeed a profound empirical reality to be investigated, bifurcation was not incompatible with the unity of the society.[12]

He concluded by noting that:

> The problem is not simply one of discerning tribal orientation within the rural society but rather of defining the North African tribe and determining its specific relationship to the central authority. If by tribe, we mean a self-sufficient social unit constituting a world unto itself – perceiving itself as the whole of mankind and recognizing no right or obligation beyond its limits – then tribes do not exist in North Africa. Furthermore, we do not see by what dialectical leap or miracle hundreds of social units, considered tribes by ethnologists, could come to recognize the authority of a state that was fundamentally exterior to them. That, historically, some tribal units have consented to the authority of the state, that others have accepted its religious legitimacy while rejecting its political control, and that a sizeable number have refused to submit to it altogether renders the problem all the more complex and demands of us a greater sociological vigilance.[13]

Indeed, almost all the English-speaking anthropologists who have studied the traditional socio-political organisation of the Maghreb had underlined the organic links binding the various segments constituting the North African societies. According to Ernest Gellner, the Maghrebi 'tribes are generally marginal or dissident groups within a wider cultural and moral continuum, which embraces both other tribes and non-tribal, urban, groups'.[14] For William Schorger,

> No rural community in the hinterland of the Mediterranean lives in any appreciable degree of isolation from a center of power and so even petty domestic decisions, made in the most torpid times, are conditioned by a general regional experience.

Society and economy before 1830

The observer is sometimes misled by the fact that a central authority may not have sufficient reason or may lack the power to interfere directly in the local affairs at particular points in time, but such lapses of attention or incapability do not result in an actual loss of contact, they simply attenuate the relationship.[15]

At any rate, the *gabyla*, forming the basic socio-political and economic unit, was sub-divided structurally into several agnatic lineages, composed of numerous interrelated nuclear or extended corporate families. A patriarch was the undisputed head of every household. The size of a tribe varied from a small cluster of hamlets dotting one or two mountain slopes to an immense unit occupying a wide region.[16] The patriarchal extended corporate family formed the elemental unit within which the basic social interaction took place: sexual intercourse, child-rearing, socialisation and economic production and consumption.

This corporate familial arrangement consisted of households that were either organised around separate hearths or lived together around a single hearth. The patterns of residence of these domestic corporate groupings varied. People either co-habited in a larger housing structure erected around a courtyard and containing several rooms or lived in widely separated dwellings, or, in the south, camped in a *douar*, an encampment of pastoral nomads. In the north almost all the houses were surrounded by gardens and orchards covered with a variety of fruit trees.

All of these basic family units were integrated structurally into multi-crosscutting patrilineal descent groups that permeated the entire social organisation of each *machta* or village. The various lineages which made up the *machta* community were incorporated into a *gabyla* that governed the various segments. Although all segmentary patrilineal societies contain inherent structural sources of friction that generate internal conflicts, their multiple cross-cutting kinship networks through a common dynamic ideology of descent act as a unifying force when the society is faced with a threat from without. As demonstrated by the stiff resistance against the invading French army (1830–71 and 1954–62), the apparent organisational weaknesses that initially encouraged the external aggressors to encroach upon the segmentary groups were transformed into highly cohesive, ramifying, voluntaristic, and resistant structures. In other words, in the face of a common enemy, the segmentary units act centripetally: the various social levels coalesce, while status and territorial distinctions fade. Conversely, when such pressures cease the innumerable societal levels and social segments are redistributed as regional nuclei, and these are reintegrated into the power groups that become loosely tied to the centralised system. In short, the structural principle of organisation in pre-colonial rural Algeria, as well as in the entire Maghreb, can be likened to

The pre-colonial economic system

a tree whose common trunk is the society itself, whose major branches are the important tribes, and whose minor branches represent the clans themselves. Such segmentation assumes a potential opposition between the parties: each unit's members tend to unite against adjacent segments and to ally with these against even larger sections.

This principle of segmentation militates against power concentration and political specialisation because loyalties and oppositions are attributed along a continuum of ordered scales . . . It is as if given this dynamics of fission and fusion, internal cohesion and reactivation of solidarities are not so much ensured by recognised authorities as by the awareness of external threat: a powerful confederation, a central government, or foreign occupation.[17]

Thus, the analysis in terms of structural segmentarity negates Marx's interpretation of the Algerian pre-colonial socio-political system. For him

the Turkish rule did not at all give rise to a feudalisation . . . the main obstacle for such a development was the strong centralisation in Algeria of the civil and military administration. This eliminated the possibility of an inheritable accumulation of local functions and the transformation of the holders of such functions into landlords, independent of the Dey in Algiers.[18]

In conclusion, as the basic social unit, the *gabyla* assumed the politico-administrative and economic roles. In fact, every *douar* and every *machta* among the sedentary population possessed a local patriarchal council called *jema'a*, which took the major decisions concerning the socio-economic and political life of their communities. The members of this assembly chose the most influential man to become their *shaykh* or *amin*. In short, rural Algerian social organisation was marked by the following features: 'Leaders emanating from the collectivity; freely debated decisions between the head of different families; a cohesive solidarity of the members of the tribe'.[19]

Even the taxes raised by the state were divided by these local leaders between the families. Practically all conflicts had to be resolved within this tribal social unit without any alien intervention, except when under certain circumstances the supreme authority of the state was resorted to. If the economic interests of the collectivity were threatened, force might be used against the encroaching party, even the state itself. Nonetheless, 'although the propensity for segmentation tends to prevent power concentration', the structural capacity 'for cohesion, activated both by feelings of external threat and the reference to a larger community and its cultural model, favours greatly the emergence of unifying leadership'.[20]

The pre-1830 rural economy

The soil was the basic factor of production, the 'foster-mother' of the Algerian pre-colonial rural communities. Ibn Khaldun wrote in the fourteenth century that:

Society and economy before 1830

It should be known that differences of condition among people are the result of the different ways in which they make their living. Social organisation enables them to cooperate toward that end and to start with the simple necessities of life, before they get to conveniences and luxuries. Some people live by agriculture, the cultivation of vegetables and grains; others by husbandry, the use of sheep, cattle, goats, bees; and silkworms, for breeding and for their products.[21]

Indeed, the organisation of economic production was concentrated on four predominant subsistence activities: agriculture, animal husbandry, horticulture, carried out on fertilised, terraced and irrigated plots of land, and the plantation of fruit trees. Geographical conditions tended to foster a broad regional specialisation of production along ecological lines. For instance, the agriculturalists of the north produced a surplus of grains and fruits that were exchanged for animal products raised by pastoralists, or certain luxury items manufactured by urban artisans. The pastoral nomads and the urban population needed these agricultural products to complement their supplies of food. In Hermassi's words:

Contrary to the stereotyped image of traditional society, neither the North African tribe nor the region could have existed with a closed economy. It was vitally necessary for the populations of both the north and the south to make regular visits to places of exchange. The Kabylia region, overpopulated and recalcitrant to central control, needed wheat products for subsistence; to that end it had to commercialise its oil and figs in the marketplaces of the Tell, and it became greatly dependent upon its relationship to this market. The tribes of the south also depended upon the market; there, they exchanged their wool, livestock and dates for grain and other items produced in the fertile regions of the north.

The marketplace, strategic as it was for exchange, was also instrumental in cementing social relationships for an otherwise dispersed and fragmented population.[22]

At any rate, the socio-economic life of the village was regulated by the code of common ideas of the producer's self-interest, the belief systems, values, the norms of behaviour that were more or less shared by certain predominant segments. The superstructure of these rural communities was, of course, moulded and determined by the historical experiences of every village and its underlying material base which made rural living possible.

The cycles of agricultural activity which constituted the kernel of a peasant society were geared to the rhythm of the changing seasons. The seasonal cycles predetermined the rhythm and intensity of work, crops and animal life.

This pre-colonial Algerian rural population was not, however, made up of socio-economically homogeneous producers who all owned their means of production. Its socio-economic stratification was characterised by three

The pre-colonial economic system

classes or fractions of classes: big landowners, peasant cultivators and impoverished and landless producers. In pre-colonial Algeria there was a landowning class

whose holdings constituted large latifundia. Most of them were absentee estate owners who lived in towns and cities; their estates were cultivated by khammassats or sharecroppers. These tenants contracted land freely and were provided with the necessary tools, seeds, and draft animals for cultivation. In return for their labour, the khammassats received one-fifth of the yield.[23]

The second category comprised a large number of producers who owned their means of production (land, ploughs and draft animals). With the assistance of their families, they produced mostly for their own consumption and for the fulfilment of obligations to the ruling groups, in the form of taxes in kind or cash. The landless families had to provide their labour for the landlords in order to eke out a livelihood, under the *khammassat*. For instance, in 1873 the French colonial authorities took a land census on the territories of 402 tribes, about half of the total tribes of that time. The result of this survey showed that 77 per cent of the heads of households owned fewer than 10 hectares each, while 21 per cent of them possessed from 10 to 40 hectares of arable land.[24] The remaining 2 per cent appear to have been landless. Moreover, all pasture lands were held in common.

Although some of these familes could have been impoverished by the French policy of land expropriation, these figures are clearly indicative of the nature and degree of socio-economic differentiation in rural Algeria. Both the economic structures and the legal system regulating property relations were capable of generating among the population a differential access to this primary resource in the environment.

According to Ibn Khaldun, 'people as a rule covet the possessions of other people. Without the restraining influence of the laws, nobody's property would be safe. This applied especially to traders and low class mobs.'[25] According to the Algerian pre-colonial law defining the status of property, one could become a rightful owner of land through the following: long and continuous occupation of a plot of land; clearing of uncultivated woodland; purchase; inheritance; and by the medium of the *maghrasa* or contract of plantation, granting the producer half of the land planted with fruit trees or other plants. An individual could also become an owner of an estate or plot of land through a juridical mechanism called *rahnia*, or mortgage of revenues of property in payment of debt in kind or in cash. However, the Algerian property law provided a legal arrangement known as *shafa'a*, whereby the co-owner of a property or a close relative had the right to retain possession of the part sold by providing the buyer with the exact sum which he had paid for it.[26] This mechanism proved useful in

Society and economy before 1830

preventing the dismemberment of familial land holdings during the colonial period.

Since pre-colonial Algeria was primarily a peasant society, land formed the basis of property relations. Hence the system of land tenure reflected strikingly the legal foundation of political economy. Land holdings were juridically and customarily divided into six different categories: *melk*, *arsh* or *sabega*, *habus*, *beylik* or *azel*, *mokhzen* and *muwat*.

Melk land was simply private property. As such it could be bought and sold. Moreover, it was not considered as a mere commodity in the capitalist sense. As early as 1837, the French colonial authority recognised it in the following terms: 'private property existed and was perpetuated in Algeria on the same bases as among us: it is acquired, transmitted and held and is recognised by long possession. Muslim testimonials, regular titles and the laws protect it and the courts assist it.'[27]

Arsh or *sabega* was owned corporately by the *kabyla* (lineage) or *machta* (village). The arable fields were temporarily divided among the heads of households, who cultivated them at their own expense. But the pastureland remained held in common. As the same document stated concerning this type of collective landholding:

Most often, particularly with regard to the Arabs who live in tents, the soil is owned in common . . . A small community knew the border between itself and the next small community; that was enough, within the territory of the particular tribe. Each individual enjoyed an equal right to the common lands, either for cultivation or pasture. This state of property, uncommon near the cities of any size, is the normal one in the most remote communities.[28]

The *habus* lands were constituted by donations in favour of religious institutions. They were intended to provide certain social services performed by various mosques. Upon their establishment they become inalienable estates that could not be sold or confiscated.

Beylik or *azel* lands were public prebends devised to provide payment for high officials. They were administered under the authority of *qaids* appointed by the *dey* or the *beys*. The *azel* lands existed only in the province of Constantine; they were divided for cultivation into three categories. One portion was given to the share-croppers or *khammassats*, who were given seeds, draught animals and food. At the end of the harvest, they received one-fifth of the total yield. They were recruited in rural areas among landless or impoverished peasants. A second part was distributed to former officers of the government. The third category was rented to individual tenants in exchange for two kinds of taxes, *okor* and *ushur* in Arabic. In certain regions the *bey* of Constantine reserved some pasture land for the grazing of the government's livestock.[29]

The pre-colonial economic system

Mokhzen is land distributed, in exchange for public service, to tribesmen who cultivated it. *Muwat* land is unproductive areas; anyone clearing and cultivating it gains title to it. The rural population has the uncontested right to use all forests and brushlands in its vicinity.

As a whole the clarity of this legal system regulating property rights led the Baron de Berthezene, who studied it in 1831, to conclude that:

> judging everything by our prejudices, we thought in taking possession of Algiers that under so despotic a government, the right of property was unknown, and that consequently all property belonged to the state. We were very surprised when we learned that among these barbarians, confiscation of property is not the inevitable consequence of political condemnation ; and that no more than among us, does might make right.[30]

This legal system on one hand, guaranteed access of the population to the cultivation of the soil for its subsistence, and on the other, it insured the urban ruling classes and all large proprietors the continuing flow of surplus products as well as income from taxation and rents.

The pre-colonial urban economy

It has been observed that the origin of a North African city has always been a market place, and not a *comitia*.[31] Nevertheless, the basic features characterising the Algerian pre-colonial urban centres were, in many ways, strikingly typical of and structurally similar to most pre-capitalist cities and towns, and no more and no less. Because of ecological conditions, the urban ruling classes encountered inevitable obstacles in exacting surpluses from the independent-minded agricultural communities located in the Atlas Mountains, and the reluctant nomadic chieftains in the Saharan steppes. As a result, the northern African cities since pre-Roman times 'could not have survived and prospered if they had not found in large-scale long-distance trade the resources that were denied them by the difficulty of extracting surplus from the cultivators'.[32]

This fact rendered the urban 'civilisation' of the Maghreb in general a 'fragile affair'. Without a permanent 'solid peasant base', the material foundation of the Algerian pre-colonial urban centres lay in mercantile activities of diverse kinds. This is why 'it was enough for trade to fall off for the states to perish, along with the cities on which they were based'.[33] Moreover, despite the shifting of the trans-Saharan trade routes to the east, the prosperity of the Algerian pre-colonial cities continued willy-nilly. And even during the eighteenth century they experienced relative economic prosperity. However, during the last decades of that century and subsequently, the urban economy of Algeria experienced a severe crisis. The

Society and economy before 1830

coastal cities underwent a process of decline and decay. This decadence was brought about by the complete loss of control of the long-distance trade and the disappearance of piracy.

On account of the increasing commercial aggressiveness manifested by the European capitalist nations, which was encouraged by the inconsequent government policy of granting import–export monopolies to their trading companies, the economic activities that had previously sustained the Algerian urban population living in the coastal cities were thenceforth undermined. As a direct result, certain coastal cities and towns lost about half of their inhabitants. Algiers, for instance, had a population of 100,000 during the eighteenth century; by 1830 it had fallen to 60,000.

But in 1830, the proportion of urban to rural population remained only about 10 per cent. The total population of the country was estimated at this time at over 3 million. The major cities in order of magnitude were:

Algiers	60,000	Oran	10,000
Constantine	35,000	Miliana	10,000
Tlemcen	20,000	Medea	10,000
Mascara	12,000	Cherchell	3,000[34]

There were numerous other cities and towns in Algeria; but their population data are not available. Most of these urban centres were prosperous and adequately built; some were even fortified. In these cities lived a socially, economically and even ethnically heterogeneous population, composed of the ruling elements, merchants, artisans and apprentices.[35] All of these social groups depended in some way on the countryside for their supplies of food and primary raw materials for handicraft manufacturing. The peasants provided raw materials and agricultural products, and the nomads escorted the trans-Saharan goods caravans. Therefore, these urban centres assumed two broadly interwoven political and economic functions. As marketing and manufacturing centres they were predestined to become significant locations where the seats of political power lay.

In fact, in the Algerian pre-colonial segmentary system of government, the cities formed the multicentrifocal points from which the administrative channels radiated over the hinterlands and out to the far limits where the bureaucratic power relationships became dilute and inarticulate, or rather inoperative. However, since most of the rural population on the peripheries of these urban centres was commercially involved to varying degrees in the national, regional and urban marketing networks, which were controlled by the ruling elements and their auxiliaries, the so-called political, economic, religious, educational and manufacturing functions of these urban centres could be considered as merely interconnected structural nodes of a single pre-capitalist state apparatus controlled by the urban political power-holders.

The pre-colonial economic system

In the cities the basic units of the social organisation were 'discretely' cemented together through the medium of kinship ties complemented by patron–client and neighbourhood relations. The urban houses contained several apartments sheltering an extended family. Various interrelated families made up a residential quarter. Every residential quarter was spatially separated from the business section of the city in a juxtaposition of similar housing structures inhabited by interrelated individual extended or nuclear families. These residential quarters were functionally isolated from the focal points of the city and possessed a few basic public facilities such as bakery ovens, baths and mosques and synagogues, but no shops or workshops were tolerated there.[36]

Commercial activities were relegated to special streets; the core of the city was usually distinguished by two equal focal points: the market area or bazaar and the principal mosque. All manufacturing and trading activities were confined to a specific area. Each trade and craft was occupied by a particular ethnic or regional group. However, work remained organised on a craft basis; production relied primarily on harnassing animate human muscular energy. Work was performed inside small-scale workshops where the master craftsman (*muallim*) was assisted by apprentices and auxiliary workers. Every skill possessed a 'syndic' who supervised the quality of the products and mediated conflicts that could emerge between the workers and their masters or between heads of various workshops. At a higher organisational level a *muhtassib*, commissioner, maintained 'law and order' in the markets and controlled the prices of the goods.

The socio-economic and political structures of Algerian pre-colonial society crumbled after 1830 under the onslaught of French colonisation. Despite its relative backwardness – compared with the European capitalist nations of the time – this society was socially integrated and economically relatively prosperous. It also possessed an adequate educational system which corresponded to the level of development attained by its productive forces.

According to the French General Pellissier de Renaud, 'primary education was as widespread as in France. There are schools that provide basic instruction in most of the villages and *douars*.' In 1834, General Valze reported that 'almost all the Arabs know how to read and write'. Ismael Urbain noted that in rural Algeria 'primary instruction was, in 1830, much more widespread that we generally think. The average number of male individuals who know how to read and write was at least equal to that of rural France [in 1845].' Furthermore, 'between 2,000 and 3,000 young men were studying in the *madrassahs*, a sort of high school in each province, and 600 to 800 were studying sciences, law and theology in some establishments of higher education'. And an anonymous note of 1848

Society and economy before 1830

stated that 'all children received primary instruction in innumerable establishments'.

However, it must be reiterated that the educational system, economy and entire social organisation of Algeria before 1830 were primarily geared to the production of use-values. Because of this the necessary political and social conditions for the development of production of exchange-values, which is a *sine qua non* of capital accumulation and hence sustained economic growth, were never created. It was such relative techno-economic stagnation that incited the French capitalist nation-state to extend its trading and fishing activities within Algeria a long time before it envisaged its colonisation, when the further expansion of these 'interests' was resisted.

Pre-1830 commercial relations between France and Algeria

Pre-colonial commercial relations between North Africa and France were the determinant factor underlying the expansion of French capitalism in the area. Trade between the Maghreb and France began during the Middle Ages and had become important by the thirteenth century. However, the nature of these trading patterns is not very well known. A list of northern African products sold in southern France during the mid thirteenth century may be indicative of this trade. A contemporary document notes that 'from the Kingdom of Fez in Africa came beeswax, leather and skins; from the Kingdom of Morocco came such products as cumin [and] raw sugar; from the Kingdom of Bougie came furs of lamb, leather, and [dry] figs which grew in the country'.[37] These trading activities seem to have been increased in volume and kept well balanced until the end of the eighteenth century, when French merchants appear to have begun to monopolise the entire North African trade. Indeed, prior to the invasion of 1830, France already owned factories and trading establishments in Algiers, but two were closed because of competition with Algerian Jews.[38] The Chamber of Commerce of Marseilles, basing its calculation on the value of exports of woollen cloth, since it almost equalled that of all other goods combined, found that annual exports ranged from 7,000 to 8,000 bales. From 1762 to 1772, exports averaged 7,000 bales. Assuming a unit price of 1,200 francs, which is the average for all qualities, a sum of 8,400,000 francs per annum is obtained. Allowing an equal sum for other goods gives a total of 19,200,000 francs; and 3–4 million francs must be added for smuggling, thus reaching a total of 23 million.[39]

In addition to these trading shops and factories, there were numerous other commercial establishments in Algeria such as those of La Calle, Annaba and Collo, owned and operated directly by French merchants

The pre-colonial economic system

through the Africa Company, which was established in February 1741. Its capital was fixed at 1,200,000 francs, divided into 1,200 shares of 1,000 francs each, of which the Chamber of Commerce of Marseilles took one-quarter. This company paid the dues agreed upon to the *dey* of Algiers and to the local authorities of Annaba, Collo and La Calle. It maintained in its factories about 300 persons: officers, soldiers, coral fishermen and workers. The Governor of La Calle was the Inspector General.

The Compagnie d'Afrique bought wheat, wool, wax and hides. In order to export these goods it had to engage in constant intrigue at the Regency of Algiers, which levied taxes for the authorisation of the company to trade there, and even for the provision of the factories. An important item of purchase was coral, which comes from the neighbouring sea. Coral was used to buy slaves from Guinea and thus promoted agriculture in the French colonies of the sugar islands; shipments were also made to China and India.[40]

Indeed, in 1826 the French consul reported that 'the commerce of this country has been ruined by the governors and military commanders'.[41] Another official document, written by the French colonial authorities in the 1830s, confirmed this consular report. Its authors concluded by stressing the fact that:

by imposing its monopoly system, and by prohibiting the export of indigenous products, the government ruined the networks of commerce and almost annihilated agriculture in the kingdom. The monopoly over coral fishing in the eastern coast and the export of wool, animal skins, wax and wheat through the port of Bone [Annaba] was granted to France (Compagnie d'Afrique) for the amount of 30,000 [Spanish] dollars per year. The *bey* of Oran also received 30,000 [Spanish] dollars from a firm for the right of export monopoly from this entire province; animal skins, wax and wool were included in these public monopolies that the government sold every year to the highest bidder . . . Export of olive oil and finished leather was strictly forbidden except when these products were destined for the provinces of the Ottoman Empire.[42]

As a direct consequence of this monopoly system that favoured the European trading companies, the Algerian merchants were eliminated from international trade. Despite the tight control of these monopolies, the French companies often complained of Algerian merchants who managed to deal directly with Marseilles themselves.[43] This situation illustrates the patterns of commercial relations between the capitalist merchants and the pre-capitalist countries ruled by quasi-despotic governments dominated by oligarchies and military chieftains. Under such circumstances, the growth of trade constitutes a necessary condition for the stimulation of capital accumulation, without which no industrial development is possible.

Given the degree of this unequal exchange between two different

Society and economy before 1830

economic systems, in 1819, the French consul, Deval, explored the possibility of France's 'possessing the stronghold of France in La Calle, with exclusive rights concerning the coral fisheries and the political control of the Mazoula Arabs'.[44] This meant the entire extension of French sovereignty over the area inland. In his audience with the *dey* of Algiers in 1827, when Deval was supposedly insulted, the *dey* declared to him that in future Algeria would not allow a single French cannon on her territory and that thenceforth French merchants trading in the Regency would be treated like all foreign traders within the country.[45] The consul reminded the *dey* of the stipulations of a treaty made between France and the Ottoman Empire in 1535, when France was granted commercial privileges within this empire, since Algeria was at that time under nominal suzereignty of the Sublime Porte. The terms of this treaty had to be respected. The irony here is that the North African regencies became completely independent from the Porte's protection in 1719; but the capitalist state clung to her advantageous treaty of 1535.

This diplomatic crisis between Algeria and France was caused by the fact that the French merchants who contracted a large number of debts in purchasing wheat for the French state from the Algerian rulers during the Napoleonic wars were instructed by their government not to pay. This decision, which provoked a political conflict leading to military hostilities, was instigated by the discredited French monarchy to punish Algeria for her cordial relations with the revolutionary regime. In fact, besides important shipments of wheat and horses, the Regency gave revolutionary France a loan of 250,000 francs in 1793 and another million francs in 1796 without charging it any interest. Needless to say, at this period revolutionary France was badly in need of this aid.[46] France was isolated by an entire hostile European continent still governed by absolutist monarchies in alliance with England, a country that had become the 'workshop of the world'. After the defeat of Napoleon, the French government of the restored monarchy refused to honour the debt or to force her merchants to pay it.

After this meeting of 27 April 1827, Deval declared that the *dey* had struck him with his fan. The French government considered that the honour of France had been insulted, and not only broke diplomatic relations with the Regency but declared a general blockade of the whole sea coast that led to the invasion of Algeria in 1830.

II

The uneven development generated by colonialism

Chapter 2

The nature of colonialism

The reasons for colonial expansion

From the outset the French conquerors intended to establish a colony in the north of Africa that could absorb a large number of idle men and women, whose main function would be to provide the *metropole* with raw materials and to be used as an outlet for dumping French manufactured goods. The major motives underlying this colonial undertaking were revealed and formulated in the conclusions of the Commission d'Afrique, which was formed in 1833 by the French government and sent to Algeria to study the advantages and disadvantages of the colonialisation of the country. Its report, contrary to what most French historians have tried to make us believe, concluded that the occupation of Algeria would be profitable economically, commercially, politically and militarily to France.

The economic calculations had belittled the value of colonies. The old nations must have outlets in order to alleviate the demographic pressures exerted on big cities and the use of the capital that has been concentrated there. To open new sources of production is, in effect, the surest means of neutralising this concentration without upsetting the social order . . . It is the surest way of preventing the seeds of hostility that are being sown among the working classes, not only against the government but also against society and against property.[1]

Later on Jules Ferry, one of the greatest theoreticians of colonisation, emphasised the importance of colonies for the economic development of modern nations:

Colonial policy is the offspring of industrialisation. There are states . . . where even agriculture can survive only if it is industrialised. Such countries can be economically prosperous only if they export; the opportunities for the employment of capital and labour will depend on the size of foreign markets . . . in this industrial age of man, social peace depends on outlets . . . we must cause fresh categories of consumers to appear in other parts of the world, for, if we fail to do so, modern society will go bankrupt.

He concluded by stating that 'one cannot be a great power if one stays in one's own backyard'.[2]

Uneven development

Since the major Algerian cities and towns were occupied before the conquest of the rural areas, we must start this chapter by analysing the nature and consequences of the colonisation of the urban centres. Our main concern is to try to comprehend the degree of destructuration of the pre-1830 society and economy and their reordering by the colonial power to meet the requirements and exigencies of total colonisation, resulting in the emergence and development of a modern colonial sector constituted by commercial agriculture, basic infrastructure, extractive industry and the beginnings of light industry. All of these productive assets were finally either inherited or nationalised by the independent state in the post-colonial period, and hence their pertinence.

Colonisation of the urban centres

From the outset, the military conquest of the Algerian cities was characterised by an unusual violence, rare in the modern history of colonialism. The capital city, Algiers, fell to French troops on 5 July 1830. A French traveller, Rozet, deplored the fact that in the suburbs of Algiers 'all the houses that were not occupied by the officers were practically demolished; the doors and beams were taken to be used for fires'.[3] By 1831 Algiers had lost 30,000 inhabitants, who were either killed or exiled. Aristide Gilbert observed in the same year that 'of a total of 5,000 buildings, 3,000 came under control of the state'.[4] As a result of this systematic confiscation of property, 'the wretched owners, the majority of whom were expropriated without any compensation, were reduced to begging'.[5] Those who were spared were eventually ruined by inflation, which was aggravated by the introduction of French currency. 'We imported a considerable volume of money into Algeria. It soon took the place of the local currency, which was declared not exchangeable.'[6] This first harsh measure ushered in the process of proletarianisation of the first Algerian producers and traders. The increasing 'inflow of European settlers undermined local commerce further . . . the removal of a large number of rich Muslims singularly diminished sales and profits; demolition for the purpose of straightening and widening streets and the increase of rents were a serious blow to the indigenous merchants'.[7]

The worsening economic situation of Algiers was described in 1846 by a military doctor in these terms:

Everything one sees here upon arrival saddens the heart: an indigenous population reduced to the last degree of misery; an innumerable crowd of starving proletarians . . . the Moorish houses, well constructed and well ventilated with pure fresh air, are disappearing every day. The fervour of construction has taken hold of the speculators.[8]

The nature of colonialism

Thus the socio-economic consequence of this military conquest has been the rise of the modern Algerian proletariat. Many dispossessed and impoverished individuals had no other way of earning their livelihood than hiring out their labour on a day-to-day basis. A large number of them became dock workers in the port of Algiers, 'whose lot does not appear to have been miserable before the occupation . . . many must have lost their resources as a result of the economic upheavals that followed the conquest of the city'.[9]

After Algiers, the French colonisation of the urban centres expanded to other cities such as Blida and Medea. When General Clauzel attempted to occupy Blida its inhabitants resisted. The General ordered his men to loot it and massacre its defenders. He noted that when he arrived there he found it 'jammed with corpses among which were those of old people, women, children and Jews. All had been defenceless.' Besides this, in 1832, the Duc de Rovigo imposed a 200,000-piastre war tribute on the two cities Blida and Kolea. When Blida refused to meet this demand, he ordered his soldiers to loot it. But when the troops penetrated into the city they realised that it was completely deserted.

The next city to be conquered, Medea, the capital of the province of Tittri, was not only totally depopulated but devastated. It was attacked and looted in 1830–1 and finally occupied in 1836. These successive military onslaughts resulted in the city's fall. General Ducrot, who participated in the previous attack as a captain, wrote:

Medea has been abandoned and the inhabitants have carried away everything. There must have been strong motives to force an entire population to emigrate in this fashion, because they are not nomads, but urbanites accustomed to leading a peaceful and easy life; people who abandoned their roofs, their paternal houses, who left their property, their industry, in order to go wandering on the plains and maybe die of hunger.[10]

In 1841, five years after its inhabitants were forced to flee, Medea was found by Captain de Smidt in total ruin. In fact, he exclaimed,

it is a good thing that in France they ignore the way this poor city has been treated; nothing remains of it but a bundle of ruins, so much debris . . . the houses have been demolished for firewood. The city was not at all badly built. A few traces of art and marble are still visible.[11]

In the eastern province the same pattern of conquest was followed. Indeed, Bijaya, one of the most prestigious medieval Algerian cities, was conquered in 1833 after a fierce street battle in which the invaders had to conquer it street by street in order to occupy a ruined city. 'This war lasted for three days and as usual it increased the ferocity of the soldiers. The entire population either perished or was exiled for ever.'[12] In 1846, when Poujoulat visited it, he stated that this city 'numbered thousands of inhabitants before our occupation. I have found there only three Arab families, about one hundred European settlers and a battalion in garrison.'[13]

The inhabitants of Constantine, the ancient city of Cirta, decisively repulsed the invading French troops who tried to seize it in 1836. This first 'expedition cost [France] about one thousand men, that is, one-eighth of the troops engaged'.[14] However, in 1837, Constantine was attacked again, and at the cost of thousands of men and women who defended it valiantly, it fell to the French. While besieged, a large number of the inhabitants were forced to flee over the gorges of the Rhummel, but many of them fell into the abyss and crashed to the bottom.

I stood on the edge of the terrifying ravines and stared at the sloping peaks over which thousands of men and women, trusting the abyss more than the mercy of the French victors, sought to escape. Their means of salvation were ropes attached to the upper walls of the rocks. When these ropes broke, human masses could be seen rolling down this immense wall of rock. It was a veritable cascade of corpses.[15]

In 1846, Constantine had lost 10,000 of its Algerian inhabitants, and the survivors were destitute. A French colonial official described their economic conditions in 1845 as follows:

Constantine is horrible to see; all buildings are falling in ruin, and half of the houses that were there five years ago have been demolished. The indigenous population is in a terrifying state of misery and deprivation . . . by expelling the traders, by taking all sorts of violent measures, we have spread misery everywhere.[16]

The urban centres of the western province were colonised, pillaged and depopulated in the same manner. In 1835 Mascara, the capital of Abdel-Kader, was completely destroyed by the bombardment of the French troops who thus avenged the crushing defeat inflicted upon them in the battle of Macta. When the Duc d'Orleans entered the city, he exclaimed:

What I saw then was the most hideous spectacle I have ever witnessed. I had never imagined what a sacked city, where numerous inhabitants have been massacred, would be like. The street that leads to the square was full of all kinds of debris; wooden beams covered with flecks of blood were still burning; everything was in disorder; not a single object remained untouched; the houses were in flame and a thousand Jews threw themselves at our feet begging for mercy: all that was left of a population which until yesterday numbered 10,000 souls.[17]

In 1833 Tlemcen was occupied and its population subjected to forced exile and the arbitrary imposition of war tributes exacted from them by General Clauzel, who was impressed with the city's prosperity. Those who could not pay in cash were forced to bring their wives' jewellery.[18] The most striking example is that of Oran, which illustrates what happened to most Algerian urban centres during this early period of French colonisation. The city was depopulated as a result of French occupation in 1831; from 10,000 in 1830 the population fell to a mere 1,000 in 1832.

In conclusion, the Algerian urban centres were impoverished and hence depopulated. The subsequent increase of the urban population was due to the migration of the rural population to the cities rather than to natural population growth.

Indeed, according to a study made by J. Ch. Boudin in 1853, the number of births and deaths among the Algerian urban population were as follows:[19]

1850		1851	
Births	Deaths	Births	Deaths
11,128	4,192	2,439	5,738

These figures give some concrete indications about the rate of depopulation of the cities as a direct result of colonisation by means of 'pacification'. The country as a whole, according to official statistics, lost 646,159 inhabitants between 1866 and 1872 alone.[20]

It should be recalled that on the eve of the French invasion in 1830, the Algerian urban centres contained an estimated 5–10 per cent of the total population. The structure and political and socio-economic function of these cities were congruent with the logic underlying a pre-capitalist, pre-industrial social praxis. Colonisation resulted in the expropriation of most of the Algerian producers as well as in the destructuration-transformation of both the pre-existing urban system and the rural landscape.

French military and economic penetration into the rural communities

The French colonisation of Algeria took place in four stages. The first phase, between 1830 and 1839, was marked by the occupation of the urban centres and their immediate hinterlands. The second phase took place between 1840 and 1847, during which the colonial army managed to extend its conquest to the fertile agricultural plains of the Tell, or northern Algeria. This period was characterised by the seventeen-year war in which the partisans of al-Amir Abdel Kader opposed the French. The third and fourth stages of colonisation occurred from 1848 to 1872 and from 1873 to 1954. All the energies of the colonial power were devoted to the 'subjugation' of the mountainous sedentary communities in the Tell, and the southern oasis-sedentary communities and pastoral nomads of the Sahara.

Uneven development

The rural populations resisted militarily the encroachment of the colonial army upon their lands until 1884. However, the backbone of the rural resistance to colonialism was smashed in 1871.

Confronted with a stiff peasant resistance, the French army adopted, from the outset, a 'scorched earth strategy' in order to 'subjugate' the peasantry and expropriate its plots of land. Many accounts regarding the application of this strategy were given by the French officers: 'More than fifty fine villages built of stone and roofed with tiles were destroyed. Our soldiers made very considerable pickings there.' And Marshall Bugeaud added in another passage: 'I began to chop down the fine orchards and to set fire to the magnificent villages under the enemy's eyes.' General Saint Arnaud described similar colonial practices in 1846: 'I left in my wake a vast conflagration. All the villages, some 200 in number, were burned down, all the gardens destroyed, all the olive trees cut down.'

> In a . . . letter you asked me what happens to the Algerian women we capture; some we keep as hostages and the rest are auctioned to the troops like animals . . . In the operations we have carried out during the last four months I have witnessed scenes that would melt the hardest heart if one had time to let them! I witnessed it all with a frightening indifference. Kill all men over the age of fifteen; take all women and children and put them on a ship for the Marquisas Islands or some other destination.
>
> The country of Beni Menseur is superb . . . we have burned everything, destroyed everything there. Oh, war! How many women and children who took refuge in the snow of the Atlas are found dead there from cold and misery!
>
> Women and children, hooked into thick bushes which they were obliged to cross, surrendered to us. We kill, we slaughter; the screaming of the terror-stricken, the dying, blend with the noise of the beasts which roar and groan from all sides; it is hell, where instead of fire that burns us, snow floods us.[21]

These war crimes were not committed because the ethical standards of nineteenth-century Frenchmen had degenerated; they were motivated by the firm conviction that the colonisation of Algeria would be in the best interests of France.

> Little does it matter that France in her political conduct goes beyond the limits of common morality at times. The essential thing is that she shall establish a lasting colony and that as a consequence she will bring European civilisation to these barbaric countries. When a project which is to the advantage of all humanity is to be carried out, the shortest path is the best. Now, it is certain that the shortest path is terror; without violating the laws of morality, or international jurisprudence, we can fight our African enemies with powder and fire, joined by famine, internal division, war between Arabs and Kabyles, between the tribes of the Tell and those of the Sahara, by brandy, corruption, and disorganisation. That is the easiest thing in the world to do.[22]

In fact, this is exactly what the French troops did, with the full support of their government. In 1841, Tocqueville observed with sarcasm that he had to report 'from Africa the afflicting notion that at this moment we are making war in a manner more barbaric than the Arabs themselves'.[23] Charles Julien tried to use Marshall Bugeaud as a scapegoat by attributing to him the responsibility for the devastation of the Algerian peasant communities. During this period 'when he was unable to vanquish the Algerians militarily, Bugeaud wanted to compel them to submit themselves by destruction and famine'.[24] He went even further than 'destruction' and 'famine' to the point of committing genocide with the full support of his government.

In fact, in 1845, Colonel Pelissier burned 1,000 persons in the grottoes of Dahra. Sergeant Moret, who executed the Colonel's order, wrote that 'the soldiers who set the faggots on fire hurried in a rage to carry the wood', and that he himself, 'furious like the others, gave a hand to the execution of the work . . . The next day . . . one thousand heaped-up corpses were found.'[25] When the news of this event reached Paris, only the Prince of Moskowa dared to denounce it as 'a murder consumed with premeditation against a defenceless enemy'.[26] To this denunciation Governor General Bugeaud replied that he would take the entire responsibility for the deed because he had 'prescribed recourse to such action as a last resort'.

This was neither the first nor the last occurrence of this kind. In fact, the previous year General Cavaignac had proceeded in the same manner among the Sbeah. Canrobert, an officer who participated in this burning, wrote that:

we blew up the entrance of the cave with dynamite and stacked faggots of brush there. In the evening the fire was set. The next day some Sbeah survivors presented themselves at the entrance of the cave requesting their protection to our advanced posts. Their companions, women and children, were dead.[27]

Colonel Saint Arnaud followed the example of his comrades at arms, Pilissier and Cavaignac, when he walled in other peasants from the Sbeah area, two months after the exploits of Colonel Pilissier.

I hermetically sealed all exits and made a vast cemetry. The earth will cover the corpses of these fanatics for ever. No one went down to the caverns; no one but me knows that there are 500 brigands under here who will not cut the throats of the French any more. A confidential report related everything to the Marshal simply, without terrible poetry and without images.[28]

These military acts were neither isolated nor accidental; they reflect strikingly the continuation of the French colonial policy by other means, judged at the time more opportune and consequential than any other course of action.

Table 2.1 *French casualties in Algeria, 1830–51*

Year	Active	Died in hospital	Killed in battle
1831	71,190	1,005	55
1832	21,511	1,998	48
1833	26,681	2,512	
1834	29,858	1,991	24
1835	29,485	2,335	310
1836	29,897	2,139	606
1837	40,147	4,502	121
1838	48,167	2,413	150
1839	50,367	3,600	163
1840	61,204	9,567	227
1841	72,000	7,802	349
1842	70,853	5,588	225
1843	75,034	4,809	84
1844	82,037	4,664	167
1845	95,000	4,664	601
1846	99,700	6,862	116
1847	87,704	4,437	77
1848	75,017	4,406	13
1849	70,774	9,744	
1850	71,496	4,098	
1851	65,598	3,193	
Total		92,329	3,336

Source: J. Ch. M. Boudin, *Histoire statistique de la colonisation en Algérie* (Paris, Bailliers, 1853), p. 53.

As a direct consequence of this kind of colonial war of conquest the total urban and rural population declined from an estimated three million in 1830 to 2,462,000 by 1876.[29] Throughout the nineteenth century the Algerian population of the urban centres, within which European quarters were established, was unable to reproduce itself demographically. Indeed, the total Algerian population did not reach its 1830 level again until 1886, when a census revealed the existence of 3,287,000 persons.[30] A process of depopulation appears to have been ushered in by such unprecedented socio-economic and historical upheavals generated by military colonisation which resulted in the dispossession of a growing number of autochthonous proprietors.

The nature of colonialism

In fact, for the expropriation of 364,341 hectares[31] of land from the rural cultivators alone between 1830 and 1851, the French government had to sacrifice thousands of soldiers. Boudin, the statistician who studied the casualties of the French colonial wars of conquest in Algeria from 1831 to 1851, established the death toll (see Table 2.1). The total number of these French casualties demonstrates the constant resistance put up by the peasantry against the invading army. The figures reveal a collective endeavour on the part specifically of the rural population to prevent the spread and consolidation of colonisation.

The French determination to colonise Algeria was revealed in an official report written in the 1840s on the necessity of accelerating the expansion of land colonisation. 'The state which gets hold of personal properties every day for the "cause of public safety and utility" must become an absolute master of the soil.' The report concluded by emphasising that 'we must face the question of colonising boldly and not stop before any troublesome consequences of an enterprise which must produce such fine and extraordinary results'.[32]

The expropriation of land from the rural population

The agents of public domain administration and their surveyors, 'armed with extraordinary powers',[33] followed the tracks of the colonial army. They accumulated through innumerable arbitrary measures – sequestration, confiscation, expropriation, *cantonnement* and the application of various property bills devised to establish 'incommutable individual property' to transform the soil into a commodity – an increasing number of hectares for the benefit of colonisation.

Thus from 1830 to 1851, 176 *centres de colonisation* were implanted for the settlers, who totalled 151,000 in 1851, of whom 33,000 were rural *colons*. Up to the 1860s the colonial state had followed an economic policy which aimed at the establishment of homestead farmers on the fertile Algerian lands. For example, between 1841 and 1851, 428,000 hectares were allocated to 15,000 settlers, averaging about 28 hectares each. However, after 1860 the colonising effort centred on the development of an agrarian capitalism based on large-scale units of production, usually managed by companies, the bulk of which fell under the control of finance capital or banks.

The constant transfer of land from the hands of the 'indigenous' peasantry to the settlers was disguised under diverse juridical trappings in an attempt to maintain a legalistic façade.

Uneven development

The legal mechanisms of land colonisation: The *sénatus-consulte*, its aims and achievements

The primary aim of this law was 'the disintegration of the tribe'. Its third article prescribed the following procedures:

(1) The delimitation of the territories of the tribes
(2) The break-up of every tribe of the Tell and other agricultural areas
(3) The constitution of individual property and its distribution among the members of the *douars*.[34]

Most *douars* were made up of segments coming from different tribal backgrounds. To quote Brenot

while the tribes [as socio-political units] were disappearing, and from their ashes the political life of innumerable douars was emerging according to the procedures and methods fixed during the application of the *sénatus-consulte*, the administrative and municipal organisation of Algeria was taking shape.[35]

In explaining the purpose of the promulgation of this law, designed to atomise the rural socio-political organisation based on the tribe, General Allard declared that 'the government does not lose sight of the fact that the general tendency of its policy should be to reduce the influence of the chiefs and to break up the tribes'.[36] And A. de Broglie, the man who played a determining role in the promulgation and application of this act, stated that this imperialist measure was aimed primarily at achieving three goals: to 'provoke a general selling-off of the land', so that, as a direct result, it would 'attract and receive immigrants from Europe'; and also to enable the colonial authority 'to disorganise the tribe', which has been the 'principal obstacle to the pacification of Algeria'.[37] For the settlers the primary goal of the *sénatus-consulte* was to abolish 'Arab communism' in order to replace it with the constitution of individual property subject to sale and purchase like all other commodities on the market. One of their spokesmen stated emphatically that once individual property was 'established in the tribe, the Europeans will quickly penetrate there. They will find the necessary land and manpower that they lack.'[38]

The purpose of the disintegration of the social organisation of the peasantry was to induce the colonised peasant to 'detach himself from the native collectivity that can [thenceforth] do nothing for him', so that in the long run he will be forced by economic necessity to 'put himself under European tutelage',[39] in the form of wage labour. Thus the application of the *sénatus-consulte* proved quite effective both in dismembering Algerian rural society and fostering the development of colonisation. As Eric Wolf put it,

this legal act accomplished two things. On the one hand it destroyed in one blow the entire pyramid of overrights which had guaranteed the livelihood of the lowly

The nature of colonialism

cultivator but which had stood in the way of making land a freely circulating commodity. On the other hand it threw all land held by Muslims upon the open market, and made it available for purchase or seizure by French colonists.[40]

In fact, according to Captain Vaissière, the *sénatus-consulte* turned out to be 'the most efficient war mechanism that one could invent against the native social structures. It was the strongest and most resourceful instrument that was put in the hands of our settlers.'[41] And another French civil servant foresaw in 1864 the consequences of the *sénatus-consulte*:

> In Arab society as we have found it, . . . everyone had his share of annual ploughing on collective property . . . At the bottom of that chaos was some guarantee of work and a certain feeling of equality; with the beginning of individualisation it will no longer be the same. Once the land is definitely acquired privately, inequality begins; on one side the owners, on the other side the proletarians.[42]

Indeed, simply as a result of the application of the *sénatus-consulte* between 1863 and 1870, Algerian rural communities as a whole lost a national average of 14 per cent[43] of their best arable lands and all the forests to the public domain, a French office of colonisation that was in charge of the transfer of land from the indigenous peasantry to the European settlers. However, according to Hermassi, 'As it turned out, the operation proved to be an example of the art of spoliation. The first *sénatus-consulte* applied to the 6,883,883 hectares possessed by the Tell communities; it left them with only 1,336,492 hectares, or 19.4 per cent of their land.[44]

At any rate, once the tribal structures, which came to be viewed as the centre of resistance to colonial expansion, were formally dismantled, the French government under Napoleon III attempted to graft the colonial administrative structures on to the traditional village socio-political organisation by trying to co-opt the *jemaa* councils.

Despite the fact that the application of the *sénatus-consulte* resulted in the confiscation of a national average of 14 per cent of the best fertile lands and all forests, the Third Republic abandoned it because it was thought of as 'pro-Arab'. After the fall of Napoleon III, a decree of 19 December 1870 stopped the application of the *sénatus-consulte*. By this date, 372 tribes had had their territories delimited according to this measure, and were broken up administratively into 667 *douars*. Instead, a more drastic measure was passed by the French parliament in 1873, which came to be known as the Warnier Law. This aimed both at the elimination of *arsh* lands, referred to by the settlers as 'collective property', and at breaking up the familial holdings still remaining impartible.

The Warnier Law of 1873

After the defeat of the peasant insurrection of 1871, and the integration of Algeria with France, the representatives of the settlers in the French parliament headed by Warnier decided to 'make the French civil code predominate' in the colony. This legal act resulted in the destructuring of the traditional Algerian land tenure system and in the application of 'the French laws in all land transactions contracted not only between individuals belonging to two different civil statuses, but also between Muslims'. Thus, under the pretext of assimilation and *francisation*, the settlers managed to persuade the French parliament to declare the systematic spoliation of the Algerian rural communities to be legal.

Since the officers of the Bureaux Arabes were made responsible both for the peasant revolt of 1871 and for the lack of rapid development of colonisation, they were disbanded. The application of the Warnier Law was entrusted to the colonial civil service so that it would be applied in thoroughgoing colonial fashion. Any protest raised by the peasants, whose lands were being surveyed and claimed, was silenced either by a show of military force or by police intervention. Indeed, since this law stipulated that unproductive and uncultivated lands must be claimed by the French office of colonisation as belonging to the state, the *Commissaires-Enquêteurs* in charge of these operations considered innumerable hectares of fallow field as uncultivated or vacant, and thus assigned them arbitrarily to the *Domaine*. Undivided familial property held in common by close relatives was split into minute plots; known *melk* landholdings were classified under the category of *arsh* lands. Speculators were even authorised to purchase them even before the law was in effect.[45]

Moreover, the cost of implementing this 'law of settlers' was solely borne by the colonised population. In fact, between 1875 and 1887, the French colonial authority exacted from the rural collectivities 750,000 francs per year to cover the costs of implementation. On the whole, these expenditures for 'the constitution of individual commutable property amounted to about one-tenth of the value of a hectare of the indigenous land'.[46] The tribes of Constantine province alone were forced to pay, between 1873 and 1881, a sum of 2,538,000 francs 'for work that benefited the Europeans alone'.[47] Through the law of 1873, the French office of colonisation appropriated 309,891 hectares out of the 2,239,092 surveyed during this period, that is, 13 per cent of the total. However, the average percentage acquired in the province of Constantine was higher: 19 per cent of the total area surveyed. But the real beneficiaries of the Warnier Law were the settlers who acquired, between 1887 and 1890 alone, 377,877 hectares for the sum of 37,413,300 francs. During the same period, the Algerian peasants managed to buy back from French speculators only 71,173 hectares for a sum of 11,043,977 francs, that is, an average of about 150 francs per hectare compared to the average of 100 francs paid by the settlers.

Another law, the 'second *sénatus-consulte*', was adopted in 1887 which fragmented 224 other tribes into 349 *douars*. Despite the fact that data concerning the populations of the Sahara and even some marginal communities of the north is scarce, Ageron estimated that between 1887 and 1934, 337 tribes were boken up into 529 *douars*. He stated that by the end of 1934, only nineteen tribes remained unfragmented and that 1,500,000 hectares were still to be reclassified and appropriated according to the new canons.[48] This 'second *sénatus-consulte* exploited the communities to which it was applied even more, leaving only 10 per cent of their initial land'. And the author noted that

Although the dispossession of land was effected according to the Napoleonic code, certain clauses of Islamic law were also employed for purposes of justification. The use of Islamic law was selective, of course; if the law favoured appropriation, it was used; if it did not, it was ignored. The French used the eminent right of the sovereign to claim lands that the pre-colonial state had never claimed. Islamic principles were, however, quickly forgotten when it came to the expropriation of religiously inalienable land, the *habous*.[49]

In implementing these French laws, the colonial administrative agents who were in charge of assigning individual property decided to ignore the present possessors of familial landholdings and instead tried to go back in time by several ascending generations to the supposed founder of the estate. They then proceeded to reconstruct the familial genealogies by eliminating various possible successors in order to revive innumerable extinguished claims, a method allowing them to divide familial landholdings between hundreds of co-owners. Since the pre-colonial legal system divided estates into two categories, direct and indirect heirs who received unequal shares, the *Commissaires-Enquêteurs* distributed titles of land on paper, which turned out to be worthless in the sense that they could not be translated into actual plots: for example, a share was fixed at 1/19,000, representing an area of 20 centiares (about one-fifth of a square yard). Thus the holders to titles were assigned parcels of land on which they could hardly put their feet.

The systematic fragmentation of familial holdings became an effective instrument of spoliation in the hands of the speculators. Usurious loans with power of redemption led to the dispossession of innumerable peasants. The speculators used every imaginable means to provoke a legal sale by auction. To obtain this they had to constrain or bribe a co-owner to sell his title either because he was unable to pay back his debts or because his credit

Uneven development

Table 2.2 *The development of colonialism*

Period	Centres created or expanded	Hectares of land distributed to settlers	French population in Algeria
1841–1850	126	115,000	56,437
1851–1860	85	250,000	103,322
1861–1870	21	116,000	129,898
1871–1880	264	401,099	195,418
1881–1890	107	176,000	267,672
1891–1900	103	120,000	364,257
1901–1920	199	200,000	633,149
1921–1933	67	270,481	733,206
Total	972	1,648,580	2,492,359

Source: A. Benachenhou, *Formation du sous-développement en Algérie: 1830–1962* (Algiers, OPU, 1976), p. 213.

term had expired. Once he became a co-owner, a speculator requested an impossible division, which always resulted in a legal sale by auction. The French court's sale by auction was a complicated legal procedure which brought about the inevitable ruin of the other co-owners for the sole benefit of the speculator who had initiated the operation. Between 1871 and 1896 alone, legal sales by auction of this kind amounted to no fewer than 17,000, which allowed private colonists to appropriate in this fashion 563,000 hectares of arable land in the most fertile areas of Algeria.[50]

The pace of colonisation accelerated after the defeat of the rebellion of 1871. By 1880 the colonial state had already distributed 880,000 hectares of fertile land, expropriated from the Algerian rural producers, to the settlers, and created and enlarged 496 *centres de colonisation*. Commercial transactions in land, transformed into a mere commodity, permitted the settlers to purchase 165,000 hectares. Over one million hectares of arable land passed from the hands of the Algerians to the settlers.[51]

From the outset expropriation from the owners of land took two distinct forms: official, and private colonisation through the market mechanism. The former was carried out by outright confiscation of land and its distribution to the European settlers. Between 1830 and 1934 the colonial state wrested 1,648,677 hectares of the best land from the Algerian owners and handed them over to the settlers. It also constructed or expanded up to this date a cumulative total of 972 *centres de colonisation*. Table 2.2 details the progressive development of official colonisation.

Table 2.3 *Land transactions between the settlers and the Algerians*

	Land sold by Algerians to settlers		Land sold by settlers to Algerians	
Period	Hectares	Cost (francs)	Hectares	Cost (francs)
Before 1877	54,990	n.a.	31,878	n.a.
1878–1898	563,762	56,495,302	131,374	20,087,471
1899–1908	277,428	31,329,295	125,794	25,887,329
1909–1914	382,749	59,271,977	79,953	28,884,400
1915–1919	80,963	34,943,880	79,608	55,245,310
1920–1934	352,896	380,607,841	250,325	400,275,674
Grand total	1,712,787	562,648,295	698,932	530,380,184

Source: A. Benachenhou, *Formation du sous-développement*, p. 217.

The expropriation of the Algerian peasantry constituted a necessary measure for colonial capitalism to concentrate land into the hands of some settlers or European companies and hence to transform the dispossessed owners into propertyless free labourers whose only means of subsistence was to sell their labour to the new owners of the means of production. Under capitalist conditions the process of appropriation/expropriation also entails commercial translations which played a determinant role in the transfer of land from the Algerian peasants, at first to the French settlers and later on to the autochthonous landlords as well. The land transactions between the settlers and the Algerians are summarised in Table 2.3.

This table reveals one of the most striking features of the commercial transactions: the unequal terms of exchange between the colonisers and the colonised. The market favours the group that possesses political power and military might. In fact, while the settlers acquired a total of 1,712,992 hectares with a mere 562,648,295 francs, the autochthonous buyers purchased only 698,932 hectares from the settlers (one-third of the land bought by the latter) for no less than 530,380 francs, which is almost equivalent to what the Europeans paid for over 1.7 million hectares!

The transfer of land from the autochthonous owners to the settlers took place as summarised in Table 2.4. By the early 1950s the French colonisers had managed to appropriate under various forms the bulk of northern Algeria. Indeed, according to the 1950–1 agricultural census the structure of landholding was as follows: eleven million hectares came to be controlled

Uneven development

Table 2.4 *Transfer of land to the settlers, 1830–1951*

Dates	Hectares controlled by the settlers
1830–1850	115,000
1851–1870	765,000
1871–1880	1,245,000
1881–1890	1,635,000
1891–1900	1,912,000
1901–1920	2,581,000
1921–1940	2,445,000
1941–1951	2,726,666

Source: René Gallissot, *L'Economie du l'Afrique du Nord* (Paris, PUF, 1964), p. 40.

by the colonial state; 2,703,000 hectares were owned by the settlers (this was the most fertile and hence the most productive land); and only 7,133,000 hectares still belonged to the Algerian landowners.[52] The cultivation of this land required the development of a basic infrastructure which was not only built by Algerian labour but also financed by taxes imposed upon the autochthonous producers.

The development of a basic infrastructure and taxation

The construction of a basic infrastructure necessary for the development of the colony required not only Algerian labour but also financial resources. The extension of land colonisation and the multiplication of French settlements throughout Algeria necessitated the development of modern communication, such as roads and railways; by 1880, 8,500 km of roads and railways had been constructed. These communication lines were designed to provide vital services to the settlers, to facilitate the military and administrative control of the 'natives' and to integrate the various local communities into the market.

Between 1830 and 1880 the cost of this infrastructure amounted to 601 million gold francs (equivalent to 103 billion francs in 1950 values). To finance such development the colonial state resorted to a special system of taxation imposed upon the Algerians from the beginning of colonisation, the *impôts arabes*. Up to 1911 the 'natives' contributed over 46 per cent of the successive budgets allocated to the development of the colony.[53]

The inequitable nature of this taxation was such that in 1880 alone, out of a total of 35 million gold francs in tax receipts, 22 million was paid by Algerians, rising to 30 million by 1887. Thus, before the 1919 tax reform, the Algerians furnished 75 per cent of the total direct taxes collected. Despite the abolition of the *impôts arabes* the total taxes of the Algerian agriculturalists rose by 19.6 per cent during the 1901–30 period.

In addition, indirect taxes in colonial Algeria, which were raised in 1918, contributed to the overwhelming majority of taxes collected. Again, they fell mainly on the Algerians, because of their number. They paid 73.3 per cent of the total collected in 1918, 72.5 per cent in 1926 and 74.6 per cent in 1929. By 1930, the Algerians paid 55 per cent of the total taxes collected in the colony. This cash flow from the 'natives' to the colonial treasury enabled the administration to continue its programme of development. Indeed, from 1909 to 1948, 449 billion old francs (1950 prices) were spent on the construction of infrastructure, social services and mine prospecting, representing an annual average of 11.5 billion.

The development of colonisation was bound to engender an increasing demand for Algerian labour. Furthermore, the policy of settlement through military conquest implied a demographic component in colonisation.

Chapter 3

Colonial development, population and manpower

The demographic aspects of colonisation

The outright seizure of buildings and businesses and land expropriation in the countryside undermined the foundations of the Algerian pre-colonial modes of production and the social system corresponding to them. This historical fact was bound to upset the economic activities of numerous small commodity producers – peasants, craftsmen and artisans – who, with the exception of the *khammassats*, controlled their own means of production. Moreover, only the bulk of urban specialists emerged as generalised commodity producers; while production for use was still prevalent in the countryside. These rural small producers were also involved to a limited degree in commodity-exchange. In effect, a peasant household had to transform some of its surplus use-values into exchange-values to be sold in the local market in order to acquire other necessary commodities which satisfied the basic requirements of their existence. At any rate, these modes of production were torn asunder by the forcible superimposition of an elaborate social system, based on large-scale commodity production. The primary natural resources appropriated from the environment through the medium of human labour were confiscated from the 'native' producers and reallocated to the increasing stream of European immigrants.

Therefore, the concept of colonisation itself entailed a demographic component in the colonising process. While France was resolving its demographic pressures by diverting its surplus population and 'troublesome' working-class elements to Algeria, the dispossessed Algerian populations were destined to bear alone the socio-economic consequences of this colonial policy. For instance, after the revolution of 1848, the French government decided to rid Paris of 20,500 workers who dared to erect barricades. It requested the national assembly to vote 55 million francs to be used for their transport costs and installation in Algeria. From the end of 1848 to 1850, these 20,500 proletarians were transformed into 'reluctant pioneers'. Upon their arrival in Algeria they were assigned to 56 *centres de colonisation* that were specially made for them. The colonial army provided them with constructed houses, arable land, instruments of cultivation,

Table 3.1 *Growth of the Algerian population*

Year	Total	Rural	Urban
1856	2,496,067	—	—
1866	2,921,246	—	—
1876	2,867,626	—	—
1886	3,827,306	3,061,091	226,126
1896	4,429,421	—	—
1906	5,231,850	3,704,453	341,691
1911	5,563,828	—	—
1921	5,804,275	—	—
1931	6,553,451	4,419,943	606,440
1936	7,234,684	4,847,814	722,293
1948	8,681,785	5,747,930	1,129,482
1954	9,529,726	7,051,796	1,397,536
1960	9,569,568*	—	—

*These figures are taken from successive censuses. Although they do not add up I could not correct them.
Source: Successive censuses.

livestock, food and spending money.[1] On 21 June, 1871, the French government granted 100,000 hectares of land in Algeria to the refugees from Alsace-Lorraine, who numbered about 8,000. They were installed in 80 *centres de colonisation*. Thus, the economic resources at the disposal of the Algerian producers were gradually eroded as countless waves of immigrants arrived in Algeria. The number of European settlers grew from 7,812 in 1833 to 984,031 in 1954.

Up to 1906, the annual inflow of immigrants into the colony far exceeded the natural growth of the European population there. A comparison between the Algerian and European populations will illustrate this point. Although the exact population of Algeria before 1830 is still a matter for debate, a large number of scholars tend to agree now with the general census realised by the French army's intelligence service under the supervision of the *bureaux arabes*, which in 1845 gave a figure of three million inhabitants. The number of inhabitants of the unoccupied territories was based on rough estimates; it could be greater than this figure indicates. Nevertheless, in 1856, when the first extensive census was taken by the colonial authorities, only 2,487,373 people, including the settlers, were still alive in Algeria. Thenceforth regular censuses were taken. Table 3.1 summarises the growth of the Algerian population between 1956 and 1960.

Uneven development

Between 1830 and 1876, the Algerian population declined, but after the census of 1881, it started to grow again. The publication of this census shook some colonial circles in Algeria. It surprised the colonial racial supremacists, who asserted that 'history is here to prove that the inferior races have always been either absorbed or destroyed by the superior races'.[2] And two professors at the University of Algiers School of Medicine, Battandier and Trabut, affirmed that the native's 'traditional laziness will condemn him sooner or later to disappear before the more active races'.[3] When events turned out otherwise and all publications of subsequent censuses indicated a steady population increase.

The colonial press was often astonished by this growth in the number of Muslim Algerians, seeking to explain it by the improvement in census procedures. This is due to the old prejudice which was still alive that assumed the slow extinction of the native by the sole fact of his contact with 'civilisation'.[4]

Indeed, the French theorists who predicted the doom of the native 'race' had based their assumptions on the actual decline of the Algerian population that occurred between 1830 and 1881. Moreover, by 1903, its birth rate had overtaken that of the European population: 32.1 per cent as against 30.9 per cent. This fact alarmed some settlers. In 1889 one of their representatives declared before a parliamentary inquiry commission that 'the natives had almost quadrupled since 1866. If they continued, in ten years they would reach ten million, and in thirty, sixteen.'

The causes of population growth under colonial conditions

There is no doubt that the increase in the population resulted in the continual immiseration of successive generations of the Algerian peasantry. However, a greater number of children was certainly considered by the adult population to be a potential economic asset. The reason for this popular belief lay in the fact that on the one hand the joint households could not keep themselves together unless they diversified their economic base by sending their surplus members out as wage labourers, and on the other, the traditional Middle Eastern and North African peasantries that owned their lands tended to favour the growth of their families because when the sons reached maturity the household might be able to expand its landholdings. As a British demographer noted:

let us look at the question from a point of view of the extended family, presuming, as is usually the case, that it is engaged in peasant agriculture. Such a family will see a child, subject to a short period of waiting, as an economic asset. By the time it has reached the age of seven, the work which it will do on the farm or in the household will exceed the cost of its keep.[5]

An additional child would make possible, and require, an increase of production both in livestock and agriculture. Thus the wealth controlled by the head of the peasant household would be augmented; the surplus produced by each member would be pooled in his hands, and the whole family, as the basic productive and demographic unit, benefit by the increase.

In the pre-colonial period this situation could go on as long as the birth rate was evened off by the high death rate. Growth of the total population was either accompanied or followed by an increase in economic production because the extraction of taxes from the countryside was relatively small and the limits of agricultural frontiers were still expandable. However, with the delimitation and confiscation of tribal territories and the imposition of new tax requirements, not only were these frontiers closed permanently but the cultivated terrain was drastically decreased by both the expansion of colonisation and depletion and erosion. Henceforth, the peasant communities lived under conditions of chronic land shortage. When the remaining arable plots were filled up, the burden of supporting a large and growing family on a fixed land base was deeply felt.

The problem which needs to be tackled now is the causes underlying this rapid demographic growth. Up to now the majority of scholars of the so-called underdeveloped countries have accounted for it in terms of the removal of the Malthusian checks: famine control through improved communication; the introduction of scientific public health services; the establishment of colonial peace; the amelioration of the standards of living; increasing per capita income in agriculture, and so on. None of these explanations can be applied to rural Algeria. According to S. H. Coontz:

it is generally held that the increase in population in colonial areas is due entirely to mortality decline resulting from the introduction of Western techniques, e.g. an improved transportation system which eliminates local famines, better sanitation, vaccines, etc. Certainly these operate to reduce mortality. However, unless in the long run there are concomitant changes in demand for labour, a continued increase in population is inconceivable. The demand-for-labour analysis suggests that more attention must be paid to factors which increase the demand for labour and reduce the average value of labour-power in colonial areas.[6]

Thus Malthusian explanations have to be rejected both on theoretical and empirical grounds. The only plausible explanation in this case might, in fact, lie in the demand-for-labour analysis or variable. The growth of the population of Algeria can in this sense be considered as a demographic response to the colonial situation which produced a high demand for labour both inside the peasant household subsistence economy and in the colonial sector. As a whole, the Algerian colonial conditions corresponded to ones which Coontz considered favourable for population growth. He stated that

Uneven development

'in demand-for-labour analysis, the situation favourable to population growth is one in which an increased demand for labour is accompanied by a reduction in the average quality (cost) of the labour-power demanded'.[7]

Demand for labour and colonisation in Algeria

From the outset the *colons* and their public officials realised the potential advantages that could be derived from the surplus labour of the pauperised population. As early as 5 March 1849 the Higher Council of the French Government in Algeria, for the purpose of inducing the impoverished peasants to till the farms of the settlers either as share-croppers or agricultural labourers, decreed that 'all natives are subject to special taxes (*Impôts Arabes*), except those employed as share-croppers on the European estates, inhabiting a house, and working under the supervision of a European landowner or his manager'.[8] In another official report sent from Algeria to the Ministry of War in Paris, it was emphatically stated that 'the advantages that colonialism could extract from the Arab workers had already been appreciated by the European landowners, who, without any exception, are already employing share-croppers on their holdings'.[9]

In urging the colonial authorities in Algeria to facilitate the utilisation of the 'indigenous manpower' on the newly established agricultural plantations and industrial enterprises implanted in the colony, the Minister of War wrote on 15 October 1851:

To attract the Arab labourer to work for the French owners . . . is the best and most proper thing to do so that French domination will be asserted definitively . . . we find in the Arab worker several essential qualities. He is sober and does not have too many needs; no matter how hard the tasks he is given to perform, he is less discontented than the European worker. He is robust and acclimatised and this permits us to count on him for all seasons. He is intelligent and docile.[10]

It must be noted that throughout the early colonisation period, the Algerian population was forced to provide labour for the construction of roads, and of *centres de colonisation* and to perform various other services without any compensation. From 1830 to 1871, forced labour was in evidence in Algeria; the 'requisition of native manpower for public utility work' was admitted by the army officers in their attempt to oppose the introduction of the Arab workers into the centres of colonisation lest they lost their free labourers to the *colons*, who at least offered some sort of wage. But on 15 October 1851 the Minister of War, who was in charge of Algeria, rejected the army's objection in the following terms:

The introduction, on a large scale, of Arab or Kabyle manpower into agricultural work is a goal towards which the administration has to concentrate all its efforts and which it has to pursue by all means in its power. It is obvious, in effect, that without this powerful auxiliary, cultivation would long be shackled by the high wages and scarcity of European workers.[11]

The Algerians worked for the settlers not only as share-croppers but as wage labourers on a daily or monthly basis. In 1851 they were paid between two and two-and-a-half francs per day. Those who worked on a monthly basis were offered only twenty to thirty francs per month. On studying the differences in wages between the Arab and the French labourers, a colonial official concluded his report by stating that:

> I have indicated what is more important, and it is easy to judge the enormous difference in the sum to be paid for the employment of an Arab labourer compared with that offered to a French labourer . . . It is sufficient to ensure that the price paid to the indigenous worker will not ordinarily exceed a quarter of that which we are obliged to give the European worker.[12]

It was recognised officially in 1851 that 'for a long time almost all the big concessionaries of land . . . in the civil territory have been using indigenous labourers for cultivation of their estates. They recruited them from everywhere.'[13]

The gradual widening of the perimeter of colonisation, which was compared by Bugeaud to a 'spot of oil', resulted simultaneously in the dispossession of the peasants and, consequently, in the increasing demand for native manpower, which played a determinant role in the development of the colony. The introduction of vineyards into Algeria in the 1860s accelerated the process of proletarianisation of a large number of despoiled peasants who were concentrated during the *cantonnement* period in rural slums. For these destitute people, the only salvation from famine, epidemics and collective despair lay in wage labour in the colonial sector. The acceptance of work, either as share-croppers or wage labourers on the confiscated plots of land and newly consolidated fields of the *colons*, was the only course to be followed under the circumstances. It was a matter of survival. The eagerness of the settlers and their government to utilise 'native manpower' to build the colonial edifice made the decision easier for the pauperised population. The situation was regarded as a means of consolidating the colonial power relations within the colony. As noted above, both the settlers and their high officials were in full agreement about the vital importance of reducing and restricting the role of the native population to that of subservient colonised manpower, to be used with careful surveillance, not to sap, but to contribute to the development of colonisation. General Bedeau stated that

> Colonisation with its requirements will be the touchstone of real submission; it will at last put the conquering people and the conquered in their rightful places . . . Only by its mass can the colony reduce them to the point where agitation is

Uneven development

impossible . . . There must be no empty space between us and the Arab population which, under careful surveillance, should supply the tribute of its labour and resources of the colony surrounding it in its growth, like the hedge around a cleared field, which is built up with the thorns that have been pulled out of it.[14]

In the long run, the exorbitant requirements of colonialism kept multiplying the ranks of the Algerian proletariat. In fact, after the defeat of the peasant rebellion of 1871, which was triggered by a series of spoliative measures directed against the peasantry during the 1860s, the core of the rural society was destroyed. The failure of the insurrection inaugurated a new period in the history of colonialism in Algeria. The peasants who were the prime movers of the revolt were finally ruined. Indeed, after this rebellion, 665,591 hectares were 'sequestered', that is, grabbed from the defeated peasantry and redistributed to the settlers. A levy of 68 million gold francs was imposed on the peasants as war compensation and paid to the colonial government.[15] Henceforth they resigned themselves to various piecemeal adjustments to the colonial system.

Besides such instances of outright seizure of their plots of land, the introduction and spread of the capitalist market plunged the peasants into a vicious circle. The international 'invisible hand' generated a

cycle which starts when the peasant is forced to sell his produce immediately after the harvest in order to pay off his debts – to sell, that is to say, at the bottom price. It continues when five or six months later he is compelled to buy the same produce back at the top price, which means at least double the figure he was given for it. It is easy to see that at this rate the unhappy man gets deeper and deeper into the hopeless difficulties.[16]

Peasants resorted to borrowing money in a desperate attempt to break the circle.

Thus, as pointed out above, colonisation entailed the expropriation in one form or another of the basic factor of production, land, from the peasantry, and its redistribution to the settlers. The transfer of this basic factor of production was followed, on one hand, by the rapid development and prosperity of the colonial sector and on the other, by an increase of the Algerian population despite the subsequent deterioration of the peasant subsistence economy. These interrelated phenomena generated a tremendous demand for labour both by the peasant household productive units and by the colonial sector. Indeed, the removal of land and labour, coupled with the exaction of taxes in cash from the traditional sector, made it imperative for the peasants to increase labour input. This was conducive to a more intensive expansion of agriculture which involved the clearing of wooded areas. The intensification of gardening and forestry on their remaining plots required more labour.

However, despite this effort to resolve the economic crisis ushered in by colonisation, the living conditions of the rural direct producers continued to deteriorate throughout the colonial period. Indeed, Algeria possessed over 8 million sheep in 1867, but by 1927 only 3.3 million, rising to 6.4 million in 1938 before declining to 6.2 million in 1955. The number of goats decreased from 3.7 million in the 1880s to 2.1 million in 1927, increasing to 3.25 million in 1938 and to 3.35 million by 1955. The number of cattle fell from one million in 1887 to 707,000 in 1927, rising to 886,000 in 1938 and 912,000 in 1955. Simultaneously, the Algerian population grew from about 4.5 million in 1906 (82.7 per cent rural) to 6.2 million in 1936 (78.2 per cent rural), 7.67 million in 1948 (74.8 per cent rural), 8.44 million in 1954 (70.5 per cent rural) and 9.6 million in 1960 (65.05 per cent rural). As a direct result, the basic resources of this growing population have become increasingly scarce. Thus, in 1871, there were 200 cattle, 1,533 sheep and 694 goats per 100 persons; by 1953 this average had fallen to 90 cattle, 631 sheep and 330 goats.

Total cereal production declined from an annual average of 19.6 million quintals between 1921 and 1929 to 14 million quintals between 1941 and 1948. The production of olive oil fell from 35,000 hectolitres in 1910 to 16,500 in 1940. The average quantity of cereals per person diminished from 5 quintals in 1871 to less than 2 quintals by 1953. Thus, shrinking resources coincided with a rapid demographic growth, and a double process of pauperisation and proletarianisation resulted.

Chapter 4

Socio-economic consequences of colonial development

The proletarianisation of the rural population

Once the capitalist mode of production was introduced into Algeria it subjected all the pre-existing socio-economic forms to the exigencies of capital accumulation for the benefit of the settlers, who, besides land and capital, needed a free labour force. However, in order to be induced to work for the colonisers as share-croppers or wage-labourers, rural producers had to be expropriated; and the socio-economic organisation of their respective communities had to be disintegrated and reorientated.

Confronted with elastic, fluid and resistant socio-economic structures, and lacking necessary credit for the modernisation of the techniques of production, the settlers resorted to the Algerian pre-capitalist contractual relations of production, namely the *khammassat* (share-cropping), as well as leasing or renting their lands to Algerian producers. In fact, by the 1880s one-third of the colonised land was either cultivated by the Algerian *khammas* or simply rented to impoverished peasants in the province of Constantine, which comprised over one-third of the entire country.

By 1930 out of 617,544 Algerian landowners, 434,537 possessed fewer than 10 hectares each, averaging 4 hectares per landowner. According to Ageron 'the threshold of malnutrition [for a peasant family] ranged from 12 to 20 hectares, depending on the regions. Economically two-thirds of the *fellahin* came to form not an independent peasantry but rather a group of semi-proletarians'.[1] Indeed, the agricultural census of 1951 revealed that 70 per cent of the Algerian landowners possessed fewer than 10 hectares of land each; the bulk of which was located either on mountain slopes or in areas receiving an insufficient annual average of rainfall. Table 4.1 details the processes of pauperisation and proletarianisation of the rural population between 1901 and 1960.

Thus, landlessness forced a large number of Algerian peasants to become either *khammas* or permanent or seasonal labourers working for the settlers. Between 1930 and 1960 alone, the number of Algerian landowners fell from 617,544 to 373,000, a 40 per cent decrease in 30 years, while the total rural population rose from less than 4.5 million in 1931 to almost 7 million in

Socio-economic consequences

Table 4.1 *The process of pauperisation and proletarianisation of the rural population, 1901–60*

Year	Peasant landholders	% change	Farmers	Khammas	Labourers	% change
1901	620,899	—	37,455	350,715	152,108	—
1910	530,211	−14.6	n.a.	426,851	207,707	36.5
1914	565,218	6.6	40,755	407,050	210,205	1.2
1930	617,544	9.3	50,771	643,600	534,000	154
1938	549,395	−11.0	n.a.	713,000	462,467	−13.4
1948	537,800	−2.1	n.a.	132,900	483,900	4.6
1954	503,700	−6.3	n.a.	60,300	571,000	18.2
1960	373,000	−25.9	n.a.	n.a.	421,000	−26.4

Sources: Adapted from Ch. A. Ageron, *Les Algériens musulmans et la France: 1871–1919* (Paris, PUF, 1968), vol. 2, pp. 226–7, and A. Nouschi, *La Naissance du nationalisme algérien* (Paris, Minuit, 1962).

1959, representing a 54 per cent increase.

As a result, the number of *khammas* went up from 350,715 in 1901 to 713,000 by 1938, decreasing to 132,000 in 1948 and to 60,500 in 1954. This fall was caused by the rapid increase of labour migration to Europe and by the modernisation, especially mechanisation, of colonial agriculture. However, some settlers continued to resort to this kind of contractual arrangement to cultivate their land. In 1950, 10,138 Algerian *khammas* were still at work on 2,218 colonial farms, 59 per cent of which exceeded 50 hectares. Table 4.1 also indicates that the number of agricultural labourers rose from 152,108 in 1901 to 534,000 in 1930, to a peak of 571,000 in 1954, declining to 421,000 by 1960. The overwhelming majority of them worked in the colonial agricultural sector which specialised primarily in the production of export crops.

Colonisation, which destroyed the previous social hierarchies of rural Algeria, generated a new socio-economic stratification. Although the two (French and Algerian) national groups appear to have constituted two distinct social classes, one dominant and the other subordinate, each ethnic grouping was also highly stratified socio-economically. Rural society illustrates this point clearly. The agricultural census of 1950–1 revealed that a different access to land existed between and within these two national groups. Table 4.2 summarises the results of this census.

The 22,007 French landowners possessed a total of 2,726,700 hectares of the best land, an average of 124 hectares per farm, while the 630,732

Uneven development

Table 4.2 *Distribution of land between Algerians and settlers and among each national grouping, 1954*

	Number of units		Area (1,000 hectares)	
Category	French	Algerians	French	Algerians
Less than 1 ha	2,392	105,954	0.8	372.0
1–10 ha	5,039	332,529	21.8	1,341.2
10–50 ha	5,585	167,170	135.3	3,185.8
50–100 ha	2,635	16,580	186.9	1,096.7
More than 100 ha	6,385	8,499	2,381.9	1,689.4
Total	22,036	630,732	2,726.7	7,685.1

Source: Gouvernement Général de l'Algérie, *Tableaux de l'économie algérienne* (1960), p. 45.

Table 4.3 *Distribution of agricultural income within Algerian rural society, 1955*

Socio-economic category	Number of persons (thousands)	Total income (billion old francs)	Per capital income (thousand old francs)
Workers:			
Permanent	100	10	100
Seasonal	500	24	40–60
Landowners:			
Small	210	43	60
Medium	210	42	200
Large	50	28	560
Colonised land		93	
Total	1,070	240	

Source: Samir Amin, *L'Economie du Maghreb* (Paris, Editions de Minuit, 1966), p. 130.

Algerian landowners had a total of 7,348,700 hectares, an average of 11½ hectares per property. Only 6,385 settlers owned no fewer than 2,381,900 hectares. Similarly, 8,499 Algerian landowners possessed 1,689,000 hectares, while 7 percent of the Algerian peasant proprietors owned less than 1 hectare each; no fewer than 53 per cent of them owned between 1 and 10 hectares, 26 per cent from 10 to 50 hectares and 4 per cent more than 50 hectares. In short, about 70 per cent of the Algerian landowners possessed only 18 per cent of the cultivable land, an average of only 3.1 hectares per cultivator. They definitely fell short of the minimum necessary for the subsistence of a productive family unit.

Furthermore, an analysis of the distribution of agricultural income summarised in Table 4.3 shows that Algerian rural society had become highly stratified by the middle of the 1950s. The modern farmers, who constituted about 4 per cent of the rural population, received 13 per cent of the agricultural income. The middle peasants represented 22 per cent of the agricultural population and received over 20 per cent of the revenue. On the bottom of the scale there were over half a million paupers who regularly alternated between their small plots of land, seasonal wage labour on the colonial plantations and unemployment. Permanent rural workers constituted a small minority.

On the whole, the Algerian rural communities, which represented 70 per cent of the total population, received only 18 per cent of the national income. The settlers, who comprised 10 per cent of the total population, acquired 47 per cent of the country's income.

One of the reasons underlying this inequitable distribution of income might be the difference in the quality of land possessed by each national group. The French settlers appropriated the most fertile areas, to the extent that the total revenue from the 22,007 French farming units was much higher than the total revenue from the 630,732 Algerian landholdings. The yield per hectare was four times greater in the colonial sector, whose production was also highly specialised in certain lucrative crops.

The specialisation of colonial agriculture

After the first twenty years of experimentation, the settlers began specialising, mostly in cereal production. By 1872 wheat cultivation covered 158,607 hectares of land, which yielded over 1.36 million quintals. In the 1880s the area devoted to wheat extended over 232,129 hectares, producing close to two million quintals of wheat. By 1910 the total surface planted with cereals rose to over one million hectares, yielding a total value of about 300 million francs. At this time the pattern of colonial agriculture was as shown in Table 4.4.

However, by 1934 the area covered with cereals decreased to 796,941 hectares, while 675,488 hectares remained fallow. By 1951–2, the figures were 824,204 and 682,034 hectares respectively.[2] As Table 4.4 shows, the second specialisation of colonial agriculture was viticulture: wine was one of the most lucrative cash crops of the colony. Indeed, the total area covered

Table 4.4 *The pattern of colonial agricultural production, 1910*

Type of plantation	Cultivated area (hectares)	Annual value (old francs)	% of total
Cereals	1,195,456	298,864,400	38
Vineyards	182,000	355,000,000	44
Industrial crops	103,151	103,151,000	13
Orange groves	10,750	32,250,000	4
Miscellaneous	355,352	10,665,960	1
Total	1,846,709	799,931,360	100

Source: Benachenhou, *Formation du sous-développement*, p. 142.

with vineyards rose from 182,000 hectares in 1910 to 399,447 by 1939, producing about 13 million hectolitres of wine for export alone. By 1960, although the growing area had declined to about 350,000 hectares, 18.8 million hectolitres were still being exported.

From the 1930s onwards colonial farmers began expanding their fruit and vegetable production. The area devoted to these crops extended from 7,500 hectares in 1938 to 34,455 hectares by 1961. These plantations turned out to be as lucrative as vineyards. Although they covered only 4 per cent of the agricultural land they were yielding over 10 per cent of the total value of agricultural production. Tobacco plantations also expanded during the twentieth century, increasing from 16,500 hectares in 1916 to 24,490 by 1930.

In sum, although certain crops such as dry vegetables almost doubled between 1938 and 1955, potatoes actually doubled and fruits quadrupled, as a whole Algerian agriculture already showed strong signs of stagnation and in some cases even noticeable regression. For example, the rapid growth of fruit production was stimulated by the extension of the irrigated area from 249 hectares in 1940 to 41,600 hectares by 1950, which was made possible by the construction of at least five major dams during the period. Nevertheless, the main products, sheep, wine and cereals, were certainly stagnating. Agronomists attributed this sluggishness to the 'strip-mining method' of cultivation practised by the settlers in an attempt to maximise their profits, to the absence of 'association between farming and animal breeding' in the colonial sector, to the reluctance of cereal growers to use chemical fertilisers and to the absolute lack of modernisation of the 'traditional sector'.

The first two explanations need to be examined in more detail. By the end of the colonial period the French agronomist Mazoyer noted that in

Table 4.5 *Daily pay: a comparison between Algerian and European agricultural wages, 1913–30 (francs)*

Year	Algerians	Europeans
1913	2.5	6–8
1920	5–6	10–12
1930	13–14	16–18

Source: A. Bernard, *La Main d'oeuvre dans l'Afrique du Nord* (Official Report) (1930), pp. 9, 32, 48.

Algeria during one century the 'search for the highest returns' from the land and the absence of an association between cultivation and animal husbandry, which prevented the regeneration of humus by the spreading of manure, resulted in the over-exploitation of the soil. This contributed to the impoverishment of the soil and hence to the decline of agricultural production.

Nonetheless, the total value of colonial agricultural production rose from over 130 billion old francs in 1932 to 155 billion by 1955. The main crops cultivated by the settlers for export were cereals, wine, tobacco, fruit and vegetables, halfa (esparto grass) and cork. Despite a slight diversification of commercial agriculture the most profitable crops remained, throughout the history of colonial Algeria, wine and cereals, representing 69 per cent of the total value. Their cultivation was profitable because of the low wages paid to Algerian workers. By 1914, 121,791 agricultural labourers out of a total of 386,000 were engaged in cereal growing, and 107,786 in viticulture. Despite the gradual mechanisation of colonial agriculture the Europeans continued to rely on a large number of Algerian labourers both on a full-time and on a seasonal basis.

Since capital accumulation in colonial Algeria was derived primarily from the agricultural sector, the bulk of the Algerian working class was cantonned in agriculture. However, this proletariat was underpaid. Table 4.5 illustrates the unequal pay of Algerian and European agricultural workers, which allowed the exaction of a substantial surplus value from the colonised workers.

In 1932, a European semi-skilled agricultural worker earned an average of 22.5 francs per day, while an Algerian semi-skilled labourer was paid only 8 to 10 francs for the same work. A European unskilled worker received 10.8 francs; an Algerian, between 4 and 6 francs per day.

Despite the progressive mechanisation of colonial agriculture the settlers continued to employ a relatively large number of labourers, especially on a

Uneven development

Table 4.6 *The use of farm machinery by settlers and Algerians, 1930*

Machinery	Settlers	%	Algerians	%
European plough	11,950	55.83	88,562	44.17
Algerian plough	4,411	1.28	339,650	98.72
Harvester (old type)	13,099	84.88	3,334	15.12
Locomobile	1,404	92.12	120	7.88
Harvester (new type)	1,388	88.70	177	11.30
Automated plough	3,360	92.58	269	7.42
Earth mover	145	99.32	1	0.68

Source: Benachenhou, *Formation du sous-développement*, p. 216.

seasonal basis. Indeed, the mechanisation of the colonial sector developed rapidly with the introduction of 'dry farming' at the end of the nineteenth century. Among the settlers the number of 'European ploughs' rose from 81,522 in 1915 to 257,000 by 1930; tractors from zero to 5,334; harvesters (old type) from 3,459 to 13,099 and harvesters (new type) from zero to 440. As Table 4.6 shows, very few Algerian large landowners had begun to modernise their techniques by the 1930s.

Between the 1930s and the 1950s the mechanisation of colonial agriculture continued. For example, the number of tractors rose from 5,600 in 1939 to 20,508 in 1955, and harvesters from nearly 500 to 3,730. By 1960 the number of tractors had reached 29,200. In short, the gradual mechanisation of colonial agriculture which had begun after the fair of 1878 also contributed to the increased pace of rural exodus. For example, one bulldozer replaced no fewer than 500 workers and one harvester, manned by only four workers, put 100 agricultural labourers out of work. As a result, by 1954, the colonial agricultural sector employed only 200,000 permanent workers, that is, those who worked at least 90 days per year. For the unemployed population the only alternative was migration, either to the Algerian urban centres, whose traditional handicrafts, education and even arts were completely undermined by colonial development, or to France in search of wage labour.

The decline of traditional handicrafts and education

The colonial power had severely hampered the urban craft 'corporations' by restrictive administrative measures, specifically those of 1838 and 1851. Finally, in 1868, they decided to abolish them altogether.[3] Gradually the Algerian handicraft industries almost disappeared.[4] 'The number of Algerian artisans declined from 100,000 in the mid nineteenth century, to 3,500 in 1951.'[5] Indeed, the opening of the Algerian market to the French speculators and the thrusting of the entire economy, without any tariff protection, first into the 'metropolitan' and then into the international market, undermined the local market for Algerian handicrafts. By 1930

all the utensils for domestic use that were manufactured by the potters, tinkers, smelters, coppersmiths and tinsmiths had been replaced by European hardware. Only a few indigenous carpenters are still found, hidden in the old quarters, manufacturing painted chests and étagères, and some turners, some ironmongers assembling and decorating fancybeds.[6]

In sum, all the Algerian traditional craft manufactures were ousted by French industrial products. Thus the integration of the Algerian economy into the 'world system' also provoked the disintegration of the pre-colonial urban activities. The collapse of the traditional urban economic organisation ushered in a process of social disintegration, accompanied by the decline of traditional centres of education such as *zauyas*, which were subsidised by regular revenue derived from *habus* lands whose confiscation by the colonial power had undermined most of the traditional social services provided in the cities as well as in the countryside.

This situation can be illustrated by the decline of traditional education. After citing several French officials reporting a relatively high rate of literacy in pre-colonial Algeria, Ageron concluded that public education was 'relatively developed in 1830' but that it 'collapsed during the period of conquest. The confiscation of mosques and public *hobus* lands by the *"domaine"* [office of colonisation] dried up the material resources that financed public instruction. It was provided free of charge' before the French-rule public schools of various levels and traditional establishments of higher education as well as Koranic schools 'were completely neglected and abandoned, except those that were directly run by the inhabitants themselves'.

In the rural areas innumerable *zaouiyas* and other primary schools which were situated close to the war zones were abandoned. The continual military operations which were carried out throughout Algeria until 1871 contributed to the destruction of others. The basic textbooks were lost during the long wars of colonial conquest. Thus on the ashes of the Algerian traditional system of education the authorities laid the foundations of a colonial education destined for the children of 'notables'. The rest of the population had to wait until the post-independence period. However, some schools for the 'natives' were set up, but their number was not sufficient to provide a basic education for all school-age children. Indeed, by 1944, only 8 per cent of them were actually attending primary school. By 1954, 85 per cent of the total Algerian population were still illiterate. The rate of illiteracy among women was between 95 and 98 per cent. According to the 1954 census, out of a total school-age population of 1.9 million, only 320,000 were having some form of schooling. Thus, only about 22 per cent of Algerian school-age children were attending school. The number attending secondary şchools rose from about 4,000 in 1950, compared with over 22,000 settlers, to 6,260 in 1954, as against 29,000 Europeans, and reached about 11,000 as against 34,000 by 1959.[7] When the war of national liberation broke out in 1954, only 1,700 students were studying in various establishments of higher education, 589 of whom were at the University of Algiers. At the time, one settler in 227 was a university student, contrasted with 1 Algerian in 15,341.[8]

A very small number of teenage Algerians were admitted to technical schools, where they acquired only the most elementary technical skills. In 1954, out of 950,000 young people, only 4,900 were being trained in these schools. By 1959, their number rose to 10,900.[9]

The teaching of Arabic, which was restricted and even banned from public schools, had to wait until 1936 in order to be authorised by the French authorities to be taught as a foreign language, even to Algerians.

However, the decline of the traditional arts (music, architecture, and so on) and crafts coincided paradoxically with the beginning of urbanisation through rural-to-urban migration. Thus, in the case under study, migration and urbanisation, besides being demographic phenomena, are first and foremost the consequences of a series of social and economic contradictions that have emerged essentially in the countryside as a result of the process of capital accumulation underlying the colonising drive. In other words, the rural-to-urban exodus in Algeria was a mere demographic expression of an ensemble of multiple socio-economic causes underlying the ejection of the peasant population from the countryside – after having disrupted and disintegrated their modes of production and social organisation – into the colonised cities and towns.

Urbanisation through migration in colonial Algeria

The process of urbanisation in the colonial period and the ensuing extension of urban networks throughout Algeria were geared primarily to the development of colonisation. The expansion of the pre-existing urban centres and the creation of cities and towns, especially along the Mediterranean coast, the high plateaus and even in the Sahara Desert, performed three essential functions: attracting French settlers and consolidating their grip on the economy and society; serving as transit stations for the colonial import–export trade of manufactured products and primary commodities such as agricultural and mineral raw materials; and serving as administrative and military centres for the alien holders of power whose control radiated over the hinterland.

In sum, the expropriation of land, the spread of the capitalist market, the imposition of taxation in cash and the gradual mechanisation of colonial agriculture, which is, in essence, a labour-saving and capital-intensive device and hence constituted a push factor for the acceleration of rural-to-urban migration, were cogent factors underlying Algeria's urbanisation. The combination of all these factors contributed to the rapid growth of a colonial-type urbanisation, without the concomitant industrialisation which alone will have provided employment for the deracinated paupers. Besides, most of the jobs created in the urban centres were given to the settlers who were also ejected from their farms by market forces. As pointed out earlier, the urban development of Algeria between 1830 and 1954 was geared primarily to the implantation of Europeans into the country, although up to the 1910s a significant number of settlers lived in rural centres of colonisation or 'groups of farms'. However, because of the process of concentration of land and capital, which began at the end of the nineteenth century but was accentuated during the First World War as a result of economic cyclical crises and drought, an increasing number of settlers went bankrupt and hence had to migrate to the cities. Between 1911 and 1921 alone, the total population of European urban communes went up from 460,000 to 512,218. By 1921, 65 per cent of the settlers lived in urban centres; the three major cities alone – Algiers, Oran and Constantine – contained 38 per cent of the European urban population. In the following years, the pace of the settlers' rural-to-urban migration accelerated.

As for the growth of Algerian urbanisation through migration, even though it started at the end of the last century, it began to accelerate during the 1929 world economic crisis. The Algerian urban population went up from 7 per cent of the total population in 1886 to 20.5 per cent by 1954. Thus, through the deterioration of the socio-economic conditions of the rural inhabitants, between 1930 and 1954 alone more than 1.5 million paupers were ejected from the countryside and moved into the major cities. As a result, between 1936 and 1954, the Algerian population of Algiers grew by 148 per cent and that of Oran, by 167 per cent. The total Algerian urban population increased from 722,800 in 1936 to 1,129,000 by 1948 and 1.6 million in 1954, that is, 18.9 per cent of the total population. In other words, the Algerian population of the urban communes went up by over 100 per cent during this period. Despite this rural exodus – which before the outbreak of the war of national liberation sent 300,000 migrant labourers to France, 90 per cent of whom were from the countryside – 1,438,000 males of working age remained unemployed in the countryside in 1954.

Uneven development

Table 4.7 *The rate of economic growth contrasted with the rate of population growth, 1880-1950*

	1880-1910	1910-1920	1920-1930	1930-1950
Average annual economic growth	2.7	2.0	2.8	0.5
Average annual demographic growth	2.7	0.5	1.2	1.8
Average annual real economic growth	0	1.5	1.6	21.3

Source: Amin, *L'Economie du Maghreb*, vol. 2, p. 98.

By 1954, close to 1.5 million Algerians lived in the 50 largest cities. On the whole, the urban population, both European and Algerian, grew from 1,838,000 in 1948 to 2,158,000 in 1954, that is, by 320,000 persons, 269,000 of whom were Algerians. Since this urbanisation through migration was not accompanied by industrialisation, the majority of the migrants remained unemployed.

The lack of industrialisation and its consequences

The situation described above shows clearly that the colonial development had engendered a profound general crisis. Indeed, agriculture, which formed the basis of this colonial economy, had been stagnating since the late 1920s. In the absence of industrialisation, the entire society was being driven into an impasse. From 1880 to 1930, the rate of economic growth hardly kept pace with the rate of demographic increase. As Table 4.7 shows, such a colonial economy was incapable of satisfying the basic needs of a growing population.

From 1930 to 1950 the gap between economic growth and population increase became negative, that is, population growth far exceeded the pace of colonial economic development. The evolution of material production indicates that the annual average rate of growth of agriculture declined to a mere 1.5 per cent; but the annual average rate of economic growth rose to 2.1 per cent during the same period. However, colonial agriculture stagnated in the 1920s. This situation may be the result of a shift in investment. From 1880 to 1950, about 1,070 million francs (at 1955 prices) were invested in agriculture, 799 million francs in infrastructure and 630 million francs in industry, including mining.

However, the rhythm of industrial investment increased significantly during the early 1940s as a direct result of the war in Europe. According to André Nouschi, 'up to 1939, Algeria imported all its manufactured consumer goods from the metropolis: from shaving soap to electric wires to textiles'. However, from 1940 to 1942, 'innumerable enterprises emerged. But because of the scarcity of capital and the mediocre quality of their products, which rendered them vulnerable, a large number of them were forced to shut down when Algeria was reintegrated into the world market between 1945 and 1954. Moreover, several big French enterprises decided to install workshops and factories in Algeria.'[10]

Since the principal function of the colonial economy was to provide the French economy with agricultural and mineral raw materials, the industrialisation of Algeria was never undertaken seriously. Thus, the quanity of iron ore extracted and shipped to the industrialised economies rose from 1 million tons in 1920 to 3.4 million by 1950. Algeria has also supplied French metropolitan industry with a variety of other minerals and, from the mid 1950s, with petroleum, natural gas and over half a million workers. By 1954, colonial agriculture exported 40 per cent of its cereals, 90 per cent of its wine and 70 per cent of its fruits and vegetables to Europe. In 1957, despite the presence of about 500,000 French troops, 51.3 per cent of total agricultural output was exported. By 1960 the share of agricultural exports of the total sectoral production was as shown in Table 4.8. Despite the fact that the number of French troops in Algeria reached 600,000, 48 per cent of total agricultural output was still exported to the developed countries primarily France.

In return, all agricultural input and equipment was imported from the industrialised countries. For example, in 1960, of the 4,885 tractors imported from abroad, 60.5 per cent came from France, 21.5 per cent from Great Britain and the rest from the other developed economies. In 1958, although 101,000 tons of superphosphates were extracted in the country, Algeria had to import all of the 178,200 tons of fertiliser it consumed that year as well as all insecticides, herbicides and fungicides used in agriculture.

No wonder the industrialisation of the country was restricted to a very few light industries. Algeria served as a protected dumping ground for unsold French manufactured goods. 'Metropolitan' interests that benefited from this situation opposed the establishment of industry in Algeria. In 1954, this opposition led one of the governors of the colony to declare that:

We are confronted with a constant hostility manifested by metropolitan industry which considers Algeria as a market of consumers. It is not willing to let an industry develop because it will deprive it of serious market outlets. I have to stress strongly to the captains of French industry that Algeria absolutely cannot be a simple consumer market for metropolitan manufactured products.[11]

Table 4.8 *The contribution of agricultural exports to total production, 1960 (billion old francs)*

Products	Total agricultural production	Total exports	%
Wine	971	1,038	107
Vegetables	369	135	37
Fruits	236	162	69
Cereals	723	82	11
Tobacco	59	49	83
Miscellaneous	835	83	10
Total	3,193	1,549	48

Source: Benachenhou, *Formation du sous-développement*, p. 361.

Under these circumstances the emergence and development of a genuine industry was completely ruled out. The share of the industrial sector in total investments rose from an annual average of 5 per cent during the 1880–1910 period to 13 per cent from 1910 to 1920, 14 per cent from 1920 to 1930, 17 per cent from 1930 to 1948 and 36 per cent between 1948 and 1955. This sharp increase was stimulated by the discovery and exploitation of hydrocarbons. As pointed out above, the annual average growth rate of industry rose by only 1.2 per cent between 1880 and 1910, by 3.1 per cent from 1911 to 1930 and by 4.7 per cent between 1931 and 1955. However, despite these growth rates, the share of the industrial sector in the total GDP represented only 10 per cent during this last year. The value of industrial production rose from 17 billion old francs in 1880 to 30 billion in 1910, 44 billion in 1930 and 170 billion by 1955. These figures reveal that the rudimentary industrialisation of colonial Algeria took place mostly during the 1940s as a result of the Second World War and the occupation of France. But once the war was over, several industrial enterprises saw their activities curtailed and several others were shut down. From 1945 to 1954, the large French industrial firms represented by Renault, Peugeot, Pechiney, Lafargue, Saint Gobain, Lessieur, La Colunaf, and the rest decided to set up local subsidiaries in Algeria, mostly to facilitate the marketing of French manufactured goods, rather than to promote local industries.

Other French concerns already controlled the mining sector; the mines of El Ouenza belonged to the Union Parisienne, the iron ore of Mokta El Hadid to the Mirabaud Group, the phosphates to the Union des Mines. In addition to this, the banking system and transport companies were under the total control of metropolitan interests.

Consequently, local capital was left only the small and medium-sized industries such as food processing, textiles and construction materials. In 1958, an industrial census revealed the existence of over 15,500 small craft enterprises, and only 9,600 industrial units. The majority of wage labourers were concentrated in fewer than 1,000 industrial enterprises. Agriculture at the time employed between 60 and 70 per cent of the active population; but it provided only 40 per cent of the GDP and a mere 22 per cent of the national income. Industry absorbed only 7.8 per cent of the active labour force. Furthermore, local industry processed only 25 per cent of agricultural products and supplied only 8 per cent of the total value of its input. Thus, the function of the colonial economy of Algeria was to export raw materials and manpower to the settlers' metropolis and to import manufactured consumer goods.

However, the ascendancy of the popular movement known as the Algerian Popular Party, from which emerged the Movement of the Triumph of Democratic Liberties (whose militants initiated the war of national liberation in 1954), changed this state of affairs. In an attempt to crush the Army of National Liberation, the French government, especially under the leadership of General de Gaulle, decided to encourage some form of industrial development designed to integrate Algeria fully into the French economy. The new economic policy aimed at the 'pacification' of the contradictions engendered by the previous colonial situation, characterised by a disarticulated economic structure and an industry devoid of any 'internal dynamics'. The French official commission that was assigned the mission of drafting a 'development plan', known as the Plan de Constantine, noted in its preliminary report that:

Algerian industry is constituted by industrial islets that are technically or geographically isolated from one another; the multiplier or accelerator effects that the economists attribute to industrial development are in the current state almost nil. The intermediary demand exerts its effects outside. The bulk of the commercial import networks are geared to export; in many cases the interests of the importers and exporters constitute serious obstacles to industrial development.[12]

In the absence of genuine industrialisation, the rural population that was ejected from the agricultural sector confronted intractable problems in the cities. This was not conducive to the easy adaptation of the rural immigrants to the growing urban centres. Among other things, urbanisation without industrialisation brought about a severe housing shortage. Besides the lack of stable employment, the colonial state did not even attempt to set up an adequate urban social infrastructure to minimise the hardships of the deracinated paupers. Indeed, when the old *casbahs* became seriously congested, the migrant families had no choice but to settle in the slum belts that were mushrooming around the major urban centres, especially in their outskirts. By 1954 a significant number of the migrants were living in shanty towns. The number of shanty towns in Algiers alone increased from 16 in 1942, inhabited by a total of 5,000 persons, to 48 in 1947, 90 in 1952 and 164 in 1954, inhabited by no fewer than 86,500 individuals out of the total Algerian population of Algiers of 293,470. Thus, over 30 per cent of the inhabitants of the capital were living in this type of habitation.[13] The most rapid growth occurred between 1945 and 1954, which saw the number of slum-dwellers grow four-fold. This urbanisation was characterised by 'slumisation' and 'shantytownisation'. The lack of industrialisation condemned innumerable migrants to permanent unemployment.

Industrial and urban employment between 1901 and 1954

In 1901, only 11,887 industrial workshops were reported in Algeria, employing 51,502 workers, including Europeans. The number of Algerian industrial workers increased from 20,535 in 1902[14] – excluding 4,531 miners – to 33,000 in 1903; then it fell to 29,984 in 1904 but rose again to 33,556, more than half of whom were unskilled, in 1905. During that year, out of 32,000 industrial units, 19,000 were operated by self-employed individuals without any additional hired labour. However, the census of 1911 indicated a rapid growth of the Algerian urban proletariat: 58,543 male workers and 21,397 female workers, totalling 79,940 proletarians. By 1935, the industrial sector employed a total of 97,910 workers, of whom 51,891 were Algerians, 36,725 were French and 9,294 were foreigners.[15] The Algerian industrial proletariat at this time was made up of 25,900 male and 25,291 female workers, of whom 24,557 were employed in textiles.

Again, the national origins of the working classes in colonial Algeria determined the daily rates of their wages. The Algerian workers were underpaid, even though they performed similar tasks. In 1929 the pay scales of the two ethnic groups working in various cities were as shown in Table 4.9. This unequal remuneration was bound to affect the living conditions of the families of the Algerian workers.

However, as a consequence of the Second World War, some industries were established. This resulted in a slight increase in industrial employment. Indeed, the 1948 census revealed the existence of 177,000 workers including French and foreigners. But 97,000 of them were employed in construction and public works.[16]

The number of urban enterprises employing wage labourers rose from 91,224 in 1948 to 98,983 in 1954, that is, an increase of $8\frac{1}{2}$ per cent. By 1954 the structure of non-agricultural employment was as shown in Table 4.10.

Table 4.9 *Urban daily wages, 1929 (francs)*

City	European workers	Algerian workers
Medea	18	11
El Asnam (Orleanville)	23	11
Annaba (Bone)	220	12
Constantine	25–30	10–12
Setif	25–30	12

Source: Jourdain, *La question algérienne* (Paris, Alcan, 1934), p. 139.

Table 4.10 *The structure of non-agricultural employment, 1954*

Sector	Number of workers
Industry	106,700
Construction and public works	99,600
Transport	32,800
Commerce	84,800
Administration	37,200
Other services	24,900
Total	386,000

Source: *Recensement du 31.10.1954*.

This table indicates that the creation of employment in the urban sectors did not keep pace with the increasing inflow of rural paupers into the cities and towns. Such a situation confirms the striking fact that in the former colonised countries the growth of urbanisation through migration is primarily caused by the decline of the economic activities of the rural communities rather than by the 'pull factor' associated with an urban industrial development.

In sum, non-agricultural jobs increased from 285,000, including those held by Europeans, in 1948, to 374,000 in 1951 and to 386,000 by 1954. In other words, in seven years only 101,000 jobs were created in the urban sectors, including mining. This was insufficient to absorb close to one million rural immigrants who arrived in the cities during the same period. Consequently, the uprooted population was not integrated into the urban socio-economic system. The majority of the immigrants eked out a precarious livelihood in the so-called informal sector. Official statistics indicate that around 1954, about 47 per cent of the Algerian labour force in the cities and towns were either jobless or irregularly employed.[17]

The overwhelming majority of the Algerian wage-earners, totalling 172,000 in 1954, working in the non-agricultural sectors, were unskilled, of whom 84,000 were actually underemployed; 95 per cent of the total unskilled and 68 per cent of the semi-skilled workers employed in the country were Algerians. The Algerians comprised only 17.8 per cent of the technicians and 7.2 per cent of the highly qualified cadres or staff.

By 1956, the colonial urban economy of Algeria was centred around 9,800 French companies employing about 225,000 workers, including Europeans, representing an average of 23 workers per enterprise. The individual European firms totalled 9,000 and employed 95,000 persons, an average of 10.5 workers per unit. By this time, statistics reveal the emergence of Algerian big merchants and industrial entrepreneurs, whose number was estimated at about 9,000. Their businesses, factories and workshops employed about 30,000 wage-earners, amounting to an average of 3.3 workers per industrial unit or commercial establishment. The self-employed totalled about 115,000 persons, only 9,000 of whom were Algerians.

Thus, in the absence of employment prospects in the industrial urban sector innumerable paupers crossed the Mediterranean in search of wage labour in the French and other European industrial conurbations.

Labour migration to Europe

The colonial economy was incapable of satisfying the basic needs of the Algerian population: employment, shelter, medical care, education and transportation. Thus, the stagnant situation of the labour market in the Algerian urban centres and the rapid deterioration of the material life of the rural communities induced an increasing number of paupers to cross the Mediterranean in search of employment in Europe. The growth of labour migration to Europe was directly connected with the development of colonialism.

Indeed, the migration of Algerian workers to Europe can be traced back to 1871, when an unknown number of labourers first appeared in French and Belgian historical records.[18] In 1905, several thousands Algerians were reported to be working in European coal mines, and in 1911 French officials revealed that 3,000 Algerians were working in France. The following year an official inquiry revealed the existence of 5,000 North Africans, the bulk of whom were Algerians. Early migration developed slowly because of administrative restrictions imposed by the Governor General of Algeria. In 1876, on the express demand of the *colons*, the Governor General promulgated a decree requiring a special travel permit for Algerians going to France. When this requirement was abolished in

1913, the movement of Algerian workers to France increased rapidly. Immediately before the First World War, 30,000 Algerians were working in France. The First World War aggravated France's need for manpower. In order to keep the war industries running, French authorities turned to the 'colonial reserve army'. In Algeria, forced recruitment brought about a 'veritable mobilisation, a civil requisition that was made possible by the sovereignty of France over the territory of the colony'.[19] This collective recruitment of colonial workers resulted in the introduction of 120,000 Algerians into 'metropolitan' France.[20]

In addition, during the First World War, no fewer than 173,000 Algerian soldiers served in the French army in France.[21] According to Ageron, between 1914 and 1 April 1917 alone, a total of 168,678 men who were either drafted or enlisted had been sent to France. By April 1917, close to 3 per cent of the Algerian population were either in the French army or working in factories in France. After the armistice some of these men returned home, but others remained as workers to rebuild the war-devastated zones. Between 1920 and 1924, 120,000 workers arrived in France. The 1929 economic crash slowed the tempo of this migration and many of the labourers already in Europe were forced to return home. The number of Algerian immigrant workers registered officially in the employment office fell from 65,000 in 1932 to 32,000 in 1936. The consequences of this economic crisis were felt strongly by these Algerian migrant workers.

The Second World War provoked far-reaching changes in the form and magnitude of this trans-Mediterranean migration. Although the French Minister of Labour had requested, in January 1940, the dispatch of several thousand Algerian workers, the military débâcle that resulted in the German occupation of France put a quick end to this request. With the ensuing disorganisation of the French economy, 10,000 Algerian workers were laid off and repatriated in the early spring of 1940. After the liberation of France, French mangement again turned to the North African labour force to reconstruct its ruined industries, communication networks and housing.

In 1947 the Algerians were finally transformed into 'French Muslims'. Although they were not granted full citizenship rights, the new legal status of Algeria allowed them to move freely between Algeria and France. Table 4.11 shows this movement of Algerian workers from 1947 to 1955.

As a result of the need of the French industrialists for manpower, the number of Algerians working in France increased by tens of thousands each year, reaching approximately 400,000 by the mid 1950s.[22] However, the Algerian workers in France continued to be considered by the employers (and the majority of the French) as a colonised labour force to be employed only 'in occupations deserted by the European workers... or in the hardest, the dirtiest and the most dangerous tasks'. This situation has been interpreted as proof that 'the "native" status follows the Algerian

Uneven development

Table 4.11 *Migratory movement between Algeria and France, 1947–55*

Year	Arrivals	Returns	Balance
1947	67,200	22,300	+ 44,900
1948	80,700	54,200	+ 26,500
1949	83,500	76,455	+ 7,045
1950	89,405	65,175	+ 24,230
1951	142,671	88,081	+ 54,590
1952	148,682	134,083	+ 14,599
1953	134,100	122,600	+ 11,500
1954	164,900	136,200	+ 28,700
1955	201,828	173,371	+ 28,457

Source: Benachenhou, *La Formation du sous-développement*, p. 370.

worker, even when he crosses the Mediterranean Sea'.[23] As a direct consequence, the Algerian worker's wages were among the lowest in Europe.

Nonetheless, the migrant workers' remittances from Europe rose from 11 billion old francs in 1950 to 38 billion by 1955. In 1954, the total income of the rural population – including peasants, permanent and seasonal labourers – amounted to 131.4 billion old francs, of which 30.9 billion was sent from abroad. In certain parts of Algeria these remittances provided 80 per cent of the income of the people. At this time such monetary transfers into the country represented more than the total wages paid by the agricultural sector to the workers.[24]

Moreover, the conditions of the migrant workers in France induced them to raise a fundamental question: total independence. For the founders of the first and only nationalist party, the North African Star (ENA), the socio-economic problems of the Algerian people which were created by colonisation cannot be resolved without eradicating the principal cause underlying them: colonialism. To attain this goal the ENA was set up in Paris in 1926 by active representatives of this uprooted proletariat, with the assistance of the French Communist Party. The experiences of these uprooted workers gave rise to the most radical nationalist movement of colonial Algeria.

The rise and development of the national movement: 1926–62

Despite serious attempts by the members of its executive committee, who were also militant in the French Communist Party, to prevent this nascent movement from demanding the independence of the country, the nationalist wing succeeded in giving it a nationalist orientation from its inception. The primary goal of the ENA was the total independence of Algeria, Tunisia and Morocco.

Moreover, the founders of the ENA formulated two types of demands: immediate and long term. In the short term, the political programme contained, among other things, the following points: (1) the immediate abolition of the 'code d'indigenats' and all repressive measures; (2) amnesty for political prisoners and exiles; (3) freedom of the press, of political association and public meetings; (4) access to all levels of education and the creation of schools teaching in Arabic; (5) financial assistance to the small *fellahin* under the form of loans.

But the ultimate objective of the partisans of the ENA was stated in early 1927 thus: (1) the independence of Algeria; (2) the withdrawal of French troops; (3) the formation of a national army; (4) confiscation of the large agricultural property grabbed by the feudalists, agents of imperialism, the settlers and by the private capitalist companies, and its distribution to the peasants; (5) respect of small and medium property holdings; (6) return to the Algerian state of lands and forests seized by the French state; (7) the taking over by the Algerian state (in full property-right) of banks, mines, railways, harbours and other public services seized by the conquerors; (8) free and compulsory instruction in Arabic at all levels; (9) the recognition by the Algerian state of the workers' rights to set up trade unions and to strike; (10) the promotion by the Algerian state of welfare programmes in favour of the popular strata.

This political programme was enriched, refined and adapted to the successive phases of the struggle for the independence of the nation. Its objectives were reformulated in the 1954 declaration of war, in the Soummam platform of 1956, in the Tripoli programme in 1962, in the Charter of Algiers in 1964 and finally in the national charter of 1976. This national charter defined not only the model of a 'non-capitalist' development and its strategy but also the type of society to be constructed by an independent state, geared to the defence of the interests of the popular strata and to the satisfaction of their basic needs.

Thus, the movement launched by the founders of the ENA from their exile did not cease until its staunch partisans wrested the total independence of the country from the colonial power in 1962. They have been the fathers of the industrialisation of the country and the nationalisation of foreign interests in the post-independence period. Despite the fact that the French government banned it in 1929, the militants of the ENA succeeded, between 1927 and 1933, in surreptitiously transplanting their new political organisation from France to Algeria. This was facilitated by the abrupt return of innumerable migrant workers who were laid off after the

Uneven development

economic crash of 1929. In 1937, the ENA was again banned by the French government. Its militants set up the Algerian Popular Party (PPA) during the same year. This involved only a change of name to circumvent certain legal complications with the French police. However, the PPA was dissolved again in 1939, but lived on as an underground political organisation until the amnesty of 1946, when it emerged into the open under the title Movement for the Triumph of Democratic Liberties (MTLD).

On 15 February 1947, the first congress of the MTLD took place clandestinely in Algiers. Two reports were presented: the first advocated political struggle by legal means and the second insisted on the return to clandestine operations in order to prepare military action. A compromise was worked out and adopted as a resolution. The congress decided to maintain the former PPA's political organisation in secret, to create a secret paramilitary special organisation (OS) devised to train the hardcore militants in revolutionary military action and to confirm the constitution of a legal movement (MTLD) to carry out a political struggle in the open, that is, by legal means.

The organisation of the MTLD was a complex political apparatus. At the top of the pyramid was the executive committee of the party, whose members came to be chosen by one of the most influential leaders who was elected by the central committee. This mode of co-option rather than direct elections, which appears to be an undemocratic way of selecting the leadership of the party, was dictated by the need for secrecy. Indeed, through the constant hostility and harassment of the colonial police, the names of the members of the executive committee had to be kept secret. The members of the central committee were organised into four major committees: press; religious affairs; organisation, election and elected representatives; and trade unions and mass organisations. The most powerful committee was the organisation committee, which was in charge of the ten provincial divisions known as *wilayates*. Indeed, the country was sub-divided into ten *wilayates*. Each *wilaya* consisted of four *dairates*. Each *daira* was sub-divided into four *kasmates*; each *kasma* was broken up into four sections; and each section comprised four cells.

Similarly, the structure of the para-military 'special organisation' extended all over the country, which was sub-divided into nine zones. Each zone was divided into two operational groups and each group was broken up into two half-groups. At the national level the leadership of the MTLD appointed a chief of staff and a deputy called 'general inspector' or co-ordinator. The council of the general staff was constituted by these two appointees and the heads of the zones.

The members of the OS were recruited from among the best elements of the party. Once incorporated, they were required to be highly secretive, dedicated, loyal, and rigorously disciplined, and to accept sacrifices of all kinds, including death. Their training involved political and military instruction both theoretical and practical. From 1948 to 1950, when it was accidentally discovered by the colonial police, the OS trained between 1,000 and 1,500 militants. The Chief of Staff of the Special Organisation was in contact with only one influential member of the executive committee of the party. Thus, although the OS was the paramilitary organisation of the MTLD, it was required to operate clandestinely even within it.

This emphasis on systematic training, organisation and secrecy was one of the main factors underlying the dynamism and resourcefulness of the wartime FLN and ALN. In addition former members of the OS became the chief organisers of the war of independence.

The complex organisation of the nationalist movement induced an American scholar to compare the structure of the MTLD to an iceberg, a small part of its bulk emerging above the surface, a political insitution seen and recognised. The submerged part was the PPA, the clandestine party machine. The MTLD was, therefore, not at all the movement it purported to be but rather the legal façade of a revolutionary party, conceived in the best Bolshevik tradition.[25]

This view completely overlooks the historical circumstances that shaped the organisational features of the political movement. Once in Algeria, this nationalist organisation acquired a hard core of militants from various social backgrounds: workers, peasants, small traders, students and petty bourgeois intellectuals. After 1944 the latter two categories figured most in the leadership. Structurally, because of the special working conditions required by long underground political activities exacerbated by constant police pressure on its militants, the PPA was organised like a pyramid. At the base there were cells of four militants linked through various levels to the executive committee. At all levels, a distinction was drawn between shock groups, militants and sympathisers, or 'elements of infiltration'. In this way the militants, cadres and leaders could be arrested and the party apparatus would keep functioning. It was this nationalist party, the most radical of them all, which appealed to the overwhelming majority of the popular underprivileged strata of the Algerian society because of its organisational rigour, ideological populism and plebeian style of political action. This ideology prevailed in independent Algeria up to its denunciation by the Benjadid regime in the early 1980s.

However, the most significant decision taken by this party during its entire history was the creation of the OS, which managed to train, between 1948 and 1950, about 1,500 militants. It was the former cadres and militants of the secret organisation that prepared, organised, carried out and led the war of national liberation under the banner of the Front of National Liberation (FLN) and its army of national liberation (ALN) from 1954 to 1962. The other political forces, such as the association of the

Algerian Ulamah, the partisans of the Democratic Union of the Algerian Manifesto (UDMA), who advocated an autonomous republic federated with France, without a foreign ministry or national army, and some members of the Algerian Communist Party, did not join the FLN until 1956, that is, when it became obvious that the country would sooner or later gain its independence. Thus, the militants and the political structure and experience as well as the programme of the ENA–PPA–MTLD not only constituted the cornerstone of the Algerian struggle for independence but also played the decisive role in the making of post-independence society, despite a series of historical discontinuities provoked by severe political crises represented by the 1954 political split of the MTLD and the 1962 crisis within the FLN. These two successive crises prevented the country from capitalising on its past most precious popular revolutionary political experience.

In conclusion, the implantation of a popular political organisation among the population, and especially among the peasantry, represented a deliberate and conscious effort on the part of the militants of the nationalist movement, and involved an attempt to restructure their society along novel alternative lines. This revolutionary political structure was from the outset conceived as a regenerative counter-structure, designed to alter the colonial status quo, which favoured a privileged foreign minority of settlers to the detriment of the autochthonous majority. Indeed, as demonstrated above, in Algeria colonisation resulted not only in the erosion of the material base but also in the simultaneous dissolution of the traditional social relations. Since the dominant colonial military and bureaucratic structures were erected on the ruins of the pre-colonial social order, the nationalist political party in the twentieth century aimed at the abolition, or at least modification, of the colonial system based on an unequal distribution of political power and economic wealth between the two national groups.

In order to effect this desired change, the radical nationalists, who learned from their own political action and that of their forefathers, devised novel revolutionary structures, in the long run capable not only of challenging the occupying power's military force but also of channelling the energy of the pauperised population in such a way as to undermine the legitimacy of the colonial authority. One of the founders of the first Algerian working-class nationalist movement, the ENA, used to reiterate the following phrase in his public addresses: 'If I were a teacher and the Algerian people were my pupils, I should have made them conjugate the verb "to organise" in the past, present and future tenses 1,000 times every day.' This emphasis on well-structured collective action is reflected in the revolutionary organisation of the War of National Liberation, which was initiated and led by the seasoned and disciplined militants of this popular nationalist movement, whose experience played a positive role in post-independence development.

The revolutionary organisation of the War of National Liberation 1954–62

By the time the French police uncovered the existence of the Special Organisation in 1950, between 1,500 and 2,000 militants of the MTLD were trained by the cadres of the OS. Some of these were arrested. Others fled to the countryside and a certain number went into hiding in the cities or left the country. In 1951 several imprisoned militants and cadres escaped from the colonial jails. This setback induced the leadership of the central committee of the MTLD, which came to be constituted by moderate elements who favoured legal means over direct action, to dissolve the special organisation.

However, the overwhelming majority of the former members of the OS kept pressuring the party not only to reconstitute the OS, but also to envisage seriously the preparation of armed struggle as the only alternative to the political stalemate. But the leadership of the MTLD continued to argue that the objective conditions for a genuine war of national liberation were still absent. During the MTLD congress held in April 1953 a severe conflict broke out between the central committee and Messali, the president of the party, who was then under house-arrest in France. This conflict resulted in a grave crisis within the MTLD that provoked the split of the nationalist party into several tendencies. The rank and file followed Messali and the cadres of the party apparatus supported the central committee. The activist former members of the OS remained neutral.

In March 1954 the central committee, which was isolated by the partisans of Messali from the rank and file of the movement, agreed to provide some aid for the constitution of a sort of national salvation committee in order to neutralise Messalist influence. Thus a four-member revolutionary committee for Unity and Action (CRUA) was set up. Mohamed Boudiaf and Mustapha Benboulaid represented the former members of the OS on this committee. The CRUA called for the preservation of the unity and integrity of the party in order to confront the colonial power. When Benboulaid and Boudiaf realised that the unity of the party was compromised by the centralists and the Messalists, they contacted former comrades from the dissolved OS, who were scattered throughout the country. A meeting of 22 former members was held in Algiers in late June 1954, during which the decision to initiate the war of national liberation was taken. Boudiaf was elected the national co-ordinator of the committee of 22 and hence empowered to choose five other persons from these 22 to constitute the council of a general staff of the future ALN as well as the political leadership of the future FLN.

The members of the committee of six were M. Boudiaf (the national co-ordinator), M. Ben Boulaid, Ben M'Hidi, M. Didouche, B. Krim and R. Bitat. They were also former members of the OS. Their immediate task was the preparation of the war of independence. They prepared the directives, defined the basic rules of conduct of the ALN and drafted the declaration of 1 November 1954, in which the objectives of the new FLN were outlined. They also had the burden of setting the D Day, which was 1 November 1954, starting at 1 a.m.

For operational purposes, the country was divided into six zones (or politico-military provinces):
(1) Aures Nemamcha in eastern Algeria
(2) Northern Constantine, also in eastern Algeria
(3) Kabylia
(4) The Algiers region of central Algeria
(5) Oran province in western Algeria
(6) The Sahara Desert

Ben Boulaid was appointed commander of zone 1; Didouche of zone 2; Krim of zone 3; Bitat of zone 4; and Ben M'hidi of zone 5. The commander of zone 6 was not designated until some time later.

Three others, A. Ben Bella, Ait Ahmed and M. Khider, were designated as FLN representatives abroad.

The Soummam congress held in August 1956 transformed the six zones into six *wilayates*. Thenceforth the politico-military structure of the former zone 2 was applied throughout all of Algeria. Thenceforth every *wilaya* was divided into at least three zones or *mantaqates*; every *mantaqa* into at least three regions or *nahayates*; every *nahaya* into at least three sectors or *kasmates* and every *kasma* into three parallel operation politico-military units. The civilian population was organised into *douars* supervised by a committee of village political commissars headed by a chairman. Every village had its own militia or *mussabbilun*. Every sector which was divided into three areas possessed at least one section of *mujahidun* ALN subdivided into three groups of 11 members.

A National Council of the Algerian Revolution (CNRA) was established. An executive committee of co-ordination and implementation (or CCE) was also set up. Its five members constituted the political leadership of the war of national liberation. With the constitution of the provisional government of the Algerian Republic in 1958, the prerogatives of the CCE were taken over by the interministerial committee of war whose members were Krim, Bentobal and Boussouf up to 1962.

In less than two years between November 1954 and 20 August 1956, revolutionary parallel politico-military structures were implanted not only in Algeria but also in France among the 400,000 Algerian migrant workers. The small bands of guerrilleros who were initially badly armed, fed and clothed saw their numbers growing rapidly into well-structured, disciplined armed groups and sections, whose members had acquired valuable

Socio-economic consequences

combat experiences in fighting the colonial army and police. They managed to arm and clothe themselves from what they seized from the French.

Between 1 November 1954 and 20 August 1956, the overwhelming majority of the rural and even the urban population had been organised and mobilised. By the beginning of 1956, the centralists, the partisans of the UDMA, the association of Ulamah and even some members of the Algerian Communist Party had joined the FLN and ALN. Thus, from the Soummam congress onwards, the basic revolutionary organisation came to be characterised by a multiplicity of parallel politico-military structures represented by the FLN and the ALN. These parallel organisations were interwoven at every level in such a way as to keep them operationally separate but structurally and functionally interrelated. At every organisational level, from the committee of the sector (and even the *douar*) or the quarter in the urban areas to the council of the *wilaya*, a body of five members was set up. Everyone was assigned specific tasks. Every chairman at every organisational level was seconded by a deputy who, in case of death or capture, would automatically replace him. Thus, organisational rigour had to to channel the energy of the combatants and militants in such a way as to compensate for the weakness and lack of military equipment of the ALN.

In sum, the emphasis was on out-organising the French colonial apparatus and its main coercive instrument, the army of occupation, rather than on out-fighting it. Contrary to the views of most western strategists and specialists on this question, the key to success in such a revolutionary war lay primarily in the structural endurance and flexibility of the organisation and secondarily on the unfailing unity and devotion of the colonised people. In order to win, the revolution embodied in its structures has merely to survive. Unable to dismantle these revolutionary structures, the French conventional war machine had to resort to the so-called counter-insurgency strategy and tactics in order to attempt to undermine the popular base of the war of national liberation. In so doing it provoked its radicalisation, which transformed it into a genuine socio-political revolution.

The collective effort of the revolutionary war of national liberation had not only shaped a national populist consensus, better known as 'Algerian socialism', but also preconditioned the achievements of the post-independence reconstruction. Despite the trauma and hardship it caused, the experience of this war moulded the minds, ideas and attitudes of an enormous number of a new breed of men and women who were compelled under exceptional circumstances to fight it. The waging of the war provided them, among other things, with valuable managerial skills for running the national economy in the post-colonial period.

III

Post-independence development

Chapter 5

The aftermath of the war of national liberation

The legacy of colonialism

On a hot summer day, 5 July 1962, Algeria's independence was finally solemnly proclaimed. Joyful crowds took to the streets throughout the country. The scenes of countless women, men, and young people[1] dancing and chanting in the crowded streets remain inscribed in my memory to this day; and yet, during this expression of enthusiastic joy a profound feeling of sadness took hold of me. I knew then what they did not: a severe crisis within the FLN and the ALN was unfolding, a crisis that might possibly undermine the achievements of eight years of war and sacrifice. Furthermore, a devastated country would need a comprehensive programme for the reconstruction of its national economy. This would, of course, necessitate political unity and stability in order to overcome the negative legacy of colonialism. However, Algeria inherited not only the negative aspects of colonialism but also a significant positive heritage that must not be forgotten.

The negative legacy of the colonial period

The war of national liberation of 1954–62, which raged most strongly in the countryside, resulted not only in the destruction of the peasant economy but also in the final dislocation of rural society. Thus, the immediate consequences of the war can be summarised as follows: about one million people were killed;[2] close to three million peasants were regrouped in the *centres de regroupement* or 'strategic hamlets', which had some resemblance to concentration camps; there were over 300,000 refugees, mainly in Tunisia and Morocco; no fewer than 400,000 prisoners were freed from colonial jails and military camps; from 1954 to 1960 alone, over 723,000 peasants fled the rural war zones to the urban centres, where they were jammed into shanty towns; no fewer than 8,000 villages and hamlets were either destroyed or burned. Hundreds of thousands of hectares of forests were burned or defoliated by napalm bombs; cultivable lands were either sown with mines or declared 'prohibited zones'; the country's livestock was

Post-independence development

almost decimated – for instance, the number of sheep declined from about seven million in 1954 to three million in 1962; and some 110 billion old francs left the Algerian banks, to which 20 billion in unpaid debts must be added.[3]

In addition to all this, some 90 per cent of the one million settlers, representing almost all the entrepreneurs, managers, engineers, teachers, professors, doctors, dentists, technicians, highly skilled workers, the most experienced administrators and clerks, had fled the country. As a result, factories, workshops, businesses, farms, hospitals and various other vital services were either completely shut down or slowed their activities, leaving about 70 per cent of the Algerian active population unemployed.[4] Even the University of Algiers library was burned and several medical laboratories were also destroyed by the OAS (the settlers' paramilitary organisation).

The settlers, who represented only 10 per cent of the total population of Algeria, received a total income of 414 billion old francs, compared with 223 billion for the remaining 90 per cent; they paid only 46.3 per cent of all taxes collected in the country, yet they consumed 60 per cent of the imported products and 40 per cent of all goods and services produced in Algeria.[5] In the agricultural sector the average annual income per person was estimated at £20.50 (AD 57.40) for the Algerians, compared with £735 (AD 2,058) for the settlers. In the non-agricultural sectors the gap was even larger; the annual average amounted to £47 (AD 131.60) for the Algerians and £330 (AD 924) for the French colonists.[6] The purpose here is to stress the weight of the settlers within the Algerian economy. As will be seen, their sudden departure in 1962 was bound to be strongly felt in all sectors.

Thus, the ravages of the war and striking socio-economic inequalities as well as profound scars and wounds left on the body of the Algerian social fabric overshadowed the constructive side of French colonialism.

The positive legacy of colonialism

At independence the new Algerian state inherited a relatively adequate techno-economic and social infrastructure represented by several modern cities and towns, containing 200,000 apartments and villas, administrative buildings, businesses, shops, schools, hospitals, hotels, cinemas, theatres and museums; a university in the capital and two annexes in Oran and Constantine; one of the most important railway systems in Africa (4,300 km); paved roads and highways (10,000 km); civil airports, harbours and an electrical network (600,000 km). In the economic field independent Algeria inherited 22,000 modern farms and their equipment, and various factories and workshops.

Moreover, this infrastructure was determined by the logic of colonial economic development geared to the extraction of raw materials and their export to Europe as well as to strategic considerations. Thus in the aftermath of the war of national liberation the Algerian economy was completely dependent on the French economy. As pointed out earlier its primary function was to provide the French economy with raw materials and a substantial number of workers. For example, 80 per cent of Algeria's total exports went to France in 1961. The large French industrial firms had felt only the need to set up local subsidiaries in Algeria, mostly to facilitate the marketing of 'metropolitan' manufactured goods rather than to promote the industrialisation of the country.[7] Since the Algerian market was reserved mainly for products made in France, the local colonial capital was compelled to invest only in the small and medium-sized light industries, such as food processing, textiles and some construction materials. The Algerian colonial economy was considered as a 'disintegrated' and 'disarticulated' underdeveloped economy. It was disintegrated in the sense that there existed no 'complementarity' between its agricultural, industrial and other sectors; and 'disarticulated' because the various branches or activities of each sector did not complement one another because of the lack of basic industry. Even the simplest machine tools had to be imported from France. There was a compounded dependence on the former colonial power: the understanding of this is vital to the appreciation of the future Algerian strategy of development, whose objective was to restructure the national economy in order to put an end to this situation. The entanglement of the Algerian economy with the French economy was strengthened during the war of national liberation.

As pointed out above, in an attempt to crush the ALN, the French government, especially under the leadership of General de Gaulle, decided to encourage some form of industrial development designed to integrate Algeria fully into the French economy. The new economic policy aimed, among other things, at the 'pacification' of deeply rooted contradictions engendered and kept in motion by the colonial situation characterised by a dependent economy. Table 5.1 shows the evolution of the three sectors of the Algerian economy between 1950 and 1962.

The noticeable growth of the role of the secondary sector in the GDP was stimulated by the development of the hydrocarbons industry, whose exploitation began in 1958. The growing importance of the tertiary sector in the GDP was primarily caused by the growth of trade and administration stimulated within the framework of the pacification of social contradictions brought into being and magnified by over one century of total colonisation. The decline of the primary sector in the GDP began in the 1920s, but accelerated from the 1930s onward. Nonetheless, in the structure of the Algerian economy before 1950, agriculture still made the largest single

Post-independence development

Table 5.1 *The structure of the GDP, 1950–62 (%)*

Sector	1950	1954	1958	1962
Primary	37	33.5	26.0	24
Secondary	27	27.0	27.0	36
Tertiary	36	39.5	47.0	40
Total	100	100.0	100.0	100

Source: Gouvernement Général, *Rapport Général du Plan*, p. 21, and *Comptes économiques, 1963–64*.

contribution to the GDP. However, as a consequence of the consolidation of the colonial state apparatus that began in 1956 with Robert Lacoste's administrative reforms, which increased the recruitment and promotion of Algerians into the bureaucracy, and the discovery and exploitation of oil and natural gas, its relative contribution dropped between 1954 and 1959 from about one-third to about one-quarter of the GDP, which rose in absolute terms from AD 6,788 million in 1954[8] to an estimated AD 14,000 million in 1959 at current prices.[9]

However, the agricultural sector at the time still employed between 60 and 70 per cent of the active population but provided only 24 per cent of the GDP and a mere 22 per cent of the nation's income. Furthermore, this agriculture was characterised by a 'dual' structure: a traditional sector which continued to produce primarily use-value or subsistence crops and a modern sector which specialised in the production of wine for export. According to official statistics the French colonial farmers were selling 71.5 per cent of their total yield on the market while the Algerian peasants and farmers combined were marketing only 28.5 per cent of their crops (8,499 of the latter owned more than 100 hectares each and hence possessed over 23 per cent of the area held by Algerians.)[10]

In sum, in 1962, the Algerian economy was characterised by inter-sectoral distintegration, inter-branch disarticulation and a striking 'extraversion'.[11]

According to official statistics, in 1963 the Algerian population totalled over 10.4 million persons excluding the migrant workers in Europe. Close to 5.3 million, representing over 50 per cent of the total population, were concentrated in five *wilayates*. Three *wilayates*, Algiers, Constantine and Oran, were inhabited by over 3.7 million, which amounted to more than one-third of the total population of the country. It is no wonder that three out of four future industrial 'poles' were to be located in these cities.

Furthermore, since colonisation had driven the bulk of the Algerian *fellahin* from the fertile plains and valleys to the mountain slopes, high densities of population were found in such *wilayates* as Greater Kabylia, Titri and Aures, which to this day contain various mountain enclaves whose integration into the national economy and other service sectors necessitates large investment in social infrastructure: roads, communications and electricity.

The social structure and the class forces underlying post-independence politics

The population was stratified socio-economically roughly as follows. In the urban districts, which were inhabited in 1962 by 3.68 million people, there was at the top of the pyramid what may, with a great deal of caution, be called an Algerian bourgeoisie. It consisted of about 50,000 wealthy merchants of all sorts, a few industrialists and real estate owners, controlling between 7,000 and 8,000 commercial concerns and small enterprises employing wage labourers; and 10,000 professionals, such as doctors, lawyers, dentists and pharmacists, who constituted the intellectual elite of this social stratum. A middle class (petty bourgeoisie) made up of retail traders, modern artisans, civil servants and other service employees numbered 185,000.

About one-third of the total population lived in the cities. Full-time active urban industrial workers totalled 110,000, as against about 400,000 migrant workers abroad. Thus, close to 70 per cent of the Algerian industrial proletariat were in exile, a fact that was found to affect the political weight of the working class. This presented the national movement with serious problems.

The urban sub-proletariat, largely of peasant origin, driven out of the rural areas during the 1940s and 1950s, and particularly between 1954 and 1962, amounted to no fewer than two million individuals, comprising over 65 per cent of all urban dwellers. The absence of employment opportunities and an adequate social infrastructure forced this pauperised deracinated mass to live in wide slum belts surrounding the cities and towns. Pierre Bourdieu and Abdelmalik Said, who carried out extensive social research in Algeria at the time, described their condition:

The most important fact about the large majority of urban immigrants is that they do not become integrated into the urban life through industrial or commercial employment. They remain separated, living in *bidonvilles* or shanty towns, with infrequent casual employment, and form a vast urban sub-proletariat ... completely at the mercy of external forces, forced into employment or at best casual labour, ill adapted to an urban economy which has little to offer them. The sub-proletariat exist without a past or future in a present that continually escapes their grasp.[12]

Post-independence development

In the countryside the following socio-economic strata or categories can be identified: about 25,000 Algerian landlords controlled 2.8 million hectares of land, representing over 50 per cent of the total arable area. Close to 170,000 middle peasant households owned between 10 and 50 hectares each; over 450,000 rural families possessed between 1 and 9 hectares; seasonal agricultural labourers totalled about 450,000; and there were approximately 130,000 permanent agricultural labourers who had been employed on the colonial estates, a small proportion of whom had been employed by Algerian landlords. The per capital income of the last three groups averaged a mere 200 new francs (AD 200) per year.

The constituent elements of this Algerian class structure as well as their roles in the war of national liberation were described and assessed in the Tripoli Programme of June 1962, which speaks of 'social strata' rather than 'social classes' because the FLN party has always denied the existence 'of classes within Algerian society':

What are the social components of this movement [of national liberation]?
Above all, they are the people as a whole and especially their most oppressed strata: first, the poor peasants, main victims of expropriation of land, of cantonment and of colonialist exploitation. These include permanent and seasonal agricultural workers; the *khammas* and the small share-croppers, the very small peasant proprietors.
Second, the proletariat, relatively few in number, together with the enormous sub-proletariat of the towns. These are made up mainly of expropriated and declassed peasants, who have often been forced to seek work far from their villages and even to emigrate to France, where they are often employed in the most menial and least remunerative work.
Third, another intermediate social category is that of artisans, junior and middle-ranking office workers, civil servants, small traders and certain members of the liberal professions constituting as a whole what might be called the petty bourgeoisie. This category has often participated actively in the liberation struggle and provided it with political cadres. Fourth, there is a bourgeois class of relatively minor importance made up of businessmen, big merchants, heads of enterprises and the odd industrialist.
To this group should be added that of the big landed proprietors and notables of the colonial administration.

These two latter social strata have participated in the movement in episodic fashion, either out of patriotic conviction or opportunism. It should be noted that excluded from these are the notorious administrative feudalists and traitors who have wholeheartedly served the cause of colonialism.

[This official document of the FLN concluded]

An analysis of the social content of the liberation struggle makes it apparent that it has been the workers and peasants generally who have been the active base of the movement and have given it its essentially popular character. Their massive participation has in turn led other social layers of the nation . . . It should be noted in this connection that in most cases it was young people of bourgeois origin who determined the adherence of the bourgeoisie to the cause of independence. The people's movement has had the effect, in the course of the armed struggle, of going beyond the objective of national liberation towards a more long-term perspective, that of revolution.

It must be recalled that this programme was adopted unanimously by the wartime National Council of the Algerian Revolution (CNRA) in Tripoli, Libya, as the new platform of the post-independence FLN party. The programme defined the main tasks of this new phase and outlined in political terms the country's future type of development. The principal objective of the Tripoli Programme was the attainment of economic independence through the nationalisation of all natural resources, foreign wholesale trade, banks and all financial institutions. Economic liberalism and a development based on the mechanisms of the capitalist market were rejected from the outset. National planning was considered a necessary alternative for the transformation of a 'dual' colonial economy and a disrupted society. The programme called for the elimination of the consequences of colonialism in the ideological and social fields by 'liquidating retrograde feudal survivals'. It also insisted on the construction of a 'socialist society' devoted to the 'service of man'.

The programme remained vague about future strategy. It considered *agriculture* to be the basis of economic growth. The strategy outlined stressed and relied on the development of agriculture rather than industrialisation. The main objectives were the increase of agricultural production, the establishment of an infrastructure and soil reclamation, protection and improvement. On the organisational plane, producers' co-operatives were to be set up. The development of industry was to be subjected primarily to the needs of the agricultural sector.

This favouring of the primary sectors goes against the theory as well as the established pattern that the construction of a socialist society requires a massive and rapid industrial development. However, the programme, like all major doctrinal documents published subsequently by the FLN party, appears very radical on paper but remains untranslatable into action. As history has shown, the Tripoli Programme, which was supervised by Ben Bella, who formed an alliance with the officers of the ALN stationed on the Tunisian and Moroccan borders and a disparate coalition made up of various politicians and opportunists belonging to innumerable political tendencies, was never implemented by his government.

In the aftermath of the war, the leadership of the FLN confronted intractable problems. This complex situation was aggravated by a severe political crisis within the FLN, which had, until then, succeeded in

Post-independence development

maintaining, at least on the surface, the unity of the various political parties, groups and factions. The crisis was provoked by the realignment of the national political and class forces. By the end of the summer of 1962, a coalition, constituted by a multiplicity of political forces representing differing social groups and coming from heterogeneous backgrounds, such as the ALN of the frontiers, the discontented partisans of the UDMA, the association of the Algerian *ulamah* and innumerable opportunists of all sorts, emerged to power. The only things they had in common were their hatred of the wartime leaders Krim, Boussouf and Bentobal, and their personal ambitions. The struggle for power in the summer of 1962 had almost plunged the country into civil war. Fortunately, popular pressure exerted upon the warring factions spared Algeria a debilitating armed conflict.

The independence of the country, which precipitated the departure of the settlers, paved the way for the quick enrichment as well as for the upward social mobility of the privileged social strata or classes which were able to take full advantage of these golden opportunities. As a result, the future status of the agricultural estates, industrial units, commercial establishments, shops and villas abandoned by the French colonists became the major issue of the day. The privileged social groups, strata and classes realised that the acquisition of this property would allow them to increase and consolidate their economic power.

The Algerian bourgeoisie, until that time in a chronic state of 'under-capitalisation' because 'it was a by-product of the colonial economy in that it was confined to areas considered unprofitable by the settlers',[13] began buying up industrial, commercial and other valued mobile property at low prices from the panic-stricken settlers. The petty bourgeoisie of shop-keepers, cafe-owners, artisans and other small-scale traders tried to purchase small commercial establishments and even take unauthorised possession of abandoned moveable property and real estate in the cities and towns. The landlords, rich peasants and some local FLN officials and ALN officers had either contemplated the possibility of purchasing farms from the European colonists or actually taking illegal possession of them. The professionals, educated people, former Algerian colonial civil servants (mostly trained and promoted during the war within the framework of the counter-insurgency strategy), FLN bureaucrats from the provisional government in Tunisia and Morocco and some educated guerrilla officers occupied the administrative structure of the former colonial state apparatus.

In addition, a new breed of *affairistes* started to become local representatives of multinational firms in Algeria. As middlemen, specialising in import–export activities, they came to play an important role in the country up to 1978, when the state monopoly on external commerce attempted, in vain, to put an end to their services and deals. (After the death of Houari Boumedienne they put their weight behind Benjadid's liberalisation drive.)

However, the Algerian agricultural and industrial workers took advantage of the political vacuum left by the crisis of the FLN, the continuing withdrawal of the French army of occupation and also the departure of the European bourgeoisie to bar the way to the Algerian privileged classes. They moved simultaneously and without waiting for any directive from above to take control of the basic means of production: land, industrial enterprises and commercial establishments left idle or vacant by the settlers.

As early as the summer of 1962, the agricultural labourers employed on the colonial farms and plantations began taking control of production. By the autumn, they set up 'self-management committees to protect their foster-mother', the land, and to continue production so that their dependent families would be provided for. As a result of this initiative to occupy the formerly colonised lands, comprising about 40 per cent of all cultivable area, employing 10 per cent of the active male population of the countryside, the big landlords and rich peasants were finally thwarted in their attempts either to rent or buy these farms.

The initiative of the agricultural labourers was immediately followed in the cities by the urban proletariat, who took control of the factories, construction sites, transport networks and some of the commercial establishments abandoned by the departed settlers. Moreover, as will be seen, the local interests of 'metropolitan' and other multinational firms were not affected by such a workers' self-management movement. Nonetheless, from the workers' point of view, the decision to take over this vacant property averted the danger presented by the 'national bourgeoisie'. Thus, the urban proletariat, with the assistance of the General Union of Algerian Workers (UGTA), which was founded by the wartime FLN in 1956, also set up committees of self-management to resume production and open communication lines.

The political crisis and its consequences

On the political level, the situation deteriorated after the cease-fire which began on 19 March 1962, as a result of the Evian-Accord, agreed upon and signed by the representatives of the Algerian provisional government (GPRA) and the French Gaullist government. Political divergences of opinion between two antagonistic factions of the FLN led to an open armed conflict in which the ALN of the frontiers, under the command of Houari Boumedienne, opposed the internal forces of the ALN of three *wilayates*:

Post-independence development

northern Constantine, Kabylia and the Province of Algiers. This conflict did not last very long; by mid September the Ben Bella coalition, which opposed the GPRA, triumphed over its opponents. A provisional political bureau, under the leadership of Ben Bella, assumed power during the summer. On 20 September 1962, the first national constituent assembly was elected in the midst of political conflict and economic chaos, and chose Ferhat Abbas as its president. On 29 September 1962, this assembly elected Ben Bella as the first president of the Algerian Democratic and Popular Republic. In the newly constituted government, Houari Boumedienne was appointed Minister of National Defence and some time later as Vice-President of the Republic. Once formed, this first Algerian government faced pressing economic and social problems that had to be at least prevented from deteriorating.

The economic policy of the Ben Bella regime: 1962–5

Upon his ascendancy to power, Ben Bella was faced with an abrupt interruption of the normal functioning of the economy and public services. With the departure of the settlers, all activities slowed down on account of the lack of experienced staff, raw materials or semi-finished products, and the drastic decline of demand. The investments projected in the Plan de Constantine ceased upon independence. Industrial production decreased drastically in all activities except petroleum production. During the second half of 1962 and the first quarter of 1963, more than 100 industrial plants were shut down, construction work stopped and contracts were cancelled. As a consequence, the total value of output declined by 35 per cent between 1960 and 1963. Construction and public works decreased from 1962 to 1963, by no less than 55 per cent, and as many as 1,400 enterprises out of 2,000 operating within this sector completely disappeared. Cement production fell from 1.3 million tons in 1962 to 0.6 million tons in 1963. Mining operations decreased by 20 per cent and metallurgical production by 15 per cent. Textile factories were operational at only 58 per cent of their capacity, and the remaining consumer goods industries at about 15 per cent. Sugar production ceased completely. The total number of Algerian industrial workers decreased from 110,000 in 1962 to 80,000 in 1963. The only sector that continued to increase its output was petroleum, because it was owned by multinational oil companies and its product was destined for export. Indeed, while the country was on the brink of national economic disaster, the net profits of the foreign oil companies operating in Algeria totalled AD 4.8 billion, of which AD 2.5 billion was actually transferred abroad.

The decline in economic production was accompanied by an

unprecedented loss of capital which was an additional severe blow to the national economy of a devastated country. In 1962 a monthly average of AD 500 million was leaving Algeria. Between 1963 and 1965, AD 4.5 billion, out of total savings of AD 10.5 billion (belonging to households, public administration and businesses) was exported. As a direct consequence the total investment in the country declined from AD 3.9 billion in 1962 to AD 1.79 billion in 1963, AD 1.30 billion in 1964 and AD 1.10 billion in 1965.[14]

The financial difficulties of the new government were compounded by the fact that the state treasury inherited from the colonial period, and remaining under French management until June 1963, was unable to collect taxes. Furthermore, public housing rents and bills for utilities such as gas, water, telephones and electricity, which were controlled by public companies and state services, were no longer paid.

Nonetheless, in December 1962 the Central Bank of Algeria (BCA) was created. During the same year a department of economic studies and planning, which was partly inherited from the colonial administration, was set up in Algiers. It attempted to formulate, within an anarchistic framework, an economic policy for the Ben Bella regime. It also helped the government to prepare the first national budget, which was discussed and adopted by the national assembly. The theoretical revenue and expenditure were estimated respectively at 2,910 million francs and 2,812 million francs.

The Ben Bella government gave top priority to the agricultural sector. Thus, 785 million francs, representing 50 per cent of the total expenditures of the budget in the fiscal year 1963 on equipment, was earmarked for agriculture. The army and the police were allocated 640 million francs, compared with 216 million francs for national education and the civil service combined.

In accordance with the Evian-Accord, France was supposed to provide up to 1,200 million francs of financial aid for the fiscal year 1963, in order to complete some of the basic projects of the Plan de Constantine. It turned out that France financed only the projects contracted to French firms operating in Algeria. Kuwait, Egypt and other countries provided about 552 million francs. The total royalties accruing to the new state from hydrocarbons amounted to no more than 220 million francs out of AD 4.8 billion net profits.

However, the tax receipts were lower than anticipated. Almost all the self-managed units were operating at a loss, to the point that French financial aid was diverted to assist workers' self-management committees as well as to meet other extra-budgetary expenditure. The economic situation deteriorated in the course of the fiscal year. Redundancy and underemploy-

Post-independence development

ment were growing rapidly, resulting in the acceleration of labour migration to France. The workers of the agricultural and industrial self-managed units, public service employees, pensioners and the retired tried for several months to receive their payments.

Confronted with this state of affairs, the government resorted to measures that were senseless politically, economically and socially. In March 1963 private Algerian cinemas, hotels, cafes and restaurants were suddenly nationalised while multinational companies and subsidiaries of French 'metropolitan' firms continued to operate freely in the country. This decision discouraged the small Algerian traders and entrepreneurs not only from investing but from supporting the regime. However, a small number of merchants were turning themselves into industrialists. The national public companies such as SNCFA (railways) and EGA (electricity and gas), were accumulating losses. And the public treasury had to subsidise the industrial enterprises operated by the self-management committees, which totalled about 50 units at this time.

In July 1963, the OAIC, the Algerian cereals board, was founded. It specialised in the import, export and processing of cereals and dry vegetables. During the same month the Algerian Bank of Development (CAD) was set up to replace the Caisse d'Equipement d'Algérie inherited from the colonial state. In August of the same year an Algerian insurance and reinsurance company (CAAR) was established by the government. In the autumn, the regime nationalised the French settlers who remained in Algeria as proprietors of farm land. In December, SONATRACH, a state company for research, production, transport, processing and marketing of hydrocarbons, was established. This national oil company played a decisive role not only in providing investment funds for the economy but also in the extracting and refining of petroleum, the liquification of natural gas, the marketing of hydrocarbons and the production of plastics and fertiliser for agriculture. Air Algérie, the Algerian state airline, was also nationalised during the same year.

In October, the Ministry of Finance promulgated a new customs and tariff code which was implemented from November 1963 and brought into existence a parallel black market in foreign currency that continues to this day. The prices of imported goods went up very sharply, provoking galloping inflation. However, this measure reduced the flight of capital slightly.

However, as will be seen, the decrees of 19 March 1963 which codified the legal status as well as defined the organisation and functioning of workers' self-management on the abandoned colonial farms provided the state with some real power to regulate the functioning of the economy. As a result of favourable weather conditions the agricultural sector's cereal yields reached a record level, 24 million tons. But this did not resolve the state's financial crisis: public expenditures averaged 250 million francs per month, while government revenues were no more than 150 million.

In addition to the French and Arab financial aid and technical assistance, the Soviet Union, the Chinese People's Republic and the United States provided some aid under various forms. The Soviet Union agreed in September 1962 to grant Algeria 500 million francs to finance the purchase of agricultural and industrial equipment from the Soviet Union, to build small dams and set up one of the major technical and scientific achievements of independent Algeria, the petroleum institute of Bou-Merdes. A loan totalling 250 million francs was also accorded by the People's Republic of China after an official visit made by Chou En-lai to Algiers. The United States dispatched 100,000 tons of foodstuffs which were badly needed just after the war.

In April 1964 the Algerian dinar was created and defined (AD 1 = 1 French franc); in August the national savings bank (CNEP) was set up; in September of the same year the national steel company (SNS) was established. Thus 1964 witnessed the launching of two major industrial projects that came to play an important role in the future economic development of the country: the construction of a steel factory in Annaba and the building of the third pipeline (Haoud el Hamra-Arzew). The first project was initiated with the financial and technical assistance of the Soviet Union and the second with the financial aid of Kuwait and the technical co-operation of Great Britain, despite France's opposition.

Indeed, when the Algerian government promulgated a new regulation compelling the foreign companies operating in Algeria to invest 50 per cent of their profits in the country and to use the dinar to pay workers and for certain services, France tried to persuade the members of the EEC, Great Britain and the USA to prevent their companies from investing in or dealing with Algeria. The British government refused to grant the French request. The construction of this third pipeline was to allow Algeria gradually to break the encirclement of its economy by France. When it was finished in 1966–7 the pipeline had contributed to the increase of Algerian oil exports and hence revenues and also to a greater control by SONA-TRACH – which was also created in 1964 – over transportation of crude oil.

The national budget of 1964 totalled AD 2,811 million. French financial aid furnished AD 850 million, the royalties paid by oil companies provided AD 270 million, the socialist sector contributed AD 90 million, the fund of national solidarity, AD 40 million, long-term loans from various sources, AD 478 million and seller's credit AD 150 million. Out of this budget AD 941 million was invested, a small improvement on the previous year. However, between 20 and 25 per cent of the budgetary targets pertaining to the purchase of agricultural and industrial equipment were attained. Furthermore the private sector, both foreign and national, which lost confidence in the Ben Bella regime, ceased to invest.

The assistance of the socialist countries of Eastern Europe allowed Algeria to receive, in January 1964, the first 148 Soviet tractors and 32 ploughs with their spare parts and several technicians to train the Algerians to operate and repair them. However, despite this aid, agricultural production began to decline because of unfavourable climatic conditions as well as managerial and technical problems. The Algerian treasury continued to contract growing debts from the French treasury. Total French financial aid amounted to 850 million francs during the fiscal year 1964, which showed a marked reduction compared with the previous year.

Both the public and self-managed enterprises experienced serious financial deficits. In addition, the private industrial units of production were either shutting down or reducing working hours. An economic recession was setting in. The country still lacked the capital, skilled and experienced manpower, technology and political and social stability which are necessary for undertaking a consequent economic development. Workers' incomes remained very low as a result of almost two years of wage freezes. Industrial workers therefore demanded a 25 per cent rise in wages in order to compensate for inflation, and UGTA organised several strikes in Algiers.

The economic situation continued to deteriorate during the third and final year of the Ben Bella regime. Indeed, of AD 3,249 million public expenditures, only AD 492 million was actually invested in 1965, that is, AD 249 million less than 1964. The living conditions of the population were growing rapidly worse. Several strikes were organised in various factories in the capital. In an attempt to avert a serious crisis the President of the Republic, who was also General Secretary of the FLN party, as well as Minister of Finance, called for a national trade union congress (of the UGTA), which was held early in 1965. Since the main purpose of this congress was to purge the leadership of the union, in his opening speech Ben Bella denounced the strikes of 1964 and 1965, and castigated the UGTA officials.

Thenceforth new competing political tendencies emerged within the regime. The so-called radical tendencies of the party and the UGTA advocated workers' self-management and the nationalisation of the means of production. A moderate wing proposed the increase of state intervention in economic management and a halt to nationalisation. Ben Bella started a series of purges within the party, the administration, the government, the army and the police. This action triggered the military *coup d'état* of 19 June 1965, which was carried out by Ben Bella's close allies in the

Table 5.2 *The structure of the GDP, 1963–5 (million AD)*

Sector	1963	1964	1965	1966
Agriculture	2,730	2,295	2,300	1,600
Mining, quarrying and electricity	340	375	400	400
Construction and public works	550	540	2,600	2,600
Manufacturing, excluding hydrocarbons	4,450	4,230	5,300	4,600
Hydrocarbons	2,810	2,265	2,100	2,700
Transport and services	1,575	1,590	5,400	5,700
Commerce	2,835	2,990		
Total GDP excluding hydrocarbons	8,860	8,810	11,000	10,300
Including hydrocarbons	11,040	11,075	13,100	11,300

Source: Secrétariat d'Etat au Plan, *Comptes Economiques 1963–1966* (Algiers, 1974).

political crisis of the summer of 1962, under the leadership of his Vice-President and Minister of National Defence, Houari Boumedienne.

At any rate, despite serious difficulties, compounded by the inexperience of the national leadership, the young and unseasoned managers and administrators and especially the lack of educated staff, engineers, technicians and skilled workers inherent in such a tumultuous transitional period, the national economy experienced some growth and development. The aggregate GDP rose from AD 13.12 billion in 1963 to AD 14.09 billion in 1964 and AD 15.23 billion by 1965. This amounted to an average annual growth rate of 7.5 per cent during the period. The gross formation of fixed capital was as follows: AD 2.71 billion in 1963, falling to AD 2.23 billion in 1964 and increasing slightly to AD 2.41 billion in 1965,[15] representing an annual average of about 17 per cent, which was small compared to the magnitude of the socio-economic problems engendered by colonial underdevelopment.

The evolution of the sectoral structure of the GDP during the 1963–5 period is shown in Table 5.2.

This was the initial economic structure of independent Algeria, the comprehension of which is vital for the evaluation of the future development of the country during the 1967–78 period and beyond. Thus, in absolute terms the value of production of hydrocarbons not only exceeded that of industry but also nearly equalled that of agriculture, which was the regime's priority sector for investment allocation.

At any rate, since the establishment of workers' self-management among the former colonial farmers was not only the show-piece of the first regime of independent Algeria, but has also affected the evolution of agricultural production since, an analysis of the genesis and development of the organisation of autogestion might allow us to comprehend at least the organisational causes of the stagnation of contemporary Algerian agriculture.

Workers' self-management in agriculture, 1962–5

On 22 and 23 October 1962, two decrees were promulgated in which, for the first time, the government defined the organisation of vacant properties and recognised the legitimacy of workers' self-management committees on vacant farms employing more than ten workers. However, once the threat of the return of the settlers was gone and the national landlords thwarted in their attempts to buy up former colonial lands (as in the case of Tunisia and Morocco), two political forces advocating opposing views surfaced: the UGTA and its rank and file favoured the establishment of workers' self-management committees, not only on these farms but in the industrial enterprises; but the emerging techno-bureaucracy preferred statism, or the organisation of state-run farms and industrial enterprises.

The struggle over the future organisation of production, both in the agricultural and industrial sectors, continued unabated. This culminated in the famous March Decrees of 1963, which were elaborated by the Bureau National des Biens Vacants (BNBV) without consulting the union leadership. As a result, they worked out a compromise that contributed to the subsequent bureaucratisation of autogestion or the so-called socialist sector of agriculture.

The first decree nationalised between 150,000 and 200,000 hectares of colonial land (it was not until 1 October 1963 that the government nationalised all landholdings belonging to 'foreigners' and incorporated them into the self-management sector, thereby increasing the number of permanent workers involved from 70,000 to 130,000; on 3 October 1964 about 200,000 hectares, 'ill-acquired' by the Algerian landlords, were also nationalised and added to autogestion). The second decree established the Office National de la Réforme Agraire (ONRA). This new institution incorporated not only the technical and administrative personnel, but also the structures of the CAPER (Caisse d'Accession à la Propriété et à l'Exploitation Rurale), an organisation set up by the colonial authorities during the war of independence as a counter-insurgency measure to implement Robert Lacoste's programme of land reform. In other words, the ONRA came to be composed of various colonial organisations such as CAPER, SAP (Société Agraire de Prévoyance) and CCSA (Caisse Central de Sociétés Agricoles), and manned by personnel inherited from the colonial period.

Although the ONRA was cast in the colonial mould and rooted in its bureaucratic tradition, it was assigned the task of carrying out the 'agrarian reform of the government and of organising the management of the farms abandoned by their proprietors'. The third decree relative to 'organisation and management' of vacant agricultural estates was set up within the institutional framework of workers' self-management. The entire system consisted of a general assembly of workers, composed solely of permanent labourers; hence seasonal workers were excluded from participation at the outset. The assembly was required to meet at least twice every three months to set priorities, goals and schedules of production of the unit – compatible with the aims of national production, accounting and financial transactions.

If there were more than 30 workers the general assembly elected a council of workers at least every three years, two-thirds of whose members had to be engaged directly in production on the farm. This general assembly was empowered by the authors of the decree to define the internal norms and regulations as well as to set targets of production, for instance, for tools, tractors, harvesters and fertiliser. It was given the prerogative of admitting new members into the farm and excluding 'wrong-doers' from it, providing that priority be granted to guerrilla veterans. It elected a management committee varying in size from three to eleven members. As in the council of workers, two-thirds had to be involved directly in the productive process. This committee was charged with the actual management and the elaboration of the production plans. As such it also was charged with implementation of the decisions of the general body, regarding the organisation of work and division of labour, loans, purchase of farm material, marketing of products and hiring of seasonal workers. It was this body that elected the president of the management committee.

Theoretically, the president was to assume an important role in the system of workers' self-management; in practice he remained a figurehead until the 1975 reform of autogestion in conjunction with the 'agrarian revolution'. This situation was determined by the appointment of a director by the MARA (Ministry of Agriculture and Land Reform) to supervise and co-ordinate these various self-management bodies. The director, a functionary of the MARA, was appointed to 'represent the state' within the unit of production and to 'ensure, under the authority of the president, the good functioning of the estate in implementing the decisions taken by the management committee and council of workers in conformity with the laws and regulations'. Although he was regarded only as a consultative member of the management committee, he was empowered to sign all principal working documents of the unit of production. He not only supervised accounting but was entrusted with all the bookkeeping documents and operations. He kept the list of the workers composing the general assembly and issued their membership cards. He determined the optimum number of workers needed and controlled the funds from which he made the major payments. Not only, then, did the power of the director overlap that of the various bodies of workers' self-management, but he was also given sufficient means to hold them under his sway.

The state maintained the right to deduct the cost of amortisation and to recover the sums earmarked for the national investment funds. The rest was used for production operating costs, including the wages of the permanent and seasonal workers which were paid either in cash or in kind, and the cost of maintenance of farm machinery and fuel, etc. The prices of the produce were estimated at the value of local market prices. Thus, the workers' initiative was, from the beginning, inserted into a constraining juridical apparatus.

As can be inferred from the description above, the institutional framework set up on paper by the authors of the decrees turned out to be complex indeed to be grasped by the illiterate members of the general assemblies of autogestion. The roles assigned to these innumerable bodies and boards that came to constitute the system of autogestion overlapped and hence paralysed the general functioning of the system from the start, facilitating the systematic intervention of the MARA through the medium of the ONRA in the internal affairs of the 'self-management sector'. The text contained various potential conflicts between the permanent and seasonal workers, the director and the president and the director and the self-management committee. These conflicts resulted eventually in the negation of the whole principle of self-management, which was based on the control of the workers over their working environment and means of production and which implied their participation in the decision-making process. Worst of all, no provision was made to ensure the representation of the producers at the national level. As a result, the 'workers' self-management committees' were bound to succumb to the onslaughts launched upon them by the partisans of statism. Hence they could not prevent, in the long run, the growing 'bureaucratisation' of their institutional environment.

The bureaucratic environment of workers' self-management

By 1965 the bureaucratic grip became so tight on the self-managed sector that the ONRA controlled everything: marketing channels; credit mechanisms; and supplying the productive units with tools, machinery and fertiliser. The ONRA took the major decisions at every level and in all economic, technical, administrative and political matters. It fixed prices, set production targets and decided on the purchase of technical means of production. It also determined wages and the number of permanent workers to be admitted and seasonal labourers to be hired. It elaborated the annual cultivation plans and even worked out the norms and regulations governing the social relations of production on the farms.

In order to overcome the resistance of the producers, the ONRA officials interfered directly in the political affairs of the workers' self-management committees by sponsoring their own candidates for the key positions. In some instances they went as far as imposing them on the labourers. When the union representatives opposed them they were either dismissed or intimidated by the directors.

In an attempt to control the activities of autogestion effectively, the ONRA established a multiplicity of specialised boards and organisations such as the ONAC (Office National Algérien de Commercialisation des Céréales), the OAIC (Office Algérien Interprofessionel des Céréales), the CORA (Coopérative de l'Office de la Réforme Agraire) and the CORE (Coopérative d'Ecoulement). However, these were co-operatives in name only; in practice the ONRA required them to deliver all the produce – including next year's seeds – to its provincial offices. Afterwards it redistributed the seeds to the producers. Nothing could be more awkwardly authoritarian and bureaucratic.

The inadequacy of these overlapping boards, which totally lacked any co-ordination, resulted in the virtual paralysis of agricultural production and distribution. They not only stifled the workers' initiative but also wasted the produce made available. For instance, the marketing channels imposed upon the workers were so slow and inadequate that a large quantity of crops perished before they were brought to market. The workers then resorted to subsistence agriculture rather than deliver their products to inept bureaucrats. As a consequence of this, many farming units were ruined and indebted, and agricultural production undermined. Cereal and wine production either declined or stagnated from the colonial period up to the end of 1965 (see Table 5.3).

The annual average returns from each hectare declined from 9.5 quintals during the 1956–61 period to 6.8 quintals in 1962, 6.2 quintals in 1963 and 5 quintals in 1964, rising slightly to 5.8 quintals per hectare by 1965 for the self-managed sector. The annual average returns of the private sector rose from 12.1 quintals per hectare in 1956–61 to 16.8 in 1962 and 16.9 in 1963, declining to 9.7 in 1964 and increasing again to 11.4 quintals in 1965. The total annual average returns on cereals per hectare of the two juridical sectors of Algerian agriculture declined slightly from 19.6 quintals during the 1956–61 period to 17.8 quintals per hectare in 1965. The annual average returns on wine on the self-managed sector increased from 45.6 hectolitres per hectare during the 1956–61 period to 48 hectolitres in 1965, after which

Post-independence development

Table 5.3 *Production of cereals and wine, 1956–65*

Annual average	1956–61	1962	1963	1964	1965
Cereals (million quintals)					
Self-managed sector	7.5	6.8	6.2	5.0	5.8
Private sector	12.1	16.8	16.9	9.7	11.4
Total	19.6	23.6	23.1	14.7	17.2
Wine (million hectolitres)					
Self-managed sector	14.4	n.a.	n.a.	9.6	12.7
Private sector	1.6	1.6	1.6	0.8	1.3
Total	16.0	12.3	12.6	10.6	14.0
Wine exports (million hectolitres)		14.6	6.8	9.1	8.2
Value (million AD)	n.a.	n.a.	221	504	552

Sources: *Tableaux economiques de l'Algérie; Annuaires statistiques.*

the average annual returns of the private sector declined from 44 hectolitres per hectare to 38. This state of affairs forced the second regime established by the *coup d'état* of 19 June 1965 to envisage new reforms in order to prevent agricultural production from falling.

From 1962 to 1966, four sectors co-existed within the Algerian economy: a workers' self-management sector made up of former colonial farms and small and medium-sized private industrial and commercial enterprises left behind by the settlers; a foreign private sector represented by local subsidiaries of French and other multinational firms; an emerging private sector owned by Algerian nationals; and a growing public sector whose assets were either inherited from the colonial power or created by the new state.

A critical assessment of the Ben Bella regime, 1962–5

What were the achievements and shortcomings of the first regime of independent Algeria in the political, social and economic fields? On the political level, Ben Bella committed a monumental mistake by allying himself and his close associates with the general staff of the external ALN that was stationed in Tunisia and Morocco, along the eastern and western Algerian borders, against the provisional government of the Algerian

Republic (GPRA), which was formed in Cairo in 1958 and hence led the war of national liberation to its ultimate victory over the colonial power. The legitimacy of this government was both historically and legally well founded. Under the leadership of this government, in which Ben Bella was one of its Vice-Presidents, the FLN became one of the most prominent movements of liberation in the third world. The effectiveness of its leadership was confirmed both on the battle fields and around the negotiating tables with its colonial foe: all the political objectives defined by the principal founders of the FLN, who initiated the war of national liberation on 1 November 1954, were attained at Evian in 1962.

However, the general staff of the external ALN failed to accomplish the main mission assigned to it by the highest institution of the wartime FLN, the National Council of the Algerian Revolution (CNRA), which represented all of the different national political forces of the country, namely to send inside Algeria the largest number of arms and men possible. This failure cannot be easily blamed on the fortification and electrification of the Maurice lines separating Algeria from Tunisia and Morocco. Despite this, Ben Bella and his close associates sided with the general staff against the legitimate leadership of the GPRA, a fact that paved the way for putschist elements within the future national popular army (ANP) which carried out the military *coup* of 19 June 1965 against Ben Bella himself.

The crisis of the summer of 1962, which was provoked by the general staff of the external ALN with the full support of Ben Bella and his partisans, had undermined the historical continuity of the national movement by opening the way for various opportunists and anti-democratic political and class forces hostile to the modernisation, secularisation and construction of a national independent economy, based upon the industrialisation of the country and devoted to the satisfaction of the needs of the people.

In the political realm, the Ben Bella regime was largely responsible for anti-democratic practices by resorting, from the outset, to purges, calumnies, blackmail and systematic intolerance of other views, opinions and attitudes even within the single party. It was Ben Bella's peacetime regime that started to imprison and torture its political opponents, a fact that was bound to facilitate the emergence of Algerian authoritarianism, which differs greatly from that prevalent in the rest of the Arab world. Indeed, despite the installation of an authoritarian state apparatus, Algerian society has remained to this day one of the most democratic in the Islamic world. By dismantling the wartime revolutionary structures and reactivating the colonial state apparatus, the first regime undermined the development of democratic institutions, traditions and practices. For example, the maintenance of the colonial administrative structures, personnel, laws, regulations and even practices turned out to be detrimental to the development of a public administration at the service of the citizens and the economy. Only the function of control was transmitted from the colonial administration. Some of the causes of the problems of contemporary Algerian public administration can be traced to this period.

In superficial ideological and political terms, the partisans of the Ben Bella regime placed a great deal of emphasis on so-called 'workers' self-management' in agriculture, industry and even commerce. However, this was only a façade. Of necessity, the workers tried to resume production in both the agricultural and industrial sectors after the settler exodus. As soon as the government moved in to 'officialise' this 'irreversible option' of 'self-management', initiative was taken away from the workers. Self-management in industry affected only the small and medium-sized enterprises abandoned by their European owners. The subsidiaries of the large French 'metropolitan' firms were not touched. These subsidiaries were the principal beneficiaries of French financial aid to Algeria. In fact, French industrial enterprises continued to play a predominant role until the nationalisation of French oil companies in 1971.

In the social field the first regime missed an excellent opportunity for promoting progressive legislation in favour of women, who played an important role in the war of national liberation; in 1962 the conservative forces within the country were on the defensive and hence could not have opposed the promulgation or sabotaged the implementation of such legislation. Despite the fact that 16 women became members of the first national assembly, only one law connected with women, making 16 the minimum age of marriage for a girl, was passed. The insistence on women's participation in the active economic life of the country was, and remains to this day, a slogan. The majority of women continue to be relegated to the domestic domain.

However, the serious difficulties encountered by the post-war leaders must be remembered. In addition to a chaotic internal situation, the first regime was confronted by strong hostility (and even outright aggression in the case of Morocco) from the two major neighbouring states of the Maghreb, which dared to claim large areas along their Algerian borders. The territorial integrity of the newly independent nation was preserved. In the field of diplomacy the Ben Bella government used the prestige and diplomatic experience of the wartime FLN skilfully and tactfully to enhance Algeria's position in the international arena. As a result Algerian diplomacy came to play an important role in world affairs, particularly during the heyday of Houari Boumedienne's presidency.

In addition, the first regime had not only managed to prevent the collapse of the administration and the national economy but had also succeeded in establishing some important public corporations, such as SONATRACH and the SNS, which came to play a decisive role in the development of the country in subsequent years. These positive results facilitated the tasks of the new leaders of industry during the 1965–6 period of transition to planned development.

The transition to a planned development based on industrialisation, 1965–6

Before formulating a plan of development based on the industrialisation of the country, Houari Boumedienne, the leader of the 19 June 1965 *coup d'état* and the future second president of the Algerian Republic, abolished political institutions such as the national assembly, the political bureau and the central committee of the FLN party. The new regime proclaimed that one of its primary goals was the construction of a state that would transcend and outlast individual leaders, and hence be capable of developing and restructuring the country. Thus it undertook a three-fold task: the construction of a pyramidal and highly centralised state in the Jacobin tradition; the gradual formation of a comprehensive policy of development for all sectors but geared primarily to industrialisation; and the relegation of the FLN party to a secondary position and the reliance on military intelligence for security and even political 'mobilisation'. In other words, the armed forces came to constitute the backbone of the Boumedienne regime, to the detriment of the development of the FLN party, a fact that undermined the development of political institutions. This was a reaction to Ben Bella's attempt to divide the army in order to weaken the political power of Boumedienne and his close associates during the last years of his regime.

However, in the aftermath of the military *coup*, economic and social conditions continued to deteriorate. Indeed, in early 1966 several industrial units shut down, and several strikes ensued that affected most factories in the region of Algiers. This unrest provoked a decline in industrial production, forcing the government to increase imports of consumer goods.

Although public expenditure rose from AD 3,038 million in 1965 to AD 3,517 million in 1966, the value of material production, excluding hydrocarbons, declined from AD 5,300 million to AD 4,600 million during the same period. The total value of the GDP declined from AD 13.16 billion to AD 12.49 billion within a year. As a result of the nationalisation of mining activities, iron ore production fell from over 3.22 million tons in 1965 to 1.75 million in 1966. More serious still, because of unfavourable climatic conditions, total cereal production declined from 17.8 million quintals to 7.7 million. As a direct consequence, the contri-

Post-independence development

bution of agriculture to the composition of the GDP decreased by AD 1,600 million in 1966 alone. Wine production fell from 14 million hectolitres in 1965 to 6.8 million hectolitres in 1966. However, the value of exports of wine rose slightly from 8.2 million hectolitres to 8.3 million. Total investments rose from AD 830 million in 1965 to AD 1,452 million in 1966; industrial investment more than doubled, from AD 156 million to AD 370 million, which indicated a clear shift in sectoral priorities. This situation implied that in the short and long run socio-economic and demographic perspectives as well as the geographic and climatic conditions militated in favour of a national economic and social development, centred on the industrialisation of the country, and required the acquisition, through nationalisation, of foreign interests in Algeria.

Indeed, according to the 1966 census, which was taken in January, one year before the launching of the first three-year plan of development – known at the time as the 'experimental plan of transition' – out of a total population of 12,096,347 (of which 3.9 million or 31 per cent lived in urban centres), 5.58 million men and women were of working age (18–65 years of age), increasing by over 175,000 entrants into the labour market every year. Only 1.7 million out of a labour force of 2.58 million were employed: an estimated unemployment rate of 45 per cent. Of the total unemployed, 288,155 persons, mostly males, representing some 21.3 per cent, were in search of their first jobs. According to the Ministry of Labour, of 706,713 recorded unemployed individuals, 38 per cent were urban and 62 per cent were rural.[16]

Of the employed population, 873,600, representing over 50 per cent, were engaged in agriculture. A large proportion of this agricultural labour force was underemployed. Any attempt to increase and diversify agricultural production through modernisation implied not only a radical agrarian reform but also the transfer of this population to non-agricultural sectors. In other words, modern agriculture was not only highly specialised in the production of export crops but also stagnating economically and hence incapable of providing additional employment. As for the so-called traditional agriculture, it was already overcrowded and the process of pauperisation was ejecting a growing number of peasants from the countryside. In fact, according to the 1966 census, the growth of urbanisation, stimulated by a rural-to-urban exodus, involved no fewer than 600,000 persons between 1962 and 1966 alone. This represented on average about 150,000 individuals arriving in the cities every year. One of the most cogent push-factors was the unequal distribution of land in the countryside. An official inquiry carried out by the Ministry of Agriculture in 1965 revealed an alarming situation.

Thus, the number of peasants owning less than 1 hectare rose from

105,954, representing 17 per cent of the landowners in 1950–1 to 134,780, who comprised 23 per cent of the total proprietors in 1965. Given the low quality of land possessed by the Algerian peasantry, and the fact that at least 18 per cent of the rural households were completely landless, the proportion of the rural paupers represented about 75 per cent of the total population of the countryside. Stagnating and even regressing Algerian agriculture could not absorb all this manpower. This state of affairs led an impartial French geographer, who taught in an Algerian university, to observe:

To overcome the state of underdevelopment in which it found itself, Algeria had to industrialise. After independence, in spite of the illusions that were held by certain people, it was obvious that this country could not expect too much from an agriculture whose potentialities, at least in the present state of Mediterranean soil and water resources, are quite limited. The industrialisation of this country is not a matter of choice. One cannot choose what is ineluctable.[17]

Chapter 6

Industrialisation as the motor of development

Introduction

The industrial revolution of the eighteenth century was the culmination of a series of developments that shaped the course of human history. It emerged and developed in one centre, Great Britain, and from there spread under various forms to the present-day industrialised nations. Its diffusion to the third world countries occurred under specific historical conditions: colonisation and economic imperialism. This resulted in the integration of the economies of Asia, Latin America and Africa into the world capitalist system, dominated by the industrialised nation-states of Europe, North America and Japan. The systematic plunder of the three subjugated continents led to the emergence of struggles of national liberation. Upon gaining independence, most third world countries realised that the overwhelming problems inherited from the past could not be resolved without comprehensive industrialisation programmes. Indeed, industrialisation is the *sine qua non* for the construction of an efficient economy, which in turn is an essential prerequisite for the existence of the kind of well-organised democratic state apparatus needed to preserve the independence of the nation.

A process of 'secondary' industrial development has been at work since the late 1940s. This has been taking place under conditions dictated by those who have monopolised industrial technology, capital and expertise. It relies heavily on the imports of all these factors of production at high prices. Since the most common mode of payment is 'credit financing', that is, high-interest loans by the banks or governments of countries that export capital goods, most 'developing countries' have become indebted. Their total debts amount to over $1,200 billion today. These conditions clearly generate obstacles to the industrialisation of the third world countries.

The industrial progress of a nation or group of nations can be measured by its share in the consumption of basic raw materials utilised by its local industries. The third world countries' share in the consumption of the world's nine major industrial minerals amounted to a mere 4 per cent in 1950 and rose only to 6 per cent by 1970, while their population comprised over 70 per cent of the total world population. The share of the capitalist nations declined from 80 per cent in 1950 to 70 per cent in 1960 and 68 per cent by 1970, while that of the socialist states rose from 16 per cent in 1950 to 26 per cent by 1970. The third world's share of the added value of manufactured goods rose from 6.9 per cent in 1960 to 8.6 per cent by 1974. That of the capitalist countries declined slightly from 75 per cent to 63.7 per cent, while that of the socialist nations grew from 18.1 per cent to 27.7 per cent.[1]

This strikingly unequal development makes the industrialisation of the third world nations an imperative. In fact, no nation can develop without the establishment of basic industries, which alone are capable of stimulating the growth of all the economic sectors and services. However, the major problems of third world industrialisation are also influenced by internal political contradictions: the absence of nationally oriented classes or political blocs.

Indeed, the history of the advanced capitalist and socialist nations indicates clearly that their industrial development was carried out either under the leadership of the bourgeoisie, one of the most dynamic and enterprising social classes in history, or under the guidance of the most conscientious and dedicated elements of society organised within a highly motivated and cohesive political movement or party. Political factors were paramount and even decisive in the mobilisation of the population, through coercion or persuasion, for the transformation of the pre-existing socio-economic structures and for the creation of new conditions favourable to the development of the productive forces and the establishment of new social relations of production. The technological component – even though it constitutes the very essence and substance of industrialisation – does not constitute an independent variable. To put it bluntly, the success or failure of industrialisation is determined in the final analysis by political factors.

Inventions, innovations and adoptions of any technology were and still are dependent variables. For instance, several crucial technological inventions, including the steam engine, had been made by the Greeks of the Hellenistic period, the Arabs and the Chinese. Frank Wright has observed that 'it is especially interesting to note that the five particularly important technical advances by means of which Europe seemed to lift itself from medieval to modern status were all Asiatic in origin – the compass, the Arabic (numerical) system, gunpowder, paper, and printing. And centuries later Asia begins to learn of capitalism from Europe.'[2] This suggests that certain political, institutional and economic factors are required.

In the case of what are now the advanced capitalist nations, industrialisation took place against a socio-political background in which the means of production and labour itself became commodities, so that the direct producers were in many cases reduced to proletarian status while the class which controlled the means of production became a national bourgeoisie.[3]

The development of capitalism as a social system was accompanied by centuries of political and social strife in which the defeated political forces and social classes lost much or all of their power. As Oliver Cox observes, 'the political organisation of a capitalist nation is thus of primary importance . . . The early capitalists put so much stress upon its significance that they seemed to think that, given favorable institutions, the economic ends would follow as a matter of course. What the great capitalists sought was the reorganisation of the government.'[4] In short, the prerequisites for the development of industrial capitalism could be stated as follows: (a) an exclusive territory, preferably with access to the sea; (b) government by a sovereign assembly of commercial and industrial oligarchs or, at least, an assembly under the immediate influence of the mercantile and industrial classes; (c) control over the leader or administrator-in-chief by election and impeachment; (d) subordination of organised religion to, or elimination of religious influences from, the politics of the state; (e) an efficient bureaucracy made up of functionaries, experts and technicians; and (f) a capitalist ethos or pattern of values, i.e., a common determination to make an active foreign trade an important instrument of industrialisation so that social status, religious and legal ideology, art, science and war all contribute to this end.[5] Those are the essential institutional mechanisms underlying the enormous productive potential of capitalism.

The inherent contradictions of capitalism resulted in the emergence and development of a socialist counter-system. As was noted earlier, industrial development in the Soviet Union and other industrialised socialist countries was the result of conscious political struggle by a social movement or party to carry out successful industrial development in order to mobilise and channel the creative energies of millions of people. Indeed, in the original version of his article 'The immediate tasks of the Soviet government', Lenin stressed that

without enrolling new sections of the people for building society, without arousing the masses to action, any revolutionary transformation [was] out of the question. The task of the entire period of building socialism presupposes the energetic participation of ever broader sections of the people in constructive work. To stimulate the initiative, energies, discipline, and responsibility of every working man means to accelerate socialist society's advance.[6]

After the October Revolution, Lenin attempted to move towards socialism by adopting a form of 'state capitalism'. By nationalising such key sectors as industrial enterprises, banking, transportation and utilities, the Soviet government would be in a position to exercise strict control over the private sector (light industries, handicrafts, agriculture). After Lenin's death an industrialisation debate began and continued until the adoption of the first five-year plan (1928-32).

This debate focused on sectoral growth strategies and hence investment priorities. There was disagreement over whether industry (the state sector) or agriculture (the private sector) should be favoured or whether sectoral growth should be balanced. The right wing of the Bolshevik party, represented by an outstanding theoretician, Nikolai Bukharin, advocated a balanced sectoral growth strategy. For Bukharin, all the economic sectors had to be developed simultaneously (although industry, as a sector enjoying the benefits of socialisation, would tend to grow more rapidly). According to him, any investment policy that favours agriculture over industry or vice versa, or one branch of industry over another, is bound to fail because of the structural interdependence of the economic sectors. He attempted to demonstrate that the industrial sector cannot function successfully without a steady flow of the agricultural products needed to feed workers and to serve as industrial raw materials. Moreover, industrialisation requires sophisticated technology which cannot initially be produced internally and which cannot be imported from abroad if agricultural surpluses are not exported to finance such imports. On the other hand, the development of agriculture requires equipment and fertiliser produced by the industrial sector, and rural workers need basic manufactured consumer products. If these capital and consumer goods are not furnished in sufficient quantity by the industrial sector, fewer of the agricultural products needed by industry and urban consumers will be produced.

According to Bukharin, the rapid growth of the socialised sectors would demonstrate by example the superiority of the socialist mode of production. Those involved in the non-public sectors of the economy would gradually join the socialised sector on a voluntary basis.

Bukharin's approach was rejected by the left wing of the Bolshevik party, represented by the distinguished economist Preobrazhensky. For the left wing, the construction of the Soviet economy had to be based upon Marx's model of expanded reproduction, according to which an economy is divided into two sectors, one producing the means of production and the other producing consumer goods.[7] The left wing wanted to give priority to the first of these sectors; they saw industrialisation as a prerequisite for the development of the other sector. Preobrazhensky envisioned two possible courses at the end of the 1920s: the Soviet economy could either continue to stagnate or even retrogress to lower levels of industrial capacity, or a 'big push' to industrialise the nation could be undertaken. In taking the latter step, which the left wing supported, halfway measures would not be sufficient, because the technological gap between the USSR and the advanced capitalist economies had become so wide that it was impossible to adopt advanced technology gradually. Furthermore, the replacement arrears of the Soviet economy had become so great that a significant increase in investment was required just to keep industrial capacity from falling.[8]

In addition, Preobrazhensky claimed that the so-called new economic policy of 1921–8 had resulted in a 'drastic disturbance of the equilibrium between the effective demand of the village and the marketable output of the town'.[9] In other words, the effective demand of the peasantry had increased substantially without a corresponding substantial increase in industrial capacity, thus creating an inflationary gap. Therefore net investment in the industrial sector had to be raised significantly to close the gap between effective demand and capacity; the inflationary effects of this industrial investment would be neutralised by altering the structure of demand significantly through reduction of consumption levels in order to increase saving. Once the new industrial capacity had been created, private consumption would rise.[10]

Thus, Preobrazhensky argued that not agriculture but industry in general and heavy industry in particular ought to be given top investment priority on the grounds that short-term benefits of investment in agriculture and light industry would be significantly outweighed by the long-term benefits of investment in capacity-expanding heavy industry. The left wing saw the Soviet Union as besieged by world capitalism and felt that the country had to rely primarily on itself for massive industrialisation. Indeed, it could not even import capital goods from the advanced capitalist powers because of the lack of foreign credit and the small size of the exportable agricultural surplus. Consequently, Preobrazhensky insisted that a foreign trade monopoly should be set up in order to ensure that capital equipment and not luxury items would be imported.

Industrialisation was to be financed by the institutionalisation of a process of 'primitive socialist accumulation of capital'. The primary goal of this process was to enable the state, not private individuals, to 'equate real savings (composed of both voluntary and involuntary savings) with the output of the capital goods sector (real investment)'.[11] Primitive socialist accumulation would transfer resources out of the private sector (primarily agriculture) into the state sector by imposing 'nonequivalent exchanges between industry and agriculture. The exchange of industrial and agricultural commodities would be nonequivalent because of the state's manipulation of agricultural prices. Once the state had eliminated the private sector as a viable threat, the socialised sector would become the source of capital accumulation.'[12]

Preobrazhensky's ideas largely prevailed and the outcome of this debate was the launching of the first five-year plan (1928–32), which gave absolute priority to massive and rapid industrialisation. The Soviet Union's fixed capital stock was to double within five years to provide the industrial base for the construction of socialism. Light industry was to be expanded by 70 per cent during the period covered by this plan. The Soviet Union's allocation of investments in subsequent years favoured industry in general and heavy industry in particular. As a result, from 1928 to 1937 industrial output rose at an average annual rate of 11 per cent, whereas agricultural production increased at an average annual rate of 1 per cent.

The structural transformation of the economy was accompanied by a shift of the working population from primary activities to secondary and tertiary sectors. The different sectoral growth rates resulted in major changes. The share of agriculture in the GDP and labour force declined from 49 per cent and 71 per cent respectively in 1928 to 29 per cent and 51 per cent in 1940. The share of industry in the GDP and labour force rose from 28 per cent and 18 per cent respectively to 45 per cent and 29 per cent during the same period. The value of heavy industry compared with total manufacturing output grew from 31 per cent to 63 per cent between 1928 and 1937 alone; whereas light industry's share declined from 68 per cent to 36 per cent.[13]

The above figures may understate the extent of structural change. According to Soviet author G. Glezerman, the proportion of 'factory workers' in the labour force rose from 14 per cent of the total in 1913 to 32.5 per cent in 1939, 48.2 per cent in 1959, and 54.8 per cent in 1968. As for the 'bourgeoisie, landowners, merchants and kulaks', their combined percentage fell from 16.3 per cent in 1913 to 4.6 per cent in 1938; and by 1939 they had disappeared from Soviet statistics.

The external factor played a decisive role in the industrialisation drive of the Soviet Union and hence in the differing sectoral growth rates of the economy. It was the continual hostility of the advanced capitalist powers that drove the Soviet Union to undertake one of the most successful rapid industrialisations in the modern world. That is why some people among the intelligentsia in the third world became fascinated by this socialist approach to socio-economic development.

Industrialisation as a process of development has taken place within specific, yet varied, historical, political, social, economic and cultural contexts. While all instances of industrialisation have certain common characteristics to which every society that attempts to industrialise must bend, any such society should still take into account its own particular resources and especially the creative potential of its people, and, at least in the long run, industrialisation ought to be adapted to local conditions, which are continually changing. Moreover, one should never lose sight of

Post-independence development

the fact that industrialisation has its specific logic, the sociological implications of which must be clearly and unequivocally understood by the power-holders who control the decision-making mechanisms. There is, neither in Algeria nor in the major third world states, no other feasible alternative to industrialisation at this stage of civilisation. The development of agriculture and other vital services cannot be envisaged seriously without the establishment of a modern basic industry that would both stimulate their growth and be stimulated by it.

The necessity of Algerian industrialisation

At independence in 1962, Algeria, which is the tenth largest state in the world, found itself a country relatively well endowed with a basic infrastructure, possessing a diversified resource base, faced with a rapidly growing population (the bulk of which was either jobless or underemployed and hence condemned to live in expanding rural slums and urban shanty towns), and the inheritor of an underdeveloped economy characterised by a sluggish agriculture and the absence of basic industry. Contrary to the views of most experts from the industrialised capitalist nations and those of their local followers, then and now industrialisation was an absolute necessity.

Indeed, the beginning of the colonial period and the subsequent integration of the Algerian economy and society into the French capitalist market ushered in a process of pauperisation. The deterioration of the living conditions of the rural population brought about a massive rural-to-urban exodus which began around the turn of the century and subsequently accelerated, especially during and after the 1930s. The urban population rose from 500,000 in 1930 to 2 million by 1960. In the absence of significant industry, these uprooted paupers either clustered (without employment prospects) in the mushrooming shanty towns and slums that were expanding within and around the urban centres, or crossed the Mediterranean in search of wage labour in French industrial conurbations. The war of national liberation had intensified the process of rural-to-urban migration. From 1954 to 1962 more than three million peasants, out of a total population of about 8.5 million, were uprooted from their ancestral villages (proclaimed prohibited zones by the colonial army) and thrown into regrouping camps. Hundreds of thousands fled the countryside to settle in the cities.

By the 1960s, Algeria's population had an overall average annual growth rate of 3.4 per cent, one of the highest in the world, and the average growth rate of the urban population was estimated at about 5.2 per cent per year as a result of the rural-to-urban exodus.

Confronted with such deeply rooted socio-economic problems, and given its important human mineral and energy potential, Algeria had no alternative to the launching of a massive programme of industrialisation. Conditions were not conducive to smooth industrial development. In fact, the country (like many developing countries) had to import technology, expertise and various other auxiliary services from the advanced capitalist nations and, to a lesser degree, from the Soviet Union. The lack of industrial experience, the existence of internal social and political contradictions accentuated by such a process of secondary industrial development, and especially the opposition of the *comprador* forces compounded by the hostile international environment shaped and dominated by world monopoly capital, were bound to generate serious difficulties.

The task of the industrialist was rendered practically impossible by the absence of a dynamic pro-industrial political force organised within a party or a national bloc, whose primary objective would have been the mobilisation of society and its resources for the construction of a viable economy capable of satisfying the needs of the population. The political nucleus that seized power and exercised it after 1965 consisted of a band of incompetent, unscrupulous and cynical ex-officers and cadres of the National Liberation Army (ALN) that was stationed in Tunisia and Morocco, a large number of whom were former professional officers of the French army who had deserted to join the Algerian external ALN once the independence of the country became inevitable.

In such a political vacuum, the Minister of Industry and Energy, Abdessalam Belaid, a former member of the radical nationalist movement (PPA-MTLD), who had experience of colonial jails as far back as 1945 and had become one of the most forceful ministers in the third world, was assigned by Boumedienne the task of formulating a strategy of industrialisation at the practical, theoretical, political and operational levels.

The Algerian strategy of development between 1967 and 1979

The strategy of development adopted was that of unbalanced sectoral growth. It involved the installation of basic industries – steel as well as machinery, metal construction, chemicals, petrochemicals and construction materials. These were referred to as basic and integrating industries, or industrialising industries, which conveys the idea that Algeria had at its disposal some oil revenue which must be invested in key industries in order to create employment for the growing population and establish a viable self-sustaining economy before the country's natural resources were depleted. Heavy industry, such as steel, would generate backward and forward links and hence stimulate the development of various branches and

Post-independence development

sectors providing iron goods, equipment and services to the iron and steel complexes, whose output would in turn furnish the raw materials and semi-finished products needed by a variety of other industries (e.g., the mechanical, construction, petrochemical and engineering industries). In return, those industries would provide not only consumer goods for the population but also necessary input for agriculture, light industries and a multiplicity of other services.

The multiplier effect of the total investment required by such growth-generating activities would, among other things, stimulate the spread of technical vocational training, the development of the social and technical services, the structural transformation of the economy and society and especially increased employment opportunities for both men and women. This would contribute to the growth of per capita income and so enhance the welfare of the population. Above all Belaid believed that the establishment of a viable economy would stimulate the development of a solid polity, capable of withstanding external encroachments and pressures. In short, the goal of industrialisation was to liquidate the colonial legacy and to resolve the major socio-economic problems facing the population before the depletion of oil, natural gas and mineral reserves.

Industrialisation under the Boumedienne regime

The main responsibility for economic construction fell on a single energetic and enigmatic man Abdessalam Belaid, the founder of SONATRACH (a national oil company) and Algeria's Minister of Industry and Energy from 1965 to 1978. His urgent task was to create order out of a chaotic scene that was becoming afflicted by the activities of a new breed of *compradors* who were in a hurry to become local representatives of multinational industrial firms and who often capitalised on their connections with highly influential officials and strong men within the Boumedienne regime.

Before developing its industrial plan, the Boumedienne regime shelved all the political institutions and organisations established under the previous regime. It then undertook a three-fold task: the formulation of the industrial policy discussed above; the construction of a highly centralised state; and the transformation of the single party (FLN) into a powerless, parallel and inert administrative apparatus. From then on, acting on behalf of society, but without consulting it, the state exercised all powers: executive, legislative and judicial. Furthermore, as the process of the nationalisation of economic assets progressed, the state became the principal agent of industrialisation and development, hence reinforcing its political, social and cultural omnipresence within society.

In subsequent years, despite the existence of deep-seated contradictions generated by this basically authoritarian but highly populist regime, the state proceeded to define a strategy of industrialisation, to make fundamental choices pertaining to sectoral priorities and to make plans for reshaping Algerian society, all without any movement towards the establishment of democratic decision-making mechanisms, particularly at the national level, that would provide for the political participation of the citizens.[14] Under these circumstances, the population became alienated from the projects dictated by the state, a fact that was bound sooner or later to undermine the regime's industrialisation effort in spite of substantial progress in the industrial field.

The first clash occurred between the Ministry of Industry and Energy and the trade union organisation (Union Générale des Travailleurs Algériens, UGTA) in 1967 over the question of industrial self-management. The UGTA demanded that workers' self-management be extended to all industrial enterprises. The Ministry not only rejected this demand but also requested the gradual ending of self-management in the industrial sector. According to the Ministry, workers' self-management constituted an anarchistic anachronism whose disappearance was necessary for the establishment of an appropriate management and the creation of an efficient industrial organisation which would not necessarily preclude genuine workers' participation in the future. The transition from a colonial economy to a planned and well-integrated independent economy would be achieved by favouring the development of large-scale public industrial enterprise which would specialise in the development and production of specific products at the branch level.

Boumedienne arbitrated this conflict in favour of the Ministry's proposal. When the trade union persisted in its demand, its national secretariat was finally dissolved. Thenceforth, the workers were further alienated from the regime and the extent of industrial self-management gradually declined. In 1969, 18,492 industrial workers (12.8 per cent of all industrial workers) were employed by self-management enterprises, a figure which had declined to 9,903 (4.7 per cent) by 1973.[15] However in 1971, the law concerning the socialist management of enterprises (or GSE) was promulgated, making workers and party officials' participation in the running of state companies an imperative.

The state-owned oil company SONATRACH, which was established in 1964 and which was headed until 1965 by Abdessalam Belaid himself, was used as a model for other national public corporations. The 1965 oil agreement with France allowed SONATRACH not only to extend participation in petroleum activities but also to increase its share of oil revenues. In subsequent years these revenues constituted the principal source of industrial investments.

Post-independence development

From 1965 to 1967 the efforts of the Ministry of Industry and Energy centred on the improvement of industrial organisation, the consolidation of existing plants and the building up of the stock of industrial equipment. This effort succeeded in reducing somewhat the difficulties that had arisen in the aftermath of independence. For instance, the textile and food industries, construction and commerce once again attained pre-1962 levels of annual production. In 1966, the industrial public sector grew as a result of the nationalisation of nine foreign mining companies. The government also expanded several small textile, leather and food-processing plants. Despite the upturn in industrial activity, a general economic expansion continued to be blocked by the lack of skilled labourers, technicians, engineers and managers, coupled with financial difficulties experienced by the workers' self-managed sector. The government sought to end stagnation by launching the country's first three-year experimental plan (for 1967–9).

The period of 'planned' industrial development

On the eve of the first three-year plan, the output of industry as a whole had not yet returned to 1962 levels. This was largely due to the fact that the formation of capital in the industrial sector fell by an average of 14 per cent during 1963–4 and by 5 per cent during 1965–6. Nonetheless, the volume of 'industrial investments rose from AD 120 million in 1963 to AD 590 million in 1964, declining to AD 394 million in 1965, but rising to AD 741 million in 1966'.[15] As will be seen in Chapter 8, agricultural investment declined drastically from AD 785 million in 1963 to AD 709 million in 1984 and to AD 329 million in 1965, increasing to AD 338 million in 1966. One of the major problems of Algerian agriculture was that unsold produce was piling up every year. It must be recalled that colonial agriculture was geared primarily to export crops such as wine, and when France closed its borders these remained in stock. Furthermore, the general economic sluggishness was aggravated by rapid population growth and high unemployment. The 1966 census revealed that those whom the census-takers regarded as the potentially economically active population (the 18–65-year-olds) totalled 5.58 million men and women, increasing by 175,000 persons per year. But only 1.5 million of a (male) labour force of 2.58 million were employed, so that the rate of unemployment was about 42 per cent. Since agriculture was unable to employ the growing rural population, the logical course of action was to establish basic industries in the big cities where millions of impoverished, formerly rural, people were concentrated.

Confronted with growing socio-economic pressures, and determined to create a new source of political legitimacy through development, the nationalist faction of the regime, represented by Boumedienne, Belaid, and

Industrialisation

the enigmatic Mohammed Ben Yahia, induced the so-called revolutionary council and the government not only to initiate a planned development centred primarily upon industrialisation but also to nationalise all the foreign insurance companies and banks. These nationalisations allowed the state to establish three banks: the National Bank, the External Bank and the Popular Credit of Algeria.

The immediate objective of the 1967–9 three-year plan was to create the basic conditions needed for the industrialisation of the country. Investment priorities were hydrocarbons (considered to be the sector of capital accumulation par excellence) and basic and integrating industry: steel, mechanical, chemical and electrical. The long-term goal of this planned development was, among other things, to strengthen the political and economic independence of the nation and to achieve full employment by the early 1980s. Since agriculture could not absorb the growing labour force, this meant that the rate of job generation in the non-agricultural sectors would have to be high enough to absorb the current jobless and underemployed population and thus to exceed the rate of growth of at least the male labour force.

An official document entitled *Perspectives septennales 1967–73*, released at the beginning of 1967, stressed that within the next seven years 'the capacity of capital accumulation, the beginning of an intersectoral integration and the educational and vocational training system must be adapted to the needs of the productive apparatus of the national economy'. A system of planning would also be set up. It was also during this year that Boumedienne secretly instructed (without the knowledge of the members of the so-called revolutionary council) his Minister of Industry and Energy to prepare the nationalisation of all industrial assets controlled by foreign firms in order to distribute them to the national public industrial enterprises. These enterprises were granted a monopoly over import, export and internal distribution so as to learn the nature and extent of the internal demand and marketing and thus to be able to launch new industrial projects and to prevent the entry of multinational firms through the medium of their local subsidiaries and their Algerian *comprador* agents. The latter were resorting increasingly to high-ranking politicians, army officers and top bureaucrats for protection and to obtain advantageous deals and contracts for the foreign firms they represented in Algeria. The decision to place all import–export trade under the control of public corporations was opposed strongly by these Algerian middlemen.

Under the first three-year plan, the industrial sector, including hydrocarbons, was allocated AD 5.5 billion out of a total projected investment of AD 9.6 billion. This sum breaks down as follows: AD 2.31 billion for hydrocarbons and AD 2.2 billion for basic and integrating industry, while of the rest, AD 500 million went to light industries (mostly food processing) and AD 400 million to mining and electricity. The regime also called upon the national private sector to invest in these light industries. Agriculture received about 25 per cent of the total projected investments.

As for the actual outcome, during the period covered by the first plan, the industrial sector absorbed a total net investment of AD 4.91 billion. SONATRACH utilised AD 2.52 billion, representing 51.3 per cent of industrial investment, for hydrocarbon development, while steel and metal construction consumed another 19 per cent and the chemical industry 10 per cent. As a whole, the industrial sector accounted for 53 per cent of the total net investment in all areas of the economy. By the end of the three-year plan, 173 projects for large-scale industry and 87 projects for small- and medium-scale industry were being implemented. Several of them were added in the course of the plan, a fact that contributed to the increase of the total estimated cost from the projected AD 5.5 billion to no less than AD 13.95 billion.

Eighty-four per cent of the total investment targets initially projected for the national economy were fulfilled by 31 December 1969. Despite this, Algeria's experience in connection with this plan highlighted one of the most serious obstacles to rapid industrialisation in subsequent years: the growing pressures exerted by the pro-*comprador* political forces within the regime and the lack of the means of implementing the industrial projects. This resulted in bottlenecks and hence galloping costs induced by long delays and by international and domestic inflation.

One important success of the first three-year plan was the nationalisation of foreign industrial enterprises and subsidiaries in Algeria and the distribution of their assets among the national corporations. This step contributed to the establishment of five new companies and to the consolidation of the nine major existing ones. In fact, from May to June 1968 alone, enterprises of 45 foreign firms, employing 7,500 industrial workers and with annual sales totalling AD 480 million, were nationalised. Thus, by the end of 1969 only about 20 French industrial enterprises, out of the 700–800 that existed in Algeria in 1962, remained under the control of their owners. In the hydrocarbons sector, SONATRACH continued to reinforce its position vis-à-vis the multinational oil companies operating in the Sahara. In 1967 the internal distribution networks of a number of British and US oil companies, including British Petroleum, Esso and Mobil Oil, were seized on the occasion of the Israeli aggression against the Arab states and then bought at a reasonable price. In 1968, 14 foreign oil companies lost their control of distribution, storage and transportation of Algerian oil and its derived products, to SONATRACH, which also took over all the reserves of natural gas, thus dashing the hopes and pretensions of French oil companies which were claiming large proportions of these important resources. In 1969, the concessions of the Sinclair Oil Corporation were nationalised. In order to increase its prospecting activities, SONATRACH set up several mixed companies in which it controlled 51 per cent of the shares. It also began the construction of two major gas pipelines, Hassi R'Mel-Skikda and Hassi Messaoud-Arzew, which allowed it to increase its control over the transport of the country's oil.

Simultaneously, SONATRACH undertook the development of the petrochemical industry, working to build industrial plants for the liquefaction of natural gas and the production of plastics, fertiliser, ethylene and polyethylene. By the end of the three-year plan, SONATRACH had increased its control over all activities and hence became the country's largest state company, employing 8,860 workers, including 900 foreigners. Since it was set up as a challenge to French oil interests in Algeria, it maintained a nationalistic outlook, a fact that enhanced its performance and industrial achievements in subsequent years. It was the only company that had no French technical experts. The value of its total output rose from AD 539 million in 1967 (compared with AD 450 million for the Algerian operations of foreign companies) to AD 2.11 billion by 1969 (as against AD 3.83 billion for the foreign companies).

The industrial public sector, including hydrocarbons and mining, was substantially expanded: its share of total annual added value rose from 28.3 per cent in 1967 to 44.5 per cent in 1969. This sector, excluding hydrocarbons, employed 42 per cent of the industrial labour force in 1967 and 61 per cent by 1970. SONATRACH's share of employment in petroleum rose from 27 to 54 per cent during the same period.

These achievements consolidated the political basis of Boumedienne's regime despite the emergence of new conflicts of interest between various social groups and political forces generated by the process of industrialisation. Indeed, all the members of the so-called revolutionary council, except its chairman, Boumedienne – who did not even deem it necessary to consult the others on the matter – opposed the nationalisation of foreign interests. They advocated a different mode of development whereby the state should have restricted itself only to heavy investments for the purpose of establishing a basic infrastructure and key industries. The remainder should have been left to private initiative. In other words, such a development was to favour the growth and proliferation of *comprador* activities that would have kept the national economy under the control of multinational firms. But, since the Ministry of Industry and Energy was the only ministerial department that presented positive gains every year, Boumedienne, who grasped the strategic importance of industrialisation, continued to support that Ministry in spite of the growing pressures exerted

Post-independence development

within the regime by the defenders of *comprador* interests and by the emerging national bourgeoisie, which controlled a growing number of light industrial establishments and the bulk of internal trade.

Throughout Boumedienne's rule there was a squabble over the functions and prerogatives of the Ministry of Industry and Energy, on the one hand, and the Ministry of Finance and the Secretariat of State for Planning, on the other. The Ministry of Industry and Energy argued that industrial planning must implement the national development priorities and goals defined by the political leadership of the state. Once approved by the Council of Ministers, the finance and planning branches of government should co-operate in expediting the fulfilment of these specific planned targets rather than perniciously depriving industry not only of the means of implementation but also of the feasibility or unfeasibility of individual projects in a disguised attempt to block the industrialisation drive.

As the Ministry of Industry and Energy saw it, planning should begin only after national economic goals had been set by the political authorities. Then the planners should formulate economic strategy, largely in terms of flexible yet binding targets for basic industries, limited only by the investment funds available. Once these funds were allocated by the state, the Ministry of Finance should authorise their expenditure without the unnecessary red tape which caused long delays in the completion of the projects already approved by the political power, a fact that was bound not only to contribute to high costs but also to slow down the process of development. As a result, the Ministry of Industry and Energy argued that state bankers and planners should not block the process of industrialisation under the pretext of preserving the so-called fundamental financial equilibria of the economy, for otherwise industrial growth would be subjected to a monetarist logic that would focus unduly on the short-term profit prospects of individual projects while tending to ignore the long-term social, economic, political, technological and cultural benefits to be derived from the industrial sector as a whole.

Meanwhile, the Ministry of Finance and the Secretariat of State for Planning, which were controlled by francophile and pro-*comprador* elements, echoed France's systematic opposition to Algeria's industrialisation and the Algerian private sector's hostility to this type of industrialisation, involving as it did the nationalisation and socialisation of the means of production. In December 1969, Boumedienne was induced to sign a drastic new fiscal law presented by the Ministry of Finance that curtailed the freedom of action of the Ministry of Industry and Energy. This led to the attempted resignation of the Minister on the eve of the publication of the first four-year plan of development (1970–3). His resignation was refused by Boumedienne. This provoked a crisis within the ruling group which was resolved by the departure of Cherif Belkacem, the Minister of Finance; but the law in question remained in effect.

These conflicts went deeper than bureaucratic territorial quarrels: they reflected the competing interests of various social and political groups. Although Boumedienne had always arbitrated, if sometimes too late, in favour of industry, he never attempted to eliminate the anti-industrialisation, pro-French, party from his regime. When one of the fathers of industrialisation told him privately that he should remove all the partisans of compradorisation from key positions within the state apparatus, he replied: 'There are certain things you don't know about', implying that these forces were too powerful to confront. Indeed, as will be seen in Chapter 13, these political and social forces, allied with *comparador* interests and domestic private capital, managed after his death not only to tip the internal balance of political power in their favour, but also to reverse the course of industrialisation easily during the preparation of the 1980–4 five-year plan. The disappearance of Boumedienne resulted in the imposition of the viewpoint of the Ministry of Finance and the Secretariat of State for Planning, which, under the disguise of preserving the fundamental equilibria of the economy, stoppped the process of industrialisation in its tracks.

The first four-year plan (1970–3)

In preparing the four-year plan of development, the Ministry of Industry and Energy clarified overall goals and refined the strategy of industrialisation. The model of unbalanced sectoral growth was, once again, adopted; top priority was given to basic and integrating industry, but light industry was not neglected. The industrial sector, including hydrocarbons, was allocated AD 12.4 billion of the total projected investments for the national economy of AD 27.75 billion, while AD 4.57 billion (16.5 per cent of total projected investment for all sectors) was earmarked for hydrocarbons, AD 5.21 billion (18.8 per cent) for basic and integrating industry, AD 1.2 billion for light industry and AD 11.4 billion for mining and electricity. Agriculture, water resources and fishing combined were allocated AD 4.94 billion, representing 17.8 per cent of the total planned investments.

One of the criticisms made by foreign observers, as well as by Algerian scholars including me, was that agriculture and other sectors were sacrificed to industry. As will be shown, however, in retrospect the reality is not only different from but more complex than the appearance. The various sectors constituting the national economy had either developed a dynamic of growth or an equilibrium of inertia and stagnation. Only the industrial sector, including hydrocarbons, had managed to generate an internal

Post-independence development

development dynamic that dared not only to challenge Algerian underdevelopment but also to pursue the struggle of national liberation into the economic field – and hence the continued defiance of the former colonial power which was determined to preserve its interests in the country. This dynamism is attributable directly to the Minister of Industry and Energy, who was a former militant of the PPA-MTLD. The other sectors, such as agriculture, public works and construction, transport and telecommunications, technical education and vocational training, public health and administration in general – which were under the management and supervision of ministerial departments headed either by the pro-*comprador* ministers or the anti-national elements that Boumedienne himself was compelled to denounce as the French party in Algeria – suffered from developmental impotence. The Ministry of Agriculture illustrates this point, as will be seen in Chapter 8. Not only did the successive ministers who were in charge of this vital sector not request sufficient investment funds to develop agriculture, but the funds allocated by the state were not used up. For instance, agriculture received 18 per cent of the projected investment during the 1970–3 four-year plan, yet only 12 per cent was actually utilised, while industry, initially allocated 44.7 per cent, increased its actual share during the plan period to 57.3 per cent. Similarly, the social sectors, such as construction, education, vocational training, welfare, local collectivities and administration, were altogether allocated a total of AD 7.4 billion of the projected investment funds, but used only 6.11 billion. Needless to say, the decline of these services eventually undermined the industrialisation drive of the country. Moreover, failure in these areas, which resulted in hardship for the population, was easily blamed on industry by *comprador* forces whose representatives controlled most of these deficient ministerial departments.

Despite the emergence of serious bottlenecks, as well as complex socio-economic and technological problems caused by the inexperience of the industrial operators and by a hostile domestic and international environment, the achievements of industry were far from negligible during the period covered by this plan. The reorganisation of the sector progressed as a result of the application of socialist management to industrial public enterprises, and the process of nationalisation went on unabated. In 1972 alone, three new national corporations were established, and three old companies were merged in order to improve their performance. In 1970, five foreign oil companies were nationalised. SONATRACH extended its control over 30 per cent of petroleum production and 60 per cent of distribution and processing. In 1971, 51 per cent of all French oil companies operating in the country were nationalised. Moreover, by the end of the new Franco-Algerian crisis brought about by this nationalisation

Industrialisation

SONATRACH controlled over 80 per cent of the oil resources in the Sahara. During 1971–2 three more French industrial firms were also nationalised.

These nationalisations contributed to the consolidation of the industrial public sector. The industrial public sector's share of production in terms of added value rose from AD 1.64 billion in 1969, excluding hydrocarbons, to AD 3.1 billion in 1973, which comprised 64.5 per cent of the total industrial added value. In the hydrocarbons sector the production of added value increased from AD 2.82 billion (compared to AD 3.58 billion for the foreign private sector) to AD 10 billion (contrasted with only AD 2.78 billion for the foreign sector) during the same period. By 1974, public industry employed 61 per cent of the total industrial labour force. SONATRACH employed 54 per cent of the labour force engaged in hydrocarbons activities in 1970, and this figure rose to nearly 96 per cent in 1974. The preponderance of the industrial sector as a whole was further affirmed during the second four-year plan (1974–7), a fact that contributed to its increasing internal difficulties and to external assaults perpetrated by *comprador* forces closely linked to foreign powers as well as various other parasitic elements determined either to halt its advance or to exploit the fruits of its dynamism.

The second four-year plan (1974–7)

The second four-year plan coincided with the unprecedented rise in oil prices – first from $3.25 to $9.25 per barrel and then to $16.20 by the beginning of 1974. This resulted in an increased availability of financial resources for industrial investment. Thus, the claim by the Ministry of Finance and the Secretariat of State for Planning that the country could not afford industrialisation because of financial constraints was finally dismissed by Boumedienne, and for a time the political forces behind the finance and planning bureaucrats lost significant ground. Projected industrial investments were revised upwards in the course of the plan. Table 6.1 shows the sectoral distribution of projected, and net, investments as well as what remained to be invested by the end of the plan period.

Thus, the second four-year plan reaffirmed the top priority given to the industrial sector and also reflected the internal dynamics of industry. Allocated 40.3 per cent of the total investments projected for the national economy, industry and energy ended up by actually investing 61.4 per cent, while agriculture and water resources were initially allocated 15 per cent, but consumed a mere 7 per cent. Instead of being rewarded for its dynamism, however, the Ministry of Industry and Energy was divided into three ministries in 1977 for political reasons.

Table 6.1 *Industrial investment under the second four-year plan (1974–7) (million AD)*

Branches	Investment projections	Net investment	Total cost of projects	Not yet achieved 31 December 1977
Hydrocarbons	19,500	36,000	63,600	27,600
Basic industry	21,900	28,460	70,960	42,500
Light industry	4,000	5,070	23,000	17,930
Mining and electricity	2,600	4,620	9,200	4,580
Total	48,000	74,150	166,760	92,610

Source: Ministère de la Planification et de l'Amenagement du Territoire, *Synthèse du bilan économique et social de la decennie 1967–1978* (Algiers, May 1980).

The period of the second four-year plan was marked by the nationalisation of the remaining foreign industrial enterprises in the country. In 1974, 20 French and 2 Belgian enterprises were nationalised, which further strained Algeria's relations with France. As noted earlier, the successive French governments opposed Algerian industrialisation; indeed, they refused to accept Algeria's economic independence. French industrialists and diplomats alike carried out a worldwide campaign to dissuade other Euro-American and Japanese firms from dealing with Algerian national enterprises. On the intellectual plane, French academics of all persuasions tried to discredit Algeria's model of development in general, and its mode of industrialisation in particular. Moreover, as we have seen, French interests in Algeria were explicitly and implicitly defended by certain Algerian ministers, high-ranking servants and even academics. In particular, the opposition of the Ministry of Finance and the Secretariat of State for planning – which were under the influence of the pro-French elements – did much to slow down the industrialisation process.

However, the experience of industrialisation pushed the Ministry of Industry and Energy and the managers of public enterprises to the forefront of the struggle against internal backwardness and against the control of the advanced capitalist countries and their multinational firms over the resources of third world countries. The mode of industrialisation chosen brought the leaders of industry into a head-on collision both with external imperialism (particularly French) and with the local *compradors* and all sorts of parasitic private entrepreneurs who used their connections with various top officials in order to get hold of the most profitable activities, either as middlemen or as sub-contractors. Boumedienne and his

Minister of Industry and Energy came to realise that, given the international balance of power and the *comprador* nature of the local bourgeoisies, private initiative was incapable of promoting a genuine national independent development. This was because, among other things, the dependent bourgeoisies would never challenge the international division of labour promoted under an unequitable world economic order imposed upon the three underdeveloped continents by the imperialist powers during the colonial period.

Algeria, which considered the nationalisation of its natural resources and other foreign assets as a necessary condition for a genuine construction of its national economy, had become increasingly aware of the obstacles posed by this old international economic order. The situation induced Boumedienne to advocate in his speech to the Conference of the Heads of States of the Non-Aligned Countries held in Algiers in 1973 and in the memorandum submitted by Algeria on behalf of the same heads of states to the United Nations in 1974, the installation of a new international economic order. This major speech as well as the memoranda submitted by Algeria to the Non-Aligned summit and to the United Nations were prepared by the Ministry of Industry and Energy, which came to play a major role in the various world conferences and negotiations between the North and the South, such as the Lima and Paris conferences held in 1975. During these conferences, Algerian experts employed by the Ministry distinguished themselves greatly.

It became obvious to the advanced capitalist countries, whose leaders had been extremely irritated by Boumedienne's address to the General Assembly of the United Nations the previous year, that if the industrialisation of Algeria were left to succeed, it might have disastrous consequences for their interests in the third world in general and in Africa in particular. Indeed, Boumedienne opened his address by stressing that:

The Fourth Conference of Non-Aligned countries [held in September 1973] noted that in recent years spectacular meetings have taken place among the great powers, announcing profound changes in international relations. However, it is abundantly clear that these initiatives correspond essentially to the aims of the developed countries anxious to find a common ground for the settlement of the serious disagreements that divided them hitherto and to create a context of co-operation for reconciling their respective interests. Tension and war have been transferred to Asia, Africa and Latin America, which have become the zones where all the contradictions of our contemporary world are concentrated and exacerbated.

Posed a quarter of a century ago by the community of nations as one of the major world priorities, the problem of development has today become that absolute priority which we must all face, and without further delay, if we wish to avert the tragic possibility that this problem might one day become a source of uncontrollable conflagration.

It must be recognised first of all that in the world in which we live all the strings of the world economy are in the hands of a minority composed of the highly developed countries. By virtue of its dominant position, this minority proceeds at will in determining the allocation of world resources in accordance with an order of priorities of its own.

And Boumedienne went on to stress that the third world countries must 'insist on being masters in their own houses, so as to collect the harvest of their natural resources and devote it to their own development. It is essential that we should not lose sight of the fact that the effort to bring the task of recovery to fruition will remain without effect so long as international monopolies and multinational corporations, those past masters of the art of making concessions in order to safeguard the essentials, continue to control the mechanisms whereby the wealth of poor countries is transferred away from them mainly by the system of price fixing for raw materials, and continue to flourish.' He added that from 1965 to 1970 alone the multinational firms of some advanced capitalist countries repatriated from the third world $23 billion out of their declared profits. The service on the $80 billion total debt amounted to about $9 billion during 1973. This constituted 'one of the factors that compel the developing countries to borrow continually and thus chronically aggravate their balance of payments positions still further'.

Boumedienne concluded by suggesting that the third world countries 'must take over their natural resources, which implies, essentially, nationalising the exploitation of these resources and controlling the machinery governing the determination of their prices; a coherent and integrated process of development must be launched, which includes, in particular, the development of all agricultural potential and the achievement of in-depth industrialisation essentially based, wherever possible, on the local processing of the natural resources, mineral or agricultural, of each country concerned'.

This position provoked the wrath of the ruling circles in the advanced capitalist countries in general and in France in particular. Indeed, according to a revelation by a former member of the US government, the French secret service suggested to the CIA in 1975 the possibility of assassinating Boumedienne in an attempt to neutralise Algeria's influence in world affairs and to put an end to its internal development. The American response to this sinister proposal was very revealing: the assassination of Boumedienne might not attain the desired goal because his regime had created a large community of interests within Algeria (meaning public companies, universities, etc.). Consequently his policies would undoubtedly continue after his death. Boumedienne himself was informed at the time by a friendly power that his life was in danger.

Despite this, Boumedienne entrusted his Minister of Industry and

Table 6.2 *Industrial investment under the 1978 annual plan (billion AD)*

Branch	Investment and re-evaluation	Actuals
Hydrocarbons	34.40	14.70
Basic and integrating industry	7.95	11.79
Light industry	8.63	3.96
Mining and electricity	4.67	22.05
Total	55.65	32.50

Source: MPAT, *Synthèse du Bilan.*

Energy and three other officials, one minister and two ambassadors (all former militants or sympathisers of the PPA-MTLD), to draft a national charter. However, the adoption in 1976 of this national charter, which stressed, among other things, the socialist character of Algerian industrialisation, accentuated internal and external pressures and contradictions whose immediate impact was not only to cause the break-up of the Ministry of Industry and Energy but also to postpone the preparation of the fourth plan of development until 1980. Indeed, after a national debate during which the majority of the people supported the socialist option and orientation of the charter, Boumedienne appeared to have backed down. As he told one of his collaborators, who criticised him for maintaining pro-western and anti-socialist elements in some strategic positions within the regime, 'There are things that you don't know.' And he added 'I lost my feet in July 1976.' The person who reported this still cannot work out what Boumedienne meant. Thenceforth, the industrial sector continued to develop in a highly disorganised and hostile political, administrative and financial environment.

The annual plan for 1978 projected a total industrial investment of about AD 55.65 billion, divided among the various branches of industry as shown in Table 6.2.

It is obvious that the development of the national economy could not have taken place in such a systematic manner without the revenue earned from the export of hydrocarbons products. Indeed, on the occasion of the inauguration of the natural gas liquefaction complex (GNL), on 21 February 1978, Boumedienne stated that

> existing proven reserves not only guarantee Algeria the ability to satisfy its own need in energy and petrochemicals for decades to come, but also ensure a high level of exports of liquid hydrocarbons and gas which will provide the means for creating and developing new and more durable sources of revenue. Consequently, in the present phase, the development of our reserves and the raising of production levels

Post-independence development

Table 6.3 *The hydrocarbons development plan (1976–2005) (US billion dollars)*

	1976–85	1986–95	1996–2005	Total
Foreign currency earnings	80.1 (40%)	83.8 (42%)	36.2 (18%)	200.1
Turnover	87.9 (35%)	101.7 (41%)	60.8 (24%)	250.4
Total investment expenditure	28.4 (85%)	3.0 (9%)	2.0 (6%)	33.4
Mobilisation of foreign loans	15.5 (90%)	1.1 (6%)	0.8 (4%)	17.4
Repayments of foreign loans	10.2 (55%)	7.3 (39%)	1.1 (6%)	18.6
Total repayment of debt	13.0 (48%)	11.7 (43%)	2.3 (9%)	27.0
Royalties	12.0 (45%)	9.9 (37%)	4.9 (18%)	26.8
Taxes on profit	30.9 (35%)	35.8 (40%)	21.8 (25%)	88.5
Net cash flow available to state	12.8 (27%)	23.4 (49%)	11.9 (24%)	48.1

Source: SONATRACH, Plan VALHYD, 1977.

are important objectives. Yet it must be emphasised that, although the reserves are considerable, they are not inexhaustible. Recourse to the stripping of our reserves in order to increase revenue can only be justified if that revenue is used wisely and efficiently, in a climate of austerity, for the creation of new resources which will be a source of revenue themselves and in their turn generate still more resources, thus safeguarding the interests of future generations.

On 1 August 1977, the proved reserves of hydrocarbons were estimated at 5,000,000 million cubic metres of gas (plus 520,000 million cubic metres of probable reserves and 299,000 million cubic metres of possible reserves), 1,023 million tons of petroleum (plus 91 million tons of probable reserves and 22 million tons of possible reserves), 159 million tons of liquefied petroleum gas (plus 42 million tons of probable reserves and 6 million tons of possible reserves) and 385 million of condensate (plus 58 million of probable reserves and 12 million tons of possible reserves).

At the specific request of Boumedienne, SONATRACH drafted the hydrocarbons development plan in the light of the proved, probable and possible reserves mentioned above and presented it to the Council of Ministers for approval. The main objectives of this plan to 1976–2005 were:
(1) The raising of the level of crude petroleum and gas production to the highest level compatible with the maximum recovery of reserves and the need to use gas in recycling, recovery and gas-lift
(2) The recovery of gas associated with petroleum production, with reinjection of this gas when an improvement of the rate of recovery would result
(3) The maximum production of liquefied petroleum gas (LPG) and condensate at the processing stage, allowing for economic constraints

Industrialisation

(4) The construction of processing plant to satisfy the external demand for liquefied natural gas (LNG)

(5) The replacement of exports of crude by exports of processed products and the satisfaction of domestic demand for refined products, fertilisers, petrochemicals and plastics.

This development plan, which would have required a total investment of 33.4 billion US dollars, was supposed to generate a total estimated revenue of $250 bn – $ bn 200.1 in foreign currency – during the 1976–2005 period. Meanwhile, the sum which would have accrued to the state treasury would have amounted to $163.4 billion. Table 6.3 summarises the development schedule of this scheme.

According to an official document 'The aim of hydrocarbons development is to accelerate the exploitation of Algeria's oil and gas reserves and to convert these resources into means of production in order to allow an improvement of the economic conditions of the Algerian people'. Ahmed Ghozali, former Minister of Energy and Petrochemical Industries, stated in 1978 that

> proven recoverable reserves of hydrocarbons in Algeria at present amount to over 12,500 million barrels of liquid hydrocarbons and 3,500,000 million cubic metres of natural gas (10 per cent of the world proven resources). Therefore, Algeria has the reserves necessary for the development of a hydrocarbon export policy which will accord with its intention of using the revenue from hydrocarbons to establish an economic infrastructure broad and powerful enough to provide the country with resources which, unlike its mineral wealth, are not subject to exhaustion.

Despite the fact that the main objective of this comprehensive plan was designed to clarify the potential financial resources of the nation and to maximise the utilisation of revenues to be earned from the export of hydrocarbons in such a systematic way as to consolidate the process of industrialisation, to develop a basic socio-economic infrastructure and to modernise agriculture, the Benjadid regime cancelled it in 1980, long before its completion. Since then the new leadership has been realising only part of this scheme in a very piecemeal and costly fashion. Indeed, as time goes by, the costs of construction and equipment keep on increasing. For instance, a 1.7 billion cubic metre liquefaction plant which cost less than $40 million in 1971 already cost $45 million in 1974, $60 million in 1975 and nearly $80 million in 1976. In subsequent years, this inflation had not only speeded up but had begun to affect the import of all capital goods, including agricultural machinery.

Aware of the stagnation of agricultural production, the Ministry of Industry and Energy financed a comprehensive technical study of agriculture for the specific purpose of developing this vital sector. The study concluded that if Algeria were to establish a network of interconnected dams along the coast and to pump water from there up to the high plateau, it could irrigate about one million hectares of land. The cultivation of this land would transform Algeria into an agricultural exporting country. When the study was presented to the Council of Ministers in 1978, Ben Chérif, the Minister of Water Resources, retorted that Algerians were not Germans. He then ordered his subordinates to burn it. The consequences are well known to all Algerians today: absolute dependence on foreign countries for food. Despite this, however, the post-Boumedienne rulers of Algeria have, since 1979, been blaming industry for all the ills of Algerian society.

From 1967 to 1979, net industrial investments totalled AD 116.36 billion, out of a total net investment in the national economy and social services of AD 238.28 billion. Some 48 per cent of the industrial investment was spent by SONATRACH in hydrocarbons development and in the petrochemical industry; the company completed 36 new projects and extended four existing ones. Basic and integrating industry consumed 33 per cent of industrial investments; electricity and distribution of gas, 5.2 per cent; and light industries, 13 per cent. From 1967 to 1979, 234 new projects for large- and medium-scale industry and 44 extensions of existing projects were completed and put into production. This rapid industrial growth was bound to generate complex managerial and organisational difficulties. Boumedienne and the leaders of public industry thought that they could overcome them by the application of a socialist management of enterprises.

The socialist management of public enterprises

In 1971 growing problems in the realm of industrial relations and management induced Boumedienne to request the elaboration of a Charter of the Socialist Management of Public Enterprises, known in Algeria as GSE. Its promulgation and implementation were intended to render industrial management more democratic and more efficient. In other words, the objectives of GSE were two-fold: to make the workers participate in the management of state enterprises and to underline the socialist character of national industry and other sectors so as to induce working men and women to win the battle of production and management.

According to the authors of the charter of the GSE, the 'state is not just an abstraction; but again it is not bourgeois in character. The state is the guarantor of the interests of the ensemble of the working masses.' It seeks the fulfilment of the 'aspirations of the people. Therefore the workers must participate in the construction of socialism. The labouring masses have the right and duty to defend their interests secured by the state socialist policies.' Workers' rights were defined as: 'a fair remuneration, a guarantee of social rights, equal pay for equal work, protection against unemployment, the setting up of training programmes and the opening of vocational training centres and the promulgation of fair standards for promotion in all areas'.

In addition, this charter called on labour and management to co-operate as equal partners in close association with the party and the single workers' trade union organisation (UGTA). The political leadership emphasised in this official document that the party, the UGTA and management must be the *motor* of workers' education and training. Accordingly, the trade union and the party ought to increase workers' competence and consciousness in order to create an alliance of co-operation between all individuals in an enterprise. Thus, it was also considered to be a school for political, ideological and social education.

Workers' participation in the management of a socialist enterprise was not limited to the organisational level, but included production workshops. The composition of the Workers' Assembly which represented the producers varied from 7 to 25 members depending upon the size and specific needs of the enterprise or production workshop concerned. A productive unit that employed fewer than 30 workers had either to be combined with another or referred to the Ministry of Labour and Social Affairs. Every worker who had been employed for at least six months had the right to vote. A candidate for the Workers' Assembly had to have been a member of the UGTA for a year, to be at least 21 years old and to occupy a permanent job. The number of candidates for the Workers' Assembly had to be double the number of members required by law. They were designated by the union officials, who were themselves chosen by the party. Once elected they had to serve as workers' representatives in the assembly for at least three consecutive years.

The Workers' Assembly, which had two representatives sitting on the management council, participated in the elaboration of the policy of the enterprise as well in the recruitment, training and sacking of workers. It held two general meetings per year at the enterprise level and four meetings at the productive unit level. In addition, a meeting was held any time it was deemed necessary by two-thirds of the members.

In order to give workers' representation and participation a permanent character, five management committees were created. The economic and social committee dealt with marketing and supply; it also controlled public resources and elaborated projects designed to enhance the profitability of the enterprise or unit. The social and cultural affairs committee was in charge of social and cultural matters. The personnel and training committee managed recruitment, wages, training programmes, fringe benefits, workers' profit sharing and hence the improvement of production. The disciplinary committee – which was the most important one – was in charge of resolving all the problems and questions pertaining to discipline, including sacking or more minor penalties. Its role was to preserve workers' rights, to protect the general interests of the enterprise and to prevent any abuse of authority or injustice. Finally, the health and safety committee ensured that the health and safety regulations were respected; it was empowered to take preventative measures to improve the working conditions of the labour force.

Although the charter of GSE insisted that the relations between the Workers' Assembly and management must be co-operative, the authority of the General Manager – who represented the state and who, in the final analysis, determined the policy of the firm under his guidance and supervision – was paramount. The document also considered that a unified system of management was necessary in order to preserve harmony within the enterprise.

The application of this law turned out to create more problems than it was intended to solve. The party, whose officials had always been close to anti-industrialisation political forces, not only chose the union representatives but also came to be represented on these same committees. The charter stipulated that if the members of a committee could not agree on a decision they should refer the conflict to a higher level for further consideration. However, the party and the union officials managed to impose a majority rule. Thus the representatives of management were put in a minority position and, since the workers' representatives within the committees owed their election to the party, their hostility to management became their only assurance of consecutive re-elections.

Consequently, the system of the GSE, which was initially conceived as a means of attenuating and resolving the conflicts between management and labour, was gradually transformed into a 'veritable war machine at the hands of the UGTA and through it the party'. Furthermore, the average Algerian worker was not interested in the actual management of the enterprise but was primarily concerned with problems generated by the backward environment, inadequate transportation, the shortage of housing and the absence or inadequacy of medical care. All these problems were engendered by the industrial environment. Thus, the failure of other branches of government to provide these vital services compelled the workers to raise these problems as demands which the management of the public enterprises had to satisfy. But when they tried, with some success, to resolve some of them, the managers were faced with unfair criticism. They were not only accused of encroaching on the prerogatives of other ministerial departments but also of creating a privileged category of workers.

Industrialisation

Needless to say, even the partial resolution of these problems had contributed to the operating costs of the enterprises, a fact that was used by the anti-industrialisation and anti-socialist elements within the power structure to denounce the low profitability, or even deficits, of this infant industry.

On top of all this, since the management of the new industrial plants were compelled by the lack of housing to favour the skilled workers in the distribution of few units of accommodation they managed, often illegally, to construct, the unskilled work force become disenchanted with the GSE. The absence of unskilled labourers from the workers' assemblies was reported by all researchers in the field of industrial relations in contemporary Algeria. The frustrations and anger of a large segment of the working class were expressed by growing incidents of sabotage and, in particular, strikes, which were (and still are) illegal. For instance, the number of reported strikes rose from 72 in 1969 to 168 in 1973 and 521 in 1977, before falling to 323 in 1978 but rising again to 870 by 1980. In 1969 only 2.7 per cent of these strikes occurred within the public sector; this proportion rose to 15.7 per cent in 1972, 36 per cent in 1977 and 45.7 per cent in 1980. In 1977, 320,000 working days were lost as a result of strikes (compared with 1.1 million as a consequence of accidents in the work-place). Although these latter figures included the private sector, which respected workers' rights in the realm of wage rates and safety regulations, they were still high enough even within the public sector to affect the pace of production as well as the rates of productivity. In these circumstances, the rate of absenteeism varied between 10 and 20 per cent, the average rate of labour turn-over reached 20 per cent and factory discipline became extremely unsatisfactory.

In spite of all this (and perhaps even because of it), the public industrial enterprises continued to offer important fringe benefits, and even higher wages, to skilled workers, for example, free transport, consumer co-operatives, canteens, health centres and vocational training centres, as well as housing for the staff, engineers, technicians, foremen and some of the skilled workers. This state of affairs led many scholars who studied Algeria's industrial relations to use such descriptions as 'the socialism of enterprises', 'peripheral Fordism' and 'social justice'. However, the political and bureaucratic environment steadily undermined the consolidation and stabilisation of this nascent industrial organisation.

The evolution of industrial production and productivity

The environmental constraints were represented by political conflicts, an inefficient bureaucracy, systematic hostility from certain ruling circles in the advanced capitalist countries who were tied closely to a local growing

Post-independence development

Table 6.4 *Annual added value produced by industry (billion AD)*

Branch	1967	Constant prices			Current prices				Average annual growth (%)
		1973	1977	1978	1967	1973	1977	1978	
Basic industry	1.6	3.3	4.9	5.9	0.8	2.2	4.3	5.7	19.9
Light industry	2.3	4.3	4.7	4.8	1.3	2.6	4.0	4.8	12.8
Mining and electricity	0.4	0.8	1.5	1.6	0.3	0.7	1.4	1.6	16.5
Hydrocarbons	14.2	21.2	22.5	24.6	2.6	6.5	23.6	24.6	22.8

Sources: MPAT, *Synthèse du bilan.*

comprador bourgeoisie, a lack of experienced engineers, technicians, managers and skilled middle-level workers and cadres and an inadequate educational and vocational training system. Besides all this, Algerian public industry was penalised by an aberrant pricing system. Indeed, the prices of the bulk of industrial products, including those imported by public enterprises to be sold in the country, were fixed by decree. Needless to say, once these decrees were promulgated, it was almost impossible to modify them because this modification required the consent of all the ministerial departments as well as the party and trade union officials. This fact forced many socialist enterprises to sell certain products below their cost of production. This anomalous situation – which was one of the main causes of the deficits accumulated by the industrial public enterprises – provided an argument for the anti-industrialisation forces, who were then able to denounce the bankruptcy of socialist industry.

Nonetheless, per capita gross industrial production rose from AD 1,159 in 1967 to AD 4,932 in 1978, representing an average annual growth rate of 14.1 per cent. Table 6.4 summarises the growth of industrial production between 1967 and 1978.

In short, in terms of constant prices, total industrial production, including hydrocarbons, rose from AD 18.5 billion in 1967 to AD 36.7 billion in 1978. Despite this, the rate of labour productivity in the hydrocarbons sector – whose total labour force increased from 5,900 in 1967 to 40,000 by 1977 – decreased from AD 2,366,666 per worker to AD 675,000 per worker during the same period. The rate of labour productivity in the non-oil industrial sector, if one takes into consideration its inexperience and its difficult environment, was better. Indeed, the total non-oil industrial labour force increased from 117,000 in 1967 to 153,000 in 1969, 233,000 in 1973, 347,000 in 1977 and 390,000 by 1978. This

Table 6.5 *Employment in the industrial public sector, 1967–78*

Branches	1967	1969	1973	1978	Jobs created 1967–78
Energy	4,543	4,928	6,619	14,255	9,112
Mining	9,022	11,859	12,834	14,432	5,410
Steel	2,200	6,248	12,075	23,378	21,578
Mechanical and electrical construction	2,000	9,892	21,637	55,328	53,328
Chemicals	1,000	3,465	5,352	13,064	12,064
Construction materials	3,100	7,041	13,329	25,600	22,500
Food industries	11,371	14,128	17,935	36,809	25,438
Textiles	6,855	9,622	12,025	20,197	13,342
Leather	1,655	2,391	2,839	6,999	5,344
Woodworking, paper making and others	1,000	4,047	8,585	18,495	17,495
Hydrocarbons	5,900	8,860	35,300	80,392	74,492
Total	48,646	82,481	148,530	308,949	260,103

Source: MPAT, *Bilan 1967–1978 – Secteur: Industrie* (October 1979).

represented an average annual growth rate of 11.5 per cent, while the average annual growth rate of production of added value was about 10 per cent during the same period. In other words, labour productivity in this sector increased from AD 36,752 per worker in 1967 to AD 37,668 per worker in 1973, before declining to AD 31,988 per worker in 1977. This can be explained by the fact that, from 1967 to 1978, the average annual growth rate of the labour force in both non-oil industry and hydrocarbons was 12 per cent, while that for added value was only about 6.2 per cent.

The share of socialist industry in total industrial employment rose from 42 per cent in 1967 to 61 per cent in 1970, 62 per cent in 1974 and 67 per cent in 1977. In the hydrocarbons industry, the proportion of the labour force employed by the state sector increased from 27 per cent, to 100 per cent during the same years. Table 6.5 summarises the structure of employment in the industrial public sector between 1967 and 1978.

It follows that the industrial investment undertaken after 1967, which made possible the installation of factories throughout the country, resulted in the growing production of innumerable and well-diversified products. Prior to the establishment of these national industries, the country was compelled to import the goods, mostly from France, in foreign currency. The hundreds of industrial products manufactured by the national public

Post-independence development

Table 6.6 *The increase in the production of certain basic Algerian industrial products, 1962–81*

Products	Unit	1962	1967	1978	1981
Crude petroleum and condensate	Million tons	20.7	39.0	57.1	46.5
LNG (liquefied natural gas)	Million cubic metres	0	1.3	11.0	12.4
Iron	Million tons	2.06	2.6	2.8	3.5
Electricity	Million kW	1,141	1,141.6	5,212	
Cement	Million tons	0.602	0.7	2.7	4.5
Pig iron	Thousand tons			357	897
Tractors	Units			3,724	4,379
Harvesters	Units			107	355
Other farm machinery	Units			348	1,641
Trucks and buses	Units		3,716	6,300	6,202
Wagons	Units		176	474	611
Motors	Units			4,896	7,057
Batteries	Billion units			40.5	59.3
Cranes	Units			0	295
Motor-cycles	Units			15,100	37,395
Cycles				27,000	20,500
Refrigerators	Thousand units			24.4	88.9
TV sets	Thousand units			23.6	145.5
Gas cookers	Thousand units			0	25,076
Wires and electric cables	Million tons		3.1	20.1	15.2
Machine tools	Units		0	500	n.a.
Fertiliser	Thousand tons		n.a.	6,331	n.a.
Refined flour and semolina	Thousand tons	450	819	1,483	1,622.2
Refined olive and vegetable oils	Thousand tons	32.7	61	199	232
Shoes	Million pairs	3.2	8.6	10.2	14.5

enterprises using Algerian raw materials, capital and labour, were, still are and will continue to be of vital importance for the satisfaction of the basic needs of consumers and the national economy as a whole. The variety of products manufactured today by Algerian basic industries, such as steel, mechanical, metallurgical, electric and construction materials, is vital for the functioning and growth of non-industrial sectors and hence for the sustenance of human material life. Indeed, these industries made possible the processing and production, distribution and storage of a variety of food products, the manufacture of clothes, shoes, hardwares and household appliances, the construction of houses, schools, hospitals, roads, bridges and dams, the manufacture of means of transportation (wagons, buses, trucks) and means of production, such as engines, tractors, harvesters, pumps, cranes and innumerable inputs needed by agriculture and other vital productive activities. Table 6.6 lists some of the most important of hundreds of new Algerian industrial products in order to demonstrate the progress by the national economy since 1962.

From the outset, Algerian industrial policy excluded the installation of plants that would only assemble imported parts. Every factory or complex had to manufacture at least 60 per cent of the basic components. This insistence on a high rate of integration, which complicated the task of the public enterprises, was intended to enhance the long-run economic and technological independence of the country and to compel the operators in this sector to train the necessary labour force so that a mastery of modern technology could take place even in the most strategic areas. This policy encountered staunch opposition from the advanced capitalist countries and in their media. But despite this hostility, the managers of the Algerian industrial sector had succeeded into converting oil revenues into a multiplicity of factories whose productive capacities could be sufficient not only to satisfy the basic needs of the population but also to meet, at least partially, the increasing demand induced by the process of development itself. One of the fathers of Algerian industrialisation told me that the completion of the initial industrial projects had 'awakened a dormant monster' (meaning demand). The domestic demand for various products evolved between 1967 and 1978 as shown in Table 6.7.

Thus, the annual growth of demand for non-durable industrial goods (foodstuffs, textiles, leather) averaged over 8 per cent during the 1967–78 period. The demand for durable consumer goods such as household appliances rose by an average of 15 per cent per year, and the demand for energy increased by an annual average of 15 per cent. The consumption of steel products averaged no less than 23 per cent per year, rising from an average of 18 kg per person in 1967 to 116 kg in 1978. The consumption of cement increased by an annual average of 18 per cent, jumping from 70 kg per person to 288 kg per person during the same period. The demand for fertilisers grew by an average of 10.5 per cent per year between 1967 and 1978. In general, the consumption of intermediary products grew by an annual average of 15 per cent. The demand for capital goods averaged between 18 to 22 per cent per year. Because of the level of development of the national economy, the bulk of these goods had to be imported from the advanced capitalist and socialist countries.

On the production side, the rates of growth of various products had exceeded the rates of demand during the 1967–78 period. This was the case for 7 products out of the 26 listed in Table 6.7. Indeed, the production of

Post-independence development

Table 6.7 *Production and growth of demand for categories of Algerian industrial products, 1967–78*

Products	Unit	1967 Demand	1967 Product	1973 Demand	1973 Product	1978 Demand	1978 Product	Annual average growth rate 1967–78 Demand	Annual average growth rate 1967–78 Product
Crude oil	Million tons	2	39	5	50.8	7.5	57.1	12.8	3.6
Refined oil	Million tons	11.2	1.8	2.3	4.7	3.9	4.3	11.3	8.3
Iron ore	Thousand tons		2,570	759	3,183	636	2,750		0.7
Phosphates	Thousand tons	51.7	211	261.4	613	321.8	1,124	18.1	16.4
Total steel and metal products (equivalent in cast steel)	Thousand tons	216	31	1,034	79.5	2,100	395.5	22.9	26.1
Metallic frames (for construction)	Thousand tons	18	6.7	72	27.3	115	46	18.3	19.1
Industrial vehicles (wagons, trucks and buses)	Units	3,500	3,478	9,500	6,100	12,000	6,044	12.3	5.2
Agricultural tractors	Units	3,000	0	5,000	388	6,200	3,820	6.8	
Electric cables	Thousand tons	3.2	2.5	10	5.9	18	10.3	17	13.8
Telephone cables	Thousand tons	1	0.6	4	2.2	7.5	4.1	20	18
Refrigerators	Thousand units	17	0	65	0	110	24.4	18.5	n.a.
TV sets	Thousand units	20	0	60	0	100	23.6	15.8	n.a.
Fertiliser	Thousand units	220	0	438	380	660	331	10.5	n.a.
Paints	Thousand units	15	11	36	27	61	57	13.6	16.1
Detergents	Thousand units	14	14.3	25	25 49.6	27.9	12.2	5.2	
Pharmaceutical products	Million AD	120	20	530	80	1,100	210	22.5	23.8
Cement	Thousand tons	850	924	2,600	1,007	5,200	2,698	17.9	10.4
Bricks and tiles	Thousand tons	400	400	850	615	1,500	1,158	12.8	10.1
Ceramic tile flooring	Thousand square metres	210	173.6	900	600	3,000	2,800	27.6	28.7
Glass	Thousand tons	17.2	13.5	59.2	14.3	92	45.8	12.3	9.1
Industrial flour and semolina	Million quintals	8	8.2	12.1	11.8	19.3	14.8	8.4	5.5
Thread (all forms and fibres)	Thousand tons	26	6.2	53	14	74	18.5	10.0	10.5
Fabrics (all types)	Million millimetres	64	25	115	98	160	122	8.7	15.5
Covers	Thousand units	800	1,050	1,350	1,364	1,600	1,630	6.5	4.1
Shoes	Million pairs	5	4.6	7.8	7.6	11.2	10.2	7.6	7.6
Papers (all types)	Thousand tons	35	35.5	96	36.8	148	73.4	15.3	14.5

Source: MPAT, *Bilan 1967–1978 – Secteur: Industrie* (October 1979).

Industrialisation

basic and integrating industry (represented by steel, metallurgical, mechanical and electrical industries) grew by an annual average of 13 per cent in real terms during the three successive plans of development (1967–78); the output of the construction material industry rose by no less than 16.1 per cent, and that of the chemical industries by 10.1 per cent. Thus, the various obstacles mentioned above did not prevent the steady growth of industrial production, particularly in the second half of the 1970s. The index of industrial production appeared to have grown even faster, rising from 120.6 (base 100 in 1974) in 1974 to 134.9 in 1976, 146.4 in 1977, 170.6 in 1978 and 197.7 in 1979. These facts refute more of the unfounded criticisms of Algerian industrialisation made by its internal and external detractors. And yet, the paralysing and parasitic environment of this infant industry prevented its managers, engineers and workers from exploiting to the maximum the substantial productive capacities installed throughout the nation.

The evolution of the industrial sector's utilisation of productive capacity was also bound to be influenced by the inadequate environment in which it had to function, at least in the short and medium terms. As a general rule, the older the industrial plant, the higher the rate of utilisation of its capacity. This is why the utilisation of plant capacities varied from one factory to another during the entire period under study, from 20 per cent to 100 per cent. This wide range was due to the fact that, by the late 1970s, a growing number of newly completed plants, particularly in the sub-sector of heavy industry, were starting production for the first time. Moreover the utilisation of the total productive capacities of light industries rose from 74 per cent in 1969 to 80 per cent in 1973, falling slightly to 76.2 per cent in 1977 and rising again to 78.8 per cent in 1978.

The former Minister of Industry and Energy was divided into three ministries in 1977. By 1980, the Ministry of Heavy Industry supervised five enterprises, the Ministry of Light Industries, 12 and the Ministry of Energy and Petrochemical Industries, two. These 19 socialist enterprises operated a total of 1,234 units, sub-divided into 482 units of production, 487 distributive and commercial units, 187 units of implementation, 60 plants in the process of completion and 18 institutes and training centres. Table 6.8 provides further information about this vital sector.

Since a macro-economic analysis may be too abstract and too general to convey the substantial progress achieved, we must try to grasp the process of industrial development in concrete terms, at the level of the public enterprise. Indeed, since the main task of the 19 Algerian public enterprises was the development of their respective industrial activities, the case studies of four of them will allow us to underline the nature, scope and achievements of industrialisation during Boumedienne's rule.

Post-independence development

Table 6.8 *Industrial units and numbers of workers under the control of the Ministries of Heavy and Light Industries and the Ministry of Energy and Petrochemical Industries*

	Ministry of Heavy Industries			
Enterprises	No. of units of production	Others	No. of workers employed	No. of basic products
SONAREM (mining)	33+1 mixt Co (Alrem)	6	14,695	11
SNS (steel)	26+2 mixt Co (Genisider, Sidal)	6	33,000	12
SN METAL (metallurgy)	19	3	14,000	13
SONACOME (mechanical engineering)	19+1 mixt Co	26	28,720	13
SONELEC (electronics)	13	1	15,421	14

	Ministry of Light Industries				
Enterprises	No. of units of production	Units in construction	Others	No. of workers	No. of basic products
SNMC (construction materials)	77	7	30	26,139	11
SNLB (cork, woodworking)	31	16	0	10,485	7
SN-SEMPAC	70	38	31	24,070	8
SOGEDIA	27	5	0	12,893	8
SN EMA (wine, mineral water, beverages)	12	6	0	4,956	6
SNTA (tobacco and matches)	16	0	3	5,990	4
SONITEX (textiles)	34	15	3	24,865	7
SONIPEC (skins and leather)	19	1	1	8,510	8
SNIC (chemicals)	16	14	3	9,587	9
SONOC (papers, etc.)	9	1	2	6,125	5
SNAT (industrial crafts)	26		0	n.a.	5
SNERI (consulting firm)		1	1		

Ministry of Energy and Petrochemical Industries	
Enterprises	No. of workers
SONATRACH (petroleum)	96,455
SONELGAZ (electricity and gas)	26,527

Industrialisation

Table 6.9 *SONAREM's production, 1966–77 (tons)*

Product	1966	1975	1976	1977
Iron ore	1,676,694	3,200,000	2,788,500	3,200,000
Phosphates	100,000	700,000	818,000	1,174,000
Barytes	20,000	68,000	65,577	42,300
Mercury	0	28,000	30,915	3,000
Lead	0	3,000	4,674	1,400
Zinc	0	15,000	18,229	5,800
Copper	0	0	1,607	1,500
Bentonite	0	0	24,514	24,400
Kilselguar	0	0	4,320	4,100
Salt	0	125,000	70,256	150,000
Kaolin	0	11,000	7,748	11,500
Felspar	0	0	456	n.a.
Celestine	0	0	6,484	5,200
Aggregate	0		472,252	480,000
Breezeblocks	0	0	383,903	n.a.
Marbleblocks (cubic metres)	0	0	8,565	n.a.

Source: Ministère de l'Industrie Lourde, *Situation et perspective du secteur de l'Industrie Lourde*, vol. 3, September 1978.

SONAREM

SONAREM (The Société Nationale de Recherche et d'Exploitation Minières) was created on 11 May 1967, a year after the nationalisation of all mining activities. SONAREM was put in charge of all mining, quarrying, prospecting and related studies, including laboratory tests and the search for new markets. Sales and distribution of raw or processed minerals in Algeria and abroad also come under the control of this company. SONAREM (with the exception of SONATRACH) occupied a strategic position in the industrialisation of the country. Situated upstream of the development process, mineral production was bound to foster the growth of various other downstream industrial activities.

Prior to the creation of SONAREM and the launching of the first plan of development, mining production was concentrated primarily on a small number of important reserves represented by iron ore at Ouenza and phosphates at Djebel Onk. However, mineral activities were then stimulated by the industrialisation drive. The installation of new extractive capacity during the two successive four-year plans of development (1970–7)

Post-independence development

resulted in rapid increase in mineral production. These extractive activities fell into three categories:
(1) Ferrous ores: iron ore, manganese, tungsten
(2) Non-ferrous ores: zinc, lead, copper, mercury, antimony
(3) Others, represented by marble, limestone, phosphates, pyrites, barytes and coal.

Iron ore was the main mineral product. Over 90 per cent of it was extracted from three mechanised surface mines at Ouenza, Boukhadra and Khanguet in north-eastern Algeria. (They are able to satisfy the needs of the steel complex at El Hadjar beyond the year 2000.) Phosphates represented the second major product, exploited at an annual rate of 800,000 tons from two deposits located in the south-east of the country: Djebel Onk and Kouif, whose phosphate content amounted to 55 per cent. The other main minerals exploited were marble and onyx extracted from quarries situated in Filfila in the east and in Kristel, Bouhanifia and Takbalet in the west. The evolution of SONAREM's mineral production between 1966 and 1977 is shown in Table 6.9.

Although SONAREM continued to export some of its extracted minerals, a growing proportion was processed and used by Algerian industry. Its general director declared in 1978 that

At present we have little interest in exporting our production as ore. Processing makes minerals profitable and thus an ever-increasing percentage of our production is supplied to the national industrial complexes (SNS, Sonatrach, etc.): in 1967, 80 per cent of mineral production was exported. Now the figure is no more than 40 per cent. This indicates a growth of the percentage used locally and illustrates the efforts the country is making to industrialise.

In the field of research and prospecting, SONAREM had at first concentrated its effort on expanding mineral production in the mines that were either abandoned or about to close down. This was followed by the initiation in 1972 of a systematic prospection campaign resulting in the discovery of some traces of gold, wolfram, uranium and tin reserves in the Hoggar mountains in southern Algeria and the discovery of the huge iron ore reserves, estimated at 3 billion tons (58 per cent ore content), at Gara Djebilet. These reserves were to be extracted in order to be consumed by the Western Steel Complex. Unfortunately, the Benjadid regime has abandoned the completion of this project.

SONATRACH

SONATRACH The state oil company, SONATRACH (Société Nationale pour la Recherche, la Production, le Transport, la Transformation et la Commercialisation des Hydrocarbures), which was established in

December 1963, was up to 1979 the largest, the most dynamic, the best organised, the best managed and the most nationalistic of the public corporations. This may be explained by the fact that it was created to challenge the interests of foreign (particularly French) oil companies in the Sahara. Until 1966, SONATRACH concentrated its efforts on increasing Algeria's share of oil revenue and consolidating itself technically and politically.

Between February and August 1967, SONATRACH had either purchased or nationalised the distribution networks of all the Anglo-American companies (BP, Esso, Mobil). On 14 May 1967, its monopoly over the distribution, storage and transportation of hydrocarbons and their derivatives was extended to cover the activities of 14 other foreign oil firms (including Shell, Beryl, Total and Algeronaphte). On 25 April 1969, SONATRACH also bought back the assets of Sinclair Oil and on 12 June 1970 it nationalised the subsidiaries of five companies: Shell, Phillips Petroleum, Drilling Specialists, SOFRAGEL (West Germany) and AMIF (Italy). The acquisition of the hydrocarbon resources was completed on 24 February 1971, when SONATRACH's participation in the subsidiaries of the two major French groups, EFL-ERAP and CFP, as well as in three smaller firms, COPAREX, FRANCAREP and EURO FREP, was increased to 51 per cent. This last nationalisation provoked a serious crisis with the former colonial power. By the early 1970s, SONATRACH had taken over 100 per cent of prospecting, transport of oil and production planning and 77 per cent of production as against 11.5 per cent in 1966.

This nationalisation process was accompanied by a new form of co-operation with foreign oil companies based upon joint-venture undertakings, especially in the field of exploration. Under this arrangement, a new mixed enterprise was set up by the two parties, with SONATRACH as majority shareholder. The foreign firm's prerogatives and obligations were fixed by the terms of the contract of association rather than by a concession.

Because of the financial requirements of industrialisation, SONATRACH had to maximise the production of hydrocarbons during the period under study. Table 6.10 summarises production between 1967 and 1978.

By 1978 the transportation of petroleum products was effected by four pipelines with a total annual capacity of about 65 million tons: the Amenas-Skikda pipeline (1960) – 15.5 million tons; the Haoud El Hamra-Arzew pipeline (1966) – 22 million tons; the Haoud El Hamra-Bejaia pipeline (1961) – 17.5 million tons; the Haoud El Hamra-Skikda pipeline (1972) – 12 million tons; and the Hassi R'Mel-Arzew pipeline (1978) – 22 million tons. Together they totalled over 3,000 km in length.

As for the transport of natural gas, the expansion of pipelines had

Post-independence development

Table 6.10 *Hydrocarbons production, 1967–78*

Products	Unit	1967	1969	1973	1977	1978
Crude oil and condensate	Million tons	39.0	44.6	50.8	53.4	57.1
Extracted natural gas	Billion cubic metres	2.9	2.9	4.8	7.9	13.2
LNG	Billion cubic metres	1.3	1.8	2.5	4.2	6.6
Refined petroleum	Million tons	1.9	2.0	4.7	4.1	4.4
Liquefied associated gas	Million tons	0.1	0.1	0.2	0.5	0.7

Source: MPAT, *Synthèse du bilan.*

reached a total annual capacity of 23 billion cubic metres by the end of the 1970s. These pipelines were: Hassi R'Mel-Arzew no. 0 (20/24) – 508 km, put into service in 1961; Hassi R'Mel-Arzew no. 1 (40) – 508 km, put into service in 1976; Gassi Touil-Hassi Messaoud (40) – 160 km, put into service in 1976, and eleven others in construction. They were to expand the pipelines by an annual capacity of 98 billion cubic metres by 1985.

The refining of petroleum products was handled by three SONATRACH refineries whose total annual capacity amounted to 5.4 million tons. The first refinery, located in Hassi Messaoud, was put into service in 1961 with an annual capacity of 225,000 tons (crude oil distillation unit and gas plant). By the end of 1978 a new distillation unit, a catalytic reforming unit and an additional gas plant were put into service. They increased the annual refining capacity of 2.7 million tons (crude oil distillation unit, catalytic reforming unit and gas plant). The third refinery, built by SONATRACH in Arzew, came into operation in 1973 (crude oil distillation unit, gas plant and plant for production of lubricants and bitumen). This refinery handled 2.5 million tons of crude oil per year. The major products were propane, petrol, butane, lubricating oil, wax and grease. The total annual production capacity of these refineries reached 30,000 tons of propane, 80,000 tons of butane, 30,000 tons of fuel gas, 130,000 tons of petrol, 230,000 tons of premium, 40,000 tons of naphtha, 150,000 tons of kerosene, 540,000 tons of diesel oil, 880,000 tons of fuel oil, 50,000 tons of lubrication oil, 2,700 tons of lubricating grease, 5,000 tons of wax, 5,000 tons of oxygenated bitumen and 5,000 tons of asphalt. Several other refineries were under construction.

By 1978 the industrial potential for gas liquefaction comprised the following:

The Arzew plant (GLIZ), which came into operation in 1964 with a production capacity of 1.5 billion cubic metres (three units). This was the first natural gas liquefaction plant in the world.

Industrialisation

The Arzew complex (LNG1), which was inaugurated in February 1978 by Boumedienne. The construction of this complex in Bethioua took 15,000 tons of concrete-reinforcing rods, 160,000 cubic metres of concrete, the moving of 2.6 million cubic metres of earth and the mobilisation of 6,200 workers. It occupied an area of 72 hectares. LNG1 comprises six liquefaction systems with an annual production capacity of 10.5 billion cubic metres, two LNG loading berths (flow of 10,000 cubic metres an hour), one sea-water catchment for cooling (175,000 cubic metres an hour) and an auxiliary power station with three turbo-generators, each with a generating capacity of around 18 million watts, fed by three 61 tons an hour boilers. The complex is supplied with natural gas by pipeline from the Hassi R'Mel field, where 14 wells produce about 2.8 million cubic metres an hour.

LNG2, which was under construction at Bethioua on a site alongside LNG1 and with an identical production capacity (10.5 billion cubic metres a year from six units). However, LNG2 differs in that it produces 360,000 tons of butane a year, 400,000 tons of propane and 3,700 tons of helium. It came into production in 1980.

The GLIK factory at Skikda, with a production capacity of 4.5 billion cubic metres (for the three units 40, 50 and 60), which started production in the late 1970s. It was a liquefaction plant (GLIK – units, 10, 20 and 30) with a capacity of 3.8 billion cubic metres a year and butane–propane separation works (300,000 tons a year). The units still under construction in 1978 included a refinery (15 million tons a year of refined products; 145,000 tons a year of asphalt; 115,000 tons a year of aromatics; 40,000 tons a year of paratylene), a liquefaction plant (KALIK – units 40, 50, 60; 4.5 billion cubic metres of LNG) and a plastics complex (140,000 tons a year of ethylene; 35,000 tons a year of PVC).

In addition, in the industrial complex and harbour of Issers, SONATRACH was constructing (in the late 1970s) an oil pipeline, an oil refinery, a liquefaction plant, a methanol works, petrochemical factories, and works for ethylene, polyethylene, ethylene oxide, PVC, butadiene, polybutadiene, polypropylene, SBR rubber, styrene, polystyrene, acrylonitrine, ammonia and phosphoric acid. The complex also included a commercial and industrial port.

Finally the methylene port of Arzew-El Djedid, which was opened by Boumedienne on 21 February 1978, comprised six methane berths (125,000 to 200,000 cubic metres), three petroleum berths (50,000 to 250,000 tons) and one PLG berth (35,000 to 50,000 tons). The annual handling capacity amounts to 40 billion cubic metres of LNG, 20 million tons of condensate and 2 million tons of LPG.

Post-independence development

Table 6.11 *Petrochemicals production, 1973–6 (thousand tons)*

Products	1973	1974	1975	1976
Plastic materials	6.0	4.0	3.0	16.0
Ammonia	82.0	19.0	25.0	25.0
Ammonium nitrate	109.0	52.0	75.0	67.0
Socium Tripolyphosphate	88.0	81.0	60.0	75.0
NPK	123.0	133.0	85.0	147.0

In addition to hydrocarbon production and refining, SONATRACH was responsible for the production and marketing of fertilisers, petrochemical products and plastics. The development of petrochemical industries was meant primarily for import-substitution. According to an official document, 'these installations are part of Algeria's industrial base as envisaged under the national development plan. They are integrated in the structure of SONATRACH as a perfectly natural extension of the company's other activities, although presenting altogether different features from the development of the hydrocarbon sector.

SONATRACH was not only providing the necessary capital for the development of the national economy but also producing and marketing basic inputs for agriculture and finished and semi-finished products for several industries.

SNS

SNS (The Société Nationale de Sidérurgie), which was created in September 1964, was assigned the task of developing the iron and steel industry. Its activities covered production, marketing (importing, exploitation, distribution), the management of existing capacity and the creation of new means of production. The SNS (like all other state companies for their respective products) was granted a monopoly of imports of iron and steel products.

From 1967 onwards, all iron and steel industry was considered as a *sine qua non*, not only for the process of industrialisation but also for the development of the other sectors, as well as for the satisfaction of the most basic needs of the population and the national economy. In accordance with the requirements of the Algerian strategy of industrialisation, the SNS gave priority to the development of flat products – the basis of downstream processing industries. This differed from the practice of most third world countries, which were advised by western experts to give priority to the production of rods.

Table 6.12 SNS production, 1969-78 (tons)

Products	1969	1970	1971	1972	1973	1974	1975	1976	1977	1978
Pig iron	180,900	408,000	333,260	399,500	361,000	293,000	402,000	412,600	389,000	450,000*
Crude steel	29,800	30,000	27,600	97,600	483,200	167,700	233,703	357,000	307,000	408,000*
Flat products	—	—	—	32,700	72,000	98,000	125,500	206,000	197,000	204,000
Metal boxes	7,400	7,500	9,500	10,100	10,300	10,100	11,200	13,233	15,600	23,000
Steel rods	42,500	44,300	39,900	36,600	38,800	39,800	45,200	45,000	55,900	95,400*
Metal drums	6,500	6,300	5,600	1,500	2,100	2,100	2,700	3,949	n.a.	n.a.
Gas cylinders	n.a.	—	—	—	3,443	3,800	5,800	3,818	n.a.	n.a.
Tubes	—	103,000	105,500	100,800	109,000	112,000	110,500	172,700	142,000	235,600
Gas bottles (units)	—	—	—	111,000	247,000	275,000	114,000	272,000	155,000	400,000*
Aluminium products	—	—	700	1,000	1,600	1,415	1,747	1,933	n.a.	n.a.

* Estimates based on the production of the first semester of this year.
Source: Ministère de l'Industrie Lourde, Situation et perspective du secteur de l'industrie lourde, vol. 3, September 1978.

Post-independence development

On the whole, despite the emergence of many problems connected with the development of an iron and steel industry, the evolution of SNS production during the decade under consideration was marked by rapid growth. Table 6.12 shows this evolution between 1969 and 1978. The same official document projected that, by 1980, the production capacity of the SNS would comprise: 1.7–2 million tons of pig iron; 1.2 million tons of rolled flat products; 230,000 tons of tubes for hydrocarbons or water; 85,000 tons of seamless tubes; 100,000 tons of cold sections and formed tube; 580,000 tons of wire and concrete-reinforcing rods; 40,000 tons of welded mesh; 1.5 million gas cylinders; 40,000 tons of metal containers; 40,000 tons of zinc; and 80,000 tons of sulphuric acid.

Since the demand for liquid steel was to rise from about 2 million tons in 1979–80 to about 5 million tons in 1984–5, and then about 10 million tons by 1990, the managers of the SNS decided to set up two additional major iron and steel complexes, one at Jijel in the east and another at Ghazaouet, in the west of the country. According to Mohammed Liassine, former Minister of Heavy Industry and former Director General of SNS, the 'abundant supply of energy should allow Algeria not only to meet its own internal demand for steel products but also to become competitive in the expanding world market'. Activities undertaken in the sphere of metallurgy and the processing of metals will aim systematically to satisfy the domestic market and keep a surplus for export.

According to plan, the Jijel iron and steel complex was to comprise three units: a pelletising plant (2 million tons of pellets – production to start in 1982), a direct reduction plant (1.2 million tons of sponge iron – 1982) and an electric steel-works (800,000 tons of billets – 1983). The aim of this integrated iron and steel complex was as follows:

to exploit Algerian natural gas and minerals (the complex was to be geared to a high consumption of electricity and natural gas and the use of high-grade ores from the Bou Khadra mine);

to free the valley of Oued El Kebir and the surrounding regions from economic isolation by creating an axis of development linking Jijel with Constantine and Skikda, and hence to stimulate the economic growth of the entire northern Constantine region, which is one of the poorest in Algeria;

to launch Algeria's iron and steel sector onto the world market (the use of domestic energy resources would enhance the competitiveness of Algerian steel products);

to satisfy internal demand for products within the range manufactured in Jijel;

to open a new sea outlet, reducing pressure on the existing ports in eastern Algeria;

to gain access to a new technology.

The new complex was to specialise in the manufacture of steel billets, 50 per cent of which would be rolled in Algeria and the rest exported. A proportion of the sponge iron manufactured would also feed the unit for the production of fine and special steels that the SNS planned to construct in Ain M'Lila. It was also anticipated that the productive capacity of the complex would later be doubled, from 1.5 million tons a year initially to 3 million tons a year after five years.

Unfortunately, this project, which was one of the best prepared, was not only modified but also transferred by the current regime from Jijel on the coast to El Milia, situated about 40 km south-east of the initial site. The transfer and modification of the initial project has delayed the construction of this badly needed complex. The preliminary work did not start until 1984-5. One of the disastrous consequences was the tripling of the total costs of the project. The second project to establish an iron and steel complex in western Algeria was simply abandoned. Yet by the 1990s Algeria will be needing more than 10 million tons of molten steel.

SONACOME

The mechanical engineering industry was initiated and developed by the Société Nationale de Constructions Mécaniques (SONACOME), which was established in 1969. SONACOME was assigned the task of setting up an autonomous and independent mechanical engineering industry capable of satisfying the present and future needs of the country (in particular the mechanisation of agriculture), while at the same time stimulating other activities through sub-contracting. It was granted a monopoly for the import of all mechanical engineering products to give it the knowledge of both the internal and external markets necessary to develop the appropriate products to meet the local demand as well as to enhance its negotiating power vis-à-vis a few powerful multinational firms – such as Renault, Mercedes and Fiat – which were, and still are, very hostile to the development of any genuinely national, integrated, mechanical engineering industry in the third world.

Before the creation of SONACOME, the mechanical engineering industry in Algeria was represented by two assembly factories, one belonging to Caral-Renault and the other to Sadab (Berliet). The former preferred to suspend the assembly of tractors in 1969 and close down its other workshops in 1970. But the latter – whose assembling of trucks, buses and

Post-independence development

Table 6.13 *SONACOME's production, 1967–78 (some products)*

Products	1967	1973	1974	1975	1976	1977	1978
Industrial vehicles (trucks, buses)	3,478	6,100	6,286	6,242	3,640	3,716	6,044
Tractors	—	388	665	1,573	1,834	2,839	3,820
Engines	—	—	882	2,024	3,402	5,673	9,459
Machine tools	—	—	—	—	69	184	534
Bicycles	—	—	189	5,702	8,042	10,180	15,005
Mopeds	—	144	1,106	5,701	9,059	18,637	30,000
Water-pumps (tons)	—	—	—	400	1,000	2,500	2,700
Steel casting (tons)	—	—	—	4,838	7,139	10,680	13,700
Nuts, bolts, valves (tons)	150	1,636	1,223	578	586	300	2,718
Hoppers and platforms	—	6,048	6,089	6,350	3,443	3,572	3,535
Trailers and cisterns	—	—	1,822	3,674	3,056	2,442	3,099
Containers	—	—	3,852	6,616	7,846	2,708	4,400
Farming instruments and machines	—	1,212	—	3,280	2,076	3,500	4,900
Harvesting instruments and machines	—	—	—	254	16	94	730

Source: MPAT, *Bilan de l'Industrie 1967–1978*, October 1978. MIL, *Situation et perspectives du secteur de l'Industrie Lourde*, vol. 3, September 1978.

cars was taken over by SONACOME for transformation into an important complex for industrial vehicles – agreed to co-operate with this newly established public company.

Between 1969 and 1978, SONACOME invested no less than AD 13 billion. This resulted in the establishment and/or modernisation of 14 complexes and productive units.

In addition, about 30 projects were either under way or about to be launched at the end of 1978. SONACOME planned that by 1980 the manufacture of the following products would start: public works appliances (at Ain Smara), mechanical scoops, cranes, fork-lift trucks, all-terrain light vehicles (at Barika 10 000 a year), private and industrial vehicles (at Setif) and parts (wheel rims, discs, springs, bearings, shock absorbers, radiators, injection pumps, and pistons).

Conclusion

In sum, the 18 Socialist industrial companies which, before their dismemberment by the Benjadid regime in 1980, were the prime movers of the development of the economy, had succeeded in setting up various industrial plants and commercial establishments specialising in the marketing

Industrialisation

and distribution of innumerable goods produced or imported, and technical training centres and institutes throughout the country. In so doing, they consolidated the political integration of the nation by cementing it with a complementary economic and social integration, vertically and horizontally, through the creation of numerous corporative communities of interests. Their emergence, multiplication and diversification, as well as their organisational consolidation, appeared to have become the surest guarantee not only for the continuation of the industrialisation of the country as well as for the defence of national interests and the improvement of living standards of the poorer strata.

Indeed, by the late 1970s, 105,836 workers were employed in heavy industries, 133,328 in light industries and 122,982 in the energy and petro-chemical industries. If the total employment in the private industrial sector is included, the result is as follows:

National industrial sector	362,146	79.0 per cent
Local public sector	22,594	4.5 per cent
Private industrial sector	77,900	16.5 per cent
Total	462,640	100.0 per cent

These socio-economic statistical data indicate that, despite serious problems inherited from the past and aggravated by a series of debilitating political crises within the FLN and the lack of experienced senior staff, engineers, technicians and skilled workers, Algeria had succeeded in launching a massive programme of industrialisation. As a result, the Algerian economy has experienced one of the highest rates of growth in the third world, stimulated by one of the highest rates of capital formation in modern economic history.

Although industry was the only sector that succeeded in fulfilling its planned investment targets, instead of praising and rewarding its outstanding performances, the political leadership that emerged to power after Boumedienne's death blamed industry for political reasons, for the so-called intersectorial imbalances. However, as will be seen in the following chapters, these imbalances were caused primarily by the low performance of the other sectors. Indeed, between 1967 and 1978, agriculture utilised only 46 per cent of its planned investment, construction and public works 57 per cent, productive services 49 per cent (of which storage and distribution were only 27 per cent), infrastructure 51 per cent, social services 37 per cent (of which housing consumed a mere 30 per cent of its planned investment) and education and vocational training 36 per cent.

Post-independence development

These figures demonstrate that even the problems of industry were created, or accentuated, by a highly deficient and non-dynamic environment constituted by the non-industrial sectors. Therefore, the recent economistic and monetarist critiques of the public industrial sector formulated by Benjadid's Minister of Planning (and then Prime Minister) Abdelhamid Brahimi and his advisers were prompted by political motives. Representatives of a new *comprador* bourgeoisie within the government, the single party and the army came to perceive the public sector in general, and industrial corporations in particular, as a serious threat to their commercial interests and political power. They feared the logic of industrialisation because it gave rise, not only to a new mode of organisation, but also to the emergence of new socio-professional categories, represented by technocrats, managers, engineers and qualified and skilled workers who would eventually have been forced to raise the question of the legitimacy of their power in society. Indeed, the process of industrialisation has always engendered radical ideological and political changes. The example of advanced capitalist and socialist countries shows that, in the realm of politics, classes and socio-professional categories associated with industry end up either by ascending to power or by sharing it with the dominant classes and social groups. The Spanish case may corroborate the hypothesis that a successful process of industrialisation is the *sine qua non* not only for the genuine modernisation of society but also for its political democratisation. It is no wonder that industrialisation has been viewed by conservative traditional elements throughout the world as subversive of both secular customs and values and outmoded traditional socio-political orders.

This historical fact explains why the success or failure of industrialisation is determined primarily by political factors. In the case under study, the partisans of industrialisation constituted a tiny minority. With the death of Boumedienne, who supported them but was reluctant to put an end to the pernicious influence of the 'pro-French party' he had often denounced publicly and of the anti-industrialisation, pro-*comprador* elements, they were eliminated from power by the new leadership. From 1980 onwards, the economic policy of the country has shifted top priority from industry to agriculture and the social services as well as to various other parasitic or premature activities that are congruent with the compradorisation of the national economy and society and particularly with the creation of the prerequisite conditions for the development of the national private industrial sector.

At any rate, in spite of some mistakes committed in the process of industrialisation, the oil revenues were invested in the country rather than placed in the banks of advanced capitalist nations. The development of this public sector not only improved the living conditions of the population, but also stimulated the emergence and rapid growth of a private sector whose specific logic was bound to end up, sooner or later, in thwarting the success of a genuinely socialist industrialisation which constitutes the *sine qua non* for national independence and social justice for all.

Chapter 7

The development of the private industrial sector

Since the colonial power precluded the industrialisation of the country, Algerian private capital, accumulated by merchants, rich landlords and a few successful artisans, was not reconverted into industrial capital. Consequently, very few industrialists emerged during the colonial period. However, the war of national liberation, and the wresting of independence in 1962, resulted in the acceleration of the development of the private industrial sector, whose economic and social weight as well as political influence have since been increasing. Since the overwhelming majority of the new industrialists came from the merchant class, their outlook, industrial strategies and activities continued to be conditioned by an underlying speculative, and even *comprador*, logic which has prevented them from becoming innovating, risk-taking and dynamic entrepreneurs. They have been interested in highly profitable small industrial ventures that would ensure quick profits in the short term to the detriment of the national economy, the work force and the consumers.

The development of the private industrial sector in the post-independence period went through three phases. The first phase, from 1962 to 1966, was marked by demagogic hostility to the development of the national private industrial sector. While the subsidiaries of multinational firms operating in the country were encouraged to reinvest at least part of their profits, potential Algerian private investors were not only thwarted but also denounced as 'fat bourgeois' who should be 'unfattened in hot baths'. However, despite this rhetoric, hundreds of wealthy merchants, enterprising artisans and rich landlords associated with influential officials and local notables managed either to acquire small factories or to establish new industrial enterprises.

The second phase, which was initiated by the promulgation of the 1966 investment decree and which ended with the launching of the agrarian revolution in 1971, was characterised by the rapid development of the private industrial sector. The majority of the industrial private plants, set up by private entrepreneurs before 1979, came into being during this period. The adoption of the national charter, which stressed that thenceforth only *non-exploiting* private property would be tolerated within

The private industrial sector

socialist Algeria, brought about a rapid decline in private industrial investment. From 1971 onwards private capital invested in the establishment of enterprises specialised in construction and public works.

The third and final phase began after the death of President Boumedienne. Only the first two phases are examined in this chapter. The last one will be analysed in chapter 13. In spite of the promulgation in 1982 of a new investment law favourable to the development of this private industrial sector, the entrepreneurs are still attracted by easy gains.

Because of the nature and extent of French colonisation, Algerian non-agricultural private capital was relegated to trading, craft and service activities. Thus, in Algeria, as in most third world countries, the development of industrial capital could not take place under colonial conditions.

However, in the case under study, a certain number of Algerian businessmen, and a few industrial entrepreneurs, managed to emerge, and even to prosper, towards the end of the colonial period. For instance, the 1954 census reported the existence of about 100 Algerian commercial and industrial establishments employing more than 20 workers belonging to Algerians. In the industrial field, 239 out of a sample of 1,514 enterprises belonging to Algerians – which were still operating in 1970–1 – were actually created before 1954. The war of independence appears to have stimulated the growth of Algerian private industrial capital. About 87 of these 1,514 enterprises were set up between 1955 and 1962. The accession of the country to independence in 1962 then paved the way for the rapid growth of private industrial capital. In fact, the 1963–5 period saw the emergence of no fewer than 258 private industrial enterprises, representing 17.2 per cent of the sample. In three years the number of enterprises created exceeded that of the entire colonial period.

Table 7.1 shows that the concentration of capital within Algeria reached dramatic proportions towards the end of the colonial era. Indeed, 2.6 per cent of the existing establishments realised 57 per cent of the total turnover while the remaining 97.4 per cent controlled only 43 per cent; and the 90,300 commercial, industrial and service establishments owned by Algerians produced only 15 per cent of the total turnover.

However, during the first years of independence, the big Algerian wholesale merchants, and a growing number of new middlemen (or *affairistes*) acquired commercial networks which were previously owned by European settlers. Thus, from the start, they were all attracted to *comprador* parasitic activities associated with import–export trade. Most of them intended to become simple local dealers representing multinational firms in Algeria.

In order to be able to regulate the functioning of the national economy and to initiate some development programmes, the state began taking

Post-independence development

Table 7.1 *The size, number and turnover of the private non-agricultural sectors in 1954*

No. of employees	No. of establishments	%	Corresponding turnover (billion francs, 1954)	%
1–4 workers	90,191	81.6	145.7	12.4
5–10 workers	8,004	7.2	70.2	6.0
11–50 workers	9,707	8.8	287.4	25.6
51–100 workers	1,418	1.3	155.2	13.2
101–300 workers	907	0.8	234.9	20.0
301–500	166	0.2	100.2	8.5
501+	120	0.1	180.1	15.3
Total	110,513	100.0	1,173.7	100.0

Source: INEP.

control of the import–export trade in certain strategic products. Several public boards and companies were set up in the subsequent years and granted full monopoly rights for the import and export of these products. In addition to this, some protectionist measures involving the import of other industrial products by the government ended up by inducing a number of merchants and artisans to invest in small light industries producing consumer goods. As a result, between 1963 and 1965, Algerian private capital had established 258 industrial enterprises. Thus, from the outset, the private-sector strategy of industrialisation was geared to import-substitution, as well as to the growing demand in goods and services stimulated by the rapid development of the public sector. As pointed out earlier, the socialistic flamboyancy and irrelevant sloganeering of the Ben Bella regime were bound to thwart the development of the private industrial sector. Only entrepreneurs who had either some influence of their own or some political patrons within the regime dared to invest in industry during this first phase.

The second phase started with the promulgation of an investment law which provided some incentives and guarantees for private investors, thus stimulating the growth and proliferation of private industries. A significant number of wholesale merchants, enterprising artisans and even rich farmers started launching industrial projects. It was estimated that between 1967 and 1974 about AD 100 billion was invested by private individuals in industry and the establishment of enterprises specialising in construction and public works. In the industrial field, no fewer than 807 private

Table 7.2 *The concentration of wholesale trade, 1969 (AD)*

Annual turnover	500,000	510,000–1,000,000	1,100,000–5,000,000	5,000,000	Total or average
No. of establishments	1,212	483	723	118	22,536
% of establishments	47.8	19	28.5	4.7	100
Grand total turnover	251,870,000	344,012,000	149,603,000	160,671,100	3,698,633,000
% of total turnover	6.8	9.3	40.4	43.4	100
Average turnover per establishment	208,000	712,000	2,069,000	13,619,000	1,458,000

Source: Secrétariat d'Etat du Plan, 1971.

Post-independence development

enterprises were created between 1966 and 1971 alone. They represented 54 per cent of the 1,514 industrial firms studied by the AARDES in the mid 1970s.

Since the wholesale merchants were the prime movers of this private industrialisation, an evaluation of their number, financial resources, trading activities and geographical distribution is in order. The Algerian wholesale traders, who replaced the settlers, continued to operate freely within the country in the post-independence period. Not only were they able to accumulate huge sums of capital to invest in industry but they could also exert a great deal of political pressure on the government either through their representatives within the regime or the manipulation of public opinion through systematically organised rumours whose aims were to discredit Boumedienne's socialistic option and hence to force the state to change its economic policy. Since they have occupied a strategic position within society, this merchant bourgeoisie have managed not only to fix prices but also to organise shortages of basic products in order to corroborate their fundamental thesis that 'socialism=shortages, inefficiency and waste'.

At any rate, by 1969, wholesale trade came under the control of a very small number of wealthy merchants. As table 7.2 shows, 4.7 per cent of commercial establishments handled no less than 43.4 per cent of the value of the products sold.

This vertical social concentration of merchant capital was accompanied by a horizontal geographical concentration. Indeed, 78.6 per cent of the wholesale traders were located in only 5 *wilayates*, while no fewer than 57.8 per cent of them were operating in two coastal *wilayates*: Algiers and Oran. The merchants of these two provinces (or rather cities) handled 75 per cent of total wholesale commercial transactions. Table 7.3 summarises this state of affairs.

The majority of these commercial establishments were selling basic consumer goods such as textiles, garments, leather, shoes, foodstuffs and household appliances. In 1969, 41 trading establishments specialised in the sale of agricultural products, 975 in foodstuffs, 646 in textiles and leather, 583 in tools and other related equipment, 149 in machines and motor vehicles, 177 in household appliances and 60 in cosmetics.

The above-mentioned geographical concentration of merchant capital in a small number of *wilayates* resulted in the concentration of the private industrial plants in the major cities. In fact, 45.8 per cent of them were located in Algiers, 21 per cent in Oran and 11 per cent in Constantine. In addition, 53 out of a total of 796 industrial projects launched by the private sector during the 1966–9 period were located in these three *wilayates*: 145 in Algiers, 313 in Oran and 75 in Constantine.

The private industrial sector

Table 7.3 *The geographical distribution of wholesale traders and their annual turnover, 1969*

Wilayates	No. of establishments	%	Producing more than AD 1,000,000 turnover per year	Total turnover	%	Average annual turnover per establishment
Algiers	1,073	44.6	31	2,194,723	59.3	1,957
Annaba	172	6.8	—	143,792	3.9	850
Aurès	49	1.9	—	21,110	0.6	479
Constantine	208	7.9	—	182.382	4.9	898
El Asnam	71	2.6	—	55,056	11.5	775
Medea	67	2.5	—	47,883	1.3	748
Mostaganem	65	2.4	1	85,087	2.3	1,372
Oasis	76	2.8	1	39,731	1.1	584
Oran	345	13.2	8	576,818	15.6	1,716
Saida	34	1.3	—	14,743	0.4	446
Saoura	26	1.0	—	11,020	0.3	423
Setif	165	6.3	—	133,456	3.6	813
Tiaret	17	0.7	—	11,346	0.3	709
Tizi Ouzou	93	3.6	—	85,394	2.3	948
Tlemcen	70	2.6	1	96,092	2.6	1,392

Source: INEAP.

As pointed out earlier, the opening of the Algerian market to French manufactured products, the dissolution of the traditional artisan corporations and the concomitant penetration of capitalist relations of production under a colonial economy undermined not only local handicrafts but also the traditional patterns of consumption. French colonial economic policy favoured the establishment of some light industries producing only basic consumer goods such as textiles, leather, shoes, processed food and detergents. Thus it is no wonder that, in 1962, textiles, garments, leather and shoes dominated the commercial activities of Algeria. The sales of appliances and other intermediary goods of various kinds grew as a result of the emergence of a new middle class engendered by the independence of the country and the subsequent socio-economic and cultural development of the society. This situation, coupled with growing import restrictions, induced a significant number of merchants, and even artisans, to set up industrial plants in order to respond to an increasing internal demand for these products.

Post-independence development

Table 7.4 *The number of private enterprises and the origins of the new industrial capital, 1954–71*

Entrepreneurs	Before 1954	1955–62	1963–5	1966–71	Total	%
Merchants	102	37	163	599	901	59.6
Artisans	51	22	18	141	232	16.0
Farmers	22	0	0	50	72	4.5
Industrialists	35	14	37	93	179	11.5
Civil servants	0	0	0	14	14	0.9
Former officers of ALN			18	0	18	1.2
Others	29	14	22	33	98	6.4
Total	239	87	258	930	1,514	100.0

Source: AARDES, Industrie privée, 1975.

The development of the Algerian private industrial sector was carried out primarily by merchants and artisans. Table 7.4 summarises the evolution of the number of private industrial enterprises between 1954 and 1971–1, as well as indicating the origins of this new industrial capital.

As table 7.4 indicates, 59.6 per cent of the entrepreneurs were merchants, 16 per cent artisans, 11.5 per cent industrialists and only 4.5 per cent farmers. Over 62 per cent of these new industrialists were either wholesale or semi-wholesale traders. No fewer than 60 per cent of them decided to produce the products they were selling. Close to 82 per cent of artisans specialised in the manufacturing of their traditional products.

Commercial capital thus played a predominant role in this private industrialisation carried out by the national bourgeoisie. Indeed, 42.6 per cent of the pre-1954 industrial firms were created by merchants, rising to 63.1 per cent of those established during the 1963–5 period and 64.4 per cent of the total enterprises set up between 1966 and 1971. Artisans come in second place: they established 21.3 per cent of industrial firms created before 1954, 7 per cent during the first phase but 15.1 per cent during the second phase (1966–71). Industrialists occupied third place in the creation of the new private industrial enterprises.

The preponderance of merchant capital is also indicated by the following figures: 298 wholesale traders owned 54 per cent of industrial enterprises employing more than 20 workers. About 256 other merchants possessed 46 per cent of those employing fewer than 20 workers. There is a noticeable trend towards the concentration of capital within this sector.

Although the private industrial firms are generally owned by close

Table 7.5 *The legal forms of private industrial firms, 1954–71*

Description	Before 1954	1955–62	1963–5	1966–71	Total
Individually owned enterprises	155	66	119	254	594
Joint-stock companies	135	75	139	541	890
No. of proprietors	271	163	340	1,634	2,408
Average no. of proprietors per firm	2.01	2.17	2.45	3.02	2.41

Source: AARDES, Industrie privée, 1975.

relatives rather than share-holders, no fewer than 890 out of 1,496, representing 63 per cent of the total reported, were registered prior to 1971 as stock companies. The rest were reported as possessed by individuals (see Table 7.5).

Finally, the majority of the 1,482 private enterprises studied had set up only single units of production. Indeed, 63.3 per cent of them employed from 1 to 19 workers, 24.7 per cent from 20 to 49 and only 12 per cent more than 50 workers. Thus most of these private industrial units resembled workshops rather than modern factories.

A study carried out by the INEAP (INEAP, *Etude sur l'industrie privée: essai d'actualisation 1969–1979* (1980)) revealed that the actual number of private enterprises totalled no fewer than 3,358 in 1966. By 1969 this had risen to 4,046. The 1971–7 period witnessed the maturation of the private industrial sector, as well as the growing verbal hostility expressed by it to the state and its single party, for both ideological and political purposes. The limits and restrictions imposed by the state upon private capital had become intolerable to the new bourgeoisie and its representatives within the state and party apparatuses.

Since the national charter was favourable only to non-exploiting property the private industrial entrepreneurs undertook a horizontal development through the multiplication of small-size units employing between one and four workers in the anterior of the country. Despite this, the trend towards the concentration of capital continued. Thus, investment per job created was seven times higher than between 1969 and 1974. Table 7.6 summarises the increase of private industrial enterprises.

The process of concentration resulted in the following situation: in 1977, 2,731 private industrial enterprises employed 66,082 workers. Thus, each enterprise employed an average of 22 workers. This must be compared

Post-independence development

Table 7.6 *The total number of private industrial enterprises, 1969–77*

Year(s)	1969	1974	1977	1969–77 %
Total no. enterprises	4,046	5,819	6,070	+50%
				1977–Total workers
No. of enterprises employing more than 5 workers	1,845	2,618	2,731	60,082
No. of enterprises employing fewer than 5 workers	2,210	3,201	3,339	6,678

Source: INEAP, 1980.

Table 7.7 *The private sector in industrial employment, 1966–77*

Sector	1966	%	1969	%	1973	%	1977	%
Energy (electricity, water)	435	8.64	289	4.70	17	0.22	—	—
Hydrocarbons	5,760	84.00	55,449	54.70				
Mining and quarrying	4,564	47.90	1,073	8.60	1,771	11.46	3,222	16.30
Steel	3,000	84.44	545	8.70	466	3.10	806	2.83
IMME (metallurgical, mechanical and electrical industries)	11,699	78.73	8,400	44.30	12,344	34.73	15,764	29.10
Construction materials	4,440	59.30	1,925	21.80	1,899	12.35	2,152	9.45
Light chemical industries	5,926	90.54	5,985	79.44	5,115	67.60	6,663	45.30
Food, tobacco, matches	8,823	44.45	7,922	29.00	12,686	41.45	12,549	28.60
Textiles	4,123	69.54	6,497	26.80	14,791	50.30	15,229	45.20
Leather and shoes	3,939	57.20	1,488	26.63	2,004	34.93	2,163	29.36
Lumber, cork and papers	7,791	63.64	7,981	52.40	6,203	49.45	7,927	33.54
Miscellaneous	404	81.00	1,603	87.20	4,615	94.90	6,280	91.20

Source: Secrétariat d'Etat au Plan, Various issues of *Enquête sur l'emploi et les salaires*.

with the situation prevailing in 1969 when 485 enterprises – out of a sample of 1,845 – employed more than 20 workers. By 1977, over 700 enterprises employed between 20 and 50 workers.

By the end of the second four-year plan, the private industrial sector employed 72,755 workers, representing 21.03 per cent of the total industrial labour force. The private enterprises specialising in construction and public works employed 105,512 workers, comprising 52.63 per cent of the work force in this sector. Table 7.7 shows the role of the private sector in industrial employment between 1966 and 1977.

Table 7.8 *The private sector in construction and public works, 1969–77*

Number of workers	1969		1974		1977	
	No. of establishments	Total employees	No. of establishments	Total employees	No. of establishments	Total employees
Fewer than 5	1,014	2,315	2,045	3,681	2,299	4,138
More than 5	1,317	86,597	1,542	90,379	1,734	101,374
Total	2,331	88,912	3,587	94,060	4,033	105,512

Source: INEAP, 1980.

Post-independence development

Because of the rapid development undertaken by the public sector in various fields, private capital had invested heavily in the establishment of enterprises specialising in construction and public works, particularly from 1970 onwards. Indeed, the number of these private firms rose from 2,331 in 1969 to 4,033 by 1977. Table 7.8 shows the contribution of the private sector in this field between 1969 and 1977.

Thus, the average number of workers per enterprise in construction and public works was twice that in an industrial firm. Indeed, each construction and public works firm employed an average of 58 workers, as against 22 per industrial enterprise. It is no wonder that this sector, from the early 1970s onwards, constituted a privileged sphere for the private accumulation of capital.

The INEAP study underestimated the importance, as well as the total number, of existing private enterprises. Indeed, the 1977 census had already revealed that the private industrial sector employed 34.4 per cent of the labour force in light industry, 52.6 per cent in construction and public works, 30.7 per cent in transport, 72.7 per cent in commerce and 69.9 per cent in other sectors excluding agriculture. Furthermore, by 1978, the Ministry of Light Industry reported the existence of 4,800 private enterprises; the Ministry of Heavy Industry identified 2,000 private enterprises; and the Ministry of Energy and Petrochemical Industries found 500 such firms (giving a total of 7,300 private industrial enterprises altogether). During the same year, about 5,000 private enterprises employed 140,000 workers in construction and public works. In commerce, 111,800 shops occupied 145,000 persons. In transport about 12,000 firms employed 50,000 workers and in the services 33,000 units occupied 130,000 persons. In 1978, 63 per cent of commercial and service activities were controlled by the private sector. As a result, by the end of the second four-year plan, the private industrial sector employed only about 21 per cent of the total industrial labour force but received no less than 34 per cent of industry's added value (excluding hydrocarbons). Table 7.9 shows the evolution of the share of the private sector in GDP between 1969 and 1977.

The drastic decline in the share of private ownership in the industrial and hydrocarbons sectors that occurred between 1969 and 1977 was caused by the nationalisation of foreign interests and the industrialisation of the country carried out by the national public corporations. Indeed, this trend is reflected in the evolution of the share of the private sector in the formation of gross fixed capital which declined in relative terms from 58.74 per cent in 1965 to 6.22 per cent in 1977. However, in absolute terms, the total value of the share of this sector rose from AD 1.45 billion in 1965 to AD 2.44 billion in 1977. This amounted to an annual average rate of

Table 7.9 *The contribution of the private sector to the GDP, 1969–77 (excluding customs taxes on imports) (%)*

Sector	1969	1973	1977
Agriculture		50.00	72.10
Manufacturing industry	56.9	69.10	27.00
Steel, metallurgical, mechanical and electrical industries	48.5	17.30	13.30
Construction materials	9.8	12.60	8.00
Chemical industries	64.4	42.10	27.20
Food industries	26.4	24.40	15.30
Textiles	57.2	65.90	72.20
Leather and skins	67.5	67.60	45.20
Lumber, papers, etc.	6.4	6.70	7.40
Diverse industries	56.9	35.70	35.60
Mining and quarrying	6.4	6.70	7.40
Energy	57.8	3.70	0.00
Hydrocarbons	82.2	21.70	17.30
Public works and construction	—	69.90	32.10
Transportation and communication	—	40.00	12.20
Services	—	75.00	81.50
Commerce	—	80.00	77.00

Source: Secretariat d'Etat au Plan, *Comptes économiques* (1974–7).

growth of 8.2 per cent. Table 7.10 shows the total annual formation of gross fixed capital (FGFC) between 1965 and 1977.

In short, the national private industrial sector, which benefited from enormous external economies, invested in light industries requiring simple technology and relatively small amounts of capital. These consumer goods industries are highly productive and profitable everywhere, but particularly under the conditions prevailing in contemporary Algeria. This high profitability has been made possible by indirect subsidies provided by the state, which has been supplying cheap raw materials, semi-finished products and energy and favourable rates of interest on loans as well as exchange rates, etc., while failing to control the prices of the goods and services produced by private firms. Thus, the economic development promoted by the state not only resulted in the installation of a multiplicity of industrial plants constituting the public sector, but stimulated the growth of a 'dynamic' private sector. In addition, a new category of Algerian *affairistes* emerged as intermediaries between the state enterprises and multinational firms. Their function, in addition to import activities,

Table 7.10 *The contribution of the private sector in the formation of gross fixed capital, 1965–77 (thousand million AD)*

Gross fixed capital	1965	1966	1967	1968	1969	1970	1971	1972	1973	1974	1975	1976	1977
Total	2,359	2,199	2,718	4,130	5,745	7,600	8,600	10,560	13,300	17,750	27,340	33,985	39,348
Public sector	944	1,261	1,968	3,330	5,045	6,093	7,215	9,122	11,800	16,000	25,340	31,785	36,900
Private sector	1,415	938	750	800	700	1,507	1,385	1,438	1,500	1,750	2,000	2,200	2,448

Source: Ilmane, 'Place, rôle et dynamique du capital privé dans le processus d'industrialisation en Algérie 1966–1977', in *Cahier du Centre de Recherche sur le Monde Arabe Contemporain* (Bruxelles, 1980).

The private industrial sector

was to ensure these foreign firms profitable contracts with Algerian public companies. In exchange for their mediating services, they received between 10 and 15 per cent of the value of the contract. The wealth amassed by these *affairistes* was important enough to allow them to constitute one of the largest and most powerful lobbies within the high spheres of the new Algerian ruling circles. By 1979 the increasing economic, social, ideological and political weight of the *comprador* private sector became such that it induced the Benjadid regime to change not only the industrial policy but also the social policy of the country, a fact that is bound to compromise the national populist consensus. This consensus resulted from over fifty years of revolutionary struggle for independence which mobilised the overwhelming majority of the urban and particularly rural popular strata. The dissolution of their craft corporations and the expropriation of their plots of land by the colonial power reduced them to miserable socio-economic conditions.

Chapter 8

Agriculture: the stagnation of production and its consequences

By 1978, Algerian agriculture had been divided into three sectors: a self-managed sector, an 'agrarian revolution' sector and a private sector. The first, which was made up of formerly colonised land, extended over 2,308,131 hectares and was organised into 2,099 units of production. The second was the result of land reform, known in Algeria as the 'agrarian revolution', which involved the expropriation of land from Algerian landlords and the setting up of co-operatives for the benefit of landless and poor peasants. It covered 1,269,446 hectares, divided into 4,992 agricultural co-operatives of the agrarian revolution (CAPRA) and 139 groupings of land reclamation (GMV). The third sector extended over 5,544,145 hectares divided into 899,545 landholdings.[1] Each of these three sub-sectors possessed its specific organisational and structural features. The cultivated area, the number of landholdings and the average surface per farming unit were as shown in Table 8.1.

These three sectors specialised in the production of specific crops. Thus, during 1978–9, the self-managed sector produced 90.2 per cent of the wine, 86.7 per cent of the legumes, 68.4 per cent of the industrial crops such as beets and tobacco, 54.7 per cent of the grapes and 44 per cent of the dry vegetables. The private sector produced 74.3 per cent of the vegetables and 60.6 per cent of the cereals. The agrarian revolution sector provided 16.4 per cent of the industrial crops, 12.2 per cent of the cereals, 12.2 per cent of the dry vegetables and 8.2 per cent of the fruit. Table 8.2 provides additional details.

This table shows clearly the heterogeneous nature of the three sub-sectors of contemporary Algerian agriculture. Their differences are rooted in their origins and development.

As pointed out above, the self-managed sector comprised all the lands that were formerly colonised by the settlers. After their departure in 1962, the agricultural labourers organised themselves into self-management committees in order to keep production going. The first regime of independent Algeria for internal and external political considerations presented workers' self-management in agriculture as a mode of socialist development. However, since this sector was the mainstay of the existing

Table 8.1 *The structure of Algerian agriculture, 1978*

Agricultural area sector (hectares)	Cultivated area (hectares)	No. of farming units	Average surface per unit
Private	3,500,000	750,000	4.7
Self-managed	2,500,000	2,071	1,250
Agrarian revolution	1,000,000	7,000	140
Total 'Socialist sector'	3,500,000	9,071	1,390

Table 8.2 *The contribution of the three sectors to agricultural production, 1978–9 (in 1,000 quintals)*

All sectors	Self-managed sector	%	Private sector	%	Agrarian revolution sector	%
Cereals 6,198	1,978	12.2	6,202	38.3	8,018	49.5
Dry vegetables 532	65	12.2	234	44.0	233	45.8
Industrial crops 1,747	287	16.4	1,195	68.4	265	15.1
Citrus fruit 4,450	229	5.0	3,937	86.7	374	8.3
Grapes 481	34	7.0	263	54.7	184	38.3
Other fruit 5,484	455	8.3	952	17.4	4,077	74.3
Wine (hectolitres) 2,710	51	1.9	2,445	90.2	214	7.9

Source: MARA, *Statistique Agricole* (1978–9).

social forces, state intervention became inevitable. Moreover, statism implied the gradual bureaucratisation of management, which ended up in the long run by stifling not only workers' initiative but also, and particularly, agricultural production. But, up to the late 1960s, given the nature of this inherited colonial agriculture and the low standards of living

Post-independence development

of the population, the major problem of Algerian agriculture was rather over-production or the inability to sell its principal crops, such as wine and fruit. This situation necessitated the reconversion or restructuring of the former colonial sector and the modernisation of the Algerian private sector.

The merit of the second regime, 1965–79, with regard to agriculture was that it tried at least to define the role of this sector within the economy and that it dared, despite strong opposition from conservative forces, to carry out an agrarian reform between 1972 and 1978. According to an official report of the Ministry of Agriculture, the role of the sector was: (1) to satisfy the needs of the population for foodstuffs, which implied the reconversion of viticulture into 'cerealculture', which was accelerated with the closing of the French market to Algerian wine; the introduction of high-yield wheat developed in Mexico; the extension of fodder cultivation to facilitate the growth of animal husbandry and the initiation of oleaginous crops; (2) to improve the income of peasant farmers in order to widen the national market.

At any rate, the first attempt to promote a planned agricultural development was made during the preparation of the three-year plan (1967–9). However, serious planning of the sector had to await the first four-year plan (1970–3) and the second four-year plan (1974–7). These two plans of development set the objectives to be attained. The main ideas expressed in them were reformulated in the national charter promulgated on 27 June 1976:

Agriculture forms, together with mineral resources and processing industries, the basis of the productive sector. But agriculture constitutes a more important source of income, in that it represents permanent wealth, unlike finite mineral resources, which ultimately get used up, and unlike industry, which is constrained by the constant need to keep up to date with technical progress, and by the risks of becoming obsolete.

The labour of a large part of Algeria's active population is devoted to this part of the productive sector, and will long continue to be so. Moreover, in the future agriculture will represent an essential source of income – when present investments in its expansion and modernisation take full effect.

If the role of mineral resources and industries is essential for the accumulation of foreign currency, the role of agriculture is primary in the generation of domestic savings. Agriculture thus constitutes one of the bases of the country's economic growth and represents a dominant factor in social progress.

In conformity with the objective of the agrarian revolution, the necessary means will be mobilised to restore agricultural labour to its proper place in society and to create economic, social and cultural conditions that will allow the development of a qualified work force with an increasingly improved status in the rural areas, to the great benefit of agricultural activity. Measures will be taken to ensure that the best workers do not continue to abandon agriculture for the other economic sectors, so

Agriculture

that agriculture can also become a real factor of progress and social, cultural and technological improvement in the heart of the countryside.

The problem of the large landholders has been resolved and exploitation of the peasants has been eradicated. The remaining difficulty – and here the solution requires a constant effort towards imaginative improvement – lies in giving the socialist agricultural sector adequate structures allowing agriculture to produce more and better, fully asserting its role in the economic structure of the country and constantly improving the conditions of the peasant farmer . . .

The private agricultural sector involves a large section of the peasantry. It must be given greater access to the means of technical improvement in farming, as well as the financing of agricultural programmes and the general improvement of agricultural productivity. As an objective of the agrarian revolution, the emphasis on the rural world will accommodate the peasant farmers in the private sector.

Nonetheless, despite such displayed official optimism, Algerian agriculture has faced intractable problems since the 1920s, some of which are caused by the geographical limitations of the country and are hence unresolvable without the systematic use of science and technology.

The limits of Algerian agriculture

The problems of contemporary Algerian agriculture have been determined primarily by many factors such as unfavourable natural conditions, erosive methods of cultivation, socio-economic disruptions associated with political upheaval, mismanagement and the lack of an industrial base and a comprehensive and appropriate agricultural policy designed to modernise, revitalise and hence stimulate the growth of production of basic foodstuffs in order to keep pace with a rapidly increasing population. In this book only the natural limits of agriculture will be discussed.

Although Algeria possesses an important agricultural potential – whose development would require a substantial amount of investment – its agriculture remains relatively limited. Indeed, in 1978, the 'useful agricultural soil' extended over 75,422 square kilometres, representing only 3.17 per cent of the Algerian national territory. More than nine-tenths of this cultivable surface was either cultivated with cereals or dry vegetables, or remained fallow. The yields depend on weather conditions. Northern Algeria, the Tell, and the steppes, comprise 19 per cent of the total area of the country, at least 40 per cent of which is not cultivable at all. The total arable lands utilised by agriculture cover only about 36 per cent of this total, 17 per cent of which consists of pasture of mediocre quality. Table 8.3 summarises the basic data concerning the agricultural potentialities and limits of Algeria.

Because of the prevalent climatic conditions, two natural processes are

Post-independence development

Table 8.3 *Agricultural potentialities and limits of Algeria, 1976 (hectares)*

	Controlled irrigation	%
Total net crop land (south)	665,000	11.5
Total net crop land (north)	7,142,000	2.3
Total net crop land	7,807,000	3.3
Total grazing land	31,597,000	
Total land area used for agriculture	39,404,000	
Total surface area of Algeria	237,807,000	

Source: La Banque Mondiale, *Algerie: Etude du Sector Agricole, Analyse des Problèmes*, Vol. II, 3 January 1979. The information was provided by the Ministry of Agriculture and Agrarian Reform (MARA).

threatening these cultivable patches: erosion and desertification. According to official statistics, every year an average of 100,000 square metres (about 40,000 hectares) of arable land is either washed off into the sea or carried away by the winds as dust. The desert has been advancing towards the northern coastal green belt by an estimated 10 kilometres per year in certain areas. This situation was aggravated by the deforestation of the country brought about by colonisation. In fact, in 1830, the forests covered over 4 million hectares; by 1952 only 3.3 million hectares remained. Theoretically, Algerian forests should cover 7 million hectares. In 1974, the wooded and forested areas covered only 12.5 per cent of the Tell and the steppes, compared with 14.3 per cent in Tunisia and 13.6 per cent in Morocco.[2]

In evaluating the achievements and shortcomings of the agricultural sector, the authorities of the Ministry of Agriculture and Agrarian Revolution noted in 1979:

that the satisfaction of the needs of the country in foodstuffs was rendered difficult by the rapid growth of demand and the limited nature of agricultural lands. The useful agricultural surface totals about 7.5 million hectares, located to a large extent in the high plains and semi-arid zones. The northern green belt – which is not large – is threatened by industrial and urban extension. The irrigated perimeters are few. They could be extended, but their extension would require important capital investment in large water resources which would necessitate the construction of large dams. Such development would be costly in the long run.

Furthermore, as Table 8.4 shows, the man–land ratio tends to diminish constantly.

The authors of the report went on to say that this situation implied that any increase in production could be obtained only by the intensification of

Table 8.4 *Man–land ratio, 1962–90*

Year	Population (million)	Land per inhabitant (hectares)	Of which irrigated (square metres)
1962	10.0	0.75	200
1966	12.0	0.63	—
1977	17.0	0.43	173
1990	26.0	0.29	150

Source: MARA, *Evolution de l'Agriculture de 1967 à 1978*, vol. I (September 1979).

cultivation, which would increase the yields of the existing usable agricultural surface. This intensification implied important investments, among other things in the extension of irrigated areas, which constitute the most important factor in efficient intensification, in the mechanisation of agricultural production and in the reduction of fallow lands, which could not be achieved without a concomitant modernisation of equipment, in the training of workers, technicians, agronomists and engineers, in the setting up of an adequate work organisation and in the provision of equitable wages.

However, the expected increase in production through the programme of intensification of cultivation could not be raised to satisfactory levels during the 1967–78 period for two major reasons. First, agriculture was not given the priority it deserved within the framework of the strategy of development. Second, the policy of agricultural development did not give enough priority to the units of production. In addition, the overall organisation of the sector, which was imposed by the administration, did not motivate the workers to produce more crops.

Unlike most academic critics of the model of Algerian development based on the industrialisation of the country, this official report, which is also critical of the Boumedienne strategy of development, concluded that 'taking into account the weak agricultural potentialities, the country's favouring industry was necessary in order to provide employment and income for a rapidly growing population'. The authors of the report overlooked the fact that the stagnation of agricultural production was attributable mostly to the incompetence and irresponsibility of the authorities in charge of this sector as well as to the hostile reaction of big landlords and their supporters to the implementation of the project of land reform. Worse than this, the authors failed to mention that through the bureaucratisation of administrative and socio-economic institutions, those in charge of agriculture were incapable of utilising the investment funds earmarked for the development of the sector.

The bureaucratisation of the workers' self-managed sector of agriculture

In November 1965, the 'council of revolution' outlined new reforms designed to resolve the chronic problems of 'socialist agriculture'. 'Considering that autogestion was never effective', this council decided to 'enrich it' by granting greater autonomy in management to the units of production and by devising 'an efficient control over it'. The workers were offered material inducements. But they were also requested to 'manifest solidarity' vis-à-vis the 'disinherited sectors'. A redefinition and clarification of roles, functions, rights and obligations was thought necessary. But the opponents of autogestion, representing private interests, expressed the desire to abolish it altogether. The anti-autogestion forces within the government even decided to return some land nationalised in 1964 from 'collaborators' of colonialism. However, at the express request of UGTA the president of the revolutionary council reversed this decision. In November 1965, he stated that 'we ought . . . to put an end to bureaucratic abuses and respond to workers' grievances by decentralising the decisions in order to control the self-managed farms better'. And again on 20 October 1965, the president declared 'we are for autogestion but not for disorder; we are for a self-management profitable both for the workers and the economy of the country, but not for an autogestion financed by the citizens'. Thus, for the regime, profitability rather than workers' control became the key issue.

To achieve this goal, material inducements both for permanent and seasonal workers were added to the system of rewards in order to increase production. At the beginning of 1969, a large number of temporary labourers who worked an annual average of at least 160 days on a mono-crop or 200 days on a multi-crop farm were offered the right to participate equally with the permanent workers in the decision-making process. Henceforth they shared equally with the full members (and in proportion to the amount a worker contributed) whatever profits were made by the productive unit. Earlier, in 1966, following a World Bank mission, a study group composed of several Soviet experts of the Gosplan were invited to Algeria. On their recommendation, the workers on self-managed farms were allotted a family garden consisting of a maximum 500 square metres on which, besides growing vegetables, they could keep chickens, rabbits and two sheep or goats. The permanent labourers were also conceded the *right* to be housed, once the needs of the 'directors and technical cadres are met'. All of the workers were to become members of a social security scheme, starting in 1971.

Although the ONRA was finally abolished in 1967, suggestions for reorganising the autogestion were not forthcoming until 1968–9. The Reform Decrees of 1968–9 aimed at granting some measure of 'autonomy of management', and at decentralising the authoritarian centralisation effected by the ONRA. Between 1962 and 1967, to reinforce its hold on the workers' self-management, the ONRA consolidated the former 22,000 colonial farms first into 3,000, and later on into a mere 1,994 gigantic macrofundia farming units totalling 2,302 million hectares and averaging over 1,000 each. In conjunction with the intended 'centralisation' the government envisaged the breaking up of these farms into smaller, more manageable units of production.

However, it appears now that this reform did not go far enough, because despite emphasis on 'decentralisation' and 'autonomy of management', the MARA inherited from the ONRA in its entirety the power to review and implement major decisions regarding agriculture. This allowed the MARA, through the directors, to run the affairs of autogestion in collaboration with the BNA (Banque Nationale d'Algérie), which, in exchange for financing its operations, was given the right to review the accounts of the self-managed farms and to keep their records audited. But the BNA ended up not only by controlling every detail regarding the utilisation of the funds it advanced, but by supervising a host of their activities. Hence in the late sixties and early seventies the control of the 'socialist sector' of agriculture fell to the MARA and the BNA, two important bureaucratic institutions.

The MARA, following the example of the ONRA, established several auxiliary boards to service the self-managed sector. The OFLA (a marketing board for Algerian fruit and vegetables) was set up as early as June 1966; in August 1968 the MARA announced the creation of the ONCV (Office National de Commercialisation du Vin); and on 3 April 1969 the ONAMA (Office National d'Approvisionnement en Matériel Agricole) was organised. Needless to say, these bureaucratic organisations, devised to market agricultural crops produced and supply the workers' self-management units with sufficient tools, seed, fertiliser and machinery, turned out to be inept, inefficient, wasteful and irresponsive to the needs both of the direct producers and the consumers.

By the 1970s workers' self-managed agriculture constituted a 'socialist' island surrounded by a stormy ocean of paralysing bureaucracy determined to assert its prerogatives, and a stagnating heterogeneous private sector. Despite the existence of a wealthy class of landlords, it remained retrograde and hence conservative in the extreme. All these factors combined to

Post-independence development

contribute both to the deterioration of the financial deficit of autogestion and to the living conditions of its labour force.

Financial and socio-economic problems of autogestion

The causes underlying the persistent financial difficulties of workers' self-managed units of production were determined by external factors. In fact, while the wages of the workers and the prices of their agricultural products were frozen during several consecutive years, the costs of other factors of production such as fertiliser, tractors, harvesters and their spare parts skyrocketed (for instance, between 1969 and 1973 alone the prices of tractors increased by 80 per cent, harvesters by 35 per cent and seed-drills by over 100 per cent). Besides, both the local private wholesale grocers and the OFLA agents began buying agricultural produce from the workers' self-management committees at low prices and selling it on the local markets at high prices; to the detriment of the direct producers and consumers, their profits seemed to have risen steadily throughout the period.

By 1975 it became clear that the 1968–9 reform had also failed to involve the workers genuinely in control of the process of production, the mechanisms of financing and above all in marketing networks designed to sell their products at fair prices. All the basic economic activities of autogestion were handled either by state boards or by private businesses. As a direct result, production kept on declining in the 'nationalised sector' and deteriorating in the peasant private sector (through neglect and lack of land reform). The blocking of the transformation of the agrarian structure has, in the long run, undermined even the process of industrialisation and hence a genuine national independent development geared to the needs of the people.

In fact, on 30 April 1975, the official newspaper, *El Moudjahid*, stated emphatically that 'From 1963 to this very day the self-managed sector has been torn by the same problems, the majority of which it has known all the time.' A new decree concerning the reorganisation of the self-managed sector was promulgated and implemented immediately in October 1975. This reorganisation consisted essentially of abolishing the office of the director and replacing it with a 'qualified technician' designed to assist the president of the workers' self-managed committee. Henceforth and without any ambiguity, the major decisions were to be debated and taken by the General Assembly, and implemented by the president of the workers' self-management committee. The trusteeship of the MARA was suppressed and replaced by a 'function of orientation, assistance, co-ordination, promotion and supervision', exercised jointly by the APC

(Assemblées Populaires Communales) and the APW (Assemblées Populaires des Wilayates). In other words, the central government finally realised the urgent need to concede a significant amount of economic and political power to the local collectivities. Financially, not only did the state dissolve or pay the deficit of autogestion, but it lowered the rate of interest on loans, increased the prices of agricultural products and devised mechanisms to stabilise the prices of the technical means of production and other industrial inputs needed by the workers' self-managed farms.

The wholesale grocers who mediated between the producers and the retail traders were suppressed; the OFLA was stripped of its role in marketing internally the agricultural products and replaced by the CAPCS (Coopératives Agricoles Polyvalentes Communales de Services). Thenceforth, the co-operative system set up to market the products of the co-operatives of the agrarian revolution also serviced those of autogestion and veterans' co-operatives. They all had to send their produce to CAPCS in order to have it distributed locally to the retail traders at the communal level. Surpluses were transmitted to departmental COFEL (Coopératives des Fruits et Légumes), charged with interregional distribution. At the national level the OFLA contined to perform import–export distribution.

The internal structure of the CAPCS was derived from that of autogestion, that is, it was governed by a general assembly which elects a management committee which chooses a president. But unlike autogestion, a director was still appointed by the MARA, and an accounting commissioner designated by the Ministry of Finance.

As usual, this reform, conceived, implemented and interpreted by the administration, failed to resolve the basic problems of the socialist agricultural sector. On the contrary, it accelerated the process of bureaucratisation which has impaired the development of both public and private sectors.

The agrarian structures and forms of production of the private sector

The agrarian structures and forms of production of the private sector, which were shaped by colonisation and the concomitant integration of the rural communities into the world market, were not modified by the state until the 1970s. As will be seen, one of the objectives of the agrarian revolution was the alteration of the agrarian status quo. Thus, as Table 8.5 indicates, the rural population continued to have a differential access to land, which constitutes the basic factor of production of the peasantry. In the mid 1960s 6 million hectares out of a total of 7.2 million in private ownership, belonged to about 200,000 landowners, while 490,000 peasant households possessed only 1.2 million hectares. These households were as

Table 8.5 *Principal characteristics of farming units in Algeria, 1968*

Size of unit	Total no.	%	Area (thousand ha)	%	Average cultivable land	% Permanent workers	% Production of hard wheat	% Production of soft wheat	% Cattle	% Tractors	% Harvesters	% Trucks	% Other equipment	% Irrigated area
Landless	130,786	20	0	0	—	28	0	0	18.0	1	0	2.4	2	0
Less than 2 ha	72,094	11	42.6	1	0.59	—	—	—	4.5	0	0	4.0	—	2
1–10 ha	89,288	13	1405.3	33	3.80	15	35	33	50.9	12	5	36.0	16	27
11–59 ha	89,288	13	1490.0	35	16.69	41	39	39	21.8	51	43	20.0	48	33
51+ ha	6,984	1	136.6	31	189.00	16	26	28	4.8	37	52	16.0	24	38
Total	388,440	58	3074.5	100	6.38	100	100	100	100.0	100	100	100.0	100	100

Source: MARA, *Enquête sur la main d'oeuvre dans le secteur privé* (1968).

poor as the 500,000 to 600,000 landless peasant families. The wealthy Algerian landlords, 4 per cent of all landowners, possessed 38 per cent of the land. Table 8.5 contrasts the structures of land ownership in 1965 and in 1973 before the implementation of the agrarian reform. It reveals that the process of pauperisation of the rural population continued during the post-independence period. The total number of microfundia owners increased from 432,270, representing 72.1 per cent of total landowners in 1965, to 563,311, comprising 79.3 per cent in 1973. The wealthy landlords totalled 16,530, representing 2.8 per cent of the landowners, and monopolised 26.6 per cent of the arable land in the country in 1965, declining to 13,174 or 1.9 per cent of the proprietors who still owned 23.2 per cent of the most fertile land.[3] The political weight of this landlord class was such that despite the fact that up to 80 per cent of Algerians were eking out a precarious livelihood from the land in 1962 and despite the striking inequalities of land distribution, the project of land reform was postponed several times before 1971–2.

Agriculture

Empirical research sponsored by the Secretariat of State for Planning during the early 1970s established that the private agricultural sector was characterised by the co-existence of three forms of production: 'domestic', 'merchant' and 'capitalist'. The 'domestic' form was defined by the utilisation of family labour, producing essentially for subsistence, using non-mechanical means of production. The family 'merchant' form was defined by the utilisation of family labour producing essentially for the market. The 'capitalist' form of production was defined by the employment of wage labour and the utilisation of mechanical means of cultivation producing for the market. Furthermore, the farming units in the domestic form of production amounted to fewer than 10 hectares; the units in the family merchant form varied in size from 11 to 50 hectares; and those in the capitalist form exceeded 51 hectares.

According to a study carried out by the Ministry of Agriculture in 1968, the rich landlords, possessing more than 51 hectares each, represented only 1 per cent of the total landowners but possessed 31 per cent of the agricultural area. Their landholdings were situated on the most fertile areas and contained relatively important irrigated perimeters. Indeed, the farms that exceeded 20 hectares of arable land possessed 38 per cent of the irrigated areas in the country, while the large landlords who owned more than 100 hectares possessed 25.5 per cent of the irrigated land.

In addition, the farmers possessing more than 50 hectares each owned 37 per cent of the tractors in the private sector, 52 per cent of the harvesters, 16 per cent of the trucks and 24 per cent of the other automated ploughing machinery and instruments. Another study showed that the landlords who owned more than 100 hectares possessed 57 per cent of the tractors in the private sector, while the small landowners possessing fewer than 10 hectares had no tractors at all. Table 8.5 present the principal characteristics of farming units in Algeria in 1968.

The landlords who cultivated more than 100 hectares each employed 86 per cent of the permanent and seasonal wage labourers of the private sector. This category of farmers sold over 70 per cent of their agricultural products in the market; they also produced 26 per cent of the hard wheat and 28 per cent of the soft wheat. However, these rich landlords controlled only 48 per cent of the cattle.

The statistical data presented above indicated that one of the major problems of Algerian private agriculture is structural. Indeed, the bulk of the landowners possessed very small farming units that were also extremely fragmented. This situation complicated and still complicates the lives of the cultivators. Indeed, *parcellement* constitutes an obstacle to the modernisation of private agriculture in Algeria. The 1950–1 agricultural census revealed that 28 per cent of Algerian landholdings were made up of more than 10 parcels. Despite this, the Ministry of Agriculture stated in 1968 that the current 'agrarian structures are suitable for a more intensive mechanisation and diffusion of various modern techniques of cultivation'.[4] This official inquiry asserted that for all of Algeria the number of parcels per farming unit averaged 3.49. The average size of each parcel was 2.25 hectares.

However, my own field work carried out during the academic year 1974–5 contradicts the findings of this official study. I found that 24.4 per cent of the 287 rural households investigated were landless, 22.9 per cent owned between 1 and 5 parcels of land, 19 per cent between 6 and 10 parcels, 12.1 per cent between 11 and 20 parcels and 1.3 per cent between 21 and 33 parcels.

Furthermore, the socio-economic conditions of the peasantry were such that an often-heard peasant expression in the rural district studied was used to describe the desperate attempt by many impoverished *fellahin* who are clinging to their increasingly unrewarding ancestral patterns of subsistence: 'We keep animals, and we are thirsty for milk; we plough fields, and we are hungry for bread.'

Indeed, the decline of traditional agriculture was accompanied by that of animal husbandry. Most oxen rented by the active *fellahin* belonged to the families of migrant workers who use the grain paid for the rental to complement their cash revenues. Livestock, which traditionally formed an important component of a rural economy, have not yet recovered from their decimation during the war, despite increased cash flow into the district.

Although the agrarian reform of the mid 1970s had contributed to the improvement of the living conditions of several thousand families, it failed to resolve the structural problems of Algerian agriculture in general and peasant economy in particular.

The objectives of the agrarian revolution

Confronted with the intractable problems of rural society, the Algerian leadership of the 1970s decided to carry out an agrarian revolution. One of the principal objectives of the reform, launched in 1971–2, was 'a just and efficient distribution of the means of production, particularly the most important of them, land, to the sector constituted by the landless and poor peasantry'.[5] The landless peasants alone numbered 600,000 families in the early 1970s. This state of affairs induced the FLN party to present the 'agrarian revolution' as 'an imperious act of solidarity between the propertied and the disinherited social strata of the nation'.

But, for Boumedienne, the agrarian revolution went with 'the industrial

Agriculture

revolution: the growth of one sector always generates a demand for the other sector and obliges it to increase its production capacity . . . the agrarian revolution, in creating favourable conditions for the economic and social development of the rural world, will therefore have an effective impact on the development of the industrial sector and on the ensemble of the national economy'.

The charter of agrarian revolution also emphasised technical modernisation, intensification of production, reduction in the import of foodstuffs and the widening of the internal market through the resolution of the problem of rural redundancy and underemployment which would result in the integration of the peasantry into the national economy. In addition, the agrarian revolution aimed at reclaiming land which had been subjected either to rapid erosion or desertification. The development of a modern agriculture would furnish certain basic raw materials for national industry. It was also intended to reinforce the political and administrative integration of the rural population into the state bureaucratic structure by strengthening the municipal organisation of every commune. The agrarian revolution was supposed to improve the standards of living of the landless and poor peasantry through a more equitable policy of income distribution, the construction of adequate housing, the provision of free health care, the general provision of education and the linking of the innumerable rural collectivities to the modern national communications networks. All this would stimulate a well-balanced agricultural and industrial development. Indeed, the authors of the charter of the agrarian revolution stressed that:

the goal . . . is first of all the modernisation of agriculture. As such it redefines the size of landholdings as well as the techniques of production to be used. Also the agrarian revolution facilitates the transformation of the structure of agricultural production: the aim is not to seek the construction of an economy cut off from the world market, it is the improvement of the productive capacities of agriculture in order to meet the food needs of a population whose very pattern of consumption evolves with the progress of industrialisation. In addition, the agrarian revolution constitutes a stimulus for industry. The modernisation of agriculture and the raising of the standard of living of the rural world will widen the internal market and favour the growth of industry.

The charter intended not to abolish private property in land but to limit the size of agricultural estates and to modernise them in order to increase production. The document concluded that 'the aim is to put an end to the complexity and diversity of the current legal statuses in order to set modern private property in land on a juridical basis . . . if the agrarian revolution does not abolish private ownership of the means of production, it has at least suppressed the exploitation of man by man'.

However, while the application of this charter was bound to affect

Post-independence development

latifundia owners by reducing their landholdings to manageable size, it guaranteed the private appropriation of land. The main purpose was to attenuate the striking socio-economic inequality which existed in the Algerian countryside to reasonable limits rather than to abolish it altogether. The large landlords affected by land expropriation in favour of the landless and poor peasants were compensated. Indeed, the landlords expropriated were to be paid the equivalent value of their land within 15 years; meanwhile the state would be paying them 2.5 per cent interest per year.

Furthermore, despite the recognition by the charter's authors that the large private estates were by-products of the 'colonial pillage', they did not intend to undermine the economic basis of the dominant Algerian agrarian class. Expropriation measures stipulated that the landlords be permitted to withhold sufficient land to provide them with an income at least three times greater than the wage of a permanent agricultural worker in the selfmanaged sector. No specification of the actual size of the area to be left for the landlord was added. The expropriated landlord was to choose the area of his farm to keep. Agricultural equipment and livestock were exempted from expropriation.

But even such a technically, economically and socially necessary reform which actually spared, to a large degree, the interests of the proprietors, was met with contempt and systematic resistance by the landlords, the urban mercantile-industrial classes and their close allies within the regime. The promulgation and implementation of this reform generated a strong reaction from conservative political and social forces which was accentuated by the adoption of the national charter of 1976. The support of the left, especially the Communist Party, could not counter-balance the increasing right-wing opposition to Boumedienne's 'specific socialism'. Thus, the balance of power within Algerian society was in favour of the landlords and a rapidly growing *comprador* class. As a result, the impact of this agrarian reform on the rural economy and class structure was limited in the process of its implementation. Nonetheless, the reform gave rise to a new juridical sector that must be assessed.

The agrarian revolution sector

The programme of the agrarian revolution was divided into three phases. In the first, arable public lands, which had previously been used for pasture or leased to private farmers, were to be given out to landless and poor peasantry whose net agricultural income did not exceed AD 3,000 per year. In the second phase all property of absentee landlords holding more than 5 hectares was to be expropriated. In addition to this, all of the large estates were to be limited. The land made available under the first and second phases of the agrarian revolution was distributed on a permanent basis, with no right of resale and with the obligation of cultivating it personally. The size of the parcels was to guarantee a net yearly income of at least AD 3,750, the legal agricultural wage of the time.

The number of recipients of the first phase totalled 54,000, and their dependants amounted to 350,000 persons, close to 45 per cent of whom had been renting their land from the communal and state authorities. These comprised only 25 per cent of the candidates officially recorded, but the number of potential candidates was much higher. On 31 December 1974, the balance sheet of this first phase was as follows: 53,674 beneficiaries, 2,316 of whom were granted individual titles to land; 788,284 hectares distributed to the members of the newly created 1,748 Coopératives de la Révolution Agraire (CAPRA), to the 601 Coopératives d'Exploitation en Commun (CAEC), to the 572 Groupements Pré-coopératifs de Mise en Valeur (GPMV), Groupements d'Entraide Paysanne (GEP), and Groupements d'Indivisaires (GI). The amount of land allocated to the landless and poor peasants during the first phase averaged 14.7 hectares per recipient. Over 8 per cent of the potential candidates turned down the state's offer to become members of the various co-operatives that were being established. A total of 1,931,146 hectares were acquired and handed over to the National Funds of the Agrarian Revolution (FNRA), of which only 1,145,376 hectares were cultivable. Approximately two-thirds of this total land recovered were represented by public land. More than one-half (55 per cent) of the useful agricultural soil that was turned over to the FNRA for distribution was public land. In other words, the private lands that were made available through nationalisation amounted to only 640,075 hectares. Three-quarters of the landholdings affected belonged to absentee landlords and 90,000 hectares (5 per cent) came from private donations to the FNRA.

These figures reveal the minimal impact of the agrarian revolution on the socio-economic structures of rural Algeria. Indeed, in order to protect themselves from the provisions of the reform bill the wealthy landlords resorted to:

(1) false declarations, or no declarations at all, of their actual landholdings that were supposed to be limited; this reporting could not be verified because of the influence of these big landowners within the Algerian government, army and single party;
(2) the existence of indivisible property enabling the 'limitable' landowners to declare as many kinsmen as necessary, as co-proprietors of indivisible lands, hence managing to circumvent the law;
(3) temporary reconversion of the system of intensive cultivation by

Post-independence development

Table 8.6 *Land ownership, 1965 and 1973*

Size in hectares	No. of farming units 1965	%	Total hectares	%	No. of farming units 1973	%	Total hectares	%
0–10	423,270	72.1	1,319,625	22.6	563,391	79.3	1,633,296	29.9
11–50	147,045	25.1	2,967,545	50.8	134,528	18.9	2,565,741	46.9
51–100	11,875	2.0	765,585	13.1	9,765	1.4	642,824	11.8
101+	4,655	0.8	786,905	13.5	3,409	0.5	622,498	11.4
Total Northern Algeria	586,845	100.0	5,839,660	100.0	711,093	100.0	5,464,359	100.0

Sources: MARA, *Recensement agricole de 1972/73*: and *Enquête de structure sur les exploitations privées 1965, Statistique Agricole*, 1968.

destroying irrigation ditches and wells in order to transform themselves into cereal growers, a device which temporarily changed the ecological nature of the soil and allowed them to prevent the limitation of their estates;

(4) the frequent use of high-ranking officials to avoid the implementation of the provisions of the agrarian revolution.

In addition, the conservative social forces orchestrated a campaign within the country devised to discredit not only the land reform but also Algerian 'socialism' and the regime associated with it. This state of affairs had affected the course of the second phase in particular and the overall tangible results in terms of the quantity of land acquired by the state for the benefit of the potential recipients on the waiting list in general. As a result the implementation of the third phase amounted to the mere establishment of some 'experimental farmers' in the steppes.

The final balance sheet of the agrarian revolution indicated that 5,980 co-operatives were established between 1972 and 1980. The CAPRA predominated with 4,305, or 72 per cent. This form of co-operative regrouped 52,000 beneficiaries, comprising 65 per cent of all co-operators. The CAPRA covered 735,906 hectares (82 per cent of the arable land allocated to the agrarian revolution). The CAEC numbered 565 co-operatives, representing over 9 per cent of all co-operatives, regrouping 18,400 beneficiaries, comprising 23 per cent of the total members, but extending only over 6.5 per cent of the area allocated to the 'agrarian revolution'. The GMV numbered 914 co-operatives, which amounted to over 16 per cent of the total, regrouping 7 per cent of the beneficiaries. They extended over 10 per cent of the arable land of the sector. GEP numbered 176 units and GI represented ten co-operators, who comprised 5 per cent of all members; but they were allocated only 1.5 per cent of the agricultural land given to the agrarian revolution sector.

The surface area of these various co-operatives averages 180 hectares per farming unit. The collective of each production co-operative averages 17 members, compared with 82 workers per farming unit in the self-managed sector. Thus, in terms of employment, in 1980 the agrarian revolution sector employed close to 100,000 co-operators and about 10,000 seasonal labourers. These 110,000 persons represented 8.2 per cent of the total active agricultural population. The state sector provided employment for 114,000 permanent and 118,000 seasonal workers, which represented 17.5 per cent, and the private sector for about 400,000 individuals, or about 74.3 per cent of the total active agricultural population.

All production co-operatives were required to become members at the municipal level of the Coopérative Agricole Polyvalent de Commercialisation et de Service (CAPCS) for efficient use of agricultural machinery and marketing of produce. A CAPCS buys a co-operative's produce and resells it to local retailers. All CAPCS units in the province (*wilaya*) were grouped together into a provincial marketing Coopérative des Fruits et Légumes (COFEL) that buys the surplus production from the various CAPCSs and resells it to retailers within the province. A national state board, the OFLA, buys the surplus from these COFELs for sale in other provinces or for export.

In sum, despite the fact that the agrarian revolution did contribute to the improvement of the living conditions of the rural population, it failed to resolve the fundamental problems of the rural society in general and Algerian agriculture in particular. In the absence of a radical transformation of the agrarian structures and forms of production of the so-called traditional sector of agriculture, a genuine rural development, which requires large sums of investment in the purchase of the tools of production, in the protection and improvement of the soil and in the planting of new plants and fruit trees, could not succeed.

Investment in the agricultural sector

In absolute terms the total amount earmarked by the state for the agricultural sector has increased from AD 2.4 billion during the three-year plan (1967–9) to AD 4 billion during the first four-year plan (1970–3) and AD 12 billion in the second four-year plan (1974–7). However, the share of agriculture within the national economy and services fell from 26 per cent

Table 8.7 *Agricultural investment during the three successive plans of development, 1966–77 (billion AD)*

	1967–9	%	1970–3	%	1974–7	%
Total economy	9.30		27.70		1,110.20	
Projected agricultural investment	2.40	26.00	4.00	18.00	12.00	15.00
Net agricultural investment	1.76	18.60	2.59	11.90	6.03	7.50

Source: MPAT, *Synthèse du bilan*, and MARA, *Evolution de l'agriculture de 1967 à 1978*, vol. I (September 1979).

to 18 per cent to 11 per cent of the total projected investments during the same time. Table 8.7 summarises the widening gap between planned and net investments.

According to a Ministry of Planning offical document, the agricultural sector was earmarked a total of AD 19.3 billion between 1967 and 1978, of which AD 6.5 billion was allocated to the development of water resources. Because of internal and external inflation, delays and so on these successive investment programmes were re-evaluated upwards on 31 December 1978, to a total cost of AD 41.6 billion. Thus, by the end of 1978, no less than AD 22.3 billion of planned agricultural investment, 54 per cent of the total, remained to be utilised.[6] According to the Ministry of Agriculture, the total net investment of the sector during the 1967–78 period amounted to AD 16.78 billion.[7] Table 8.8 shows the net annual investment in agriculture from 1967 to 1979.

These statistical data refute the various criticisms made by innumerable academics, politicians and observers – both Algerians and foreigners – regarding the alleged negligence of the public agricultural sector during the 1967–78 period of development. The major problem of agriculture was accentuated by the incompetence of the political authorities, managers and administrators who were in charge of this sector during the period under study. In an underdeveloped country like Algeria, everything needs to be developed, from the training of farm mechanics to the construction of dams and the improvement of crops through seed selection. Since the leaders in charge of the various sectors of the economy had to undertake many activities, not only were they bound to compete with one another for scarce financial resources, skilled labourers, engineers, managers, administrators and so on, but they had to create or train them in order to enhance the overall performance of their respective sectors and their development.

Thus the low absorptive capacity for investment in the agricultural sector was such that even the planned objectives for the purchase of farm

Table 8.8 *Net agricultural investment within the national economy, 1967–79 (million AD – current prices)*

Year	Total economy	Agriculture	% of total
1967	2,416	576	23.8
1968	3,061	547	17.9
1969	4,008	641	16.0
Total	9,485	1,764	19.2
1970	5,610	644	11.5
1971	7,088	847	11.9
1972	9,614	1,148	11.9
1973	12,000	1,443	12.0
Total	34,312	4,082	11.8
1974	17,808	1,729	9.7
1975	25,670	2,040	7.9
1976	26,020	1,981	7.6
1977	36,900	2,257	6.1
Total	106,398	8,007	7.8
1978	55,710	2,905	5.2
1979	65,129	3,548	5.4

Source: MARA, *L'Evolution de l'agriculture*.

machinery were not attained during the successive plans of development. For instance, during the 1970–8 period only 72 per cent of the projected targets for the purchase of tractors and 63 per cent for harvesters were attained.

Table 8.7 shows the gap between the model of development of agriculture adopted by the government, which was aimed at the intensification of modern means of production, and the implementation or translation of this model into action. And yet, the state gave top priority to the mechanisation of the public agricultural sector.

The private sector, which badly needed farm machinery and other related tools, was not sufficiently encouraged by the government to modernise its basic methods of production. Table 8.9 shows its rate of acquisition of farm equipment. Thus, during the second four-year plan the acquisition of farm equipment by the private sector declined drastically.

As a result the overwhelming majority of the private cultivators continued to use draught animals. According to the 1972–3 agricultural census, only 21 per cent of the farmers utilised mechanical or motor machinery. Furthermore, for the rest of the peasantry the characteristic agricultural device remains the scratch-plough, called locally *mihrath*,

Post-independence development

Table 8.9 *Acquisition of farm equipment by the private sector, 1967–77*

Type of equipment	1967–9	1970–3	1974–7
Harvesters	678	61	41
Tractors	5,001	939	295
Harvest tools and instruments	1,023	159	146
Tools for soil working	1,907	955	226
Cover crops	1,139	667	63
Ploughs	2,682	974	126
Trailers	472	451	620

Source: 1967–74: *Annuaire statistique de l'Algérie*; 1975–7: MARA, *Bilan 2ème Plan Quadriennal.*

Table 8.10 *Acquisition of farm machinery and equipment, 1973–7*

	Co-operative units of production	CAPCS (marketing and service co-operative)
Harvesters	469	1,044
Harvesting tools	4,125	5,519
Tools for soil preparation	2,850	2,234
Cover crops	3,346	4,370
Ploughs	4,599	6,014
Spraying tools	4,284	1,830
Trailers	2,969	3,013

Source: 1967–74: *Annuaire statistique d'Algérie*; 1975–7: MARA, Bilan du 2ème Plan Quadriennal.

which is a simple representative of the *aratrum* of the Romans. It is the oldest form of plough known in history and its form has remained basically the same, essentially a crooked stick. The cultivator takes hold of one end, and the other is shod with metal; the plough is drawn by a pair of draught animals, usually oxen.

To assist the private agriculturalists the state distributed free of charge during the second four-year plan 7,165 ploughing tools and instruments and 6,591 ploughs. However, this aid was insufficient; the private sector remained seriously under-equipped, a fact that hindered agricultural

Agriculture

Table 8.11 *Consumption of insecticides, fungicides and herbicides by the self-managed sector, 1970–7*

	Unit	1970–3	1974–7
Insecticides	Hectolitres	47,191	215,087
Fungicides	Quintals	3,210	5,012
Herbicides	Hectolitres	9,700	13,720

Source: S. Bedrani, *L'Agriculture algérienne depuis 1966* (Algiers, Office des Publications Universitaires, 1971), p. 41.

production. The agrarian revolution sector acquired more farm machinery and equipment between 1973 and 1977 than the private sector, for a smaller area. Table 8.10 summarises the statistical information available.

The utilisation of industrial inputs

The authorities in charge tried to encourage the planters and cereal and vegetable growers of the public and private sectors to utilise industrial input in order to increase production and to improve the quality of the products.

The state sector increased the quantity of industrial inputs, especially fertiliser, during the three plans of development. As a result, the consumption of fertiliser rose from 52 million 'fertilising units' in 1966 to 67.1 million in 1970, to 152.4 million in 1972 and 188.5 million in 1974, but fell to 166.1 million in 1977. In 1966 the self-managed sector utilised an annual average of 48 fertilising units per hectare, increasing to 110 in 1972, 131 in 1974 and 215 in 1978 (as against an annual average of 1,464 per hectare in Greece, 1,805 in Italy, 787 in Spain and 695 in Portugal). It becomes obvious now that the development of agriculture cannot be envisaged without the industrialisation of the country, especially the establishment of chemical, metallurgical and mechanical industries.

The consumption of insecticides, fungicides and herbicides by the sector evolved as shown in Table 8.11.

Although the exact use of fertiliser and other chemical inputs by the private sector is not very well known for the 1966–77 period, it was estimated that the consumption of fertiliser was as shown in Table 8.12 between 1969 and 1978.

The use of this vital input was far below the international norm. Furthermore, the annual quantity consumed kept declining from an

Post-independence development

Table 8.12 *Utilisation of chemical fertiliser by the private sector, 1969–78 (in 1,000 fertilising units)*

	Total fertilising units	Index base 100 in 1969
1969	8,350	110
1970	6,750	81
1971	15,800	189
1972	23,850	285
1977	37,172	445
1978	53,347	626

Source: 1969–73: MARA, *Bilan du 1er Plan Quadriennal*, 1977–8: *Statistique agricole* (1979 and 1980).

estimated total of 20,000 tons of fertilising units during the 1969–70 harvest season to 6,750 tons in 1970–1; it rose to 52,347 tons in 1978.

However, despite this relative increase in the utilisation of fertiliser, the private sector continued to trail behind the self-managed and agrarian revolution sectors. Although it comprised 59 per cent of the agricultural area by 1977–8, it utilised only 27.9 per cent of fertilisers consumed by agriculture, rising to 29.8 per cent in 1978–9. Nonetheless, this modest growth would not have occurred without state subsidies: between 1973 and 1977 alone, the government provided 40,260 private agriculturalists with 73,000 tons of fertiliser free of charge. But this quantity could fertilise only 91,000 hectares (at two quintals per hectare).

On the whole, when the government realised the growing demand for foodstuffs, especially cereals, it decided to distribute fertiliser free of charge to all the three sectors in order to intensify production. For example, during the second four-year plan (1973–7) the state's distribution proceeded as shown in Table 8.13.

Despite the government incentives, only 10 per cent of the private agriculturalists used fertiliser in the mid 1970s. However, the quantities consumed certainly increased between 1966 and 1977, particularly during the second four-year plan. The use of insecticides, fungicides and herbicides remained relatively insignificant, yet even there the consumption of the private sector rose slightly – the value of these products purchased by individual farmers increased during the 1971–9 period.

The mechanisation of agricultural production, which constitutes a *sine qua non* for modernisation, regressed between 1967 and 1977. Indeed, the total number of tractors possessed by each of the three sectors fell from

Table 8.13 *Distribution of fertiliser by the state to the three sectors of agriculture*

Total	Self-managed	Agrarian revolution	Private
Fertiliser (1,000 quintals) 1,176	40	406	730
Number of recipients 50,610	552	9,798	40,260
Number of recipients of insecticides, fungicides and herbicides 31,982	786	10,347	20,849
Selected seeds (Mexican wheat – 1,000 quintals) 509	24	160	325
Number of recipients 52,212	708	11,648	39,856

Source: MARA, *Bilan du 2ème Plan Quadriennal*.

Table 8.14 *The number of tractors owned by the three sectors, 1969–77*

Sector	1967	1972	1973	1977
Private sector	18,960	14,337	14,355	10,104
Self managed sector	18,762	17,251	18,974	18,764
SAP (Sociétés Agricoles de Prévoyance)	1,919	2,000	2,000	—
Production Co-operatives (Agrarian revolution)	—	—	1,458	5,954
CAPCS	—	—	651	4,578
Total	39,641	33,588	37,438	39,400

Source: MARA, *Bilan du 2ème Plan Quadriennal*.

39,641 in 1977 to 33,588 in 1972, rising to 39,400 by 1977 (old trailers and other farm machinery become obsolete or worn down). Table 8.14 provides further details.

The number of tractors owned by the private sector almost halved during the period under consideration. Although in certain regions up to 60 per cent of the farm machinery of the CAPCS was utilised in exchange for rent payment, the decrease in farm machinery possessed by the private agricultural sector had serious repercussions on production. The total number of tractors rose from 29,200 in 1959 to 39,400 by 1977. However, because of bureaucratic and technical deficiencies, a significant proportion of them were either too old and hence obsolete or out of service because of the lack of spare parts and experienced mechanics. In 1967, 19.76 per cent of the tractors of the self-managed sector were less than six years old, rising to 55 per cent by 1970 and 63 per cent by 1972, of which 17 per cent were out of service (as against 19.3 per cent in 1967).

Within the framework of the government's policy of 'intensification' of cereal production, the Ministry of Agriculture decided to introduce and generalise the so-called 'Mexican wheat' that was supposed to provide high returns. The area sown with Mexican wheat extended from 5,000 hectares in 1969 to 400,000 hectares in 1973, and to 600,000 hectares by 1977, including the private sector. However, results fell short of expectations. As in most of the third world countries, the 'green revolution' amounted to nothing because of the lack of an adequate industrial base, the archaism of the agrarian structure and the scarcity of qualified and skilled workers, which hindered the development of agriculture.

The development of animal husbandry through the import of cattle

Since peasant agriculture continued to depend largely on draught animals, its association with the keeping of livestock is vital for the economic survival of rural communities. However, in 1966 a plague almost eliminated farm horses and mules. In the late 1960s their numbers began to increase slowly. For instance, in 1954, Algerian farmers owned a total of 203,000 horses, declining to 124,000 during the 1966–9 period; the number increased to 139,000 during the 1970–3 period, 145,000 during the 1974–7 period and 149,000 in 1978. The number of mules declined from 595,000 to 489,000, rising to 533,000, 636,000 and 886,000.[8]

As a result, the state allocated a substantial amount of money to the import of milch cows. Because of the ineptitude of the leaders and managers of the sector, not even the targets for this were attained (see Table 8.15), which shows that only 35.7 per cent of the planned objectives were actually achieved. According to the Ministry of Planning, 'The absence of cattle-sheds in sufficient quantity constituted the principal obstacle for the development of livestock breeding in the public sector.'

Agriculture

Table 8.15 *Imports of cattle, 1967–77*

	1967–9	1970–3	1974–7	Total
Target	13,750	20,000	32,000	65,750
Actual	8,972	9,200	5,360	23,532
% of actual	65.2	46	16.75	35.7

Table 8.16 *The growth of livestock breeding on self-managed farms, 1967–77 (thousands)*

	1967	1968	1969	1970	1971	1972	1973	1974	1975	1976	1977
Cows	12.2	10.6	16.6	16.9	20.0	21.5	26.2	29.8	35.5	37.7	37.7
Sheep	125.0	75.8	80.9	88.3	101.5	153.9	205.2	223.0	246.2	246.7	279.8
Goats	3.0	0.8	0.9	0.3	0.3	0.2	0.3	0.6	0.4	0.4	0.5
Mares	—	—	—	1.1	1.3	1.1	1.1	1.1	0.8	0.7	0.9
Mules	14.0	8.5	10.2	6.2	6.8	5.6	6.0	5.7	5.5	5.1	4.6

Sources: MARA, 1967–9, *Statistique Agricole*, Series B; 1970–7, *Statistique Agricole*, Series grise, *Etudes et enquêtes*.

Nonetheless, the self-managed farms managed to increase their livestock. Table 8.16 summarises the evolution of animal husbandry of this sector. This table indicates that the number of milch cows more than tripled, while that of sheep nearly tripled. However, the needs of the rapidly growing population were increasing even faster. Fortunately the private sector took advantage of the rising meat prices to increase its numbers of livestock during this period (see Table 8.17).

These official statistics – which do not reflect the reality of the situation because private farmers and peasants have always under-reported the actual number of animals they own – indicate that the rate of growth between 1966 and 1976 was relatively very small compared with the rate of growth of the population, as well as the increasing demand for meat and dairy products in the country. Indeed, the number of milch cows rose by 22 per cent in ten years, sheep by 28 per cent and goats by only 5 per cent. On the whole the average annual growth rate of these animals did not exceed that of the population, which rose by an annual rate of 3.3 per cent during this period. The agrarian revolution sector possessed only 5,290 cows and 260,480 sheep by the end of 1979. The co-operators of this sector seemed to

Post-independence development

Table 8.17 *Livestock in the private sector, 1967–79 (thousands)*

	1967–9	1970–3	1974–7	1978	1979
Milch cows	481	541	607	719	777
Index base=1967–9	100	112	126	149	161
Sheep	4,242	4,862	5,498	6,164	7,106
Index	100	115	130	145	167
Goats	1,415	1,490	1,489	1,623	1,796
Index	100	105	105	115	126
Horses	99	113	112	111	124
Index	100	114	113	112	125

Sources: Statistiques agricole, Series A and B, several issues covering this period.

be attracted not by animal husbandry, but by the cultivation of basic crops for the market, which necessitates the development of irrigation.

The extension of irrigated areas

Since the amount of yearly agricultural harvest depended on the annual quantity of rainfall, the state decided that in order to increase production, the irrigated area must be widened. The leadership had set specific targets for the extension of irrigation, especially during the period of the two four-year plans, 1970–7. From 1970 to 1973, the state set itself the task of irrigating a total of 40,000 additional hectares. However, only 13,500 hectares, representing 34 per cent of the target, were actually added. During the second four-year plan, of a projected total of 80,000 hectares, only 20,000 hectares, or 25 per cent, were irrigated; and irrigated lands were lost to urbanisation and industrialisation.[9]

Indeed, in 1978, in an official document entitled *Bilan du 2ème Plan Quadriennal*, the Ministry of Agriculture, in an obvious attempt to cover up its inefficiency, estimated that 250,000 hectares of agricultural land, including 10,000 hectares of irrigated perimeters, had either been used and/or were about to be used for the extension of urban growth or industrial

Table 8.18 *Irrigated crops in the private agricultural sector, 1966–79 (average annual hectares)*

	1966	1967–9	1970–3	1974–7	1978	1979
Summer cereals	1,080	1,256	1,750	1,010	170	310
Winter cereals	74,490	71,043	59,142	18,447	3,330	3,110
Fruit trees	51,050	52,016	63,387	79,020	72,140	86,420
Vegetables	16,990	28,910	40,367	41,577	53,080	59,650
Industrial crops	1,170	1,586	2,425	1,825	2,160	2,350
Vineyards	920	853	1,147	1,415	470	500
Miscellaneous	3,420	2,603	3,480	3,862	3,950	4,170
Total	149,120	158,267	171,698	147,156	135,300	156,510
Index (100=1967–9)	94.2	100.0	108.5	93.0	86.0	98.0
Total without winter cereals	74,630	87,224	112,556	128,709	131,970	153,400

Source: MARA, *Statistique agricole*, Series A and B, several issues.

development. These highly exaggerated figures were refuted by a thorough study carried out by the Ministry of Light Industry.[10] The authors of this investigation concluded by conceding that only 25,000 hectares were already taken or about to be taken from agriculture, during the entire 1962–80 period, by industry and hydrocarbons. To be more precise, from 1962 to 1977 only 17,685 hectares were utilised by industry. The loss of irrigated land resulting particularly from the mobility of the people concerned to protect and maintain irrigation facilities was certainly aggravated by the loss of water resources, mostly to urban centres.

Nonetheless, the irrigated perimeters of the self-managed sector rose from an average annual area of 119,300 hectares during the 1967–70 period to 151,700 hectares during the 1973–3 period, falling to 140,000 hectares during the 1974–7 period and to 136,200 in 1978.[11] However, this rate of growth is quite insufficient. Moreover, according to Hamid Temmar,[12] the total area irrigated in the north alone increased from 104,000 hectares in 1966 to 112,000 in 1970 and 210,000 in 1973, falling to 200,000 in 1976.

The private agricultural sector was granted by the state-owned National Bank of Algeria (BNA) AD 98 million for the development of irrigation. But the amount of state loans to this sector declined drastically after 1973. However, private farmers continued to widen the areas cultivated with irrigated crops in the subsequent years as a result of self-financing investments in this field.

Table 8.19 *Sectoral distribution of irrigated areas, 1976*

	Self-managed	Agrarian revolution	Private	Total
Controlled irrigation				
In south	3,280	14,490	58,560	76,330
In north	14,500	113,460	72,460	200,420
Sub-total	17,780	127,950	131,020	276,750
Winter cereals	5,360	2,240	19,180	26,780
Total reported irrigation	23,140	130,190	150,200	303,530

Source: Banque Mondiale, *Algérie, Etude du secteur agricole* (1979).

The cultivation of irrigated crops by the private-sector farmers evolved as in Table 8.18 between 1966 and 1979.

The private sector took better advantage of the market conditions. Since prices of fruit and vegetables rose sharply the irrigated area cultivated with vegetables almost quadrupled between 1966 and 1979, while that of fruit trees extended from 51,050 hectares in 1966 to 86,420 hectares in 1979, a growth of 36 per cent. The irrigated areas of the agrarian revolution sector also expanded between 1973 and 1979 from 2,785 hectares to 47,040 hectares.

When a team from the World Bank carried out a technical analysis of the Algerian agricultural sector during the mid 1970s, the Ministry of Agriculture provided it with the statistical information in Table 8.19 concerning the respective irrigated areas of each sector.

Of these irrigated lands, fruit trees cover the widest area, 55.7 per cent of the total, followed by vegetable plantations, which extend over 28 per cent, and winter cereals with 8.8 per cent. Table 8.20 provides further details of the irrigated areas devoted to Algeria's basic agricultural crops.

According to this study, if Algeria completes the planned projects for water resource development, it would extend the total irrigated area to 680,000 hectares. Moreover, as pointed out above, a former minister of the Boumedienne government informed me in 1982 that another thorough study made by an international firm at the express demand of the former Ministry of Industry and Energy showed that if the country were to construct a network of interconnected high dams along the coast and to pump the water up to the high plateaus, no fewer than 800,000 hectares of land would be irrigated by the year 2000. The total cost of this project would amount to about $5 billion, which would develop a comparatively expensive agriculture. However, this comprehensive programme of

Agriculture

Table 8.20 *Basic irrigated crops of Algeria, 1976*

		%
Summer cereals	1,080	0.4
Winter cereals	26,780	8.8
Fruit trees	169,180	55.7
Vegetables	34,950	28.0
Industrial crops	6,890	2.3
Vineyards	8,580	2.8
Other	6,170	2.0
Total	253,630	100.0

Source: Banque Mondiale, *Algérie*.

irrigation would transform the Algeria of the years 2005–25, whose total population would by then exceed 35 million, into a country self-sufficient in food. When it was presented to the government in 1978 for the approval the Minister of Water Resources and Environment, a right-winger called Ahmed Ben Cherif, closely tied to *comprador* circles, opposed it. In an attempt to justify his opposition he exclaimed 'the implementation and completion of this scheme presupposes that Algerians must be as organised, skilled, disciplined and hard-working as the Germans'. Ben Chérif went as far as ordering the top executives to 'burn the documents containing this feasibility study' instead of trying to implement the project, which was, and remains to this very day, highly suited to the development of water resources and irrigation. Instead, the current regime brought in some US firms to implement an insignificant number of agricultural schemes in the desert similar to those developed in California. However, the US example shows that no country can have a viable agriculture without the continual development and expansion of a basic and adequate industry, which constitutes the *sine qua non* of the modernisation of society and hence the consolidation of national independence. In other words, by halting the industrialisation of the country the Benjadid regime had already undermined the necessary modernisation of agriculture.

Furthermore, given the climatic conditions prevalent in contemporary Algeria, the optimum utilisation of water resources is of vital importance to the provision of urban centres, industries and particularly agriculture. If unattended, unprotected and unpreserved Mediterranean soil, like that of Algeria, is as finite as oil, natural gas or any other mineral resource. Such impoverished soil needs to be improved and restored.

Post-independence development

Defence and restoration of the soil

As early as 1963 a programme of defence and restoration of the soil, better known as DRS, was launched. Its objective was to protect the soil against erosion and to improve its quality so that returns from the land would be raised. From 1963 to 1969, an annual average of only 7,000 hectares were actually restored and hence protected from further deterioration. To compensate for the destructive effects of erosion alone, an annual average of 40,000 hectares should be restored.

The private sector's performance during the first three-year plan was even worse than that of the public sector. Indeed, it managed to restore or renovate only about 11,000 hectares between 1967 and 1969, which amounted to an annual average of fewer than 3,700 hectares.

Aware of this high rate of erosion, the Council of Ministers assigned to the Ministry of Agriculture the objective of restoring and protecting one million hectares of land between 1970 and 1980, in areas receiving annual average rainfall of 400 mm. In the long term the government envisaged the prospect of reclaiming up to 80 per cent of the 29 million hectares of northern Algeria, of which 15 per cent needed immediate restoration and protection.[13]

Thus, from the first four-year period onwards, clearly defined objectives were assigned to the Ministry of Agriculture and the private sector. From 1970 to 1973, a total of 53,150 hectares were restored, or 59 per cent of the target. The public sector was responsible for 24,800 hectares and the rest were the work of the private farmers. During the second four-year plan the performance of both the state operators and private farmers improved markedly. Table 8.21 confirms this progress.

During this period the government devised a new programme of soil improvement whose method differs from that of DRS. This method consists of enriching the sub-soil. A total of 58,120 hectares were treated between 1974 and 1977, 58 per cent of which was done by the private sector, 37 per cent by the agrarian revolution sector and the remainder by the self-managed sector. In order to succeed these two methods require consistent effort at preserving all types of existing plants and trees, and introducing new ones.

A programme of reforestation was conceived as complementary to land reclamation and soil improvement. The authorities concerned believed firmly that in the long run the only solution to galloping erosion which has devastated the existing arable land would be the replanting of trees of various kinds. The government estimated that the long-term objective would be to reforest 4 million hectares of land; 2 million hectares on steep slopes that are favourable to reforestation; 0.5 million hectares in areas

Agriculture

Table 8.21 *Objectives and fulfilled targets of the second four-year plan in the protection and restoration of soil by sector, 1974–7*

	Self-management	Agrarian revolution	Private sector*	Total
Target	54,200	178,000	247,000	479,200
Actual	37,400	135,000	191,300	363,700
Rate of target fulfillment	69%	76%	77%	76%

* The state financed all of the private sector's operations for soil protection and restoration as well as 'soil improvement', which started during the 1974–7 period.
Source: MARA, *Bilan de l'exécution du 2e Plan Quadriennal* (1974).

Table 8.22 *Areas reforested, 1963–8*

Year	Government programmes	Popular campaigns	Total
1963	5,400	1,100	6,500
1964	7,000	3,700	10,700
1965	18,000	19,200	37,200
1966	7,500	11,900	19,400
1967	20,000	15,500	35,700
1968	21,000	14,900	35,900
Total	78,900	66,300	145,400

Source: Temmar, *Stratégie de Développement*, p. 78.

which were already designated for replanting before 1970; and 1.5 million hectares for the reconstitution of forests that were seriously damaged in the past.

From 1945 to 1969 only 163,000 hectares were reforested, 89 per cent of them after 1962. From 1963 to 1968 the government programmes and popular campaigns achieved the results shown in Table 8.22.

During the first four-year plan the government planned the reforestation of 335,000 hectares. However, only 64 per cent of the target was attained.

If compared to the second four-year plan, the period of the first four-year plan showed remarkable achievements in this field. Between 1974 and 1977 the government projected the reforestation of 735,000 hectares, divided

Post-independence development

between 335,000 hectares for the planned programmes, and 400,000 for the special programmes. However, only 166,000 hectares were replanted with trees, or 22.6 per cent of the target.

The main reasons for this were essentially administrative. In spite of official pronouncements emphasising the urgency and importance of a global policy of reforestation, the means and resources provided by the Ministry of Agriculture and other authorities concerned were utterly inadequate to satisfy the needs of the country. Besides, they were rendered totally inefficient by their mismanagement by the bureaucracy and the lack of qualified staff and workers; and the newly planted forests, which require a great deal of care and protection from fires and parasites in order to grow and mature, were left to themselves. Hence human effort and financial resources were almost entirely wasted.

The planting of fruit trees increased substantially. The total area planted with fruit trees, including vineyards, was 189,000 hectares during the 1966–9 period, 249,000 during the 1970–3 period and 289,000 during the 1974–7 period. The area devoted to olive trees grew by 55,000 hectares, palm trees by 19,000 hectares and other fruit trees, including vineyards, by about 26,000 hectares.[14] According to the Ministry of Agriculture a total of 115,000 hectares were planted with fruit trees between 1970 and 1977.[15] Even the new private-sector plantations were financed by the state. The substantial number of new fruit trees contributed both to ecological improvements and to the renewal of old plantations.

However, as will be shown, some of the major problems of Algerian agriculture were caused by the low skills of the work force, compounded by the inadequacy of top management in the state sector. The successive Ministers of Agriculture and the state bureaucracy which were supposed to promote the development of agricultural activities ended up by undermining the growth of this vital sector. They did not attempt to reverse negative trends, such as the ageing and 'disqualification' of the labour force, the wage gap between agriculture and the other sectors of the economy and the bureaucratisation of the agricultural environment, represented by the Ministry, the marketing boards, the banks and so on.

The lack of skilled workers, training and the problems of staffing and employment in agriculture

Because of the mediocrity and short-sightedness of the successive Ministers of Agriculture, the management of this sector has been unable to create the necessary conditions for its modernisation. This situation was not conducive to the emergence of a forceful development programme comparable to that of industry. The leaders and managers of this primary sector did not

Table 8.23 *Minimum wages, 1963–78 (AD)*

Sector	1963	1968–71	1972–3	1974–5	1976	1977	1978
Agricultural	7.54	8.0	9.8	12.25	15.30	20.00	28.00
Non-agricultural	10.86	—	13.84	16.64	19.20	25.28	33.68
Difference	3.32	—	4.04	4.39	3.90	5.28	5.68

Source: MARA, *L'Evolution de l'Agriculture.*

(and still do not) understand that the growth of agricultural production would not only necessitate the establishment of a modern basic mechanical and chemical industry in the country, but would also imply the industrialisation of agriculture itself. This would require, among other things, not only that skilled workers be induced to stay on the farms by offering them at least equal advantages with the workers of non-agricultural sectors, but also the opportunity to learn all the necessary skills associated with the development of agriculture. The political short-sightedness of the Ministry of Agriculture is evidenced by its wages policy. Indeed, not only were the wages of the agricultural workers frozen for over ten years, but they were lower than those of workers in other sectors. Table 8.23 summarises the evolution of the minimum wage for one eight-hour working day between 1963 and 1978.

In 1974, a presidential decree was promulgated which made the minimum wage of all sectors the same. Yet the authorities in charge of the agricultural sector did not insist on its prompt implementation. Since no protective measure was taken to provide some additional incentives designed to reward the direct producers for increasing agricultural production, a growing number of the skilled young workers were pushed out of agriculture by the bureaucracy of this sector.

By the late 1970s only a 'residual' labour force remained on the farms. Indeed, the 1972–3 agricultural census revealed that 32.9 per cent of the workers of this sector were more than 59 years old, compared to 23.6 per cent in 1968. In strategic areas this situation was even worse. For example, on certain workers' self-managed farms in the Mitidja, one of the most fertile areas in the country, the proportion of permanent workers over 60 years of age increased from 15 per cent in 1971 to 39 per cent in 1973.

This state of affairs was aggravated by the high rate of illiteracy and the low levels of skills of this 'residual' agricultural manpower. For instance, in 1968, 84 per cent of the heads of farming units were illiterate and during the 1968–72 period 83 per cent of the permanent agricultural labourers of the Mitidja could not read or write. About 76 per cent of the heads of farming

Table 8.24 *The number of agronomists and technicians qualifying, 1967–77*

	1967–9	1970–3	1974–7	1977
Engineer-agronomists	—	341	2,049	327
Technicians	188	1,490	2,309	842

Source: MARA, *L'Evolution de l'Agriculture*, vol. 2.

units in this area were also completely illiterate.[16] In 1975–6, 81 per cent of the total national agricultural labour force remained illiterate.[17] The 1977 census revealed that 71.1 per cent of the rural population were still illiterate.

In order to upgrade the skills of these agricultural workers who were supposed to self-manage the modern farms inherited from the settlers, the authorities in charge of the sector proceeded to set up specialised training institutions, particularly after 1966. Indeed, from 1962 to 1966 only an institute of agronomy which specialised in the training of agronomists and technicians of agriculture existed. It trained 82 agronomists and 137 technicians during this period. In addition, 462 technical agents and 12,586 assistant managers, clerks, accountants, and so on were trained in various establishments. However, the needs of the state sector alone were estimated in 1966 to be 3,870 agronomists, 10,000 technicians and 30,000 technical agents.[18]

From 1967 to 1971, the centres of vocational training for adults trained 12,340 persons, which fell far short of the 30,000 needed. However, from 1972 onwards there was a serious effort to train people. Table 8.24 gives details of the number of agronomists and technicians who qualified between 1967 and 1977.

About 70 per cent of the target for the training of agronomists was attained during the first four-year plan (1970–3), but only 30 per cent of that for the training of technical agents and skilled workers. As can be seen, the authorities in charge neglected the training of middle-level staff, technicians and skilled workers. For instance, in 1971, the technical agents formed 78 per cent of all staff, falling to 53.5 per cent by 1977. The proportion of agronomists rose from 8 per cent to 21.3 per cent, and that of technicians from 14 to 30 per cent during the same period.[19]

Unfortunately, the system of education that trained these agronomists and technicians inculcated in them the 'mentality of the cadres' (or the privileged), a fact that induced them to exhibit a negative attitude towards manual labour and a feeling of superiority over the field workers.[20]

This prevented them from resolving the serious technical problems of

Agriculture

Table 8.25 *The structure of agricultural employment, 1966–77*

	1966	1977
Employers (units)	4,981	1,594
Independent farming units	362,384	255,252
Co-operators	—	74,252
Permanent workers	212,824	192,604
Seasonal workers	571,475	114,000
Home helps	145,732	52,768
Trainees	40	742
Not reported	1,627	678
Unemployed	—	328,174
Total	1,299,063	1,020,064

Source: Les Recensements, 1966 and 1977.

agriculture in collaboration with the field workers by capitalising on the latter's experience. After they had qualified, the authorities in charge assigned them, in many cases, to administrative and managerial tasks instead of in the productive units. According to a survey, of 200 agronomists and 400 technicians studied, none of the former and only a dozen of the latter were actually assigned to work on the farms. By 1977 only 52 agronomists and 60 technicians were actually working in the productive units, representing 2.4 per cent of the agronomists and 2.3 per cent of the technicians employed by the public agricultural sector. The rest of them were performing bureaucratic tasks, which amounted in many instances to the administrative control of the labour force employed by the workers' self-management committees.

The modernisation of agricultural production has resulted, in both the advanced capitalist and socialist countries, in the transfer of the labour force from the primary sector to the secondary and tertiary sectors. This trend is apparent in Algeria, where agricultural employment has been declining since 1962. Between 1966 and 1977 the structure of agricultural employment was as shown in Table 8.25. Agricultural employment decreased by 278,727, that is, 21.4 per cent of the total population employed in this primary sector of the economy. The table shows that about one-third of the active rural population remained jobless in 1977; in addition, a large proportion continued to be underemployed.

Overlooking the striking fact that since the 1920s the 'push-factors' (landlessness, redundancy and underemployment) have been more decisive than the 'pull-factors', the critics of the Boumedienne strategy of development attributed the continuation of the agricultural exodus to the indus-

Post-independence development

trialisation drive. According to these critics, industry had attracted agricultural workers by creating jobs and offering higher wages and other advantages. The development of a modern country could not be based upon agriculture: not only because any meaningful development of this primary, relatively backward sector requires the existence of a basic industry, but also because its modernisation implies the utilisation of labour-saving means of production and hence a large number of the rural active population must be transferred to the secondary and tertiary sectors. This could not be achieved without the industrialisation of the nation, which constitutes the *sine qua non* not only for the development of the economy but also and particularly for the growth of agricultural production.

The evolution of agricultural production between 1967 and 1978

Because of the lack of water for irrigation, Algerian agricultural production continued to be dependent on weather conditions, with the direct result that the volume of crops harvested at the end of every harvest season fluctuated from one year to the other. For example, the annual production of cereals averaged 18.7 million quintals during the three-year plan (1967–9), 19.3 million quintals during the first four-year plan (1970–3) and 19 million quintals during the second four-year plan (1974–7). However, the total annual yield of these crops varied from 16.4 million quintals in 1967 to 26.8 million quintals in 1975 and to 11.4 million quintals in 1977.

Consequently, the yield per unit area varied from one year to the next and one sector to another. For instance, during the 1974–5 harvest season the returns varied from an average of 8.3 quintals per hectare in the workers' self-management sector to 5.6 quintals in the agrarian revolution sector and 5.2 quintals in the private sector.

The stagnation of cereal production coincided with a growing demand for cereals, a fact that contributed to the multiplication of cereal imports. Between 1967 and 1978 the volume of imports of cereals tripled. In 1967, imports satisfied only 23 per cent of the national demand, rising to 60 per cent in 1978. In 1967 for every 100 kg of flour and semolina consumed in Algeria, 28 kg were imported. By 1978 the imported proportion reached 65.5 kg out of every 100 consumed. The annual average imports of cereals between 1967 and 1978 were as follows:

1966–9	7.4 million quintals
1970–3	8.0 million quintals
1974–7	16.1 million quintals
1978	22.1 million quintals

Source: Ministère de la Planification et de l'Amènagement du Territoire, *Bilan économique et social (1967–78).*

Table 8.26 *Vegetable production, 1967–78 (1,000 quintals)*

Crop	1967	1978	Average annual growth rate (%)
Potatoes	2,035	4,729	8.0
Tomatoes	691	1,043	4.0
Melons and watermelons	1,357	1,420	Negligible
Onions	387	901	8.0
Artichokes	269	206	Regression
Carrots	385	329	Regression
Green beans	66	66	Stagnation
Other vegetables	532	1,643	10.5

Source: MPAT, *Bilan économique.*

The production of wine

From 1962 to 1977 about 150,000 hectares of vineyards were reconverted into cereal and vegetable crops and fruit tree plantations. However, the substitution of these crops and plantations has created more human and economic problems than it has solved. By 1979, the area cultivated was 208,570 hectares. However, the level of productivity per unit area declined from 45 hectolitres per hectare in 1961 to 21 in 1975 and 9.9 in 1978. The total quantity of wine produced decreased from 15.6 million hectolitres in 1975 to 1.8 million by 1979.

The production of dry vegetables

The production of dry vegetables had increased noticeably during the period. However, because of growing demand, the state had to resort to imports. The annual average production of dry vegetables rose from 404,000 quintals during the 1967–9 period to 440,000 quintals during the 1970–3 period and 667,000 quintals during the 1974–7 period. Between 1967 and 1977 the annual growth rate averaged 5 per cent. The bulk of this progress was achieved during the 1973–7 period, when the annual growth rate averaged 12 per cent.

As a result of the growth of production of dry vegetables, the volume of imports declined from an annual average of 54,000 quintals during 1967–9 to 37,300 quintals during the period of the first four-year plan. In other words, imports represented an annual average of 12 per cent of the national consumption during the 1967–9 period and only 9 per cent from 1970–3. However, between 1974 and 1977 the imports of dry vegetables averaged

Post-independence development

402,000 quintals per year, or 38 per cent of national consumption. By 1978, 44 per cent of local demand was satisfied by imports.

The production of green vegetables

The production of fresh green vegetables increased from 654,000 tons in 1967 to 1,045,000 tons in 1978 – an annual average growth rate of 5 per cent. Potatoes, tomatoes, melons, watermelons and onions represented 80 per cent of vegetable production in 1978. Table 8.26 summarises the evolution of vegetable production between 1967 and 1978. During the 1967–9 period the country was self-sufficient in fresh green vegetables. During the first four-year plan an annual average of 7 per cent of national consumption was imported from abroad, rising to 8 per cent during the 1974–7 period, that is, from an annual average of 450,000 quintals in 1970–3 to 970,000 in 1974–7. By 1978 close to 10 per cent of national consumption was imported.

The production of fruit

Fruit, date and olive production grew slightly or stagnated during the period under consideration. Table 8.27 summarises annual average production between 1967 and 1977.

Similarly, the production of industrial crops either progressed or stagnated, and even declined in some instances. The production of processed tomatoes rose from an annual average of 37,400 tons between 1967 and 1973 to 70,900 tons between 1974 and 1977. The production of tobacco decreased from 6,000 tons between 1967 and 1969 to 3,500 tons during the 1970–3 period and 2,500 tons from 1974 to 1977. Sugar beet also declined, from an annual average of 73,400 tons during the three-year plan to 56,100 tons during the first four-year plan, rising slightly to 57,300 tons during the second four-year plan. Consequently, sugar imports rose sharply from an annual average of 215,000 tons during the 1967–9 period to 240,000 tons during the 1967–9 period, 370,000 tons during the 1974–7 period and 420,000 tons in 1978. In other words, imports provided 95 per cent of the national consumption of sugar in the 1967–9 period and 98 per cent in 1978.

In sum, since agricultural production stagnated or even regressed in some cases, the state had to resort to importation to feed the population. This resulted in growing food dependence; and Algeria, which has been a pastoral country since time immemorial, became an importer of meat from the 1960s.

Agriculture

Table 8.27 *Annual average production of fruits, dates and olives, 1967–77 (million quintals)*

	1967–9	1970–3	1974–7
Fruits	6.20	5.84	6.20
Dates	1.60	1.30	1.50
Olives	1.42	1.49	1.77

Source: MPAT, *Bilan économique*.

Livestock

The bulk of Algerian livestock are privately owned. State intervention aimed particularly at the development of large-scale poultry-farming units. The main problem of animal husbandry in Algeria was connected with the fact that two-thirds of the herd were breeding milch-cows, 95 per cent of which were local stock; improvement through cross-breeding with European stock progressed slightly during the period under study. Since Algeria has specialised in dairying, beef production has developed little in recent years.

Milk production rose from 482 million litres in 1968 to 700 million by 1977, representing an annual average rate of growth of 5.0 per cent. Because of a high rate of demographic growth and the improvement of the living conditions of the population, this local milk production was insufficient to satisfy the national demand. Hence the authorities concerned had to resort to imports: in 1968 Algeria imported 213 million litres of milk from abroad, rising to 302 million by 1973 and 677 million in 1977. The annual rate of growth of milk importation averaged 14 per cent during the period under study. The contribution of imports to the national consumption of milk increased from 31 per cent in 1968 to 35 per cent in 1973 and 19 per cent in 1977, when, for every 100 litres of milk consumed in the country, 49 litres were imported from abroad.

Meat and poultry production

Meat and poultry production increased from 100,000 tons in 1968 to 127 tons in 1973 and 188,000 tons in 1977. The annual average growth rate was 7 per cent (13 per cent for poultry production) during the period. For poultry the country managed to remain self-sufficient up to 1978; however, meat imports rose rapidly between 1967 and 1978. In 1968 Algeria imported only 5,000 tons of meat, rising to 100,000 tons in 1977.

Table 8.28 *Annual average imports and exports of foodstuffs, 1966–77 (million AD)*

	1966	1967–9	1970–3	1974–7
Imports: (value)	731	731	925	4,049
Index (base=1967–9)	—	100	127	554
Exports: (value)	931	717	736	612
Index	—	100	103	85

Source: MPAT, *Statistique agricole* (various issues).

Nonetheless, national production continued to meet the bulk of local demand. In 1968 1 per cent of consumption was supplied by imports, increasing to 11 per cent by 1977.

Egg production too failed to keep pace with the rapid growth of demand. In 1968 Algeria produced 10,500 tons of eggs, rising to 12,000 tons in 1973 and 15,000 tons by 1977. As a direct result of this, the importation of eggs increased considerably during the period. Indeed, imports went up from 500 tons in 1968 to 13,400 tons by 1977, that is, by a factor of nearly 2.7. Imports accounted for only 5 per cent of national consumption in 1968, rising to 47 per cent by 1977.

Thus, confronted with stagnating agricultural production and with rapid growth in demand, accentuated by one of the world's highest demographic growth rates, as well as by the improvement in the level of consumption of the population as a whole, the authorities opted for an easy solution: importation of food from abroad instead of a policy for the development of food production. The immediate consequences were a critical food dependence and a concomitant growth in the value of food imports. The import and export of agricultural products are summarised in Table 8.28.

The widening gap between the supply of foodstuffs and the demand for them was caused by two essential factors: population growth (3.2 per cent per year) and a popular policy of income distribution and employment. The population rose from 12.5 million in 1967 to 17 million in 1977 and 18.3 million by 1980. Thus, between 1967 and 1980 the country had to feed more than 6 million additional persons. The number of employed individuals increased from 1.7 million in 1967 to 2.3 million in 1977, reaching 3 million in 1980. As a direct result, the disposable income of households rose from AD 15.5 billion in 1969 to AD 75.4 billion in 1979 (see Table 8.29).

As will be seen, the total income of wage- and salary-earners increased by a factor of 10.8 in less than 12 years. This would not have been possible without the industrial development of the country at that time. However,

Agriculture

Table 8.29 *Growth of household income, 1969–79 (million AD)*

	1969	1973	1977	1979
Wages paid	7.4	12.1	26.1	46.0
Income of entrepreneurs	5.0	6.7	11.0	21.5
Transfers	3.1	6.6	7.0	7.9
Total	15.5	25.4	44.1	75.4

Source: MPAT, *Comptes économiques*.

the authorities of the agricultural sector failed to modernise and develop agriculture in order to meet the growing demand for food, a fact that ended up by undermining the process of industrialisation itself. Indeed, large sums were spent on food imports instead of being invested in productive activities. By 1978 the total value of food imports (excluding butter and oil), exceeded AD 5 billion, about one-fifth of the value of hydrocarbon exports. Thus, the situation of agriculture was, and remains to this very day, catastrophic. As in most third world countries, the problem of Algerian agriculture has become so grave that it would be impossible to solve in the short term. It was caused primarily by the non-utilisation of credits earmarked for agricultural development, an inadequate price policy for agricultural products and a stifling bureaucratic interventionism by the Ministry of Agriculture, the National Bank of Algeria and innumerable national boards that, instead of providing the indispensable services for the normal functioning and development of the sector, ended up nearly choking agriculture to death.

Chapter 9

Education and development

The experience of industrialised societies, capitalist and socialist alike, indicates that in modern times education and vocational training have played a major role in their social, economic, technological and cultural development. The growth of education was closely related to the process of industrialisation and technological innovation. Industrialisation has necessitated a far wider range of occupations requiring the acquisition of technical expertise and scientific knowledge as well as a host of social skills that are crucial to the management of productive activities, to the running of basic services and to the administration of society as a whole.

Thus, the process of industrialisation generates an increasing demand for ever higher levels of technical, scientific and liberal education. Educational and vocational training institutions have to keep pace not only with technological innovations, the endless accumulation of technical expertise and scientific and non-scientific knowledge, but also with the socio-economic development of the country, by providing it with highly trained workers, technicians, engineers, scientists, managers, administrators, writers, artists and social scientists. However, these institutions cannot fulfil their functions without long-term planning. Because of the dialectical relations between education, economy and society, a planned development requires 'the output of skilled people' whose training must be consciously geared to the economic and social priorities of the society. In accordance with such developmental requirements, independent Algeria set up a four-tier educational system based upon primary schools, middle schools, high schools and universities and other specialised institutions of higher education.

At first the authorities of the newly independent state tried to adjust the colonial educational system to the new situation while preparing for reform. By the mid 1970s the new Algerian system of education consisted of a primary education of six years for the 6–13 age group; an intermediate education of four years, a secondary education of three years and a university education of four years. Despite its democratisation, this system remained highly selective. The passage not only from one level to the next but also from one year to the next was by taxing examinations.

Education and development

Because of a high rate of pupil failure in examinations, which resulted in a growing number of dropouts, and also because of the inadequacy of this system, the authorities decided in 1974–5 to introduce a radical reform of primary and intermediate education. These levels were combined into one single level of nine years, called the 'fundamental polytechnical school'. This reform was implemented in 1979–80.

When this reform was put forward the government stated that the tasks of the educational system were many. It must ensure the development of the child's and citizen's personality and his preparation for active life; ensure the acquisition of general scientific and technological knowledge; and respond to people's aspirations for justice and progress.

Furthermore, this reform bill stressed that every Algerian has the right to education and vocational training. Education is compulsory for all school-age children from 6 to 13 years. The state guarantees equal opportunity for the admission of pupils to post-primary education. Education is free at every level and in every type of educational institution. Arabic must be used as the medium of instruction at all levels, in vocational training centres and in all subjects.

The expansion of education in the post-independence period, 1962–79

One of the major obstacles to the development of the country in the post-independence period was a high rate of illiteracy among the population. In 1944 only 8.8 per cent of Algerian school-age children were enrolled in schools, rising to 14.6 per cent by 1954. By 1961 only 300,500 Algerian children were attending school. The number of school-age children (6–13) who were not receiving education was estimated at 1.5 million.

It is no wonder that by 1966, close to 6 million Algerians over the age of ten were completely illiterate. About 75 per cent of the population were illiterate. The rate of illiteracy varied in accordance with age, sex, socio-economic status and region. For example, in the age group 0 to 14 years, 49 per cent were illiterate, as against 95 per cent for the age group 55 and above; 63.3 per cent of the males were illiterate, compared with 85.9 per cent of the females; 89 per cent of farmers could not read and write, as against 64.5 per cent of industrialists, traders and artisans. Table 9.1 shows the geographical distribution of illiteracy within the country. The rate of illiteracy also varied within the provinces themselves. In the peasant villages the rate averaged 88.4 per cent, while it was 78.6 per cent in the small towns of the interior and 59.6 per cent in the urban provincial capitals.

Thus, from the outset, the new authorities of the educational system

Table 9.1 *Geographical distribution of illiteracy, 1966*

Province	Rate of illiteracy	Province	Rate of illiteracy
Algiers	55.9	Oran	63.7
Annaba	—	Saida	85.1
Aurès	79.2	Saoura	80.4
Constantine	75.3	Setif	80.1
El Asnam	83.5	Tiaret	83.9
Medea	86.0	Tizi Ouzou	75.3
Mostaganem	77.8	Tlemcen	75.3
Oasis	77.5		

Source: RGPH, 1966.

were faced with a difficult task. They had to reform the colonial educational system in order to adapt it to the new situation and to attempt gradually to set up a new system capable of providing modern basic instruction for a rapidly growing number of school-age children. The educational system inherited from the colonial power was French in its programmes, orientation, tradition and language, and a large proportion of its teachers were French.

The pre-existing educational infrastructure could accommodate during the 1962–3 school year only 777,636 children at the primary level, 30,790 pupils at the middle school level, 19,999 students at the high school level and 3,718 students at the university level. Since the French teaching staff and administrators had left the country, the question of 'Algerianisation' was raised from the outset. Indeed, 27,000 out of 30,000 colonial teachers fled Algeria in the summer of 1962. To replace them, innumerable Algerian teachers, instructors and monitors were recruited.

Despite an intensive recruitment drive Algerian teaching staff represented 64 per cent of teachers needed by primary schools. In order to resolve this staffing problem, the requirements for recruitment were ignored, which was bound to affect the quality of education provided. But there was no alternative. Out of the 19,908 new teachers, including foreigners, 22 per cent were classified as teachers, 41 per cent as instructors and 37 per cent as monitors. In other words, only one-fifth possessed the necessary qualifications to teach; most recruits had no teaching experience.

The curriculum of the secondary schools was characterised (from the sixth grade onwards) by two co-existing programmes. A programme of general education prepared the pupils for higher education and a technical education programme of a shorter duration specialised in teaching basic skill to the less successful. But once they obtained a *Certificat d'aptitude professionnelle*, they were cast on to the labour market without any possibility of continuing their education further. So-called technical education was reserved for the victims of a highly selective educational system. Because of this the Algerian authorities were compelled to devise some partial reforms in order to try to adapt this inherited system to the new conditions, that is, to meet the requirements of development and modernisation. Indeed the Tripoli programme of the FLN stressed that 'Algerian culture will be national, revolutionary and scientific'.

As early as 1962, a Higher Commission for the Reform of Education was established. During its first meeting on 31 December 1962, the essential objectives of the future Algerian system of education were defined as follows: progressive Algerianisation and Arabisation; unification and homogenisation of the system; emphasis upon vocational, technical and scientific training; and democratisation and universalisation of primary education.

Algerianisation of the teaching staff

The Algerianisation of the teaching staff was one of the major preoccupations of the authorities in charge. The number of foreign teachers was decreased from 7,212 out ot 19,908 in 1962–3, to 4,859 out of 36,255 in 1968–9 and to 984 out of 76,025 by 1977–8, or 1.3 per cent of the total. The Algerianisation of the administration was achieved earlier than that of the teaching personnel and curricula. The Algerianisation of the curricula came about empirically and unevenly; certain subjects such as history and geography were not only Algerianised but also progressively Arabised. By the late 1960s a significant number of text books were already written by Algerian teachers in order to adapt their content to the national historical reality. For example, the teaching of the French language was modified by introducing as basic reading texts written by Algerian authors.

In order to prevent the standards of education from deteriorating, the authorities responsible attempted to remedy the existing deficiencies by setting up special programmes designed to upgrade the quality of teachers. To achieve this goal teacher handbooks for in-service training were prepared. They explained to the inexperienced instructors and monitors the purpose of a course, how it should be taught and how the interest of the pupils can be aroused and maintained. Most of these teaching staff consisted of the dropouts of the system, that is, those who failed to pass their examinations at the end of middle school and high school.

Through these in-service training programmes innumerable instructors and monitors were upgraded, promoted and tenured. The number of certified teachers of primary education rose from 3,286 in 1962-3 to 16,260 by 1977-8, and that of instructors increased from 9,366 to 44,869 during the same period. Despite this progress, the problem of teacher training continued to plague primary education up to the late 1970s, when finally several institutes of education (*instituts de technologie de l'education*) were completed and began training teachers. The progressive Algerianisation was accompanied by the gradual introduction of Arabic as the language of instruction.

Arabisation

The Arabisation of primary education began as early as 1962-3, when the teaching of the Arabic language was made compulsory in all the programmes and at every level. The newly established curriculum devoted seven hours per week to Arabic, and the time allocated to the teaching of the French language was reduced. In addition, by 1964-5 the first grade was entirely Arabised. In the other grades the time assigned to teaching in Arabic was increased from seven to ten hours per week. Mathematics was taught in the first grade in Arabic and from the second grade onwards in French. By 1967-8 the second grade was also Arabised completely, and from then on both in the first and second grades of primary education, 20 hours of teaching were done in Arabic. As a result the number of teachers who taught in Arabic rose from 3,432 in 1962-3 to 22,797 in 1969-70 and to 49,128 by 1976-7, representing 69.60 per cent of all teachers, while the number teaching in French increased only from 16,456 to 21,370 during the same period. For the third and fourth grades, 15 hours of teaching were done in Arabic and 20 hours in French. Thus, despite the progressive introduction of Arabic as a medium of instruction at the lower grades of primary education, the French language continued to prevail in the fifth and sixth grades up to the late 1970s.

Prior to 1971 the Arabisation of education proceeded both horizontally and vertically, that is, by subject-matter and by grade. Gradually a dual system emerged and took shape, particularly at the middle and high school levels. The authorities concerned created two sections: a bilingual section and an Arabic section. In the former the pupils were taught scientific subjects in French and other subjects in Arabic, while in the latter they were taught all subjects in Arabic, and French was taught as a foreign language. Since the best Algerian teachers used French as their medium of instruction, the pupils in the bilingual section received a better education. Furthermore, bilingualism contributed to the career success of the graduates of this section. By 1979, over 70 per cent of the teaching staff were teaching in Arabic. In the middle schools, 52.6 per cent of the students were studying in Arabic and in high schools, 57.1 per cent.

In short, the policy of Arabisation was applied empirically, that is, without taking into consideration the basic requirements for its success. The error turned out to be costly in human, social and economic terms. In the absence of qualified teachers, adequate textbooks, laboratories, and even classrooms, the quality of education was impaired, a fact that undermined particularly the scientific and technical option. For example, in the secondary and intermediate cycles the number of pupils who chose non-scientific and non-technical subjects increased by 54.3 per cent during the 1974–8 period. Enrolment in scientific and technical education rose by an insignificant 1.6 per cent during the same period. The proportion of Arabised pupils preparing for their high school diplomas (*baccalauréat*) in mathematics and science fell from 42.5 per cent of the total in 1974 to 28.8 per cent in 1977. In a country like Algeria the dissemination and mastery of modern science and technology constitute a *sine qua non* for a genuine socio-economic development for the benefit of the people.

Scientific and technical subjects

Despite the official emphasis on the teaching of modern sciences and techniques at every stage of education, the authorities failed to attract students to secondary technical schools. They went as far as transforming existing schools into either middle or high schools offering a general education.

Prior to the 1971 reform of education, the so-called priority given to science and technology amounted to a simple modification of the teaching schedule. The number of hours devoted to science and mathematics courses was increased. For instance, mathematics took up 22 per cent of the pupils' time. At one time the authorities transformed about 30 high schools into experimental establishments in which the teaching of technology was emphasised rather than the general classical education that prepared the students for admission into the universities. However, this experience was discontinued. This failure explains in part the decline in the number of students attending middle and secondary technical schools after 1973.

Thus, contrary to the national objectives of development and the so-called scientific and technical bias of educational policy, the number of pupils in technical education declined from 72,549 in 1973–4 to 11,806 in 1976–7. The level of secondary school enrolment in general classical education increased by 85.7 per cent between 1974 and 1978, while enrolment in technical education rose by only 16.4 per cent.

As will be seen, this resulted in marked shortages of skilled and technical

Post-independence development

workers which have continued to hinder the development of the country to the present time. Indeed, while the demand for middle-level manpower was increasing at a very rapid pace, because of the industrialisation of the country, the partisans of the former association of the Algerian *ulumah* who controlled the Ministry of Education proceeded to dismantle technical education. This created serious manpower shortages for the economic sectors and for basic technical services.

The closing of the technical schools was presented by the education authorities of the time as a necessary measure designed to enhance the 'democratisation of education'. Indeed, during the colonial period technical education was reserved for pupils coming from the underprivileged social classes and strata. This historical background was used as a pretext for transforming a significant number of secondary technical schools into middle and high schools.

The democratisation of education

Because of the popular character of the national movement that led the country to independence as well as the socio-economic conditions of the bulk of the population, the universalisation of education implied its democratisation. To be more precise, the state had to try to guarantee equal opportunity for all children by offering financial aid to pupils and students coming from the popular strata. As a result of a serious effort to universalise education, the rate of school attendance of school-age children (6-13 years of age) rose from about 25 per cent in 1962-3 to 71.05 per cent by 1977-8 (83.8 per cent for boys and 58.3 per cent for girls). This fell short of the first four-year plan (1970-3), which projected that by 1973-4 all 6-year-old children and by 1978 all school-age youngsters would be attending classes. The high rate of demographic growth rendered this target unattainable.

The number of pupils enrolled in primary schools increased from 777,737 in 1962-3 to 1,323,203 in 1965-6, of whom 504,552 were girls. Table 9.2 summarises enrolment in primary schools between 1966-7 and 1977-8.

This rapid growth of enrolment in primary education did not keep pace with the increase in population. Indeed, the total number of school-age children rose from about 2.43 million in 1962-3 to 2.87 million in 1966-7 and 4 million in 1977-8.

The number of students in the middle and high schools combined rose from 51,014 in 1962-3 to 100,082 in 1964-5 (71,379 boys and 28,703 girls). For later years, see Table 9.3.

The proportion of girls increased from 20 per cent in 1966 to 37 per cent by 1979-80. During this school year the number of pupils in secondary schools reached 90,000. The annual average growth of enrolment in the

Education and development

Table 9.2 *Pupil enrolment in primary education, 1966–78*

Year	Boys	Per cent	Girls	Per cent	Total
1966–7	857,242	62.6	513,115	37.4	1,370,357
1969–70	1,058,153	62.6	630,870	37.4	1,689,023
1972–3	1,351,862	61.2	855,031	38.8	2,206,893
1976–7	1,653,885	59.4	1,128,159	40.6	2,782,044
1977–8	1,712,508	59.2	1,181,576	40.8	2,894,084

Source: Ministère de l'Education, *Bilan* (December 1979).

Table 9.3 *Secondary school pupils, 1966–78*

	1966–7	1969–70	1972–3	1976–7	1977–8
Middle schools	145,363	199,708	307,198	488,293	596,652
High schools	18,196	34,139	53,655	124,626	145,066
Total	163,559	233,847	360,853	612,919	741,718

Source: MPAT, *Bilan économique*.

middle schools was 12.9 per cent during the 1967–77 period (11.2 per cent during the three-year plan, 15.4 per cent during the first four-year plan and 12.3 per cent during the second four-year plan). The annual average growth rate in high schools was 17 per cent during the 1970–7 period, 12.8 per cent during the first four-year plan and 23.5 per cent during the second four-year plan.

The Algerianisation of the teaching staff of the middle and high schools did not progress as fast as in primary education. Nonetheless, the proportion of Algerians rose, as Table 9.4 shows, from 32.8 per cent in 1967–8 to 81.6 per cent in 1977–8.

Because of the high rate of population growth the universalisation and democratisation of education required considerable human and financial resources. For instance, the number of primary schools increased from 2,759 in 1962–3 to over 8,000 in 1977; that of high schools from 30 to 175; teachers' institutes from 6 to 50. By 1976–7 the number of middle schools reached 806. Between 1970 and 1978, over 14,000 classrooms out of a planned 32,097 were in use.

It is no wonder that by the mid 1970s about 30 per cent of the national budget was devoted to education and vocational training. For example,

Post-independence development

Table 9.4 *Algerian teachers in middle and high schools, 1967–78*

Year	Middle school teachers	Per cent of total	High school teachers	Per cent of total
1967–8	2,227	32.8	1,098	36.8
1970–1	3,256	46.8	1,397	44.5
1974–5	7,516	67.0	2,077	44.0
1977–8	16,053	81.6	3,286	46.7

Source: MPAT, *Avant-projet de bilan social, 1967–78* (December 1979).

capital investment in educational infrastructure rose from AD 170 million in 1964, representing 15.4 per cent of the state's total capital investment, to AD 665 million in 1963, comprising 15.9 per cent of the state's capital investment, and reached AD 1 billion in 1977, amounting to 7.8 per cent of the state's capital investment. The operating expenditure of the Ministry of National Education increased from AD 323 million in 1963, representing 11 per cent of the state's operating costs, to AD 980 million in 1970, comprising 22 per cent of the government's operating expenditure, and to AD 2.8 billion in 1977, which amounted to 17.5 per cent of the state's operating budget. In sum, over AD 24 billion was spent on education in 14 years (1963–77); AD 8 billion was devoted to operating costs and AD 6 billion to capital investment for the establishment of the necessary infrastructure. These total costs averaged over AD 1.7 billion per year during the period under consideration.

To assist the children from poor families, the state provided scholarships, free meals, textbooks, and school clothing. For instance, in 1970, 700,000 sets of school clothing were distributed free of charge. In 1975, 61.33 per cent of the pupils attending middle and high schools were on government scholarships. But this percentage fell in relative terms to 52.9 per cent in 1978, even though the total number of pupils had increased significantly. Since education is totally free these scholarships were intended to provide their beneficiaries with living expenses.

In sum, the main goal of democratisation of education was to create favourable conditions for the pupils and students coming from 'popular origins' so that they could have access to all stages of the educational system, including the university. However, despite undeniable progress, the government failed to provide equal educational opportunities for all children, regardless of their social and geographical origins. Indeed, most of the students who received higher education came from educated upper- and middle-class families.

Table 9.5 *Pass rates in various examinations, 1978–9*

Examination	No. of candidates	No. of pupils admitted	Passes (%)
Entrance to the first year of middle school	366,045	194,172	53.04
Certificate of primary education	233,109	85,285	36.90
Certificate of intermediate education (4th year of middle school)	165,193	42,846	25.93
High school diploma (*Baccalauréat*)	57,076	14,585	25.55

Source: *Annuaire statistique de l'Algérie* (1981), 95.

An evaluation

Despite the human and financial resources allocated to education during the period under consideration the returns were not as high as expected. For instance, the pass rate in two key examinations declined from 41.8 per cent in 1967–8 to 36.6 per cent in 1977–8. Table 9.5 shows that in spite of democratisation the new educational system turned out to be highly selective.

In short, of 100 pupils enrolled in primary schools, 20 would drop out before the end; and 40 would fail to pass the examination for the certificate of primary education, which meant that they would not be allowed to stay at school. Of the remaining 40 pupils about 18 would be admitted to high schools, 16 of which would be candidates for the *baccalauréat* examination. The pass rate was 25 per cent in 1978–9. This meant that only 4 pupils out of 100 would have the chance to go to the university.

While the demand for senior staff, engineers, technicians and skilled workers was growing rapidly, the proportion of pupils enrolled in technical schools fell to 7.6 per cent of the total. The severe shortage of skilled manpower hampered the process of socio-economic development of the country.

Education was unevenly developed, with the cities benefiting more than the rural population. The regional disparities were not reduced. For instance, the rate of school attendance of school-age children varied and continues to vary from one province to another. In 1977 in the *wilayates* of Algiers and Oran 85.5 per cent were attending schools and in the *wilayate* of Constantine, 83.5 per cent, compared with 42.7 per cent in Djelfa, 53.5 per cent in Adrar and 56.6 per cent in Mostaganam. Furthermore, the quality

Post-independence development

of education in the interior of the country and in the rural areas is inferior to that of the towns.

This inter- and intra-*wilayate* inequality has been compounded by social discrimination based on sex. Boys continued to be more favoured than girls by the parents. Some of them compel their daughters to stop going to school once they reach the age of 13. Many young women, even if they manage to learn a skill are not allowed to work outside the home, either by their parents or by their husbands.

By 1977–8, 83.8 per cent of school-age boys were attending school, as against 58.3 per cent of girls. In the rural areas, particularly in the south and the east of the country, only a minority of girls attended school. For example, no more than 23.3 per cent of school-age girls were attending school in the *wilayate* of Djelfa, 30.6 per cent in the *wilayate* of Adrar and 36 per cent in the *wilayate* of Tebessa during the 1977–8 school year. It is not surprising that at university level the proportion of female students was only 23 per cent during the same year. As long as the Algerian woman is subjected to the strict rules of tradition, and hence relegated to the home, the country will never be able to modernise its society and develop its economy.

Higher education

In 1962, Algeria inherited a university located in Algiers and two annexes, one in Constantine and the other in Oran. As shown in Chapter 2, during the colonial period access to higher education was the privilege of a tiny minority of Algerian students, usually from wealthy families, whose riches were acquired through collaboration with the colonial authorities. The number of Algerian students in the institutions of higher education declined from 589 in 1954 to 267 in 1956, rising to 814 in 1959 and 1,372 in 1961. The sharp decrease in 1956 was caused by the students' strike in connection with the war of national liberation. Indeed, the Algerian Students' Association, which came under the control of nationalist elements, asked the high school and university students to give up their studies in order to join the ranks of the FLN and ALN.

In the autumn of 1962, 3,718 Algerian students registered at the university. During the colonial period the majority of Algerian students were studying law and the humanities.

In the post-independence period several specialised institutes and schools of higher education were established in order to train a sufficient number of technical, administrative and managerial personnel to run the economy. For example, in 1963–4 the Algerian Centre for Hydrocarbons and Textile Studies and the Institute of Management and Planning were set up. In 1964 several other establishments of higher education were created, such as the Polytechnical School of Algiers, specialising in civil and mechanical engineering, mining and geology, and telecommunications, the National Institute of Agronomy and the National School of Administration. Many other institutions of higher education were added later. In 1969 the two regional annexes of the University of Algiers in Constantine and Oran were transformed into universities. In 1974 the University of Science and Technology of Algiers was inaugurated, followed by the creation of several other universities, in Tlemcen, Annaba, Tizi-Ouzou, Sétif and Batna, for instance. The construction of these specialised schools, institutes and universities was stimulated by a growing demand for higher education.

Between 1962 and 1971 the organisation and curricula of the universities remained almost unaltered. The classical education offered by these institutions of higher learning was not only highly selective but also unresponsive to the developmental requirements of the country. This situation induced the newly created Ministry of Higher Education to devise a comprehensive reform programme designed to adapt the curricula of the various institutes and departments, which had also been created by this reform measure, to the needs of the economic sectors and services. The time devoted to 'practical studies' and laboratory work was increased. The duration of the academic year was increased by two months. Thenceforth, the institutions of higher education were assigned the task of training a sufficient number of highly competent 'cadres' who were supposed to be immediately 'operational' upon leaving. Priority was given to 'science and technology' so that the process of industrialisation would be mastered. This reform attempted to consolidate the democratisation of higher education by the creation of favourable conditions for the admission of both students from 'popular origins' and girls. The number of students registered in the national universities increased from 3,718 in 1962–3 to 55,148 in 1978–9.

In fifteen years (1962–77) the number of university students multiplied by a factor of 14.6. The annual average growth of students of higher education was 10 per cent during the three-year plan (1967–9), 25.7 per cent during the first four-year plan (1970–3) and 14.7 per cent during the second four-year plan (1974–7).

The democratisation of higher education was accomplished by the provision of scholarships and accommodation to students coming from poor families. In 1967, 40 per cent of all students were on government scholarships, rising to 65 per cent by 1978, when the state spent AD 280 million on scholarships. The budget for scholarships increased eight-fold during the 1970–7 period alone. By 1978, 22,300 students, representing 43 per cent of the total, were housed by the universities and specialised institutions of higher education, as against 29 per cent in 1971.

Post-independence development

The total number of women studying at the universities increased six-fold in ten years. Their proportion stagnated, progressing by 2.3 points during the 1967–78 period, that is, rising from 21 per cent of the total to 23.3 per cent.

The increase in the student body was accompanied by a rapid growth in the number of university teachers, from 224 in 1962–3 to 6,396 in 1978–9, of whom 2,571 were foreign (40.2 per cent of the total). The number of Algerians increased from 339 in 1967–8 (48.9 per cent of the total) to 3,850 in 1978–9 (60.2 per cent of the total).

The Arabisation of higher education presented and continues to present serious problems; the authorities appear to have Arabised the ideological disciplines first, such as philosophy and history. For the social sciences, represented by economics, political science, sociology and law, each department or institute was required to set up two sections: one in French and the other in Arabic. This dual system was abolished in 1980 when all the first-year courses in social sciences were Arabised. However, the teaching of sciences continued to be carried out in French. By 1984 all courses in social sciences were Arabised.

In 1971, 8 per cent of the students were studying in Arabic. By 1978 this proportion had risen to 32 per cent, the majority of them in the humanities, social sciences and law. Only 16.5 per cent of the Arabised students in 1978 were studying scientific and technical subjects. These students were destined to teach in high schools. The major obstacle to the introduction and generalisation of Arabic in the universities was the absence of scientific books and articles in the Arabic language. The authorities concerned refused to take this fact into account. The long-term consequences of this refusal are bound to be disastrous for the future of higher education.

The number of university graduates rose from 98 in 1963–4 to 4,956 by 1977–8, of whom 907 graduated from medical schools, 546 from engineering departments, 815 from science institutes, 606 from economics and business departments and the rest in the social sciences and humanities.

Graduates in sciences and engineering increased from 100 in 1969–70 to 1,131 in 1977–8 and from 208 to 802 respectively. However, this spectacular growth did not resolve the problem of manpower shortages in their fields. A total of 27,500 students graduated from the universities between 1967 and 1978, two-thirds during the second four-year plan (1974–7). However, 54.6 per cent of the graduates were in social sciences and humanities. Out of this cumulative total, 5,600 doctors, representing 22 per cent of all graduates, finished their degrees during the two successive four-year plans (1970–7).

However, the proportion of students studying exact sciences and technology has been increasing since the early 1970s, while the proportions of

Education and development

those enrolled in non-scientific and technological establishments has been decreasing. In this field restructuring has been taking place within the universities. Indeed, the proportion of students enrolled in the departments of social sciences, law and humanities declined from 55.2 per cent in 1972–2 to 38.70 per cent in 1980–1. However, medical and biological sciences continued to attract a large number of students. (The pre-medical students are enrolled in biological sciences.) The proportion of students studying medical and biological sciences rose from 25.38 per cent in 1971–2 to 28.9 per cent in 1980–1.

In sum, apart from the medical schools, higher education failed to provide the necessary qualified manpower, represented by scientists, engineers, managers and technicians, required by the rapid industrialisation of the country. These professional categories constitute in any social system not only the backbone of industry but also the dynamic agents of modernisation and development.

Adult education

Despite a high rate of illiteracy, adult education was neglected between 1962 and 1969. However, both the first and second four-year plans envisaged 'literacy campaigns' to reduce the rate of illiteracy, which at the time affected no less than 70 per cent of the adult population. The 1970–3 plan projected that 1 million persons would benefit from this programme; the 1974–7 plan, 300,000. The target group was represented by the young active adults of the 'organised sectors'. The results were very disappointing. Only 16.6 per cent of the targets were attained during the three successive plans, 1967–77.

Adult education by correspondence and television was organised, but the results were even more disappointing. For example, the 1970–3 plan projected that the number of students who would follow this type of education would reach 200,000 by 1973. However, in the 1974–5 school year only 16,299 students were officially enrolled, rising slightly to 20,967 by 1977–8. These two programmes of adult education were conceived as a means to raise the level of skills and culture of the active population. They were supposed to be accompanied by vocational training both in the workplace and in specialised vocational training centres.

Vocational training

In this field also Algeria inherited some facilities from the colonial power that were used as a basis for the development of a network of vocational training centres. The socio-economic development undertaken required the vocational training centres to provide qualified manpower, particularly to industry; hence the need for new training establishments. Their goal was to satisfy the country's need for skilled workers and technicians in various fields.

From 1962 to 1968 the trade schools and other vocational training centres trained 45,000 skilled workers and salaried employees, 7,800 technicians and foremen and 1,400 middle-level cadres and senior staff. On the eve of the launching of the three-year plan, 1967–9, 35 vocational training centres were operating at only 56 per cent of their capacity. These centres were under the control of the Ministry of Labour and Vocational Training. During the three-year plan, of the 17 centres to be constructed only 5 were achieved by 1970.

Confronted with a growing shortage of skilled labour, various ministries decided to set up their own training institutions. The Ministry of Industry and Energy established 8 specialised schools and institutes, the Ministry of Agriculture, 17 centres and the Ministry of Public Works and Construction, among other things, the school of civil engineering.

From 1967 to 1969, 48 additional vocational training centres and trade schools were established by various ministries. The Ministry of the Interior set up 10 centres, the Ministry of Agriculture, 12 and the Ministry of Transport, 14, for example. These new centres increased the training capacity of the country from 14,500 persons per year in 1967 to 25,700 in 1969.

During the first four-year plan (1970–3) the planners projected that 176,690 persons were to be trained. However, only 127,981, that is, about 72 per cent of the target, were actually trained, of whom 16,150 were senior staff and engineers. This figure included the graduates of the Ministry of Higher Education and of the specialised institutes and schools under the auspices of various ministries and public enterprises, as well as the graduates of teachers' colleges. Nonetheless, only 50 per cent of the planned number of workers for industry were actually trained during this period, a fact that slowed down the process of industrialisation.

During the second four-year plan (1974–7), 72 new training centres were opened. This plan projected the training of 160,000 persons. By the end of 1977, only 125,000, which represented 78 per cent of the target, were trained, of whom 28,400 graduated from teachers' colleges. By 1977–8, 68,930 persons were enrolled in vocational training centres and teachers' colleges.

From 1967 to 1978 about 230,000 had received some training (excluding higher education), of whom 70,000 were graduates of the institutes of education. The numbers of graduates were as follows: 33,970 during the three-year plan, 66,479 during the first four-year plan, 101,036 during the

Table 9.6 *The growing shortage of manpower, 1970–7*

	Senior staff and engineers	Technicians and foremen	Qualified workers
Technical co-operation	14,200	1,500	3,400
Needs of the economy	67,140	94,000	243,000
Planned training projects	(60,180)	(48,680)	(232,030)
Achieved goals	48,940	27,950	169,040
Deficit	32,400	67,550	77,360

Source: MPAT, 1979.

second four-year plan and 27,985 in 1978. As a direct result, the number of instructors of vocational training centres rose from 720 in 1967 to 3,168 in 1978, that is, by a factor of 4.4.

However, since the classical vocational training centres were incapable of satisfying the growing needs of industry, the public enterprises were compelled to train about 40,000 persons during the same period (7,908 were trained by light industries, 20,687 by heavy industries and 10,621 by the energy and petrochemical industries). In addition, industry had trained 3,013 persons abroad between 1967 and 1978.

Indeed, the shortages in manpower increased dramatically during the 1970–7 period (see Table 9.6). The short fall was no fewer than 177,910 persons. This state of affairs indicates that the Ministry of Labour and Vocational Training and the Ministries of National Education and Higher Education were unable to provide the national economy with a sufficient and adequately trained work force. They failed to gear the vocational training programmes to the specific needs of industry and other key activities. This failure induced the Ministry of Industry and Energy to envisage the development of its own vocational training centres. Unfortunately for the country, this imaginative initiative gave rise to vocational training programmes to the specific needs of industry and other key activities. This failure induced the Ministry of Industry and Energy to envisage the development of its own vocational training centres. Unfortunately for the country, this imaginative initiative gave rise to determined opposition from the Ministries of Education, Labour and Vocational Training and Higher Education and the Secretariat of State for Planning. Once more industry was compelled to shelve a vital project which would have made it possible to train at least 100,000 persons per year.

According to the former Ministry of Industry and Energy:

Post-independence development

When we realised that the classical type of vocational training centre was incapable of providing industry with the necessary skilled and qualified manpower we decided to launch a project to establish our own vocational training facilities. We contacted French and Italian enterprises which had long experience in training their own labour force as well as East Germany's authorities on vocational training. They provided us with advice and documentation. Then we carried out a technical study which allowed us to make an inventory of all existing and potential jobs. We even took into account the manpower requirements of all future industrial projects. This allowed us to determine the needs of the industrial sector, estimated at over 50,000 persons per year. When we took into consideration the needs of other sectors (including the private sector) we realised that we needed to train about 100,000 persons per year.

Even the World Bank agreed to provide us with a loan to finance this project. However, when we presented it to the Council of Ministers, we were faced with strong opposition from the Minister of Education, the Minister of Labour and Vocational Training, etc. on the grounds that our project was too costly and that they could do something better and cheaper. The result was that our project was shelved but nothing was done to attenuate the growing shortage of skilled manpower. When the rate of school failure reached alarming proportions in 1978, Boumedienne stated in the cabinet meeting that anyone who could do something in this field must start immediately. He died a few months later.

This problem remains unresolved to this day. The five-year plan (1980–4), which contained less ambitious objectives than the previous plans, projected that the national economy would be needing 650,000 skilled and qualified workers during this plan period. This meant that the authorities of education and vocational training had to provide an annual average of 130,000 skilled and qualified workers between 1980 and 1984.

In sum, quantitatively the achievements in the fields of education and vocational training were remarkable. In financial terms, close to AD 12 billion was invested during the 1967–78 period: AD 8.1 in primary and secondary education, AD 2.3 billion in higher education and AD 1.5 billion in vocational training. By 1980 the number of pupils, students and trainees totalled 4,291,495 persons:

Primary education	3,118,827
Intermediate education	802,482
Secondary education	227,402
Higher education	72,200
Vocational training	84,738
Total	4,305,649

Source: *Annuaire statistique de l'Algérie* (1981).

However, the quality of this education and vocational training remained inadequate and poorly adapted to the actual needs of the national economy.

This lack of suitability gave rise to redundancy or underemployment, particularly among the graduates of higher education. Moreover, a narrow operationalism emphasised by all the successive reforms of primary, secondary and higher education turned out to be in disharmony with the ideological orientation of education. The insistence on the clinging to 'our traditions, values, and customs' and on the 'return to the religious sources' of *Al-Assalah* resulted in a sort of retraditionalisation of the objectives of teaching. The combination of educational functionalism and traditionalism was bound not only to weaken the role of education in the development of the productive forces but also to prevent a genuine cultural revolution from taking place. The subjection of education to an instrumental developmentalism, whose aim was the modernisation of the economy through the installation of industrial plants and a related infrastructure, was accompanied, paradoxically, by a strong resistance to cultural change. Indeed the process of industrialisation requires an unconditional acceptance, acquisition and mastery of modern sciences, technology, secular ideas, values and attitudes towards nature, history, social relations, organisations and practices. In other words, the modernisation of the economic sectors cannot succeed without the internalisation of a rationalist and modernist ideology.

Conclusion

A process of development cannot succeed without the concomitant modernisation and secularisation of the national culture of an underdeveloped society. The educational and vocational training institutions of Algeria were supposed to play an important role in its elaboration, systematisation, propagation and internalisation by present-day young people and its transmission to future generations. Since the Algerian system of education was conceived by the political leadership as a state system, whose principal mission was to carry out a 'cultural revolution' within the country, it was expected either to transcend or minimise the negative influences of an underdeveloped socio-cultural environment characterised, among other things, by a retrograde and authoritarian power relationship at every level of society, a fact that made horizontal communication almost impossible. Under such circumstances, the educators themselves, who received an inadequate education, needed, first of all, to be educated. It might be that 'the coincidence of the changing of circumstances and of human activity can be conceived and rationally understood only as revolutionising practice'.[1] However, in the field of education, the social practice that prevailed in the country was, and continues to be, determined by an archaic ideology imposed in primary and secondary schools by some formerly influential members of the association of the Algerian *ulamah* who became the principal theoreticians of educational philosophy in contemporary Algeria. Since these pseudo-theoreticians were either ignorant of or impermeable to modern 'western' ideas, philosophies and values, they succeeded in making Algerian schools provide one of the most retrograde and conservative educations in the world. In so doing, the schoolteachers who were supposed to be agents of Boumedienne's 'cultural revolution' reproduced the archaism and prejudices of the Algerian family, whose social conservatism is unique in the Mediterranean world.

Consequently, this underdeveloped society, whose leadership was and continued to be incapable of comprehending the nature of education, affected the performance of the eduational system. The second-rate quality of its graduates hampered their performance in the field of development; which shows how an underdeveloped country is trapped in a vicious circle. Since educational institutions turned out to be mere reflections of an underdeveloped socio-cultural environment, they were bound to fail either to inculcate in the minds of the pupils and students adequate technical expertise and an accurate knowledge and understanding of modern life, culture, thought, sciences and technology or to induce them to adopt new attitudes and values congruent with the exigencies and requirements of industrialisation.

Chapter 10

Post-independence urbanisation and the housing crisis

Since the conditions that stimulated the rural-to-urban exodus during the colonial period were not altered immediately after independence, a growing number of rural paupers had no alternative but to move into the cities. However, the process of ejection from the countryside subsided slightly in the late 1970s. This might be attributable to regional programmes devised by the government in favour of the most depressed rural regions of the country, and to a serious attempt to spread the new industrial plants throughout the country. The agrarian revolution launched in 1971 was also designed to reduce this rural-to-urban migration.

Between 1966 and 1973, about 840,000 individuals migrated to the urban centres. This represents an annual average of 120,000 migrants, compared with an average of 150,000 between 1962 and 1966. (This decrease was more than compensated for by the cross-Mediterranean exodus that led hundreds of thousands of workers to north-western Europe.) The average annual growth rate of the rural population was 2 per cent, as compared to a national average of 3.2 per cent. The urban population grew by an average of 5.1 per cent per year during the 1966–73 period. The rural exodus contributed 25 per cent of the growth of the urban population. From 1973 to 1978 the rural population still increased by an annual average of 2 per cent, despite the fact that the demographic growth rate remained constant. Consequently, migration still constituted 24.6 per cent of the total growth of the urban population during the same period. In other words, between 1967 and 1979, 1.3 million persons moved from the countryside into the cities. As a result of all this, by 1979 the overwhelming majority of the heads of households had rural origins.

In 1976, 82.94 per cent of the migrants were concentrated in the six major cities. Over 69 per cent were in three: 42 per cent in Algiers, 18.02 per cent in Oran and close to 10 per cent in Constantine. Original urban households comprised only one-fifth of the population of Algiers, Oran, Constantine, Tiaret and Batna.

The average growth rate of urbanisation between 1966 and 1977 has been estimated at 5.1 per cent per year, compared with a total population growth

Post-independence development

rate of 3.2 per cent. In 1966, the populations of the four cities with more than 100,000 inhabitants were as follows: Algiers, 994,000; Oran, 326,000; Constantine, 246,000; and Annaba, 152,000. By 1977, eight major cities inhabited by more than 100,000 people contained 46 per cent of the total urban population; and the 25 largest cities inhabited by more than 50,000 persons comprised 63 per cent of the urban population. The concentration of the population into the cities and towns resulted in a severe housing crisis.

Rapid urbanisation and the housing crisis

The departure of the settlers left housing which was swiftly filled by the Algerian population. However, by the mid 1960s the demand for housing increased drastically. The 1966 census revealed the existence of 1.98 million housing units occupied by 2.28 million households. The deficit in accommodation was set officially at approximately 300,000. Each housing unit was occupied then by an average of 6.1 persons; over 45 per cent were constructed before 1945; 45.6 per cent had no running water; more than 60 per cent were not connected to the sewerage system; 59.7 per cent had no electricity; and more than 25 per cent were huts and shanties. The 1977 census revealed the existence of 2.2 million housing units, which amounted to a total growth of 1.3 per cent since 1966. During the same period the population increased by over 40 per cent. The average number of persons per housing unit reached 7.1. Out of these 2.2 million housing units 55.2 per cent had no running water, 51 per cent no electricity, 87 per cent had no gas and 60 per cent no sanitation; 50 per cent were over thirty years old. The average number of persons per room rose from 2.6 in 1966 to 3.2 in 1977. This overcrowding was caused by the fact that, while the average growth rate of new housing units rose by about 1 per cent per year between 1963 and 1978, the annual demographic growth averaged 3.2 per cent. From 1968 to 1978 only 152,959 housing units were constructed, 83,191 rural and 69,768 urban. By 1979 the number of persons per housing unit exceeded 8. The deficit was officially set at 700,000 housing units so as to preserve the situation of 1966.

It must be noted that the 1977 census revealed that 83 per cent of urban families lived in accommodation varying from one to three rooms, compared with 86.2 in 1966; 14 per cent in accommodation with four to five rooms, as against 10.9 per cent in 1966; and 3 per cent in more than six rooms, compared with 2.9 per cent in 1966. This situation was caused primarily by the Under Secretariat of State for Planning, which has been controlled by pro-French techno-bureaucrats since its inception in the 1960s. Its officials refused to authorise the allocation of funds for the

Urbanisation and the housing crisis

construction of new accommodation on the basis of the 'theory of constructed space'. According to this theory, the homes already constructed in the country will suffice to house Algerian familes in the coming decades. This refusal compelled the public companies – which were assigned the mission of developing the economy – to build housing units for their own growing numbers of employees without the consent of the planners. Unfortunately for the potential beneficiaries, the Ministry of Public Works and Housing demanded the strict application of an existing law which bans any other authority from constructing public accommodation. During a heated debate within the Council of Ministers, some pro-*comprador* ministers responded to the Representatives of Industry, who insisted that industrial workers must be provided with adequate accommodation, by stating plainly that the 'state should not do everything for these workers'. It was the same individuals who not only criticised the strategy of industrialisation after the death of Boumedienne, but also blamed industry for draining the financial resources of the state and for sacrificing the basic needs of the people. As a consequence of such practices, overcrowding for the overwhelming majority has become intolerable, and inequality in housing continues.

Since migration and urbanisation always entail structural changes, an examination of the family structure and pre- and post-migration socio-professional status may allow us to delineate some of the major modifications in the social structure of the population involved.

Structural changes in the urban setting

A study carried out in 1978 by the AARDES revealed that the family structure of migrants in the cities tends towards nucleation. Out of a total sample of 140,793, 63.29 per cent were nuclear families, 32.26 per cent were extended and individuals living alone numbered 6,335. Of the migrants who moved into the cities prior to 1930, 14.06 per cent, which represented a total of 3,834, were nuclear, 37.03 per cent were extended families and 13.88 per cent were living alone. The migrants who have arrived in the cities since 1971 are: 14.56 per cent living alone, 59.21 per cent in nuclear families and only 26.20 per cent in extended families. It is among the families that arrived in the cities between 1931 and 1953 that the nuclear family represents the predominant type. Despite its transplantation into the cities, the extended family continued to exist even though its survival appears to be dependent on the housing crisis which forced innumerable families, despite serious internal tension, to continue to live in that way. Table 10.1 details the migrant family structure in the urban setting.

Post-independence development

Table 10.1 *Classification of migrants according to date of arrival in Algiers and type of family*

Dates	Alone		Nuclear family		Extended family		Total	%
	No.	%	No.	%	No.	%		
Before 1930	1,065	13.76	3,834	49.54	2,840	36.70	7,739	100
1931–1953	994	3.01	22,081	67.02	9,869	29.95	32,944	100
1954–1961	639	1.91	20,945	62.48	11,928	35.59	33,519	100
1962–1966	923	2.03	29,820	65.52	14,768	32.44	45,511	100
1967–1970	852	6.15	8,875	64.10	4,118	29.74	13,845	100
Since 1971	1,065	14.71	4,260	58.82	1,917	26.47	7,242	100
Total	5,538	3.93	89,815	63.38	45,440	32.27	140,800	100

Source: AARDES, 1979.

Since the family structure of the migrants in the cities may be determined by socio-economic factors, a look at the type of housing may explain this phenomenon. Indeed, the above-mentioned sample for the city of Algiers alone reveals that 62.9 per cent of those inhabiting villas are organised into nuclear families, while 35.09 per cent live in extended families and only 1.98 per cent live alone. In contrast to this, 86.94 per cent of the families inhabiting what were referred to in this study as 'inadequate independent lodgings' live in nuclear families and only 13.03 per cent are still structured into extended families. Table 10.2 analyses the type of housing and family structure of migrants in the cities of Algiers and Constantine, which may be representative of the other cities as well.

As this table shows, the nuclear family predominates among inhabitants of the shanty towns of Constantine, and to a lesser extent in those of Algiers. The table also indicates that, in comparison with those of Algiers, in Constantine 55.54 per cent of the residents of villas, but only 18.17 per cent of the residents of shanty towns, live in extended families. In other words, although there is probably a correlation along class lines between the type of housing and family structure, it is not as conclusive as one would expect. The material constraints associated with the housing crisis seem to force families to keep on living together despite the friction thus created. Indeed, my own research in a rural district shows that the family structure had become predominantly nuclear. In 1974, over 88 per cent of the households were nuclear: urbanisation did not completely alter the family structure.

Table 10.2 *Types of housing and family structure*

Type of housing	Alone		Nuclear family		Extended family		Grand total	
	Total	%	Total	%	Total	%	Total	%
Algiers								
Villa	1,213	11.31	6,745	62.90	3,763	35.09	10,721	100
Adequate independent	1,369	8.17	10,579	63.13	4,828	28.80	16,756	100
Inadequate independent	—	—	1,420	86.94	213	13.03	1,633	100
Collective (apts.)	3,621	3.43	67,237	63.72	34,648	32.83	105,506	100
Shanty towns	355	5.74	3,834	62.06	1,988	32.17	6,177	100
Grand total	6,538	3.93	89,815	63.79	45,440	32.17	140,793	100
Constantine								
Villa	—	—	396	44.43	495	55.54	891	100
Adequate independent	—	—	2,687	53.74	2,244	46.05	4,851	100
Inadequate independent	33	1.88	1,221	69.80	495	28.30	1,749	100
Collective (apts.)	825	3.52	14,619	62.39	7,986	34.08	23,430	100
Shanty towns	66	4.54	1,122	77.26	164	11.89	1,452	100
Grand total	924	2.85	20,045	61.66	11,384	35.46	32,373	100

Source: AARDES, 1979.

A look at the occupations of the migrants prior to their departure for the cities may reveal the nature of this rural-to-urban exodus, and the upward social mobility it entailed. The AARDES study, which concerns 164,963 male heads of households, indicates that 33.51 per cent (55,279) of these migrants were peasants practising subsistence agriculture. By 1966, 4.8 per cent of these peasants continued to eke out a livelihood from agriculture, decreasing to 0.52 per cent by 1976. This should be contrasted with the migrants who worked as service personnel prior to their departure, totalling 3.4 per cent, increasing to 16.45 per cent in 1966 and 22.36 per cent in 1976. The percentage of the rural migrants that were engaged in commerce and administration rose from 3.36 per cent before departure to 10.47 per cent in 1966 and 13.15 per cent in 1976.

Post-independence development

The bulk of the migrants left the primary activities associated with agricultural production in favour of the non-productive tertiary sectors. Nonetheless, this geographical mobility appears to have involved a social mobility as well. The number of middle cadres increased from 0.84 per cent prior to departure to 4.02 per cent in 1966 and to 5.88 per cent in 1976. The number of higher cadres rose from 0.16 per cent to 2.74 per cent in 1976. Traders increased from 3.65 to 8.62 per cent in 1976. The number of unskilled labourers increased from 6.66 per cent to 13.10 per cent, but that of skilled workers rose from 3.31 per cent before their departure to 14.88 in 1966, and 18.55 per cent in 1976. Thus, migration and urbanisation resulted in the acquisition of higher socio-professional status for innumerable individuals. However, a large number of them are still subjected to precarious conditions in the overcrowded urban centres.

This migration of an increasing number of rural inhabitants into the cities is not only rooted in the economic history of Algeria but is also directly associated with the inadequacy of agricultural policy. The devaluation of agricultural labour began with the expropriation of the basic means of production of the rural producers and their subsequent transformation into an exploited work force. The diminishing returns of agriculture, caused primarily by soil exhaustion brought about by overcultivation, and the fragmentation of landholdings forced innumerable peasants to abandon their fields and become wage labourers either in Europe or in the Algerian urban centres. This process has continued in the post-independence period. In spite of the agrarian revolution, which aimed, among other things, at the construction of a thousand villages in order to prevent the migration of the rural paupers, a mass exodus went on unabated. It was caused mostly by both wage and income differentials between the agricultural sector and the industrial and tertiary sectors. The result is that the agricultural activity of the so-called traditional peasant sector has been undermined. Even the reproduction of the labour force of the modern agricultural sector represented by the so-called workers' self-managed farms is in jeopardy. The remaining current agricultural labour force is a 'residual' one, that is, mostly made up of the old, unskilled and unfit. Because of the wage differentials, agriculture could not compete with industry or other skilled work.

Even in the rural communities, the size of the non-agricultural population has increased rapidly, from 1.6 million in 1966 to 2.1 million in 1977. This situation, aggravated by the lack of a comprehensive, well-planned and implemented agricultural policy, has not only undermined the supply of foodstuffs to the urban population but has contributed to its unprecedented growth. The lack of development in the non-industrial sectors, such as agriculture, fishing, water resources, transport and housing, together with rapid demographic growth, has fostered the under-development of the productive forces and a 'wild urbanisation'. This has engendered intractable problems in all social fields. It was this very lack of foresight and planning that permitted the acceleration of cross-Mediterranean labour migration throughout the sixties and early seventies. Today the problem of the Algerian migrant workers in Europe, which was inherited from the colonial era, is still awaiting a satisfactory solution. The recent serious French threat to deport the transplanted migrant labourers posed grave problems, both to the people concerned and to the Algerian government. Despite almost two decades of 'rapid development' and talk about the imminent repatriation of the migrants, 920,380 Algerian nationals are still permanently residing in Europe. If they were to be returned abruptly the Algerian urban crisis would be aggravated further.

Indeed, the rapid urbanisation of Algeria through migration has brought about a kind of cultural ruralisation of the cities. Today the cities are experiencing intractable problems associated with congestion, the general absence of basic hygiene, scarcity of housing, water, recreation facilities and transportation and inadequate social services, most of which are overloaded. The concentration of population into urban areas has resulted in the erosion of the existing habitat through the over-crowding of the housing units and the lack of maintenance caused by the fact that the inhabitants are of a rural origin and on low incomes and that most of the buildings are state owned, which means that neither the population nor the state authorities think of them as a perishable national heritage that has to be preserved and transmitted intact to future generations.

In sum, because of a high rate of demographic growth as a result of which 60 per cent of the total population are under 20 years old, this severe housing crisis is bound to worsen between now and the year 2000. Indeed, since the total Algerian population will rise from 22.45 million in 1986 to 35.87 million by the year 2000, the country will have to construct no fewer than 6 million housing units. In 1982 an official document of the single FLN party estimated that over 2 million families were in urgent need of accommodation. This fact alone militated in favour of the continuation of the rapid industrialisation of the country undertaken by the Boumedienne regime. Once again, it must be reiterated that, in a third world country like Algeria, industrialisation is the necessary condition for the improvement of the standards of living of its inhabitants, the socio-economic and political integration of their society and the consolidation of the national independence of their state. Furthermore, housing, trans-

Post-independence development

portation, the level and quality of food intake, education, sanitation and so on are the overriding factors determining the state of health of any modern human population, and they too cannot be improved without the establishment of modern industry.

Chapter 11

Public health since 1962

The state of health of a population is a reflection of the level of development attained by its society. Besides the ravages of war and its trauma, the majority of the Algerian population was afflicted in 1962 by various diseases associated with underdevelopment. These diseases were usually caused by malnutrition, lack of public sanitation and hygiene and inadequate housing, compounded by an inadequate health service. The most common diseases were (and continue to be) measles, typhoid, dysentery, tuberculosis, meningitis and cholera.

The departure of the French settlers was strongly felt in this field. Of 2,500 doctors who were practising in the country in January 1962, only 600 remained by July of the same year, of whom 285 were Algerians. This gave an average ratio of one doctor per 100,000 inhabitants. The rural areas and small towns had no doctors and almost no medical facilities. The paramedical staff numbered only 1,380 in 1962.

The physical facilities were represented by 156 establishments, divided into 143 hospitals, one cancer centre, and 13 clinics. The number of hospital beds amounted to 42,787. Health centres totalled 188, consultation rooms 1,016, dispensaries 150 and sanitation offices 5.

The health service inherited from the colonial period was divided into three sectors. The public service was managed by the Ministry of Health, the dispensaries of free medical assistance were administered by the municipal authorities and the school health centres were under the control of the Ministry of Education. Private offices functioned in accordance with a liberal traditional model. However, all these services were unequally distributed within the country. There was no co-ordination or functional relationship between the sectors, a fact that prevented them from developing a common programme of action devised to meet the demands of the population.

The efforts made during the three successive plans (1967–77) to meet the health needs of the population aimed at providing the country with an adequate and dense network of small units and other medical facilities capable of assuming the protection and improvement of the population's health. The implementation of free medical care was to be the cornerstone

Post-independence development

of the reorganisation and development of the national public health service.

From 1967 to 1973 the newly established health service was organised into sectors. This reorganisation resulted in the extension of health services to the interior of the country and even to rural areas. By 1973 the government promulgated a law instituting free medical care in all public health services. During this period a series of health campaigns were launched, the most successful of which was the anti-tuberculosis campaign. The other major campaigns were anti-trachoma, anti-malaria, anti-rickets and a campaign for the improvement of mother and child health. In 1969 a public board, the Central Pharmacy of Algeria, was granted the monopoly for import and manufacture of drugs. In 1971 medical studies were reformed, rationalised and modernised, a fact that accelerated the training of medical staff in subsequent years.

From 1974 onwards, this new public health service consolidated. In 1975, the major health problems of the population were delineated and appropriate strategies were proposed to resolve them. During the 1978–80 period the development of the basic infrastructure was increased. The health service was divided into 195 sectors devised to provide comprehensive preventive and curative medicine. Each sector covered an average of 100,000 persons. These health sectors are centred locally around a hospital and comprise a certain number of care and preventive medical units under the supervision of this hospital. With the advent of free medical care, this structure assumed an important role. In addition to its curative and preventive functions, the health sector was assigned the task of taking care of the problems of epidemiology and public sanitation over a certain area.

Since the European settlers were concentrated in the urban centres along the coast, the infrastructure, represented mostly by hospitals, was initially sufficient. The Algerian authorities concentrated their effort on the extension of health facilities to the interior of the country and on the training of medical staff, including doctors. Thus the major objective of the three-year plan was to extend light medical facilities geographically – mostly polyclinics and health centres – and to reduce regional disparities through the establishment of new medical centres for diagnosis, preventive action and care. At this time the 'heavy structure' represented by hospitals appeared to be sufficient. However, despite this, the planners projected the construction of ten hospitals. But only two were built during the next two successive four-year plans (1970–77). The projected construction of 82 health centres and the 109 polyclinics was not completed until 1977.

The first four-year plan (1970–3) projected the construction of 8 new hospitals, 24 polyclinics and 232 health centres. This 'light' infrastructure was more adequate than large hospitals for providing primary care to the local population. Only two hospitals were built during the plan period. The

Table 11.1 *Medical infrastructure, 1962–79*

Year	Population (millions)	Health sectors	Number of hospitals	Number of beds
1962	10.4	—	156	42,782
1966	12.0	—	163	39,418
1974	15.6	143	163	41,728
1979	18.3	161	167	44,885
In construction	—	—	Several	11,600

Year	Polyclinics	Health centres	Consulting rooms	Socio-medical centres
1962	—	188	1,016	—
1966	—	256	1,081	—
1974	106	556	1,402	—
1979	160	653	1,305	859
In construction	115	160	130	

Source: Union Médicale Algérienne, *L'Organisation de la lutte anti-tuberculeuse en Algérie* (1985), p. 47.

second four-year plan (1974–7) maintained the same objectives: 7 hospitals, 154 polyclinics, 317 health centres and almost 600 examination rooms were to be built. However, these planned targets were not attained. Out of AD 4.64 billion earmarked for the development of medical infrastructure during these successive plans, only AD 1.33 billion was actually utilised, representing 29 per cent of the total allocated. Here, as in the other non-industrial sectors, the developmental performance of the authorities in charge was very indifferent.

Nonetheless, as Table 11.1 shows, the number of hospitals rose from 156 in 1962 to only 167 by 1979, while the number of polyclinics rose from 0 to 160, that of health centres from 0 to 644 and that of socio-medical centres set up by social security, public enterprises and institutions, from 0 to 859. In addition, 58 maternity hospitals were constructed during the three plans (1967–7) and 39 were under construction.

The most striking progress appears to have been achieved in the training of doctors and paramedical staff. Indeed, the number of Algerian physicians increased from 285 in 1962 to 4,605 by 1979, and that of paramedical personnel from 250 to 31,742. See Table 11.2.

In addition, there were 1,005 dentists, 721 pharmacists and 227 mid-

Post-independence development

Table 11.2 *The number of doctors, pharmacists and dentists, 1962–79*

Year	Algerian MDs	Foreign MDs	Total	Inhabitants per physician	
				Algerian MDs	Total
Doctors					
1962	242	937	1,179	29,301	7,835
1965	304	1,115	1,419	38,977	8,007
1967	417	1,036	1,453	30,136	8,649
1969	519	1,179	1,698	25,718	7,861
1973	1,241	1,226	2,467	12,139	6,107
1977	3,026	1,295	4,321	5,637	3,947
1979	4,561	1,785	6,346	3,969	2,853
Pharmacists					
1963	70	194	264	149,285	51,225
1967	160	84	244	78,543	51,504
1969	292	46	338	48,551	41,943
1974	441	64	505	45,376	38,043
1977	866	40	906	19,697	18,828
1979	1,001	50	1,051	18,086	17,225
Dentists					
1963	36	175	211	290,277	69,205
1967	86	78	164	146,127	76,628
1970	171	84	255	80,403	53,917
1974	410	84	494	37,885	31,443
1977	813	120	933	20,982	18,283
1979	1,305	121	1,426	13,873	12,695

Source: MPAT, *Séries statistiques 1967–1982* (October 1984).

wives in 1979. In the subsequent years the graduates of the medical colleges and various other schools under the auspices of the Ministry of Health increased rapidly. However, the professional qualifications of these medical staff were often inadequate.

The rapid development of the national health service was made necessary by the growing demand of the population for medical care. The number of medical examinations and visits increased from 1.5 million in 1965 to 17 million in 1979. The total value of drugs sold by the Central Pharmacy of Algeria increased ten-fold during the 1967–78 period, rising from AD 115 million in 1967 to AD 1,355 million by 1978. However, because of the

Public health since 1962

existence of a private health sector, only a quarter of this amount was prescribed by the doctors of the public sector, and hence provided free of charge to the patients. Most of these drugs were imported from the Common Market countries. The value of drugs produced by Algeria by the Central Pharmacy rose from AD 31 million in 1972 to AD 108 million in 1978, representing only 8 per cent of the total.

In sum, despite these quantitative achievements in the development of medical facilities and in manpower training, the Algerian national health service has been faced with intractable problems. The health policy of the Boumedienne government was marked by a striking ambiguity regarding the private sector. The Ben Bella government abolished private health care in 1964. After the *coup d'état* of June 1965, a compromise was worked out. From 1966 on a growing number of doctors were allowed to open private medical offices; many work on a part-time basis for the public sector. The rest of their time is spent in their private offices. Among other things, this system allowed them to use public facilities for their own private gains. This ambiguity was bound, sooner or later, to undermine the 'socialist sector'. Indeed, peaceful co-existence between these two conflicting sectors – private and public – could not be balanced out. The number of part-time Algerian doctors rose from 335 in 1972 to 768 in 1977, that of pharmacists from 194 to 303 and that of dentists from 128 to 261. By 1974 the number of Algerian medical doctors who worked as full-time private practitioners reached over 2,000. The contradiction between the private and public sectors prevented the government from establishing one single national health service capable of responding to the needs of the citizens. The absence of a single policy and the dichotomisation of the health service contributed to the concentration of Algerian MDs in the major cities. The state had to resort to foreign co-operation in order to man rural and small-town medical facilities.

As Table 11.3 shows, by the late 1970s almost half of the doctors were concentrated in only three major cities. This state of affairs induced the Ministry of Health to resort to compulsory administrative assignments for newly graduated doctors to the interior of the country for a specified period of time. Although this 'zoning' policy made it possible for the authorities to send doctors to 'marginal' communities of the interior to work for at least two years, it undermined the long-term development of the health services. Since the medical staff concerned knew that their stay was temporary, they did not devote their time and energy to developing these local medical facilities. Confronted with the refusal of Algerian doctors to settle in these underprivileged areas, the state resorted to the importation of foreign medical teams and individual doctors.

The growing demand of the population for medical treatment, coupled

Post-independence development

Table 11.3 *The concentration of doctors in the major cities during the mid 1970s*

City	Population	Number of doctors	%
Algiers	1,523,000	1,016	31
Oran	576,000	322	10
Constantine	426,000	197	6
Total	2,525,000	1,535	47
Rest of country	1,489,000	1,758	53

Source: Ministère de la Santé.

with the congenital inefficiency of the bureaucracy, compounded the problems of the national health service. For instance, the 'free' national health service turned out not to be free. The operating costs of the public, and even the private, sectors were financed by social security funds deducted from workers' pay. Indeed, the share of social security in the financing of operating costs rose from 23.49 per cent of the total in 1974 to 35.13 per cent in 1978 and 49.13 per cent in 1983. Nevertheless, working people, like the rest of the other social strata, benefited from this 'socialist' health service. The following indicators confirm this: the average rate of mortality fell from 16.3 per cent in 1964 to 8.6 per cent by 1978, while life expectancy rose from an average of 53.5 years to 62.82 years. However, despite this undeniable progress, the overloading of the health services, which is attributable to administrative mismanagement, resulted in a great deal of confusion, nervousness and even hardship. This situation was used by the advocates of the private medical sector to discredit the 'socialist sector'. Public care had been undergoing a process of creeping 'liberalisation' since the death of President Boumedienne, a reflection of the compradorisation of the economy and society.

The Benjadid regime had reversed the strategy of the development of the health service, which was geared to the establishment of an extensive network of 'light infrastructure', represented by small and widely distributed clinics and health centres providing primary care and preventive services. From 1980 onwards the Ministry of Public Health began the construction – without any adequate planning and preparation – of a 'heavy infrastructure', represented primarily by large hospitals equipped with 'heavy', complex and highly expensive imported medical technology. In addition, this current regime, by accelerating the process of 'privatisation' of medical care, will soon undermine the substantial gains achieved by the Algerian popular strata in this vital field. Indeed, after increasing the share of social security in the financing of the public health service to about 80 per cent of operating costs, and compelling patients to pay all the fees for laboratory analyses, it is now considering the idea of transforming hospitals and other medical facilities into financially self-supporting and profit-making services. A new breed of monetarist techno-bureaucrats, who have been encouraged by the Prime Minister's inner circle as well as by the presidency, are advocating the idea that every public activity must become profitable in order to justify its existence. But as everybody knows, the only unproductive and unprofitable services are represented by the bureaucracy, the growing number of police and the corrupt officers of the army. These are the services that have been 'booming' since the emergence of Benjadism. They are still hiring an increasing number of people and offering very attractive salaries. The top bureaucrats of the administration, the senior staff of the security services and the high-ranking officers of the army are not only enjoying all sorts of privileges but are also receiving the highest incomes in the country.

By 1987, the number of doctors reached over 18,000 (as against 4,561 in 1978, thanks to the reform of medical studies of 1971); that of dentists, pharmacists and medical staff more than quadrupled. Unfortunately for the underprivileged population, the creeping compradorisation of the economy and society stimulated the privatisation of the health service, which provoked the destabilisation of the system as a whole.

The subsequent breaking down of planning and the termination of the policy of equal distribution of medical facilities and staff throughout the country resulted in the growing concentration of doctors, dentists, pharmacists and other medical staff in the major cities, to the detriment of the small towns and rural communities. This privatisation has been undermining the performance and efficiency of the public health service, which provides medical care for the popular strata of society. The private sector has been draining the best and most qualified and experienced staff, whose training was paid for from public funds.

Chapter 12

The growth of employment, income and consumption

The goal of development is, among other things, the improvement in the living conditions of the population. The national charter of 1976 stressed that the objective of Algerian 'socialism' is to 'ensure to the maximum to every citizen adequate consumption, clothing, health, education, culture and leisure'. No citizen can enjoy a decent life without employment.

One of the major objectives of the three successive plans of development was to create jobs. The number of employed persons rose from 1.72 million in 1966 to about 2.83 million by 1978: that is, close to 1.11 million new jobs were created, representing a growth of 64.5 per cent. Employment increased by 9.8 per cent during the three-year plan (1967–9), 15.3 per cent during the first four-year plan (1970–3) and 21.4 per cent between 1974 and 1977. Table 12.1 shows the employment structure between 1967 and 1978.

This table reveals that the proportion of workers employed by three key non-agricultural productive sectors (hydrocarbons, industry, construction and public works) rose from 22.3 per cent of the total in 1967 to 42.5 per cent by 1977. The proportion of the labour force employed in the services declined. Employment in administration remained very important. The active agricultural population stagnated to about one million during the 1966–77 period. This active agricultural population was made up of peasants and farmers, permanent and seasonal workers and rural paupers who worked occasionally in agriculture. The proportion of the labour force engaged in agriculture fell from more than 50 per cent in 1966 to 30 per cent in 1977; and redundancy and underemployment in this sector persisted.

Because of the massive investments made by the state during the 1967–78 period, 84 per cent of all jobs were created in the public sector, outside agriculture. As a direct result, the proportion of wage- and salary-earners rose from 67 per cent of the total active population in 1967 to 76 per cent in 1977. The creation of jobs in productive sectors was considered the best way of distributing income to the population.

As a result of the development of the country, the total national revenue rose from AD 15.63 billion in 1967 to 91.17 billion in 1978. This amounted to a growth of 483 per cent, representing an average annual growth rate of 17.4 per cent during the period. The total gross income of households rose

Table 12.1 *Non-agricultural employment, 1967–77 (thousands of persons)*

Sector	1967	%	1969	%	1973	%	1977	%
Agriculture	824		934		873		800	
Hydrocarbons	6	0.7	8	0.8	22	1.8	40	2.8
Industry	I	13.4	153	16.1	223	17.7	347	18.8
Construction and public works	71	8.2	82	11.7	190	15.3	364	19.7
Trade	179	20.4	182	17.8	192	14.1	212	11.5
Transport	53	6.0	64	6.6	85	6.9	140	7.6
Services	142	16.3	152	15.0	163	12.2	205	11.1
Administration and others	206	35.0	318	32.0	434	32.1	542	29.3

Source: MPAT, *Synthèse du bilan économique* (May 1980).

Table 12.2 *Income patterns, 1967–78*

	1967	1970	1974	1977	1978
Gross household income (AD billion)	13.5	17.7	27.8	45.2	55.0
Wages and salaries (AD billion)	5.8	8.4	15.8	26.2	33.4
Gross income of entrepreneurs (AD billion)	5.0	6.2	8.2	12.5	14.0
Transfers (AD billion)	2.7	3.1	4.6	6.6	7.6
Household consumption (AD billion)	9.8	13.4	22.8	38.9	47.9
Per capita household income (AD)	1,072.0	1,290.0	1,792.0	2,570.0	3,075.0
Per capita household consumption (AD)	781.0	987.0	1,478.0	2,281.0	2,688.0
Average wage paid per month (AD)	411.6	500.5	742.8	1,081.7	1,269.7
Income of entrepreneurs and self-employed persons Per head per month (AD)	730.0	885.0	1,117.0	1,646.0	1,832.0

Source: MPAT, *Bilan économique*.

from AD 13.5 billion in 1967 to AD 55 billion in 1978. The income derived from wages and salaries increased from AD 5.8 billion, distributed among 1.77 million workers and employees, to AD 33.4 billion, received by almost 2.2 million employed persons during the same period. For instance, during the three successive plans (1967–77), employment increased by 76 per cent and the amount of wages and salaries paid by 156.3 per cent. Table 12.2 summarises income patterns during the 1967–78 period.

In 1967, 46.3 per cent of total income was received by entrepreneurs and self-employed persons, who then comprised 33 per cent of all income-receivers. By 1978 both the proportion of their income and their number declined to 29.5 per cent and 22.5 per cent respectively. The average monthly wages and salaries combined rose from AD 411.6 in 1967 to AD 1,269 in 1978, while the average monthly income of entrepreneurs and self-employed persons increased from AD 730 to AD 1,832. The ratio between the two income categories was reduced from 1 to 2 in 1967 to 1 to 1.5 in 1978.

Table 12.3 reveals that a noticeable increase in income took place during the period under consideration, both in current and constant prices. For example, between 1967 and 1978 per capita income in constant prices rose by an annual average of 10 per cent, and total wages and salaries grew by an annual average of 17 per cent. Per capita annual average household consumption increased by 1.5 per cent in current prices and by 11.9 per cent in constant prices during the same period. The total amount of wages and salaries grew by an annual average of 13 per cent between 1967 and 1969, by 13 per cent from 1970 to 1973 and by 21.8 per cent during the 1974–7 period. Table 12.3 summarises the growth of wages and salaries, employment and wage rates during the 1967–77 period.

As Table 12.3 shows, the total amount of wages and salaries paid increased by 350.3 per cent, employment by 76 per cent and the successive increments of wages and salaries by 156 per cent during the first decade of planned development. By 1978 agriculture provided 14 per cent of total wages and salaries, industry 15 per cent, construction and public works 17.1 per cent, transport and communication 6 per cent, services 25.4 per cent and administration 22.5 per cent. The public sector contributed 60 per cent of the GDP as well as providing 85 per cent of total wages and salaries and 60 per cent of employment. Thus the development of the public sector played a vital role in the generation of the living conditions of the population. Table 12.4 highlights the sectoral growth of income of self-employed persons and wage- and salary-earners between 1967 and 1977.

In order to off-set inflation and improve the standards of living of low-income groups, the state increased the national guaranteed minimum wage by 66 per cent during the 1967–78 period. The net average wage grew

Table 12.3 *The growth of total wages and salaries, employment and the wage rate, 1977/67*

	Total wages/salaries 1977/67	Total employment 1977/67	Wage rate 1977/67
Agriculture	122.1	−13.5	156.0
Non-agricultural sectors	320.2	184.0	48.0
Administration	322.6	105.4	106.0
Total	350.3	76.0	156.0

Source: MPAT, *Bilan économique*.

by 68 per cent during the same period. The increase in the national minimum wage was as follows:

	Non-agricultural Sector, AD/hour	Agricultural Sector, AD/day
April 1963	1.36	—
June 1964	1.36	7.54
June 1972	1.73	9.80
January 1974	2.08	12.25
February 1976	2.40	15.30
October 1977	3.16	20.00
May 1978	3.69	24.00
November 1978	4.21	28.00
January 1980	4.21	33.00

In addition, total state transfers rose by a factor of over 2.5 between 1967 and 1978. From 1974 to 1980 wages increased rapidly. The national minimum wage doubled, while the agricultural minimum wage increased 2.7 times. The two were made equal in 1980. As a consequence, the purchasing power of the population has risen appreciably during the period under consideration. Prices had almost doubled between 1969 and 1978, while gross pay tripled. As a result, real purchasing power grew by 48 per cent during the same period, representing an annual average growth rate of 4.45 per cent in gross terms and 2.13 per cent in real terms.

Post-independence development

Table 12.4 *The growth of disposable income, 1967–77 (AD billion)*

Sector	1967	1977	Public sector, 1977
Agriculture	1.9	5.3	1.3
Industry	1.6	6.1	4.6
Construction and public works	1.1	6.5	4.6
Transportation and communication	0.6	2.2	1.9
Commerce and services	3.7	10.3	1.7
Administration	2.0	8.3	8.3
Total	10.9	38.7	22.4

Source: MPAT.

In an attempt to reduce the inequality of income, the government increased the wages of low-income categories more rapidly than those of other income groups. Despite this, the gap between the lowest and highest incomes widened between 1968 and 1979. The monthly average wage rose from AD 750 to AD 1,066 between 1968 and 1976, representing an annual average growth rate of 4.5 per cent. The annual average net wage increased from AD 6,149 in 1973 to AD 10,372 in 1977 and reached AD 12,815 by 1978, while the minimum national guaranteed wage rose from AD 3,600 to AD 6,000 and then AD 9,000 during the same period. In the urban centres studied the gap between low- and high-income groups narrowed slightly. The income of the inhabitants of Algiers increased by an annual average rate of 5.89 per cent, and that of the other 12 major cities by 9.89 per cent (see Table 12.5).

In 1968, 74.8 per cent of all low-income (less than AD 8,000 per year) households studied received 48.4 per cent of all income. In 1976, 29.7 per cent of these low-income households received only 10.1 per cent of total income. In contrast to this, in 1968, 6.9 per cent of the high-income households (AD 15,000 to 50,000) received 22.3 per cent of total income. In 1976, 32.78 per cent of the high-income households received no less than 63.05 per cent of total income. The income of senior staff in 1968 was 6.7 times higher than that of the workers, declining to 5.13 times higher by 1976. Table 12.6 shows that inequalities of monetary resources persisted despite serious attempts to reduce the inequality of income between the various socio-professional categories.

The annual average income of wage- and salary-earners was 40 per cent less than that of non-agricultural self-employed people and entrepreneurs. The average annual income of entrepreneurs in industry and construction

Table 12.5 *The distribution of annual income in the major cities, 1968–76*

	1968		1976	
AD	% Households	% Income	% Households	% Income
0–4,000	45.6	19.8	10.30	1.60
4,001–8,000	29.2	28.6	19.40	8.55
8,001–15,000	18.3	29.3	38.50	31.50
15,001–30,000	5.5	15.3	26.20	35.40
Over 30,000	1.4	7.0	5.60	18.90
Over 50,000	n.a.	n.a.	0.98	4.05

Source: AARDES, *Eléments sur l'emploi et les revenus dans les principales villes d'Algérie* (January 1969).

Table 12.6 *Income distribution, 1977*

Socio-professional category	Total income (AD million)	Population	Average income of an active person (AD)
Wage- and salary-earners	26,176	2,014,000	12,997
Self-employed, entrepreneurs	11,066	487,064	22,720
Agricultural	3,515	255,252	13,771
Industrial, construction and public works	1,328	10,453	127,045
Others	6,223	221,359	28,113

Source: Les comptes économiques.

and public works was six times higher than the annual average of self-employed persons and entrepreneurs in agriculture and 21 times higher than the minimum national wage. There was a wide gap between the annual average per capita income of the urban population and that of the rural dwellers. Table 12.7 shows this persistent and unequal distribution of income within the country.

In 1973, 40 per cent of the income of the rural population was derived from agriculture, 20 per cent from non-agricultural activities, 20 per cent from workers' remittances from abroad and 20 per cent from state

Post-independence development

Table 12.7 *Comparison of average annual urban and rural incomes, 1973 and 1977*

	1973 (AD)	1977 (AD)	Annual average growth rate (%)
Urban per capita income	2,300	—	—
Per capita consumption	1,860	2,300	5.5
Rural per capita income	—	—	
Per capita consumption	540	780	9.6
National annual average per capita income	1,200	—	—
Per capita consumption	1,160	1,560	7.6

Source: MPAT, *Bilan économique*.

transfers. By 1979 there was a wide gap between the lowest and the highest income groups in the poor regions of rural Algeria. The poorest 10 per cent of families received only around AD 2,000 per year, which amounted to a per capita income of only AD 289. In contrast, the richest 10 per cent of families received an annual income exceeding AD 30,000 per household, that is, AD 4,347 per person per year, fifteen times that of the poorest rural households. Moreover, the per capita income in these poor rural areas was about 25 per cent lower than that of the annual average income of the rural 'well-off' families. That of the rural poor families was 70 per cent lower than the average national per capita income.

Nonetheless, the living conditions of the majority of the population, even of these poor rural zones, were improved by the development drive. Indeed, over 63 per cent of the active population derived their income from wage labour.

This income distribution policy resulted in the amelioration of the per capita food intake of the population. Indeed, the per capita consumption of the principal foodstuffs – cereals, meat, milk, potatoes, fats and sugar – increased during the post-independence period. Table 12.8 summarises the per capita consumption of these basic foods between 1938 and 1979.

Food intake remains insufficient quantitatively (2,400 calories per day) and qualitatively. Nonetheless, from 1955 to 1979 the per capital consumption increased by 38 kg for cereals, 8.4 kg for meat, 32.3 kg for milk and 10.9 kg for potatoes. Moreover, the improvement of per capita consumption was due primarily to the growth in the consumption of cereals (+300 calories), fats (+246 calories) and milk (+59 calories). On the whole, average food intake rose by 40 per cent after 1962.

Table 12.8 *The consumption of basic foodstuffs, 1938–79 (kg)*

Dates	Cereals	Meat	Milk (litres)	Potatoes	Fats	Sugar
1938	143	6.7	—	13.5	3.70	10.5
1955	147	6.6	21.00	23.5	5.28	16.8
1979	185	15.0	61.35	34.4	15.29	15.6*

* This is an underestimate.
Source: H. Ait Amara 'Système Alimentaire et identité culturelle', in *La Révue du C.E.N.E.A.P.*, No. 3 September 1985, p. 72.

However, the expansion of wage labour involved mostly male workers. The employment of women either as waged or salaried workers outside the domestic domain has stagnated since 1962.

The employment of women outside the home

In Algeria, as in the rest of the Islamic world, women have been relegated to the home (or private realm) since the Abbassid period. By the end of the Middle Ages, Muslim women, in urban areas as well as among rural wealthy families, came to be restricted to domestic tasks. Their confinement to the private realm prevented them not only from participating in public life but also from developing their intellectual potentialities. In modern times, the exigencies of modernisation and socio-economic development require the full participation of the female half of the population: hence the necessity of women's legal and social emancipation.

As pointed out above, the introduction of capitalist relations of production into Algeria resulted in the emergence and multiplication of a modern proletariat which included a certain number of women. By the twentieth century innumerable women were compelled by economic necessity to leave their homes in search of wage labour. In 1925, the number of women employed in the industrial sector totalled 25,291. In addition, several thousands were working as domestics in European families and many more as seasonal agricultural labourers on colonial plantations. The number of women working outside as wage labourers has increased in subsequent years.

In the post-independence period the percentage of women workers has either declined or stagnated. In fact, in 1966 the proportion of women in the total labour force represented a mere 5.2 per cent, rising slightly to 5.9 per cent in 1977 and reaching 7 per cent in 1982. In other words, in eleven

Post-independence development

Table 12.9 *Women in employment, 1966–82 (% increases within total work force)*

Sectors	1966	1977	1982
Services	62.20	75.00	79.00
Agriculture	21.90	5.59	3.37
Industry	15.40	17.36	14.32
Construction and public works	0.50	2.05	1.47

Source: Ministère du travail, *Evolution des problèmes de l'emploi en Algérie*, (1976) and ONS, *Statistiques* no. 3 (1984).

years the growth of the female labour force rose by only 0.7 per cent. By the late seventies and early eighties the employment of women speeded up. It increased by 7.6 per cent during the 1977–82 period. The employment of women within the national economy between 1966 and 1982 is shown in Table 12.9.

According to this table the majority of women were employed in the non-productive sectors. Furthermore, in 1982, 83.4 per cent of them were employed by the public sector, as against 78.7 per cent in 1977. The private sector continued to employ several thousand women without declaring them, particularly in the textile industry. Nevertheless, despite over two decades of socio-economic development, the employment of women in the public realm remains insignificant. Indeed, between 1966 and 1977, only 47,786 women were added to the total working females and 106,553 during the 1978–82 period. Today, between 200,000 and 300,000 women are working outside their homes (as against over 3.6 million housewives in 1977).

Almost all women employed outside their homes are still compelled to carry out double tasks. Once a woman's day's work is over, she has to perform her traditional domestic duties upon her return home. These working women, who are still not only faced with strong hostility from their families and from society in general, continue, in many cases, to do equal work with men for unequal pay. Despite their skills, experience and seniority, they are rarely promoted to supervisory and executive positions. However, as long as society persists in subjecting half of the most industrious sector of the population to a subservient position, it will never be modernised, developed and genuinely free and independent from external interference and encroachments.

In sum, despite the persistence of inequality of income, the 'populist' policy of the Boumedienne regime resulted in a relatively equitable distribution of income among the population. If the rate of demographic growth had been slower, the living conditions of the average family would have improved greatly. In fact, the proportion of households of more than seven persons grew by 47 per cent in the urban centres and by 30 per cent in the rural areas during the 1966–77 period. Yet, despite this high rate of demographic growth, the average number of persons under the charge of an employed individual fell from an average of 6.2 persons in 1967 to 5.2 by 1978.

In spite of such positive results this 'populist' employment policy has been denounced by the current regime, which considered it to be the main cause of the problems of the Algerian economy. Since 1980 the principle of full employment has been abandoned. Some members of the group in power consider that unemployment would be the best means of disciplining the workers. This constitutes a serious deviation from the ideology of the radical national movement which emerged from the North African Star and led the country to independence. In addition, the development of the most productive sectors of the economy has been seriously compromised by the new economic policy of President Chadli Benjadid, which is based on the compradorisation of economy and society. This trend is bound to undermine even the achievements of the 1967–78 period in the industrial field. Indeed, since 1979 a process of 'deindustrialisation' has been set in motion. If it is not reversed, it will compromise the chances for the overall development of the country and hence undermine the standards of living of the rapidly growing population.

Chapter 13

The new economic policy and its implications

The sudden death of President Boumedienne and the coming to power of Colonel Chadli Benjadid in early 1979 resulted in unexpected disruptive changes instead of a peaceful succession. In less than two years the strategy of development, the model of growth, the priorities, the overall objectives of industrialisation, the social policy and the political ideology of the state were revised and reversed without encountering a strong collective opposition. However, these changes were predetermined by the contradictions of the previous regime, which had stimulated the development of a 'socialist sector' as well as a 'dynamic' private sector. It assembled into a single party and a highly centralised state, heterogeneous groups with different ideological outlooks and representing contradictory class interests. Thus, despite its positive results, the development undertaken strengthened anti-democratic and anti-progressive forces that were, and still are, opposed to industrialisation, progress, secularisation and hence the modernisation of society. The consolidation of these class forces and social groups gave rise to Benjadidism, which questioned the possibility of a genuine national development based on industrialisation under the aegis of the state.

Before the death of Boumedienne an evaluation of the 1967–77 period of development was in progress. It was conceived as a necessary constructive critical assessment of this experience, whose aim was to delineate the achievements and shortcomings of this first crucial period of planned development in order to correct the errors and distortions made by 'economic operators' or engendered by such a rapid growth. However, the internal situation and the international juncture delayed the completion of that study until after Benjadid succeeded Boumedienne in 1979. Even while the late president was still lying in hospital, the members of the so-called revolutionary council, which included the principal contestants for his succession, M. Yahiaoui, A. Bouteflika and Ch. Benjadid, met to discuss the new situation created by Boumedienne's serious illness. They all agreed during this meeting that Boumedienne's policies must be reversed and abandoned. But they did not dare to reveal this fateful decision to the people. Thus, after Benjadid's election to the presidency of

The new economic policy

the republic and to the general secretariat of the single FLN party, the evaluation of the economic and social development of the previous decade provided the new regime with an excellent opportunity to play down the achievements of industrialisation and to highlight and exaggerate its shortcomings.

This so-called evaluation was intended to discredit the strategy of development adopted by the Boumedienne regime and to downgrade its results. Indeed, the authors of this document stated in the introduction that 'The conduct of our development was accompanied by grave distortions and profound imbalances both on the economic and social planes and even certain deviations which may compromise dangerously the construction and consolidation of our development and hence put a brake on the very dynamics of the revolution.' They went on to denounce 'the permanent triumphalism and self-congratulation' of the previous regime and its 'occultation of errors and weaknesses'.

After this denunciation, the critics of the economic and social development undertaken between 1965 and 1978 singled out the socialist industrial enterprises. According to the Ministry of Planning, which was headed by a protégé of the new President, these enterprises have not only been unprofitable but were also incapable of reducing their 'alarming deficits' to 'amortise their investment funds' and to 'redeem their debts' borrowed from the state banks. 'The reasons for these disequilibria were due', according to the authors of the evaluation, 'to a series of interconnected factors', of which they chose to cite only

> the investment overcosts and the long delay in realising the industrial projects, the slow pace of production during the initial phase of the operation of the new plants, the overconsumption of raw materials (caused by defective installations), excessive importation costs, over-manning of the productive units, the low productivity of labour, a bad work organisation, the insufficient qualifications and the inexperience of the labour force, the absence of material inducements, the existence of social problems . . .

In addition, the bureaucrats of this Ministry and their political bosses asserted that the bulk of the difficulties of the public enterprises were caused by the fact that they tried to assume a 'multiplicity of functions': development, importation, production, marketing, training, transportation, housing, medical care and leisure. They also attributed the 'problems' of these socialist corporations to their 'monopoly position' and particularly to their 'gigantism', a fact that allowed them, according to these critics, to 'constitute states within the state'.

The real aims of all these gratuitous armchair criticisms of the public enterprises of the industrial sector were masked behind ideological and

Post-independence development

Table 13.1 *The new structure of national enterprises, 1984–5*

Supervising ministries	No. of enterprises	
	1984	1985
Urbanism, construction and housing	125	129
Public works	34	34
Water resources, environment and forests	48	49
Heavy industry	44	41
Energy and petrochemical industry	28	30
Light industries	48	52
Agriculture and fishing	20	21
Transportation	24	24
Commerce	29	30
Culture and tourism	29	29
Finance	12	14
Public health	5	5
Planning and territorial organisation	2	4
Youth and sports	1	1
Higher education	1	1
Post office and telecommunications	2	2
Information	8	8
Total	460	474

Source: MPAT, 1985.

demagogic slogans, such as for 'a better life' and in search of 'the satisfaction of the needs of the citizens'. Despite the fact that the only way to satisfy such needs was the consolidation of these enterprises and the continuation of the industrialisation drive, the regime decided to break down these effective tools of production and development.

Indeed, under the pretext that the existing public companies had become gigantic, the regime proceeded, on the advice of military intelligence, to restructure them in order to reduce their sizes into meaningless so-called functional enterprises so that they would supposedly be transformed into 'manageable small entities and hence easily controllable'.

Without any preliminary research, without any attempt to try this reform on a few enterprises whose restructuring could be justified *a priori*, and without consulting the parties concerned (management, unions, workers), the 66 existing national public corporations were broken down into 474 specialised mini-enterprises. (Table 13.1 gives details.) The 19 existing public industrial companies, which constituted the backbone of

Table 13.2 *The number of new public enterprises at the wilayate level, August 1985*

Wilayate	No. of EPWs*	No. of EPCs**	Wilayate	No. of EPWs	No. of EPCs
Adrar	18	17	Constantine	24	17
Chlef	20	26	Medea	14	46
Laghouat	15	08	Mostaganem	18	20
Oum El Bouaghi	23	21	M'Sila	21	22
Batna	22	45	Mascara	15	39
Bejaya	18	32	Ouargla	15	07
Biskra	17	32	Oran	23	21
Bechar	16	20	El Bayadh	12	11
Blida	19	21	Illizi	05	02
Bouira	16	21	Bordj Bou Arreridj	14	11
Tamanrasset	12	10	Boumerdes	19	31
Tebessa	23	19	El Tarf	10	18
Tlemcen	25	32	Tindouf	05	05
Tiaret	26	38	Tissemsilt	09	19
Tizi-Ouzou	24	52	El Oued	08	18
Alger	61	26	Khenchla	04	17
Djelfa	19	18	Souk Ahras	04	10
Jijel	17	16	Tipaza	13	33
Setif	15	33	Mila	09	18
Saida	15	14	Ain Defla	14	25
Skikda	19	24	Naama	10	13
Sidi Bel Abbes	17	32	Ain Temouchent	07	24
Annaba	17	13	Ghardaia	10	08
Guelma	15	27	Relizane	07	28
Total				779	1,060

Source: MPAT, 1985.
* EPW: Public enterprise of the wilayate.
** EPC: Public enterprise of the commune.

the national economy and the driving force of development, were split into 120 mini-enterprises whose headquarters were scattered throughout the country, without the creation of the minimum conditions for their most basic operations.

On 2 July 1974 Algeria was divided administratively into 31 *wilayates*; each *wilayate* sub-divided into several *dairates*, totalling 160 and each *daira* into several communes, totalling 704. On 4 February 1984, the Benjadid regime decided to extend the number of wilayates to 48 and that of communes to 1,541. This administrative reform followed the 'destructuring' of the public enterprises and their ensuing multiplication. As a direct result, the total number of local public enterprises under the control of the *wilayates* and communes was multiplied by over three in less than three years, rising from about 500 in 1979 to 1865 in 1985. Table 13.2 indicates the final result of this irrational process of institutional segmentation.

In atomising the public enterprises in this fashion, the regime had undermined not only the process of development but also the resolution of some difficult managerial and organisational problems. In a country where inter-ministerial, inter- and intra-enterprise co-ordination was almost impossible – because of red tape and bureaucratic inefficiency – the government proceeded to multiply the micro-economic units of management.

A new five-year plan (1980–4) whose slogan was 'for a better life' was prepared and adopted at a congress of the country's single party. The principal objectives of the new plan were 'the reduction of tensions generated by unbalanced growth and the creation of the necessary conditions for the widening of the national market, investment and production' and the 'adaptation of the educational and vocational training system to the needs of the national economy'.

In the industrial field, the five-year plan began by denouncing the priority given to industrialisation up to 1979. It asserted that, although the biggest part of the financial, material and human resources of the nation was concentrated on the industrial sector, this sector did not sufficiently control its production machinery. It had few means for the design and implementation of its investments and it still called to a considerable extent upon outside technical assistance. Furthermore, it was strongly concentrated in the north of the country, in poles whose influence crippled the utilisation of good arable land to the detriment of a national land development policy. In other words, according to the plan, the problems of agriculture are caused by industry. Therefore, the new economic policy ought to reverse the order of priorities in favour of agriculture. The new industrial policy froze all important projects devised by the former regime to complete the projected industrial system. It aimed at 'rationalising' the functioning and management of the existing industries by 'the intensification of the use of the means of production, a better programming of production and a better control over . . . management capacities'.

Considering that the former regime's 'populist' social policy regarding employment and income distribution had induced the managers of the industrial public sector to overstaff the plants, the new political leadership stressed the following principles:

Greater efficiency in employment was needed in order to avoid redundancy of personnel and to aim at greater productivity

The level of wages must be linked with production and quality

Non-productive jobs would be limited to the number required for the good operation of the unit

The creation of new jobs should result directly from the growth of the economic surplus.

Furthermore, in the coming decade (1980-90) the industrial productive apparatus would be geared to:

the new priority sectors: housing, farming, hydraulics, economic and social facilities

meeting the population's need for industrial goods

developing facilities for accumulation.

Having shelved the most significant industrial projects that would have ensured and enhanced the success of the country's industrial take-off, the planners, in accordance with the directives of the new ruling group, emphasised that 'the present plan should pay special attention to small industry; on the grounds that it generates, not only jobs where lesser skills are required, but also various products and tools for the citizen's everyday use'.

To attain this goal, the private sector was invited to invest in order to contribute its share to industrial development in the following fields:

(a) Final processing
(b) Metal, mechanical and electrical industries, general mechanics, nut and bolt works, the screen-cutting industry, light hardware and ironmongery
(c) Sub-contracting through the supply of spare parts, small tools and instruments required by the public sector-plants, and the manufacturing of these items on a small scale to ensure a greater flexibility, particularly in mechanical, electrical, electronics and metallurgical industries.

Thus, the private sector was offered the most profitable downstream light industries. All over the world, these industries, which use simple technology, provide the highest rate of profit in manufacturing.

The private sector since 1979

After 1979 the new regime adopted a favourable attitude towards the national private sector. The resolution of the extraordinary fourth congress of the party of the FLN was followed by a decision of the central committee about the role and place of the private sector within the national economy. Thenceforth the government tried to integrate private initiative into the

Post-independence development

national planning of economic development. These decisions culminated in the promulgation of a new investment law in August 1982 which provided some incentives for private investors. In 1983 the government set up a special board (OSCIP) designed to orientate and to co-ordinate the investment of the national private sector.

The various pressures exerted by the private entrepreneurs in general, and *comprador* elements in particular, resulted in the shift of the economic policy of the nation. The new bourgeoisie, closely linked to conservative elements within the government, the party and the army, wanted not only some clearly defined space within the national economy but also some real assurances, guarantees and advantages in order to be able to use its accumulated capital. In 1980, the bank deposits of the private sector amounted to AD 12.60 billion. Indeed, since the promulgation of the 1982 investment law an increasing number of industrial projects are being submitted for approval either by the national investment commission (CNI) or by the *wilayate*'s investment commissions, which are empowered to approve smaller projects whose individual cost would not exceed AD 3 million.

In 1982 alone the national commission approved 104 private industrial projects. Their total investment costs amounted to about AD 370 million, and the average cost per project was AD 3.5 million. These projects, which would create 2,400 jobs, were in the following industries: construction materials, 27 per cent; food industries, 21 per cent; textiles, 19 per cent; metallurgical, mechanical and electrical industries, 3 per cent; others, 30 per cent. The geographical concentration remained almost unaltered. In fact, 48 per cent of the projects were located in four cities: Blida (17 per cent), Oran (13 per cent), Algiers (11 per cent) and Annaba (7 per cent).

In 1983, 376 projects were authorised by the CNI, whose total investment costs totalled AD 1.2 billion. Once completed, these projects would create about 7,000 jobs. The total investment of each project averaged AD 3.2 million. Food industries attracted 29 per cent, textile and light chemical industries 14 per cent, metallurgical, mechanical and electrical industries 12 per cent, construction materials, 13 per cent and others, 32 per cent. The geographical distribution of the projects was modified slightly in 1983. Some new *wilayates* attracted a growing number of private investors: for example, Mostaganem attracted 9 per cent of the total projects while Setif and Mascara had 7 per cent each. However, over one-fifth of the projects, representing one-third of total investments, were located in three cities: Algiers, Oran and Blida.

By 1984, the CNI approved 642 projects, which required a total investment of AD 2.2 billion. The average cost of each project was AD 3.4 million. These private industrial projects would create close to 12,000 jobs.

The new economic policy

The breakdown by industry as follows: food and light chemical industries, 15 per cent; metallurgical, mechanical and electrical industries, 12 per cent; construction materials, 12 per cent; textiles, 12 per cent, hotels and quarrying, 9 per cent and others, 40 per cent.

In sum, in the years 1982–6 the CNI approved 2,835 industrial projects, which necessitated a planned investment of AD 9.31 billion intended to create 51,400 jobs. In providing certain incentives such as tax exemption during the first five years and credit facilities with a low interest rate, the government expected that the private sector would create employment in the interior of the country in order to halt labour migration into the coastal cities. However, the preliminary results turned out to be very disappointing. The new facilities offered by the government to the private sector encouraged the entrepreneurs to re-equip their plants. The new technology happened to be labour-saving and capital-intensive, a fact that has certainly contributed to the increase of unemployment, especially among the new entrants into the labour market.

The total number of workers employed by the private sector appears to have declined from 72,755 in 1977 to 48,474 in 1980 before rising slightly to 56,131 in 1982. The situation has not improved since then because most projects launched during the 1982–6 period are not yet completed. These long delays were caused by bureaucratic blockages and an underdeveloped technical environment.

While employment in private industry was stagnating, turnover was increasing rapidly – from AD 5.74 billion in 1979 to over AD 8 billion in 1982.

Despite the multiplication of small private industrial enterprises the process of the concentration of capital appears to have accelerated in the 1980s. In 1982, 1,847 enterprises out of a total of 5,707 employed from 1 to 4 workers; 2,847 from 5 to 19; 721 from 20 to 49; 214 from 50 to 99; 60 from 100 to 199; 17 from 200 to 499; and one more than 500. During that year, the private industrial firms employing more than 30 workers possessed 56.3 per cent of the assets.

By the early 1980s the private sector was represented in the industrial, construction and public works sectors by a total of over 12,000 firms. The annual average of new enterprises was 600 during the 1962–82 period. By 1982, the private sector as a whole produced 30 per cent of the national added value outside agriculture. One year earlier, the private industrial entrepreneurs controlled 2.3 per cent of the total formation of gross fixed capital, employed 25.78 per cent of the industrial labour force and produced 33.6 per cent of the value of national manufactures.

In food industries the private sector possessed 4 per cent of capital stock, employed 34 per cent of the labour force and produced 57.4 per cent of added value. In textiles, with a share of 6.5 per cent of capital stock, it employed 45 per cent of the labour force and produced 51 per cent of added value. It must be noted that the private sector is concentrated in these two consumer goods industries, which accounted for 66.6 per cent of its production.

It follows that, although the Algerian new industrial bourgeoisie is driven by the profit motive, its socio-economic and political behaviour is still conditioned by a *comprador*, speculative, Levantine and submissive logic. The private industrial sector is situated downstream of the public sector. The latter produces and furnishes the inputs, which require costly investments and complex technical and organisational skills, to the former at lower prices, often below production costs. Once the materials are processed and transformed into consumer goods, these private manufacturers sell them at the highest prices possible in a highly protected national market. The state never tried to devise a national price policy; this allowed the private investors to impose upon the consumers some of the highest rates of profit in the world, varying from 60 to 120 per cent.

Because of the incomplete nature of the industrialisation of the country undertaken by the public corporation, Algerian private industrial enterprises were still, in the early 1980s, 100 per cent dependent upon imports of technology and spare parts. They also continue to import 54.79 per cent of their semi-finished products from abroad. The state external bank offers them one of the most favourable exchange rates in the world. Furthermore, the new industrial bourgeoisie is strongly opposed to a Sadat-style opening of the national economy for multinational firms. However, the majority of the industrial entrepreneurs interviewed recently are favourable to some form of association with foreign capital. In this respect this new industrial bourgeoisie would like to play a *comprador* role. So far, its industrial experience has not transformed it into a nationally oriented dynamic class, determined not only to play an economic role in the construction of a capitalist economy but also to push for the establishment of a liberal democracy.

On account of industrial inexperience and political insecurity, the overwhelming majority of private investors are attracted by activities that will ensure them quick profits with little risk. As a result, they continued to behave like speculators concerned only with business opportunities that offer them the highest rates of profit in the short term. In order to attain this goal these industrialist-speculators seek a powerful protector within the regime, either through a marriage alliance or through association-corruption. In other words, the Algerian industrial bourgeoisie, like all the third world bourgeoisies, is interested primarily in the accumulation of wealth rather than in the construction of an independent, prosperous and free

The new economic policy

society. Indeed one of the most conscientious industrialists noted recently that 'our entrepreneurs are money-makers [*faiseurs d'argent*] rather than industrialists'.

Paradoxically, the so-called 'liberalisation' has been accompanied by the deterioration of the political and administrative environment of the economy as a whole. Indeed, bureaucratic red tape has become so stifling that it is almost impossible for both public and private sectors to operate normally. Most of the private projects launched during the 1980–4 plan were not completed during this period. Corruption and nepotism have become mechanisms of the state so that private investors are being compelled to associate with highly placed officials in exchange for assistance in the resolution of complex 'multi-level' bureaucratic blockages. But corruption does not stop at this stage; it is extended to contractual relations between the private and public sectors.

In order to obtain advantageous contracts with the public sector, private entrepreneurs have been forced either to pay state officials for their co-operation or to associate them with their lucrative, parasitic activities. This 'Levantinisation' of the public administration led a private entrepreneur to inform me that the ruling group in power had 'sabotaged' Boumedienne's 'socialism' and had already succeeded in 'deforming' the current 'economic liberalism' at its birth. Indeed, genuine capitalism presupposes the existence of specific rules of the economic game and their strict observance, particularly by the state, as regulator of the economy and guarantor of the functioning of the market, so that competition between the various private enterprises is encouraged. Free competition is bound to benefit not only the public sector but also the consumers.

Furthermore, the new regime decided to give top priority to agriculture, to the detriment of basic industry. The five-year plan stressed that, in the long run, the 'development' of agriculture is based on the following:

> In order to foster specialisation, based on the exploitation of the major three climatic areas of the country . . . the agricultural activities of the peasant communities must be developed in close co-ordination with the other activities . . . the complementarity of the steppes, the high plains and the Tell should be gradually developed. The main goal lies in the reintegration . . . of the association of arable farming, animal husbandry and arboriculture on the one hand and the association of irrigated crops and dry crops on the other hand.

The setting up of a new system of organisation was supposed to enhance the management of public farming units. All the obstacles hampering the supply of inputs, production and the marketing of produce were to be rapidly eliminated. This resulted in the abolition of CAPCS and the privatisation of marketing channels, a fact that allowed private dealers to accumulate handsome profits from their speculative buying and selling activities.

The planners recommended the following steps:

The development of water resources and the expansion of irrigated areas (first through the improvement of the existing networks and then through the extension of collection mainly in small water systems)

The continuation of intensive efforts for soil improvement and preservation and the extension of forests in connection with the major agricultural projects in the south and the north

A rational land occupation that must be improved on the basis of appropriate adaptations to the ecological conditions of various regions, with a view to intensifying production and developing the association arable farming–animal husbandry–arboriculture and giving priority to fodder and food crops and to semi-intensive and intensive stock breeding

The development of livestock on a large scale and the introduction of fruit arboriculture

The renewal, maintenance and adaptation of the mechanical materials and equipment to the real conditions of production in order to improve productivity

The increase of productivity and yields of cereals through the use of industrial inputs, selected seeds and better management.

It is ironic that, although the planners began by substituting agricultural development for industrialisation, they ended by admitting that industrial inputs are vital for the increase of agricultural production and productivity. They also ignored the fact that the massive utilisation of chemical inputs and other mechanical means of production are capital-intensive and labour-saving and thus conducive to the displacement of the agricultural population.

The restructuring of public enterprises

In the midst of their struggle to overcome underdevelopment, and confronted with the initial refusal of the bulk of foreign engineering firms, which had previously controlled the Algerian market, to sell their technology and technical expertise to Algeria, the Ministry of Industry and energy had granted monopoly rights to the nascent public enterprises for the import, marketing and production of their projected products. This measure allowed these national companies to reduce the role of the middlemen in import-export activities, to compel foreign firms to sell their industrial equipment and technical expertise to Algeria and, in particular, to learn the nature of the Algerian market and hence the exact demand of the consumer in the national economy. Such information helped to elaborate new industrial projects designed to satisfy these national needs by new projected national production. However, the granting of monopoly rights was strongly denounced by the local *compradors* and their representatives within the power-structure. When they failed to reverse this decision, they intensified their campaign through rumours against industrialisation and industrialists. The current re-structuring of these public enterprises is now intended to suppress their monopoly rights over import–export activities and the direct marketing of locally produced and imported industrial products.

Despite the high-sounding economic arguments derived from criticisms of the performance and functioning of the public industrial enterprises, the policies advanced by the Benjadid regime in favour of their restructuring were prompted by purely political considerations. Every well-informed individual knew that the major problems of these public corporations were caused by the underdeveloped nature of the industrial environment. Therefore a genuine concern for their resolution would have required not the dismantling of the public enterprises, which constituted the prime movers of development, but the rationalisation and dynamisation of their political, social, bureaucratic, cultural and technical environment.

Instead of adjusting this paralysing environment to the exigencies and requirements of industrialisation, the post-Boumedienne political leadership chose to do just the reverse. By subjecting the logic of industrial development not only to the logic of an underdeveloped society but also to narrow and selfish private interests, the new leadership was bound, sooner or later, to undermine the process of a national development genuinely geared to the satisfaction of the needs of the popular strata.

The experience of industrialisation was a very recent one; it covered less than a decade (1970–8). In addition it took place within an unfavourable internal socio-cultural and technical environment and an external context hostile to the development of the third world countries. Yet despite this, the public companies managed to install an industrial apparatus and also to develop the material and human resources, capable of operating it and, eventually, of reproducing it. In this attempt to overcome an underdeveloped socio-economic and cultural reality, the public enterprises gave rise to a small group of highly experienced cadres, who provided the intellect behind development in the various basic industrial branches. By breaking up these public corporations, the new regime dissipated a vital national asset, a fact that was bound to compromise the further industrialisation of the country.

Furthermore, given the inadequacies of the industrial environment, the public enterprise had to train, to house and to provide transportation and medical care for their workers and staff. In such a context industry could

Post-independence development

not be expected to yield huge financial gains in the short term. Its primary function was rather to generate the changes necessary to modernise an underdeveloped society. This initial objective was attained: the public enterprises engendered an entire industrial population, represented by experienced managers, engineers, technicians, foremen, skilled workers and labourers. In so doing, they contributed to the raising of the scientific and technical levels of society as well as to the improvement of the living conditions of the people and so laid a solid foundation for the mastery of advanced technology, the *sine qua non* for the construction of the national economy and the modernisation of culture. The industrialisation of the country should be considered one of the greatest achievements of contemporary Algeria.

In 1982, in answer to the question 'what were the achievements and short-comings resulting from the rapid industrialisation of Algeria?', one of the most experienced industrial planners and managers replied:

The main achievements are represented by the fact that we were able to start from nothing and to create an industrial base. This was the most important achievement. We were able to build innumerable plants specialising in the manufacture of almost all basic products. And I think that now we are mastering almost all the basic technologies. This means that in the future we have to continue our efforts, we have to increase our capacity, we have to improve our efficiency . . . The most difficult tasks have been done. It's clear that this was a very costly experience. We made a number of mistakes. We made bad choices. But this was the learning process. It was costly. We are not highly efficient . . . However, this overall experience was wonderful. It was a permanent challenge on every front, in every area. We had to overcome all the problems of building the plants. By the late 1970s, we had to overcome all the problems related to their management and maintenance.

We encountered a number of problems we had never heard of before and our engineers had to overcome new problems they had never experienced before. So each time, each day, each case was a challenge for any one of us. We had also to analyse all the efforts, all the choices and all the mistakes we made in order to take a better advantage of our industrial experience and capitalise on it. Now, if we are to build another plant, it's obvious that we'll build a better plant in a shorter time at less cost.

This experience allowed us to increase our technological capital which we can now use to design other projects and other plants. This was the main feature of the 1967–79 period . . . It was costly and we are still not highly efficient, but when we look at what happened during this past twenty years, what does it mean for a country like Algeria? It's almost nothing. In twenty years we were able to establish this industrial base in a basically agricultural underdeveloped country. Now we still have at least twenty years more to increase our efficiency, to increase our mastering of technologies and to develop new technologies by ourselves . . .

This experience may be considered by certain people to be costly. But, let's say that the overall costs of industries were x billion dollars, and we could say to a country, 'would you agree to pay this x billion dollars and be sure that in twenty years, you would be an industrialised country?' Well, no country in the world would refuse such a proposal.

Indeed, according to most historians of modern industry, the experiences of industrialisation of the advanced capitalist and socialist countries required more than two generations to succeed. Consequently, the political leadership's decision to restructure the public enterprises violated the logic of modern industry. This restructuring could have been thought of in terms of redefining the functional relationships between these public corporations so that they could improve their industrial organisation, resolve some serious management problems, master the existing technologies and start innovating in all these fields.

However, the political leadership's solution amounted to a systematic segmentation of the public enterprises which they presented to the nation as a panacea. Instead of allowing the managers and workers of this infant industry to overcome the difficulties inherent in its growth and development, the regime decided to impose from above a measure designed to simplify the operation and functioning of an embryonic economic system. According to a former industrialist, 'in a world that requires complexity, the current political leadership believes it can find a panacea in simplification'. Indeed, the world industrial experience has shown that most successful processes of industrialisation were made possible by the emergence and consolidation of firms which were flexible, efficient, well organised, well articulated, solid, highly complex, multi-functional and hence multi-structured. In an underdeveloped state, the imposition of microscopic enterprises was bound to hamper the development of the economy. A mosaic of autonomous micro-economic structures, geared to the maximisation of immediate financial gains, obviously cannot propel the industrialisation drive. The logic of industry universally subordinates the administrative, political, cultural and social environment to the requirements and exigencies of the rational functioning of the economy, and not the other way round. Thus, the restructuring of enterprises reveals an attitude that refuses to confront industrial complexity and a vision of organisation and management of a modern enterprise which could not transcend the traditional family shop.

The outcome has been disastrous. Instead of promoting decentralised decision-making, the suppression of the function of co-ordination at the branch level, and the multiplication of micro-centres of economic activities without providing them with the power and capacity to take decisions and co-ordinate these activities, makes the ministry the supreme arbiter and co-ordinator of a chaotic situation. Instead of the announced decentrali-

Post-independence development

sation of decision-making, the restructuring of enterprises resulted in a creeping centralisation of power. Since a ministry is incapable of arbitraring or co-ordinating or taking a decision on its own, it has been compelled to refer all the growing problems to the presidency, whose decisions have created more problems than they have resolved because of its remoteness from the economic reality of these new microscopic enterprises. This state of affairs has thus reinforced the bureaucratisation of economic life.

However, this decision was not dictated by sheer ignorance of industrial dynamics. On the contrary, those who advised it knew well – and the current rulers of Algeria appear to have agreed with them on its implications – that industrialisation promotes a vertical socio-political and economic integration of the local population through the modern institutions associated with it. Indeed, the various public industrial corporations engendered not only complex organisations, but also corporative groupings which became countervailing centres of power, a fact that was bound to reduce the direct intervention of the political potentates in the mangement of these institutions and to contribute in the medium and long terms to the emergence and development of democratic institutions. Thus, the Algerian rulers, like most despotic Arab monarchs, came to view the growth and development of these enterprises, not as cogent means of cementing a vertical national integration of society, but as a threat to their power. Despots have never encouraged the autonomisation of centres of decision, be they industrial, financial, commercial, social or political. For Benjadid's advisers, the atomisation of the public corporations constituted an old political device used by 'oriental despotic' governments to prevent the development of modern corporate communities of interest, represented by the socialist enterprises, whose operations were bound, sooner or later, to compel Algerians to get rid of their traditional inertia. Accordingly, the restructuring of public companies was preceded by a drastic shift in the orientation and hence priorities of development.

The sectoral priorities of the Benjadid regime and the disastrous consequences of the new economic policy

The planners, in accordance with the political directives of their new masters, projected the investment targets for the 1980–4 period as shown in Table 13.3. The share of industrial investment was reduced by almost 20 per cent over the 1978–9 period and that of the hydrocarbons and petrochemical industries by no less than 50 per cent. In other words, investment priorities were reversed, a possibility that had been anticipated as far back as 1967. However, the eventual shift in investment priorities envisaged in the previously mentioned *Perspectives Septennales* issued in that year was

Table 13.3 *The projected investment structure of the first five-year plan (1980–4)*

Sector	AD billion	%
Industry	154.5	38.6
(of which hydrocarbons)	63.0	15.7
Agriculture, fishing, forestry	24.1	6.0
Water resources	23.0	5.7
Transport	13.0	3.3
Economic infrastructure	37.9	9.5
Housing	60.0	15.0
Education, vocational training	42.2	10.5
Social infrastructure	16.3	4.1
(of which public health)	7.0	1.7
Collective equipment	9.6	2.4
Enterprises of implementation	20.0	5.0

Source: MPAT, *Le Rapport général du premier plan quinquennal 1980–1984*.

one that would have consolidated the overall development of the country without halting the process of industrialisation. The new post-Boumedienne economic policy, on the other hand, derided the notion of 'industrialising industry', denouncing it as an imported foreign model and considering a pause in industrialisation as a necessary condition for the development of agriculture and the social sectors and the satisfaction of the needs of a population of over 20 million, 60 per cent of whom were under 20 years of age.

When the senior staff of the industrial enterprises tried to moderate the zeal of Abdelhamid Brahimi, the Minister of Planning, who was assigned the mission of atomising the public corporations, the government reacted hastily but brutally. At the beginning of the five-year plan (1980–4) a systematic campaign of denegration of 'operators' of the public industrial sector was launched during a national conference on development, presided over by Benjadid. After three days of denunciations and unfounded accusations, the bulk of the cadres of the nation realised that the new political leadership was determined to destroy the national enterprises. In spite of intimidation, the majority of the people in charge of the public sector continued to voice their opposition to the new economic reforms. The government reacted by denouncing the wasteful management of industry. Several managers and senior staff were even arrested under the pretext of corruption or mismanagement. This affected the integrity of the heads of industry, discouraged the workers in the sector and hence undermined the entire development drive. Indeed, the slow pace of development of the national economy and the persistent regression of the social sectors represent an alarming index of the disorganisation and demobilisation of the economic agents of the country. Since 1979 none of the planned objectives has been fulfilled.

In fact, during the 1980 year plan, which inaugurated the first five-year plan (1980–4), out of AD 20.03 billion projected for industrial investments, only AD 16.79 billion (84 per cent) has actually been invested. Agriculture consumed only 47 per cent of the funds allocated; water resources, 66 per cent; construction and public works, 50 per cent; transport and tourism, 50 per cent; storage and distribution, 36 per cent; housing, 66 per cent; vocational training, 35 per cent; and public health and social infrastructure, 44 per cent. In other words, from the outset, this plan was marked by a fall in the rate of industrial investment and a further regression of the newly proclaimed high-priority sectors. The rate of growth of the GDP, excluding petroleum and natural gas, rose by 7 per cent in 1980. The total value of industrial production increased from AD 12.9 billion in 1979 to AD 14.9 billion in 1980, representing a rate of growth of 14.28 per cent, even though the target was 51.5 per cent. The rate of utilisation of productive capacity also declined in several branches.

This trend continued during the 1981 annual plan. Net industrial investment fell by 21 per cent compared to 1980, the hardest hit branches being textiles (-31 per cent), petrochemicals (-28 per cent), mechanical industry (-21 per cent) and the steel and light chemical industries (-19 per cent). In short, apart from 'local industries' and construction materials, the rate of net industrial investment utilisation declined dramatically in all other branches. The energy and petrochemical industries consumed 61 per cent of the planned investment, heavy industries 19 per cent, and light industries 18 per cent.

The rate of net investment in the so-called 'priority sectors' did not improve at all during the annual plan of 1981. For example, only 50 per cent of the projected investment earmarked for housing, public health and youth was utilised. The authorities of economic infrastructures consumed 31 per cent of the planned investment; those of education and vocational training, 42 per cent; those of social infrastructures, 36 per cent; those of water resources, 43 per cent; and those of administrative infrastructures, 45 per cent.

The information available for 1982 reveals that the stagnation of the national economy continued to be accompanied by declining rates of net industrial, agricultural, infrastructural and social investment. According to highly exaggerated estimates based on the preliminary results of the first three-quarters of 1982, the rate of investment utilisation for the national economy averaged 80 per cent, ranging from 60.7 per cent for the 'means of implementation' to 88.4 per cent for the 'means of transportation'. However, since the final results for the entire year were much lower than anticipated, the Ministry of Planning withheld their release at the end of the year. Nonetheless, an official government document admitted that 'the pace and level of the utilisation of planned investment remains far below targets', especially in the new high-priority sectors such as agriculture, housing, water resources and other vital social services.

Total economic production stagnated also. The growth rate of the GDP during 1982 was estimated at 7.2 per cent, which is very low if the total amount of past investment is taken into consideration. Several industrial plants established by the previous regime started production during this year.

With the disorganisation of public enterprises brought about by the so-called 'restructuring' of the public corporations, the apparatus of industrial statistics was severely damaged. Furthermore, from 1983 onwards, the authorities in the Ministry of Planning began either to manipulate or to conceal compromising economic statistics. The annual plans stopped providing detailed information about the performances of the previous ones. They included only national, overestimated, rates of net investment for the first three-quarters of the year. The final results were kept secret. It became very difficult even for an Algerian researcher to obtain information.

The only source of information about the performance of the economy during the period 1979–84 comes from an internal document produced by the Ministry of Planning. As the figures in Tables 13.4 and 13.5 show, the annual rate of growth looks good when measured in current prices (some 15 percent) but much less good if constant prices are used (only 4.3 per cent). The same tables also reveal details about changes in the sectoral composition of the GDP during the same period. They show, for example, that the share of industry (excluding hydrocarbons) in real terms, rose from 12 per cent in 1979 to 15.3 per cent in 1984. This increase was rendered possible by the completion of the industrial plants set up by the previous regime. The contributions of the other sectors have either declined or stagnated. For example, the share of agriculture decreased from 9.5 per cent to 8.6 per cent and that of hydrocarbons from 29.6 per cent to 23.7 per cent during the same period. The total taxes on hydrocarbons rose from AD 37.7 billion in 1980 to AD 51 billion in 1981, declining to AD 41.5 billion in 1982 to AD 37.7 billion in 1983 and increasing to AD 43.8 billion by 1984. Instead of being invested in productive activities, these revenues were primarily used for operating the state machinery and other current expenditures. The total amount of government expenditures went up from

Post-independence development

Table 13.4 *The structure of the GDP, 1979–84 (AD billion in current prices)*

	1979		1984		Annual average variation	Variation of added value	
	Value	%	Value	%		Value	%
Agriculture	10,776	9.5	19,710	8.6	12.8	8,934	7.8
Industry	13,570	12.0	29,690	13.0	16.7	16,120	14.1
Hydrocarbons	33,535	29.6	63,030	27.7	13.4	29,495	25.7
Construction and public works	18,119	16.0	38,190	16.7	16.1	20,071	17.5
Transportation and communication	6,726	6.0	12,240	5.4	12.7	5,514	4.9
Trade	16,790	14.8	32,070	14.1	13.8	15,280	13.5
Services	5,105	4.5	9,530	4.2	13.3	4,425	3.9
Total added value	104,621		204,460		14.3	99,839	—
Taxes	6,072	5.4	18,630	8.2	24.3	12,558	11.0
Customs duties	2,514	2.2	4,730	2.1	13.5	2,216	1.9
Total GDP	113,207	100.0	227,820	100.0	15.0	114,613	100.0

Source: MPAT, 1985.

Table 13.5 *The sectoral growth of the GDP, 1979–84 (AD billion constant prices)*

	1979		1984		Average annual variation	Variation of added value
	Value	%	Value	%		
Agriculture	10,776	9.36	12,101	10.4	2.4	1,325
Industry	13,570	11.79	21,400	18.4	9.5	7,830
Hydrocarbons	53,535	46.52	33,072	28.4	−6.7	20,463
Construction and public works	6,726	5.8	8,758	7.5	5.4	2,032
Transportation and communication	nd	nd	nd	nd	nd	nd
Trade	16,790	14.6	20,744	17.8	4.3	3,954
Services	5,105	4.4	6,395	5.5	4.6	1,291
Total added value	104,621	92.5	125,848	88.0	0.6	4,032
Taxes	6,072	5.3	9,544	8.2	9.5	3,472
Customs duties	2,514	2.2	4,414	3.8	11.9	1,900
Total GDP	113,207	100.0	116,428	100.0	4.3	1,340

Source: MPAT, 1985.

AD 21.6 billion in 1979 to no less than AD 51.8 billion by 1984, representing an annual average growth rate of 19.1 per cent.

Despite a sharp fall towards the end of the first five-year plan, the total value of household consumption rose in real terms from AD 56.2 in 1979 to AD 76.5 billion by 1984, which amounted to an annual average rate of 6.4 per cent, corresponding to less than 3 per cent per person. The GDP per capita went up from AD 6,250 to AD 10,730 in current prices.

However, the overall rate of net investment utilisation during the 1980–4 plan for the national economy turned out to be only about 68 per cent of the target: of the total AD 459.2 billion earmarked for investment during the first five-year plan, only AD 345 billion was utilised.

The disastrous consequences of the new economic policy are revealed by the following results: the industrial public sector, whose share in the total projected investment was revised downwards from 38.6 per cent to 28 per cent, realised only 68.1 per cent of its planned target; agriculture and forestry attained 66.3 per cent; fishing, 42.4 per cent; transport, 63.8 per cent; and means of implementation, which was supposed to increase the absorptive capacity of the national economy, 62.6 per cent. It must be noted that industry, which had a high absorptive capacity in the past, was brought down to the level of the other sectors. Not a single new industrial project was launched during the 1980–4 plan. The total industrial investment of AD 120.74 billion was used to complete projects started in the 1970s. The gradual entry into production of the new plants contributed – in spite of the chaotic situation created by the so-called reorganisation of the enterprises – to a noticeable annual growth of industrial production. However, because of the relatively massive investment of the late 1970s, the rates of growth were expected to be much greater. The Ministry of Planning kept lowering the production targets in order to cover up the immediate consequences of the dismantling of public enterprises.

Nonetheless, the production of the national public corporations increased by an annual average of 8.3 per cent during the 1980–4 period. The growth of production of manufacturing industries average 13.8 per cent per year and hydrocarbons 1.9 per cent. The annual average growth of industrial output of the various branches was as follows: chemical industries, 19.13 per cent; textiles, 15.8 per cent; steel, metallurgical, mechanical and electrical industries, 14 per cent; water and power, 12.6 per cent; lumber, cork and paper, 11.70 per cent; leather and shoes, 9.2 per cent; food industries, 8 per cent; construction materials, ceramics and glass industries, 7.9 per cent; and mining and quarrying, 3.5 per cent.

It is in the field of hydrocarbons that the industrial policy of the 1970s has produced the most positive results. Indeed, through the development effort undertaken by the national oil company, SONATRACH, which

Post-independence development

Table 13.6 *The production of hydrocarbons, 1979–84*

	Unit	1979	1980	1981	1982	1983	1984
Crude oil	Million tons	52.5	47.2	37.6	33.5	31.3	33.3
Condensate	Million tons	4.3	4.3	8.8	12.3	13.7	14.0
GPL	Million tons	0.8	1.0	1.3	1.6	1.5	2.8
Natural gas	Billion cubic metres	21.4	21.3	45.7	63.1	70.7	73.2
GNL	Billion cubic metres	19.7	10.7	12.3	16.8	25.9	20.1
Processed oil	Million tons	5.3	9.8	12.9	18.5	17.0	19.1

Source: MPAT, 1985.

aimed at the diversification, re-evaluation and processing of hydrocarbons, the structures of production and exportation were modified during the early 1980s, a fact that minimised the impact of the world economic crisis as well as the fall of petroleum prices. Table 13.6 shows the production of hydrocarbons between 1979 and 1984.

The various projects of development launched by SONATRACH in the late 1970s resulted in the diversification of products derived from the hydrocarbons industry. Algeria's dependence on crude oil and natural gas has been reduced. By 1984, 57.8 per cent of the petroleum products were processed inside the country.

A schematic evaluation of the results of some of the new priority sectors, particularly agriculture, reveals the extent of the disastrous consequences of the new economic policy. For instance, in the agricultural sector this economic policy started in 1980 by liberalising the marketing networks of agricultural products, dismantling the CAPCS in 1981, selling their equipment to the private sector and restructuring the self-managed sector and the co-operatives of the agrarian revolution farming units. The latter were divided into 3,429 smaller productive units so that they could be easily managed. In addition, 0.7 million hectares were distributed by the state of private farmers, most of them members of the co-operatives of the agrarian revolution. The five national boards that assisted the former self-managed sector were sub-divided into 14 new boards, each of them specialising in specific tasks.

Finally, in September 1987, the government, without any preparation, published a decree authorising the Ministry of Agriculture to sell the usufruct, the farm machinery and all related equipment and tools as well as buildings located within the so-called self-managed sector to the agricultural workers. The funds needed for these transactions are to be lent to the buyers by the state bank of agricultural development.

The new economic policy

The constitution prohibits the sale of former colonised land nationalised by the state in 1963 and the leadership does not yet dare to remove this clause. Therefore, this interministerial decree allowed the president of the republic to circumvent the law and to impose a compromise on the procomprador political forces who wanted to privatise these public farms and on the partisans of the maintenance of the status quo. However, since the president favours the former over the latter, these fertile lands which were seized from the French settlers (who expropriated them from the Algerian peasantry during the 1830–1962 period) in the aftermath of the revolutionary war when the balance of power was in favour of the popular strata are eventually going to be sold to the new comprador bourgeoisie.

From 1980 onwards the private agricultural sector was offered more incentives to produce than the public and co-operative sectors. For instance, imports of farm machinery by the private sector rose sharply between 1980 and 1984. In four years the private farmers received 27,000 tractors, 4,000 motor cultivators and 12,000 lorries for transportation and livestock farming, and the 10,000 tractors possessed by the CAPCS. The private farmers' share of fertiliser and other industrial inputs rose from 28 per cent in 1977–8 to 42 per cent in 1980–1.

However, instead of increasing the production of basic food crops, the private farmers specialised in the cultivation of speculative products such as watermelons, melons and fruit, a fact that has accentuated the crisis in Algerian agriculture and hence contributed to the increase in food imports. Indeed, according to the *Bilan agricole*, established by the Ministry of Planning in the autumn of 1984, the Benjadid government planned an annual average production of cereals of 30 million quintals during the 1980–4 period. However, cereal production averaged only 17.3 quintals per year during this period. As a result, while local production of these crops had provided 52 per cent of the national consumption in 1979, it declined to only 20 per cent by 1984. The annual average returns per hectare fell from 6.2 quintals per hectare during the 1969–77 period to 6 quintals per hectare during the 1979–84 period.

Wine production declined from an annual average of 3.8 million hectolitres during the 1974–7 period to 2.6 million hectolitres in the 1979–83 period. The annual returns averaged 18.6 hectolitres during 1974–7, falling to 13.7 hectolitres per hectare in the 1979–83 period. Milk production decreased from 700 million litres to 658 million, while imports rose from 677 million litres to 958 million litres between 1977 and 1983. By that year, 62 per cent of the national consumption was imported from abroad. Although the production of vegetables rose slightly from an annual average of over 1 million quintals during the 1974–7 period to 1.25 million from 1979 to 1983, Algeria had to import 3.5 million quintals of potatoes in

1983 alone. While the production of watermelons rose by about 115 per cent, imports of vegetables tripled between 1980 and 1984, increasing from an annual average of 1 million quintals during 1974–7 to 2 million during 1977–83. More serious still, the imports of basic cereals, mostly wheat, averaged 17.3 million quintals during the 1974–7 period, rising to 26 million quintals during the 1978–83 period. The total value of imported foodstuffs jumped from AD 5.1 billion in 1979 to AD 8.8 billion in 1984, representing an annual average growth of 11.5 per cent. In financial terms, the value of these imports averaged AD 9 billion per year and represented 17 per cent of the total imports of the country during this period.

The leadership that came to power after 1978 exploited the desires of the population in general, and the new middle classes in particular, for certain consumer goods. While the process of development was being reversed, the new rulers stressed their willingness to satisfy the 'needs' of the people. Since the reform of the national enterprises undermined the entire economy, the Benjadid government resorted to imports in order to satisfy these 'needs', a fact that diverted the financial resources of the state from productive investment to the import of consumer products. Indeed, the death of Boumediene occurred after a decade of rapid development which contributed to the enrichment of private business and to the rising expectations of labouring men and women. The policy of austerity amounted to a sort of forced saving as a result of the scarcity of consumer goods. Although the president became very popular throughout the country, most people were extremely frustrated. Taking advantage of this situation and the 1979–80 sharp increase in oil prices provoked by the outbreak of the Iraq–Iran war, the new leadership raised the slogan 'for a better life' at the extraordinary congress of the single FLN party, held in 1980. An anti-scarcity programme (PAP) designed to import consumer products was adopted by the council of ministers. Furthermore, Algerians were not only authorised to travel freely abroad but also allowed to convert an annual sum of AD 1,000 per person into foreign currencies. Innumerable local state-owned supermarkets were rapidly built and filled with imported consumer goods. For over a couple of years the new Algerian middle classes indulged in high consumption made possible by savings accumulated during the period of austerity and ambitious investment projects. As a result the total value of imported goods rose from AD 32.4 billion in 1979 to AD 51.2 billion in 1984, representing an annual average growth of 9.5 per cent during the first five-year plan. Table 13.7 summarises the growth of imports.

The data summarised in Table 13.7 corroborate my two principal theses relating to the ending of economic development through industrialisation and to the gradual compradorisation of the Algerian economy and society

The new economic policy

Table 13.7 *Imports, 1979–84 (AD billion current prices)*

Category	1979	1980	1981	1982	1983	1984	1980–4
Food, beverages, tobacco	5.1	7.6	9.1	9.3	9.7	8.8	44.5
Energy and lubricants	0.6	1.0	1.0	0.8	1.0	1.1	4.9
Raw materials	1.7	2.3	2.7	2.5	2.9	3.2	13.6
Semi-finished products	7.7	9.9	12.1	11.0	12.1	15.2	60.3
Capital goods	12.4	12.7	16.3	16.5	15.8	15.6	76.9
Consumer products	4.8	6.9	7.4	9.1	8.0	7.2	38.6
Miscellaneous	0.07	0.08	0.1	0.3	0.3	0.1	0.9
Total	32.4	40.5	48.7	49.5	49.8	51.2	239.6

Source: MPAT, 1985.

since the advent of Benjadidism. The share of the value of capital goods in the total bill of imports fell from 38.3 per cent in 1979 to 30.5 per cent in 1984. The nature of equipment brought in from abroad has changed. Most of these capital goods are represented by construction engines and vehicles. Once the 'boom' is over they will be left to rust. Simultaneously, the share of consumer goods in the total value of imports increased from 14.8 per cent to 14.6 per cent during the same period, representing an annual average growth rate of 8.5 per cent. In addition, the share of raw materials, semi-finished and intermediary goods jumped from about 27.4 per cent in 1979 to 36 per cent in 1984, that is, from AD 9.4 billion to AD 18.4 billion. The increase of the total value of these imported industrial goods averaged 14.3 per cent per year. This fact militates in favour of the acceleration of the process of industrialisation designed to reduce the dependence of the national economy on the external market.

The total value of imports rose by an annual average of 15.6 per cent, while the total value of exports increased by only 12.1 per cent during the 1980–4 plan. The volume of these exports rose by only 2 per cent per year. Therefore, the actual growth of exports is due primarily to the price of hydrocarbons (in US dollars), which rose by an annual average of 7.5 per cent, and to the increase of the value of the dollar in relation to the dinar by 512 per cent per year during the same period. Consequently, the current fall in the prices of crude oil, accompanied by the decline of the US dollar in the world financial market, will probably compromise the few chances left for the development of the country before the final depletion of its oil and natural gas reserves.

In short, the current regime has not only reversed the country's industrial policy but has also undermined the performance of existing

Post-independence development

Table 13.8 *The creation of jobs in the non-agricultural sectors, 1980–4*

Sectors	No. of jobs created	Growth rate (%)	%
Industry	93,679	4.3	13.3
Construction and public works	218,000	8.4	31.1
Transportation	36,000	5.1	5.2
Trade-services	124,000	4.8	17.7
Administration	230,000	6.6	32.7
Total	701,619	6.1	100.0

Source: MPAT, 1985.

industry by its erratic reform, the so-called 'restructuring' of public enterprises, and has proved incapable of even maintaining agricultural production at its 1974–7 level. The development of such a vital sector requires not only the consolidation of industrialisation but also the nurturing of a breed of men and women capable of comprehending the significance, exigencies and implications of a planned development geared to the consolidation of the nation's economic independence and to the satisfaction of the needs of the citizens.

Indeed, it must be recalled that in the Algerian context, the basic aim of development up to 1979 was the improvement of the living conditions of the popular strata of society through the creation of employment in productive activities. As a result, by 1984, the number of the employed totalled about 3.7 million persons. During 1980–4 employment grew by an annual average of 4.2 per cent. Even the low targets set by the planners were not attained. Demographic growth went on unabated: the total population rose from 18.3 to 21.6 million during this period, representing an average of 3.17 per cent per year. Most of the jobs created were in the non-productive sectors. Table 13.8 summarises the data pertaining to the creation of employment in the non-agricultural sectors during the first five-year plan.

The proportion of the labour force employed in agriculture fell from 32 per cent in 1979 to 26 per cent in 1984. The non-agricultural sectors – excluding administration – employed 47.6 per cent of the total labour force in 1979 and 51.4 per cent in 1984. Public administration employed 20.4 per cent in 1979 and 32.7 per cent in 1984: it is now employing over one-third of the total labour force. After criticising the previous regime for the creation of unproductive jobs, the current regime ended by doing worse.

Table 13.9 *The employment structure, 1979–84*

Sector	1979	1980	1981	1982	1983	1984
Agriculture	969,172	968,702	962,848	960,000	960,000	960,000
Industry	401,428	431,488	458,145	468,346	474,571	503,634
Construction and public works	437,009	468,498	503,864	522,241	608,826	652,526
Transportation	128,892	140,037	146,741	150,974	158,340	165,885
Trade-services	469,750	486,823	506,584	541,180	568,332	603,509
Administration	615,000	660,000	750,000	752,000	797,000	845,000
Total	3,021,251	3,155,548	3,394,741	3,394,741	3,567,069	3,730,554

Source: MPAT, 1985.

Finally, because of the dynamics of development generated by the process of industrialisation initiated by the previous regime, the proportion of highly qualified and skilled manpower rose slightly during the 1980–4 period. The structure of this qualified and skilled work force was as follows:

	1980	1984
	(%)	(%)
Senior staff	2.2	2.8
Highly qualified technicians	3.2	5.3
Technicians (IV)	7.9	8.0
Other skilled manpower	21.2	26.0
Total	34.5	42.1

The growth of education since 1979

The number of pupils and students reached 5.13 million by 1983–4, as against 4.04 million in 1979–80, amounting to an annual average rate of growth of 6.2 per cent. In five years about 521,000 persons graduated from the institutions making up the education system, 42,675 of them from the universities. Thus, a quarter of the total population is attending classes. However, it must be stressed that the quality of this instruction has been deteriorating dramatically in recent years. The diplomas and degrees

Post-independence development

granted are becoming without any real value to the graduates as well as to the economy and society.

The number of pupils enrolled in primary and middle schools increased from 3.79 million in 1979–80 to 4.66 million by 1984–5, an annual average growth of 4.2 per cent. The planners projected an annual increase of 4.3 per cent in the number of primary pupils, but only 2.2 per cent was achieved. The annual average increase of pupils enrolled in middle schools was 11.2 per cent instead of the 10.3 per cent projected by the planners. As a result, the rate of school attendance of six-year-old children rose from 82.5 per cent to 85.8 per cent and that of six- to thirteen-year-olds from 77.3 per cent to 81.7 per cent during the same period.

The number of pupils in primary school classrooms is reported to have fallen from 57.97 pupils in 1979–80 to 48.55 in 1984–5. In fact, because of the projects inherited from the past, about 17,289 classrooms were built during this period. Furthermore, in 1979, there was an average of 35.8 pupils per teacher, falling to 30.6 per cent by 1984–5 in primary schools; in middle schools this ratio was brought down from 29.63 to 24.54. More than 30 per cent of educational establishments have abandoned the double shift. This was rendered possible by the increase in the number of the teaching staff, whose levels of qualification are also reported to have risen. Indeed, the proportion of qualified schoolteachers went up from 25.9 per cent in 1979–80 to 57.2 per cent in 1984–5 while that of instructors fell from 64.2 per cent to 48.26 per cent of the total teaching staff. The number of monitors decreased from 6,000 to 639 during the same period. However, this quantitative progress resulted from a policy of administrative promotions rather than qualifications. In addition, innumerable experienced male teachers have either left the educational system or have been promoted to administrative jobs because of the invasion of the profession by women. Indeed, by the early 1980s about 40 per cent of the teachers were women.

The proportion of girls in schools and universities continued to increase slightly. In primary education, their proportion rose from 41.6 per cent of the total enrolled pupils in 1979–80 to 43.02 per cent in 1984–5, and from 38.7 per cent to 40.91 per cent in middle schools. At the secondary school stage the proportion of girls increased from 34.79 per cent to 41.36 per cent.

The number of students enrolled in high school reached 365,000 in 1986/7. Between 1979 and 1984–5 it grew by an average of 14.3 per cent a year. Of this, technical secondary school enrolment rose by an annual average of 27.3 per cent, but still only 11.9 per cent of high school students were enrolled in technical schools in 1984–5. The student–teacher ratio stagnated in the secondary schools during the same period, rising from

19.79 students per teacher in 1979–80 to just 19.88 in 1984–5. As a result, in 1986, about 80 per cent of high school students failed their final baccalauréat examination, and were thus unable to proceed to higher education.

The proportion of secondary school teachers teaching in Arabic rose slightly, from 50 per cent in 1979–80 to 57.12 per cent in 1984–5. The proportion of 'Arabised' students in general secondary education increased from 63.3 to 65.1 per cent, but in technical high schools this proportion rose from 7.1 per cent to 28.4 per cent. However, on the whole, because of a number of highly qualified and experienced Algerian high school teachers and administrators trained by the French during the colonial period, secondary schools are still better run than the institutions of higher education.

The growth of student numbers continued during the five-year plan. The total number of students enrolled in the universities and specialised colleges and institutes of higher education increased from 61,610 in 1979–80 to 166,600 in 1986–7. Most students are still attracted by medical, biological and social sciences as well as the humanities: 36.5 per cent were studying medicine and biology in 1984–5, while 29.9 per cent were studying social sciences. The proportion of students in science and technology rose from 12.8 per cent in 1979–80 to 25.1 per cent by 1984–5. This progression resulted from the introduction of compulsory orientation of students towards some strategic disciplines such as various branches of engineering.

The total number of faculty members increased from 3,309 in 1979–80 (including 1,514 foreign teachers) to 12,000 (1,942 foreign) in 1986–7. The rate of Algerianisation was as follows:

	1978–9 (%)	1984–5 (%)
Professors	52.8	61.5
Associate professors	31.3	24.3
Assistant professors	58.5	73.8
Assistants	61.4	95.0

Thus, the lower grades are more Algerianised than the grade of associate professor. The inadequacy of the administration of higher education, the absence of minimum conditions for teaching, the inexperience of the Algerian teaching staff and particularly the hasty, unplanned and unprepared Arabisation introduced in 1980 are factors underlying the deterioration of the quality of education and training provided by the universities. The political leadership appears to be concerned primarily with quantitative results for propaganda purposes.

The number of students studying in Arabic at the universities rose from 13,561 in 1978–9 to 33,400 in 1984–5, an increase of 146 per cent. By 1985 close to 32.5 per cent of students were Arabised: 95 per cent of social sciences students, 45 per cent of biological and physical science students and 20 per cent of postgraduates.

The number of Arabised teaching staff rose from 623 in 1978–9 to 2,200 in 1984–5. The student–teacher ratio remained virtually unchanged: there were 18.62 students per teacher in 1978–9, falling slightly to 18.1 per teacher five years later.

The number of women attending the universities kept rising, to reach 30 per cent of the student population in 1984–5. However, unfortunately for the development of the nation and the emancipation of women, the majority are becoming housewives on graduation.

By the middle of 1980s, it became evident that these quantitative achievements were not going to be followed by qualitative improvements. The educational and vocational training system remained inadequate, inefficient and costly. The returns of the 33 per cent of the national budget allocated annually to education and vocational training have so far been extremely low for both the population concerned and for the economy. For instance, the number of dropouts from the fundamental and secondary schools greatly exceeds the number of graduates. In June 1987, only 38,000 students officially passed the baccalauréat examination out of a total of over 193,000 candidates. However, only 13,000 were given passing marks by the teacher who examined them. Thus no less than 25,000 students were 'redeemed' for political reasons by the authorities in charge. The examiners were requested to lower the passing mark in order to increase the rate of success.

Higher education, instead of subjecting the endogenous underdeveloped socio-cultural reality to its own universal logic, exigencies and requirements in order to mould and transform it, was driven by those in charge, particularly since 1979, into succumbing to its pre-existing socio-cultural surroundings. In other words, since most Algerians were forced to cling to their customs, traditions and social values in order to preserve their national identity and culture, threatened by the French policy of assimilation, Algerian society became one of the most conservative societies in the Mediterranean basin. Consequently, its demands and expectations of higher education and even the individual aspirations and hence the personal life projects and strategies of its members are still shaped by traditional logic, socio-economic orientations and norms.

The new economic policy

The Algerian universities, like all other institutions, are in deep crisis. The absence of the strict minimum conditions and prerequisites for research, documentation, teaching and studying have limited their access to historical, sociological, philosophical and humanistic knowledge, as well as to modern technological and scientific knowledge.

If the mission assigned to the universities is to raise society's consciousness and understanding of itself, of its culture and experience as well as of other people's cultures and experiences and also to teach the students how to master modern science and technology in order to increase the production of goods and services, they have failed, for political reasons, to fulfil it.

Through the momentum set in motion in 1962, the number of graduates from the institutions of higher education totalled 42,675 during the 1980–5 period. However, a growing proportion are either jobless or underemployed. This situation has been created by the halting of the industrialisation of the country and the monetarist measures introduced by the government. This bleak situation may explain the total absence of references to the results of the first five-year plan in the document outlining the educational targets for the second five-year plan.

The second five-year plan (1985–9)

As a consequence of the disappointing results of the first five-year plan, the government decided to assign 'realistic' objectives to the second five-year plan. In the autumn of 1984, the government announced that AD 660 billion would be invested during the plan: Table 13.10 summarises the investment allocations.

Thus, the priority sectors continued to be social infrastructure, agriculture, water resources, education, vocational training and local collectivities. All that is required of industry is the 'widening and diversification of the supply of products through the improvement of labour productivity and the efficient use of the existing plant capacities', which are expected to rise from 60 per cent in 1984 to 85 per cent by 1989. In other words, new industries would not be established.

Another new priority is the creation of the prerequisite conditions for the development of the private industrial sector. Indeed, the second five-year plan insists that the 'national private capital' be encouraged to 'complement the public sector' by investing particularly in 'sub-contracting productive activities'.

Post-independence development

Table 13.10 *The programme of national investment during the second five-year plan (1985–9)*

Sector	AD billion	%
Agriculture, water resources	79.00	14.4
Agriculture	30.00	5.5
Water resources	41.00	7.4
Fishing	1.00	0.2
Forests	7.00	1.3
Industry	174.20	31.6
Hydrocarbons	39.80	7.2
Means of implementation	19.00	3.5
Transport	15.00	2.7
Storage and distribution	15.85	2.9
Post office and telecommunications	8.00	1.4
Economic infrastructures	45.50	8.3
Social infrastructures	149.45	27.2
Housing	86.45	15.7
Education, vocational training	45.00	8.2
Public health and social protection	10.00	1.8
Other social services	8.00	1.5
Collective equipment	44.00	8.0
Total	550.00	100.0

Source: MPAT, Deuxième plan quinquennal 1985–1989.

In addition, the second five-year plan aims at fulfilling the following targets:
The reduction of the import of technical assistance and other services
A 20 per cent increase in the export of non-hydrocarbon products
A better mobilisation of internal resources which constitute a necessary condition for improving the capacity of internal capital accumulation
A growth of production in excess of the increment of revenues and domestic consumption. At the moment the pace of consumption

Gross income per capita is expected to increase from AD 6,550 (AD 545 per month) in 1984 – which placed Algeria third in Africa after Libya and South Africa – to AD 7,540 (AD 628 per month) in 1989. The annual average per capita consumption, now estimated at AD 5,700, is expected to reach AD 6,500 during the same period.

Finally, the annual average rate of growth of the economically active population is projected to rise by 4 per cent – 9 per cent for women (whose total number would increase from 390,000 to about 610,000 by the end of the plan).

The pace of development of human resources will also be accelerated in the coming five years. The total number of school attendants and vocational training should reach 6.5 million by the end of the plan, 1.4 million more than in 1984. This would necessitate the recruitment of 100,000 teachers, 60,000 by the Ministry of Vocational Training alone, in order to train 83,000 technicians and 40,000 highly qualified and skilled workers. The existing universities and other establishments of higher education will have to make room for no fewer than 160,000 students by 1989, representing a 43 per cent increase during the plan period.

In short, it appears that the more the socio-economic reality escapes the present leadership, the more it resorts to words in an attempt to transform it, through the magic of numbers. The harsh reality of the new model of development is represented, among other things, by the following figures: in 1985 alone, the value of food imports amounted to AD 10 billion, while the price of hydrocarbons fell from over $30 a barrel to about $14 a barrel. Furthermore, the atomisation of non-agricultural public enterprises and the concomitant suppression of their development 'functions' resulted in a dramatic slow-down of the rates or productive investment. According to an executive of the State Bank of Development, only 30 per cent of the funds earmarked for investment in 1985 was actually utilised, most of it on non-productive activities.

It is not surprising that the results of the first three years were very disappointing indeed.

From 1979 to 1985, the Benjadid administration, its single party and the media kept reiterating to the Algerians that the growing development of the country and the rising standards of living of its population were unparalleled in the third world. Indeed, while the new Algerian middle classes were enjoying their holidays abroad and their imported consumer goods, food riots broke out in the neighbouring states: Tunisia, Morocco and Egypt. The administration also insisted on the fact that the leadership succeeded in protecting the economy from the devastating impact of the current world economic crisis. This was made possible by the necessary and opportune reforms undertaken by the regime during the early 1980s. These reforms had, supposedly, resulted in the setting up of rationally organised enterprises and other related commercial, financial and social institutions that had enhanced the efficiency and performance of the national economy.

The unfolding of a profound crisis which affected the functioning of every institution was hidden behind such deceptive propaganda and ideological smokescreens. The destabilisation of the public enterprises had already undermined the performance of the industrial sector. This low performance was reflected strikingly in the disappointing results of the first five-year plan, whose terminal year coincided with the down-turn in crude

Post-independence development

oil prices. The leadership expressed its preoccupation by blaming the Algerian workers for their own mistakes. The congress of the single party held in 1984 substituted 'work and rigour to guarantee the future' for its 1980 slogan 'for a better life'. This substitution indicated that a gloomy prospect for the future was unfolding rapidly.

Despite its high sounding pronouncements concerning the need to prepare the Algerian economy and society to face the post-petroleum era, nothing of any consequence was actually done to reduce the absolute dependence on the export of hydrocarbons. From 1984 onwards the sharp fall in oil prices was aggravated by the decline of the value of the US dollar on the international foreign exchange markets. Since the regime insisted on indexing the prices of natural gas with those of crude oil during the 1979–80 period, export revenues were quickly reduced. By 1985, the president, in a televised speech to the nation, finally admit that the impact of the world economic crisis had hit the Algerian economy very hard. Thenceforth the blame was put on the world economic crisis. This speech generated a general panic throughout the country, resulting in long queues in front of supermarkets and grocery stores for the purchase of imported basic foodstuffs such as cooking oil, sugar, coffee and black pepper. The upper and middle classes started hoarding large quantities of storable products, which aggravated the shortages. The state supermarkets, so pompously inaugurated, become almost empty. This stimulated the growth of the black market which had so far specialised in the sale of scarce imported consumer goods.

At this juncture the leadership and the media chorus advocated 'firmness and rigour' to overcome the effects of the world economic crisis on the national economy. By the end of 1985 the Algerian popular strata found themselves in the midst of a deepening crisis which eroded their standards of living. The official rate of inflation rose by 12.5 per cent in 1986. This contributed to a 1 per cent decline in per capita consumption during the same year.

Once the initial panic subsided, the government took additional measures to reduce both imports and spending. The budget for the 1986 fiscal year was cut by 15 per cent. The planned investment projects were modified, postponed or cancelled. The imports of vital capital goods, semi-finished products and spare parts were either curtailed or suppressed. The authorisation granted by the government in the early 1980s to individual citizens to order spare parts directly from France, payable in AD was withheld. The annual foreign currency allowance was finally abolished. Thenceforth only the citizens that have foreign currency deposits in the local Algerian banks are allowed to travel abroad.

As a consequence, the total value of imports fell from AD 59.5 billion in

1985 to AD 47 billion in 1986, a decrease of 21 per cent, declining to an estimated AD 39 billion by 1987, representing a fall of 17 per cent over the previous year. The total value of exports decreased from AD 69.2 billion to AD 41 billion, amounting to a 41.08 per cent fall, rising to an estimated sum of AD 42 billion by 1987, which represented a mere 2.4 per cent increase over the previous year during the same period.

The reduction of imports affected two key items: capital goods (equipment) and semi-finished products (including raw materials). Indeed, the former were cut by 29 per cent in 1986 and by 31 per cent in 1987. These two categories are vital not only to the development of the economy but also to the operation of the productive activities. The imports of foodstuffs were reduced by 12.6 per cent and 11.8 per cent; the industrial consumer products by 19.3 per cent and 10.7 per cent during the same years. Nevertheless, in spite of these cuts, the balance of payments deficit still amounted to AD 6 billion in 1986 alone. Furthermore, although public expenditure was also reduced by 15 per cent, the budget deficit represented the equivalence of about 5.5 per cent of the GDP during the same year.

The reduction of imports, particularly of semi-finished products, which are necessary for the operation of the apparatus of production, had affected the growth of the economy. Indeed, the growth of the GDP (in current prices) declined from an annual average rate of 15 per cent during the 1979–84 period to an insignificant 0.3 per cent by 1986. In volume, it fell from 5.2 per cent in 1985 to 2.9 per cent in 1986 and to an estimated 2.7 by 1987 against an annual average rate of 5.8 per cent during the first five-year plan (1980–4). The gross fixed capital formation fell for the first time in the post-independence period by 3.4 per cent in 1986 over 1985, and would decrease by an estimated 6 per cent in 1987.

Thus, none of the projected targets was attained during the first three years of the second-five-year plan (1985–9). This low performance was bound to generate, sooner or later, an explosive social and economic situation.

The predictable negative effects of deindustrialisation engendered by the shift in development priorities and the ensuing restructuring of the public enterprises had accelerated the rates of redundancy and underemployment which were drastically reduced during the 1970s. In 1985 only 122,000 jobs were created, falling to 116,000 in 1986 (the new entrants into the labour market numbered 173,000 during this year) and to an estimated 110,000 by 1987. In short only 57 per cent of the planned objectives were attained. According to an official document, the number of jobless workers rose from 658,000 in 1984 to 838,000 in 1986. In order to appreciate the magnitude of this figure, it must be recalled that the implementation of the 1980–4 plan resulted in the creation of 703,000 jobs, necessitating no less than AD 344.8 billion gross investments. This amounted to an annual

Post-independence development

Table 13.11 *Manpower balance sheet: 1986–99*

	1986	1989	1999	Total growth 1989–99	Annual average growth rate %
Agricultural employment	1,000	1,049	1,425	,376	3.1
Non-agricultural employment	2,958	3,211	4,854	1,643	4.2
Industrial employment	527	580	930	350	4.8
Construction & public work	661	675	965	290	3.6
Services	813	873	1,356	483	4.5
Administration	955	1,083	1,603	520	4.0
Unemployed	838	1,190	2,062	872	5.6
Total active population*	4,794	5,450	8,341	2,891	4.3
Employed	3,956	4,260	6,279	2,019	3.9
Total population	23,285	25,400	34,500	11,215	3.2

*Owing to the status of women the active population differs from the working-age population.

average of AD 68.96 billion.

The increase in new entrants into the labour market constitute a time-bomb for the current regime. Indeed, according to an interministerial document, by the year 2000, the potentially active population (15–64 year olds) will total about 19 million. Since the authorities expect only 692,000 women to join the labour market, which might be an erroneous supposition, the manpower balance sheet would evolve between 1986 and 1999 as in Table 13.11.

Severe pressures on the economy will be exerted by the growing number of young people who will be flooding the educational and vocational training facilities, the labour market and the real estate market. Indeed, in 14 years, 11.5 million individuals are going to be added, that is half of the present population. The age group 0–14 years will number about 15 million people by the year 2000, comprising 43.4 per cent of the total population. The age group 15–19 years will comprise over 3.64 million, representing close to 11 per cent of the total population.

Thus, by the turn of the next century strong pressures will be exerted on existing and potential resources. The demand for foodstuffs, shelter, transport, medical care, schooling, culture, leisure, and entertainment will increase commensurately with this demographic growth. The total value of the annual consumption of households will develop between 1987 and 1999 as in Table 13.12.

Table 13.12 *Total value of the annual consumption of households, 1987–99 (AD billion, 1985 prices)*

	1987	1989	1994	1999	Annual average growth % 1989–99
Foodstuffs	78.0	83.20	99.2	143.3	4.10
Accommodation and utilities	9.25	9.85	13.6	20.3	7.50
Furnitures and appliances	11.20	12.25	16.9	25.3	7.60
Transportation and telecommuncation	12.00	13.10	17.5	26.4	7.25
Medical care	4.45	4.80	6.3	9.0	6.50
Cigarettes and matches	3.95	4.10	4.8	5.5	3.00
Leisure, culture, education	10.30	11.10	14.6	21.3	6.75
Clothing and shoes	11.20	11.85	14.4	18.0	4.25
Others	3.30	3.45	4.2	5.4	4.60
Total	143.60	153.70	191.5	256.3	5.20

Furthermore, in order to provide the new families with shelter, more than 5.53 million housing units have to be constructed between 1985 and 2000. In 1987 Algeria had to produce 1.6 million tons of cereals to satisfy 36.5 per cent of consumption. The remainder was imported. Owing to the authorities' decision to reduce the proportion of cereals in the average diet and their gradual replacement by vegetables, meats, dairy products and fish, the future needs for these staples will rise by only an annual average growth rate of 1.13 per cent between 1989 and 1999. Yet to meet this projected stagnant demand and to reduce the food dependence on the international market by at least 39.5 per cent, Algerian farmers must produce by the year 2000 no less than 13.86 million tons of cereals. In other words, in order to supply 76 per cent of the national consumption of these products, Algerian cereal production must maintain an annual average rate of growth of 7.6 per cent between 1987 and 1999. Given the geographical limitations, the structural problems and the technical weaknesses of Algerian agriculture, this target is unattainable. One of the manifold contradictions of the economic policy of the current administration pertains to the following paradoxical reasoning: the government intends both to intensify the mechanisation of agriculture in order to increase production and to create additional agricultural employment by an annual average growth rate of 3.1 per cent during the 1986–99 period. Needless to say that

Post-independence development

in both the capitalist and the socialist countries, the modernisation of agriculture involved the introduction of capital-intensive and labour-saving means of production. Hence the transfer of a large proportion of the agricultural population to the secondary and tertiary sectors has occurred in all the developed economies of the world.

How can the Algerian government reverse this general modern trend? Wishful thinking of this sort cannot resolve the complex problems of the growing rate of redundancy, accentuated by a rapid demographic growth, the premature halting of industrialisation and the decline of productive investment, caused by the recent collapse of hydrocarbons export revenues, aggravated by the fall of the US dollar. This situation is complicated by the rising price of industrial technology, engines and technical know-how, which are still imported in hard foreign currencies from abroad. Indeed, the average investment cost (in current prices) for creating a job rose from AD 98,000 in 1967 to no less than AD 740,000 by 1986.

During the last twenty years Algerian economic and social development generated about 2.32 million jobs. The official demand for employment totalled over 2.49 million, that is 93 per cent of this expressed demand was satisfied. In order to keep the 1987 level of employment, which is very low, because only about 20.9 per cent of the total population is working to support the remaining 79.1 per cent, close to 4 million jobs have to be created between 1985 and the year 2000 (against 1.5 million during the 1970–84 period). Given the current investment costs, the creation of these 4 million jobs will require an annual average investment of AD 200 billion during the period under consideration. Thus, the financial constraint is considerable. This will affect the future orientation and pace of development.

In 1983, the Benjadid administration projected a total investment of AD 1,800 billion between 1990 and 1999. However, in 1987 the so-called 'impact of the world economic crisis on the Algerian economy' compelled the planners to bring down this total investment target to AD 1,200 billion during the 1988–99 period, comprising only an annual average of AD 100 billion. Table 13.13 indicates the sectoral allocation of the projected investment during the 1988–99 period.

The proportion to be allocated to productive sectors will increase from 42 per cent in 1985 to 60 per cent by 1999. Hydrocarbons export revenues will finance about AD 536 billion, household savings AD 242 billion and the remainder will come from other sources. The returns on this planned investment are expected to total AD 694 billion between 1988 and 1994 and AD 506 billion during the 1995–99 period.

The overall objective of the planned investment is as follows: to sustain a

Table 13.13 *Sectoral allocation of investment, 1988–99 (AD billion in 1987 constant prices)*

	1988–1994	1995–1999	1988–1999
Agriculture	103	104	207
Hydrocarbons	68	30	98
Industry	156	114	270
Construction and public work	20	16	36
Services	45	40	85
Sub-total	392	304	696
Non productive sectors	302	202	504
	694	506	1200

certain degree of economic growth in order to guarantee a minimum satisfaction of the country's needs; to create at least 2.3 million jobs in an attempt to attenuate the rapid growth of unemployment, which will affect more than one third of the active population by 1991. Thus the FLN party's commitment to full employment and an equitable distribution of income has been gradually discarded. This has broken up the national consensus which emerged from the revolutionary nature of the war of independence. To justify this political and ideological discontinuity, the Benjadid administration invoked a host of arguments: low productivity of labour, high demographic growth, overstaffing (which in 1987 allegedly involved about 500,000 workers, whose wages and social costs amounted to AD 15 billion per year, an annual average cost of AD 30,000 per worker, but these figures are deliberately exaggerated for political purposes; they have no statistical foundation) and shrinking financial resources, aggravated by the existing foreign debt.

With regard to the debt, whose exact amount has been kept secret by the current administration inside Algeria, the country was told in 1979–80 by the new leadership that it had reached, under the previous regime, an 'alarming level'. The Minister of Planning assured me then that the government had decided not only to put an end to additional borrowing but also to repay the debt already contracted.

The foreign debt issue, which was presented as a threat to the independence of the country, was used to justify the government's decision to cancel or postpone strategic industrial projects, designed to complete the industrialisation of the nation, the only course capable of guaranteeing its security and the welfare of its citizens in the coming decades. Among the most significant projects cancelled during this period I mention only three:

the planned construction of GNL III, the steel complex of the west and the complex of heavy mechanical and electrical equipment (CEMEL). To finance this kind of highly productive investment project, the public companies concerned contracted several loans from various foreign banks. When Boumediene died in December 1978, significant sums were already in the hands of the national banks waiting to be invested. The post-Boumediene administration cancelled many such important projects, but did not consider it necessary to return the borrowed funds to the foreign banks. The government used some of them to complete pre-existing projects. The remainder was spent on the import of consumer goods and the construction of monuments for the martyrs ('factories, schools, hospitals are the best monuments for our martyrs'), palaces, public parks, supermarkets, commercial centres and even a north American shopping mall that came to be called Riad El Fath. This shopping mall and the national monument beside it were built in the heart of Algiers by a Canadian firm and financed by a loan contracted by Sonatrach in Canada for the construction of GNL III, which would have generated about $ 1 billion net revenue per year. Thus, Riad El Fath has become the symbol of a distorted and aborted national development. It also announced the beginning of a process of indebtedness, without a concomitant industrialisation.

Despite frequent references by the current administration and its media to the 'disindebtedness of the country', the national foreign debt rose from about $ 11.15 billion at the death of Boumedienne to an estimated $ 20–21 billion by 1986. During this period the nation experienced a creeping indebtedness accompanied by an alarming deindustrialisation. In 1987, the debt service amounted to no less than about AD 27 billion.

The financial constraint, which has been partly aggravated by the government's own policies (represented, among other things, by a 10 per cent reduction in petroleum production when prices of crude oil reached over $ 40 per barrel), the restructuring of public enterprises, the untimely change of development priorities and the resort to massive imports of consumer goods will be used as a strong argument in favour of belt-tightening measures. The scarcity of capital will be invoked by the current leadership to decrease public expenditures, to cut the social services, to change the model of development, to promote both foreign and local private investment, to alter the policy of income distribution and to compress consumption through a drastic reduction of imports and a rapid increase of exports. For instance, the annual average growth rate of the value of imports will rise by 2.5 per cent and that of non-hydrocarbon exports will go up by 23 per cent during the 1988–99 period. However, the current emphasis on the export of locally produced consumer goods is in

The new economic policy

total contradiction with the objective of Algerian development. Since the national demand has so far exceeded domestic production of goods and services their export will create tensions and frustrations within Algeria. This situation will stimulate further the development of speculative activities, parallel clandestine marketing networks, commercial nepotism and corruption, a fact that accelerates the process of compradorisation of the economy and society. In the recent past the number of parasitic elements specialising in highly speculative transactions and self-employed persons rose from 480,000 in 1977 to 720,000 in 1985. These informal trading activities have contributed to the devaluation of productive wage labour. For instance, in 1984, one single transaction involving a refrigerator, which took less than two hours to carry through, brought to the petty speculator more than one month's wages for a skilled worker. Yet the Algerian ministry of heavy industry has just committed itself to export in 1988 alone the equivalent of one year's production of refrigerators to Libya while countless Algerian families are looking desperately for them.

In conclusion it should be understood that every process of industrialisation involves mistakes, sacrifices and hardships. Not a single industrialised country has escaped this. It is wrong to denounce these mistakes without regard to their context. Algeria has no acceptable alternative to industrialisation. Even if the present lack of forward motion is just a pause, the new entrants to the labour market cannot wait; their number grows every year. Is the development of agriculture sufficient by itself to offset the situation and to resolve the problem facing Algeria's society? Would any responsible person think that the satisfaction of the most elementary needs of a population (shelter, clothing, transportation, health care, education, culture and leisure) can be provided without an efficient industry?

If the industrialisation drive had not been abruptly interrupted by the current regime, Algerian industry would be able today to satisfy the basic needs of the national economy and hence of the society as a whole. The full maturation of an industrial development programme requires at least 40 years. To nip the process of industrialisation in the bud is a monumental error because it not only destroys any chance of economic well-being but also discourages and demoralises the nation. Such a nation must meet the challenge of industrialisation in order to resolve its fundamental problems and develop a necessary self-confidence.

What is preposterous about the new economic policy adopted in the 1980s lies in the striking fact that once the process of industrialisation has reached a 'repetitive stage' (that is, the multiplication of the existing plants throughout the country), the industrial population which it has generated acquires valuable experience, enabling it to move successfully to a higher stage. But the Benjadid regime decided not only to halt industrialisation

Post-independence development

but also to discredit it altogether. In 1982, a Greek industrialist reported to me a conversation he had had with the head of a French delegation of industrialists on a visit to Algiers. This Greek businessman was told: 'Thank God! The Algerians have at last realised that their mentality is incompatible with large industrial complexes. If they give up heavy industry and shift their development priorities to light industries and other sectors, we'll keep the Algerian market for our heavy industrial products and we'll sell them our equipment and services so that they can develop these new priority sectors.' The Greek added, 'I am a capitalist, but if I were an Algerian I would do the opposite.' However, the current Algerian leadership's shopkeeper mentality is incapable of grasping either the significance of industrialisation or the importance of heavy industry. In other words, the premature halt of the process of industrialisation under any pretext was bound to undermine the development of the economy and hence to condemn future generations to hardship, deprivation and a humiliating neo-colonial dependency on the former colonial power.

Conclusion

Three successive, conflicting, and interactive factors, or legacies, have contributed to the making of contemporary Algeria. A pre-1830 traditional heritage, which outlasted the colonial onslaughts and plunders, continues, at the ideological or superstructural level, to precondition the collective consciousness, social behaviour and practices of the present-day population. A colonial legacy, despite the deep scars it has left on the social fabric, is still permeating and influencing all aspects of everyday life. Egalitarian attitudes and political ideology, inherited from the Berber gentile village democracy, were modified and adapted by the nationalist movement to the exigencies of a political struggle carried out by a modern class party. Finally, the country was strengthened by the historic experience of the revolutionary war of liberation. This heritage not only determined the progressive social policies of the state up to 1979–80, but also constrained the first two regimes to respect the national populist consensus which emerged from the war experience. Furthermore, the armed struggle, which was carried out between 1954 and 1962 and was fought primarily by militants and freedom fighters coming from the popular strata of society, had also compelled the first regime to nationalise in 1963 all the farms belonging to the former settlers and the second regime all the industrial, financial and natural resources. Finally, it induced them to rely on voluntaristic campaigns of mobilisation rather than on coercion for the post-independence economic reconstruction.

However, the political and ideological weaknesses and contradictions of the nationalist party (ENA–PPA–MTLD) in general and the FLN in particular were bound to complicate the Algerian revolution and change its course.

Paradoxically, both Boumedienne's rise to leadership in the early 1960s and the Benjadid's current policy of 'deboumedianisation' were made almost inevitable by these basic flaws underlying the FLN as an independentist movement, devoid of any ideological or political coherence. Indeed, being a mere coalition of heterogeneous political parties and tendencies this wartime front failed to generate or shape politically a homogeneous, experienced and cultivated or ideologically coherent elite,

Conclusion

independent of the army, the comprador bourgeoisie and the influences of foreign powers.

Boumedienne's conception of power and his particular strategy of concentrating it in his own hands as well as preserving it throughout the manipulation of the various factions within the FLN party, the state apparatus and the army, reinforced the anti-socialist, anti-popular and anti-nationalist class forces. The co-existence within the regime of the representatives of these class forces, having different social bases, which allowed Boumedienne to divide and rule, had favoured the reinforcement of the conservative tendencies, because they were strengthened and consolidated by the growing number and wealth of the new comprador bourgeoisie and middle classes. This situation ushered in contradictory processes of rapid development at the infrastructural and industrial levels and ideological deviation, stagnation and even regression at the superstructural levels. In other words, the modernisation of the productive forces was neither accompanied nor resulted in the expected cultural transformation which would have induced the new elite of such a conservative underdeveloped society to accept the sociological implications of industrialisation and its principal prerequisite: modernity and all its philosophical, religious, institutional, socio-behavioural and techno-economic ramifications.

All this may explain why the economic and social policies as well as the political practices and tactics of the second regime (1965–79) culminated, as a direct result of its deep-seated contradictions, in a legal Algerian Thermidor, without the emergence of an Algerian Napoleon. The main objective of this Thermidor was to reverse all the progressive policies in favour of the popular strata, denounced by the new potentates as motivated by a creeping, unprofitable populism which must be banned for ever and replaced by profitable public and private enterprises driven by the profit motive, regardless of the long-term economic, political and social consequences.

Recently, the term 'socialism' was discreetly dropped from official documents of the administration and the party. The media were also instructed to stop referring to socialism as the social and economic doctrine of the country, yet economic liberalism has not been officially substituted. The abolition of Boumedienne's socialism and populism will not resolve the fundamental problems of Algerian society in the coming years. On the contrary, the experience of neighbouring countries, such as Sadat's Egypt, shows that these problems are going to worsen. The post-Boumedienne reforms have been consolidating the gains of the new comprador bourgeoisie and those of the most parasitic elements, which were prevented in the aftermath of independence from imposing their solutions on the popular strata.

Conclusion

Thus we are far removed from 1962, when the balance of power was in favour of the development of the public sector: the capitalist path was presented then not only as synonymous with brutal exploitation of man by man, but also as conducive to a neo-colonial dependence and hence to a reproduction of colonial capitalism which brought about the underdevelopment of the country. It must be recalled that the Algerian strategy of development during the 1967–78 period was designed to resolve the problems created by colonial capitalism and to prevent the restoration of a neo-colonial capitalism that has pushed the third world into an economic impasse.

The colonisation of the traditional economic activities resulted in the disintegration of the socio-economic structures based upon them. Algeria was one of the longest (1830–1962) and most extensively colonised countries in the Arab world. It must be reiterated here that, from the outset, the French confiscated urban businesses and residences, dismantled the craft corporations, imposed their currency as the medium of exchange, opened the borders to European settlers, manufactured goods and banks and subjected the Algerian people to direct rule. By 1962, the settlers controlled 3.04 million hectares of the most fertile lands. The colonial state possessed 11 million hectares (mostly forests and pastures). The Algerians were left with only 7 million hectares, located mostly on slopes, in mountainous regions and other unproductive areas. In addition, the settlers owned up to 95 per cent of the industrial production and all banks and other modern services, and provided over 70 per cent of the civil servants. To put an end to this state of affairs, a long political struggle was not enough. A popular war of national liberation had to be fought during which about one million out of nine million Algerians sacrificed their lives.

During the colonial period, the principal contradiction was between the bulk of the colonised social classes and strata and the overwhelming majority of the colonisers, who perceived themselves, and were also perceived by most Algerians, as constituting the ruling class. However, after independence, when the Europeans fled the country, the main contradiction came to be between the Algerian social classes and strata which owned or controlled the means of production and those which were economically dispossessed and politically powerless. This contradiction was accentuated by the departure of the settlers from Algeria in 1962, which created a golden opportunity for the social mobility of innumerable members of the various Algerian social classes and strata.

What was at stake in 1962 was not only the immediate control of the 'vacant property' but also the model of development, and hence the type of society, to be constructed. Thenceforth, Algerian politics, like the politics of every third world society, were bound to be conditioned by the existing

Conclusion

class forces, whose social bases were rooted in the country's colonial history, as well as by the balance of power between contending class forces.

To bar the way to the privileged classes and strata, the agricultural and industrial workers moved to take control of the basic means of production – land, industrial enterprises and commercial establishments. The agricultural labourers formed self-management committees to protect their 'foster-mother', the land, and to continue production to provide for their dependants. The urban workers, with the assistance of the General Union of Algerian Workers (UGTA), also set up self-management committees. However, the UGTA, which has often been manipulated, paradoxically, by both left-wing groups and conservative elements within the state apparatus, was integrated into the single-party system in 1969 as a so-called 'mass organisation'. Thenceforth, the members of the executive board were imposed by the leadership of the party.

Between 1962 and 1965, the economic policy of Algeria was geared primarily to the reactivation of the industrial, service and mining sectors and to the reorganisation of colonial agriculture. Although workers' self-management in the public sector was proclaimed as the foundational option of 'Algerian socialism', it was, in fact, never completely applied. The subjective populism of the short-lived Ben Bella period (1962–5) was supplanted by a global economic policy based on the nationalisation of the productive assets and their management by the public companies under the aegis of the state. Thenceforth, a mode of development – whose economic coherence appeared to be flawless but which was, in fact, being undermined by conflicting interests defended by various factions within the state apparatus, each of which wanted to apply its own mode of development – was imposed by the Boumedienne regime on the entire civil society. However, despite these deep-seated contradictions, the goal of Boumedienne's strategy of economic growth was the consolidation of the independence of the country and the satisfaction of the needs of the popular strata through the creation of employment in productive activities and the provision of basic social services. Indeed, a few months before his death, Boumedienne declared that the application of social justice benefits all Algerians: 'Our motto is education for all, books for all, health care for all and dignity for all.' He went on to stress that the children of the unemployed and poor persons 'must not only be educated' but also 'promoted to the highest positions possible'. He concluded by stating that the 'millions of workers, peasants and young people constitute the pillars of our regime', which defends their interests.

As a result of the populist ideology inherited from the nationalist movement, Boumedienne continued the tradition of a charismatic leader who relied on the 'mobilisation of the masses' rather than on the easy

Conclusion

solution of resorting to coercion, threats and punishments. This led him to dynamise and use the 'mass organisations', represented by the trade unions (UGTA), the National Union of Algerian Peasants (UNPA), the National Union of Algerian Youth (UNJA) and the national Union of Algerian Women (UNFA), as the principal organisations designed to mobilise the population for the 'struggle against underdevelopment and imperialism'. Through these mass organisations the regime diffused 'mobilising slogans' which propelled a social and popular dynamics which was necessary for the pursuit of the national development undertaken and whose objective was the construction of socialism. Although this form of socialism was authoritarian, it has a genuinely popular basis.

The movement of national liberation had contained a 'populism' which became one of the most pervasive features of Algerian society. This ideology not only conditioned the collective behaviour of the population but also determined all the political, social, cultural and economic policies of the nation during the first eighteen years of independence, and hence legitimised the very exercise of power. The entire civil society has also functioned by 'mobilisation' rather than by the 'law of value'. As during the period of the struggle of national liberation, the Algerian people were incited to carry out battles (of production), to launch campaigns, to confront imperialism and to win victories over the external enemy and its internal allies. The entire society was set in motion in order to carry out various actions defined and orchestrated by a charismatic leader who behaved 'as an "animator" of a client collective rather than as a classic head of state'.[1]

Boumedienne, in spite of the fact that he had either promoted or maintained innumerable opportunists, former collaborators with the French and partisans of the former conservative religious association of *ulamahs* to the leadership, was a staunch populist-nationalist fully committed to the development of the economy and to the modernisation of society provided that it enhanced his own power and authority.

The Boumedienne regime (1965–78) faced intractable problems: an agriculture specialising mostly in export crops, a backward industry and high rates of unemployment and underemployment. This situation induced his government to opt for a strategy of planned development based on the industrialisation of the country and geared to the construction of a socialist society. This decision was followed by the launching and implementation of three successive 'revolutions', industrial, cultural and agrarian, and three consecutive plans.

As a consequence of the massive development undertaken by the state, 1.11 million jobs were created, representing an increase of 64.5 per cent during the period. Thus, the official rate of unemployment was brought

Conclusion

down from 70 per cent in 1964 to less than 19 per cent in 1978. The number of industrial workers rose from 117,000 in 1967 (13.4 per cent of the total labour force) to 390,000 by 1978 (18.8 per cent). The social landscape also changed rapidly during the period. The number of working women rose, multiplied and diversified: women become workers, technicians, engineers, cadres, doctors and dentists. Most families received more than one wage because of their large size. The baby-boom which was provoked by the end of the war and the independence of the country continued at an annual average of 3.2 per cent, thanks to the progress achieved in the fields of public hygiene, income distribution and health care. The gross rate of mortality decreased from 16.3 to 8.6 per cent, while the average life expectation at birth rose from 53.5 to 62.83 years. The total population increased from 12.6 million in 1967 to 18 million in 1978. More than half of it came to be concentrated in the coastal cities of the north. The minimum monthly wage grew rapidly, while the total household income rose sharply. All the classic socio-economic indicators revealed that the living conditions of the population had improved.

However, these achievements masked the emergence, and the aggravation, of some serious problems caused by the inertia of the non-industrial sectors, such as a shortage of housing and agriculture. In a political system where the media and all other channels of information are manipulated by the state apparatus, the collective consciousness, and even the decision-makers, remained insensitive to the negative consequences of certain inter-sectoral imbalances and gaps resulting from the differing efficiency of the various ministerial departments and services. For example, in 1960, 60 per cent of Algeria's exports were represented by agricultural products, but this had fallen to the insignificant proportion of 0.7 per cent in 1980. Furthermore, agricultural production had stagnated and even declined in the case of certain products. As a consequence, the country had become dependent on the world market for most agricultural products (cereals, dry vegetables, meat, milk, sugar, tobacco.) Meanwhile, because of the miserable living conditions of the rural population engendered by colonial plunder, a rural exodus went on unabated in the post-independence period. This resulted in the depopulation of certain marginal areas of the hinterland and in the uncontrolled growth of the cities, where innumerable families were being concentrated within widening slum belts and shanty towns. The active agricultural population declined (from 50 per cent of the total labour force to 861,000, 28 per cent) during the same period. In other words, all the jobs created were in the non-agricultural sectors.

Despite the seizure of the lands of the former settlers, the agrarian problem caused by colonisation remained unresolved through a stagnating production and through striking socio-economic disparities in the country-

Conclusion

side – for instance, on the eve of the agrarian revolution initiated in 1972, 4 per cent of the landowners possessed 38 per cent of the land. The Algerian landlords at first opposed any attempt at land reform, and when the agrarian revolution was finally imposed by the state they succeeded in minimising its scope and impact through their representatives within the power structure.

By 1979 the agricultural sector consisted of three sub-sectors: private, self-managed, and agrarian revolution. This fragmentation has complicated the development of agriculture as a whole. The chronic stagnation of agricultural production has been caused primarily by the absence of a coherent agricultural policy that takes into account the specificities of these sub-sectors, as well as by the staunch opposition of the conservative class forces to genuine land reform. This state of affairs led a local representative of the Ministry of Agriculture to exclaim to me: 'the problem of agriculture has been its over-politicisation'.

The way in which the agrarian revolution was implemented allowed the big landlords to minimise its impact, either by fictitious sales to kinsmen and loyal retainers or by the giving away of the less fertile lands in order to keep the most productive areas. Since the landlords were compensated, the majority of them managed to diversify their economic activities by investing either in commerce or transport and distribution. Although the economic impact of the agrarian revolution was minimal, its effects on class structure were decisive. Most of the landlord class were transformed into new rural bourgeoisie or entrepreneurs whose economic base lay in non-agricultural activities. A large number of this rural parasitic bourgeoisie often got hold of various activities such as transport, distribution, trade and construction. Their links with the new urban *comprador* bourgeoisie, wealthy traders and dealers, private industrialists, army officers, and the state bureaucracy were strengthened.

The two decades of development ushered in, on the one hand, a rapid process of socio-economic structuration, and on the other, the specific logic underlying private accumulation which eventually undermined the 'Algerian socialist transformation'. Not only did private capital – which specialised in parasitic activities downstream of the public sector – succeed in appropriating a major part of the national social surplus value but it also tipped the political balance in its own favour. Indeed, since the death of Boumedienne and the resurgence of the right in the advanced capitalist countries and in the Arab world, a realignment of political forces along ideological and class lines has been set in motion within Algeria.

Despite Boumedienne's insistence that he would 'never leave behind an Algerian Sadat', the post-Boumedienne regime changed its 'pillars'. It removed the workers, peasants and young people and replaced them with

Conclusion

compradors, middlemen, dealers, contractors, entrepreneurs, private industrialists and all sorts of opportunists in search of rapid enrichment to the detriment of the development of the national economy. The Benjadid regime consolidated the interests of parasitic anti-national and anti-popular class forces represented within the power structure by a political coalition led by obscure former officers of the ALN, who were stationed during the war in Tunisia. This alliance of conservative social forces consists of partisans and sympathisers of the former Association of the Algerian *ulamah* (financed and supported since its foundation in 1931 by an archaic rural and urban traditionalist bourgeoisie), former Algerian officers of the French army who deserted towards the end of the war from Germany in order to join the external ALN in Tunisia and Morocco, descendents of the wealthy families who collaborated with the colonial power and other disparate opportunistic elements. This situation led one of the surviving leaders of the war of national liberation to tell me that 'There were those who made the revolution, those who were moulded by it, and those who were excreted by it. It is the latter who are in power today.' This is why they have driven the country once more into a historical cul-de-sac.

Indeed, halting the development of the public industrial sector was bound eventually to compromise the economic viability of society and hence the political independence of the new nation. The atomisation of the public companies turned out to be detrimental to the growing Algerian population and yet beneficial to internal *affairistes* and other speculators, as well as to some external multinational firms, especially French, which have always viewed industrialisation in all their former colonies as a serious threat to their interests. In fact, despite its seeming dynamism, the Algerian industrial private sector is still determined by a pre-existing mercantile speculative logic rather than being driven by a productive logic similar to that of mature industrial capital. Today the Algerian economy is being pushed by a coalition of disparate conservative and even archaic class forces through a process of compradorisation which is undermining the dynamics of a genuine national and popular economic and social development, the cornerstone of the independence of a free, prosperous and democratic society. However, in the absence of an enterprising national industrial bourgeoisie, a modernising, dynamic middle class and a powerful, skilled and experienced working class, such a strongly desired genuine national development cannot take place, and hence freedom, prosperity for all and democracy cannot be realised in the short term: 'Only from the vantage point of these classes can a plan for the total organisation of society even be imagined.'[2]

The structural characteristics and ideological outlooks of the current Algerian class forces have been determined by the unfolding of historical

Conclusion

evolution shaped by the nature and level of the development of the productive forces. This is an objective reality that cannot be wished away, but which should be analysed, understood and transformed by a continual political struggle.

Notes

Introduction

1 Quoted by O. Cox, *Foundations of Capitalism* (New York, Philosophy Library, 1959), p. 21.
2 Karl Marx, *The Eighteenth Brumaire of Louis Bonaparte* (New York, International Publishers, 1972), p. 120.
3 A. Gunder-Frank, 'Liberal anthropology versus liberation anthropology', in *Latin America: Development or Revolution* (New York, Monthly Review Press, 1969), p. 58.
4 Anthony Smith, *Social Change* (London, Longman, 1976), p. 12.
5 S. Amin, *Développement inégal* (Paris, Minuit, 1973).
6 R. Gallissot, 'L'Algéria précoloniale', in *Sur le féodalisme* (Paris, CERM, 1974).
7 A. Benachenhou, *Formation du sous-développement en Algérie: 1830–1962* (Algiers, OPU, 1976).
8 M. Bennoune, 'The origins of the Algerian proletariat', *Dialectical Anthropology* (1976), 201–24.
9 E. J. Hobsbawm, *The Age of Revolution 1789–1848* (New York, Mentor, 1962), p. 90.
10 S. Amin, *The Maghreb in the Modern World* (Harmondsworth, Penguin, 1970), p. 105.
11 Charte nationale (Algiers, Editions du FLN, 1976), p. 119.
12 Ibid., p. 22.
13 Benaouda Hamel, *Système productif algérien et indépendance nationale* (Algiers, OPU, 1983), vol. 1, p. 106.
14 Charte nationale, p. 121.
15 Ibid., pp. 121–2.

1 Algerian society and economy before 1830

1 'Capitalism' is used here in a positive sense; it is one of the most dynamic and liberating socio-economic systems known in history.
2 Barrington Moore, *Social Origins of Dictatorship and Democracy* (Boston, Beacon, 1966), p. 108.
3 Elinor G. Barber, *The Bourgeoisie in 18th Century France* (Princeton University Press, 1952), pp. 145–6.
4 In 1811 Napoleon ordered Boutin to establish a plan for the military invasion of

Algeria for the purpose of creating a 'French Gibraltar' on the North African coast. This strategic study and military preparation, known as the 'Boutin Plan', was followed in 1830. M. C. Sahli, *Décoloniser l'histoire* (Paris, Maspero, 1965), p. 91.
5 These figures are taken from X. Yacono's 'Apropos d'un grand livre d'histoire de l'Algérie', *La Revue d'histoire moderne et contemporaine*, 11–12 (1964–5), 272–3.
6 Y. Lacoste, A. Nouschi and A. Prenant, *L'Algérie passé et présent* (Paris, Editions Sociales, 1960), p. 152.
7 The so-called Turkish troops in pre-colonial Algeria amounted to an insignificant 3,661. Marcel Emerit, 'Au début du XIXe siècle: Les tribus privilegiées en Algerie', *Annales* (January 1966), 45.
8 Abdellah Laraoui, *L'Histoire du Maghreb* (Paris, Maspero, 1970), p. 240.
9 André Raymond, 'North Africa in the pre-colonial period', *Cambridge History of Islam* (Cambridge University Press, 1970), p. 282.
10 Elbaki Hermassi, *Leadership and National Development in North Africa* (Berkeley, University of California Press, 1972), pp. 8–9.
11 David M. Hart, 'The tribe in modern Morocco: two case studies', in *Arabs and Berbers*, ed. Ernest Gellner and Charles Micaud (Lexington Books, 1972), p. 25.
12 Hermassi, pp. 9–10.
13 Ibid., p. 13.
14 Ernest Gellner, 'Saints of the Atlas', in *Peoples and Cultures of the Middle East*, vol. 1, ed. Louise Sweet (Garden City, The Natural History Press, 1970), p. 205.
15 William D. Schorger, 'The evolution of political forms in a North Moroccan village', *Anthropological Quarterly*, 42 (July 1969), 264.
16 Hart, p. 25.
17 Hermassi, p. 13.
18 Quoted by Gallissot in 'Le Système foncier en Algérie au moment de la colonisation française', in *Sur le féodalisme*, (Paris, CERM, 1974), p. 129.
19 Lucette Valensi, *Le Maghreb avant la prise d'Alger, 1770–1830* (Paris, Flammarion, 1969), p. 34.
20 Hermassi, pp. 13–14.
21 Ibn Khaldun, *The Muqadimah*, translated from the Arabic by F. Rosenthal, edited and abridged by N. J. Dawood (Princeton, 1967), p. 91.
22 Hermassi, p. 27.
23 M. Bennoune, 'Socio-economic changes in rural Algeria: 1830–1954', *Peasant Studies Newsletter*, vol. 2, no. 2 (April 1973), 12.
24 Valensi, p. 45.
25 Ibn Khaldun, p. 313.
26 Louis Vignon, *La France dans l'Algérie* (Paris, Hachette, 1887), p. 27.
27 Ministère de la Guerre, *Tableau de la situation des établissements français dans l'Algérie* (Paris, Imprimerie Royale, 1838), p. 256.
28 Ibid., p. 257.
29 *Archives Nationales de France* (hereafter ANF), 80 1805.

Notes to pages 26–38

30 Baron de Berthezène, *Dix-huit mois à Alger* (Montpellier, August Ricard, 1831), p. 200.
31 Louis Massignon, 'Enquête sur les corporations musulmanes et de commerçants au Maroc', *Revue du monde musulman*, tome 58 (1924), p. 70.
32 Ahmed el-Kodsy, 'Nationalism and class struggle in the Arab World', *Monthly Review* (July–August 1970), 11.
33 Ibid., 17.
34 All of these figures are taken from Lacheraf, Julien and Valensi. Lacheraf estimated the population of Oran to be 40,000, but Valensi gave only 9,000 and Julien, 10,000.
35 Augustin Berque, 'La Bourgeoisie algérienne', *Hisperis*, tome XXXV (1948), 5.
36 Valensi, pp. 50–8.
37 Quoted by Régine Pernoud, *Histoire de la bourgeoisie en France* (Paris, Editions de Seuil, 1960), p. 100.
38 Charles Issawi, ed., *The Economic History of the Middle East, 1880–1914* (University of Chicago Press, 1966), p. 35.
39 Ibid., p. 35.
40 Ibid., p. 34.
41 Quoted by Ernest Picard, *La Monnaie et le crédit en Algérie depuis 1830.* (Algiers, 1930), p. 32.
42 ANF 80.
43 Issawi, p. 34.
44 Quoted by Sahli, p. 90.
45 Ibid., p. 94.
46 Ibid., p. 93.

2 The nature of colonialism

1 *ANF*8010.
2 Quoted by H. Brunschwig, in *French Colonialism* (New York, Praeger, 1964), pp. 83–4.
3 Rozet, *Voyage dans le régence d'Alger* (Paris, Arthur Bertrand, 1833), tome 1, pp. 223–4.
4 Quoted in Mostefa Lacheraf, *L'Algérie: Nation et société* (Paris, Maspero, 1965), p. 57.
5 Ibid., p. 57.
6 Berque, 'La Bourgeoisie algérienne', 14.
7 Quoted in Lacheraf, *L'Algérie*, p. 158.
8 Ibid., p. 159.
9 Charles A. Julien, *L'Histoire de l'Algérie contemporaine* (Paris, PUF, 1964), p. 72–3.
10 General Ducrot, *La Vie militaire du General Ducrot, d'Après sa correspondance, 1839–1871* (Paris, Plon, 1895), tome 1, p. 93.
11 Quoted in Lacheraf, *L'Algérie*, p. 166.
12 General Daumas et Fabar, *La Grande Kabylie, Etudes historiques* (Paris, Hachette, 1847), p. 115.

Notes to pages 38-46

13 M. Poujoulat, *Etudes Africaines* (Paris, Hivert, 1847), pp. 219-20.
14 Maurice Wahl, *L'Algérie* (Paris, Alcan, 1903), p. 135.
15 Poujoulat, *Etudes*, p. 43.
16 Quoted in Lacheraf, *L'Algérie*, pp. 170-1.
17 Duc d'Orleans, *Récits de Campagne* (Paris, Calmann Levy, 1892), pp. 139-40.
18 Camille Rousset, *L'Algérie de 1830 à 1840* (Paris, Plon, 1900), tome second, pp. 53-4.
19 J. Ch. M. Boudin, *Histoire statistique de la colonisation en Algérie* (Paris, Bailliers, 1853), p. 53.
20 *Résultats statistiques du dénombrement de la population* (Alger, 1954), p. XIX.
21 All cited in Bennoune, 'Socio-economic changes', 14-15.
22 Quoted by Charles H. Favord, *Le FLN et l'Algérie* (Paris, Plon, 1962), p. 31.
23 Quoted in Julien, *L'Histoire*, p. 316.
24 Ibid., p. 316.
25 Quoted ibid., p. 320.
26 Ibid., p. 320.
27 Quoted ibid., p. 320.
28 Saint Arnaud, quoted ibid., p. 320.
29 Benachenhou, *Formation du sous-développement*, pp. 90-1.
30 Ibid., pp. 90-1.
31 John Ruedy, *Land Policy in Colonial Algeria* (University of California Press, 1967), p. 101.
32 Quoted by Michel Launay, *Les Paysans algériens* (Paris, Le Seuil, 1962), p. 126.
33 Ruedy, *Land Policy*, p. 35.
34 ANF80 524. As a result, between 1863 and 1938, in northern Algeria alone, 707 tribes were delimited and broken up into 1,196 *douars*. By 1956, out of a total of 801 tribes, only eight had not yet been broken up; one in the Province of Algiers and seven in the Province of Oran.
35 H. E. L. Brenot, *Le Douar: Cellule administrative de l'Algérie du Nord* (Alger, Victor Heintz, 1938), p. 24.
36 Quoted ibid., p. 22.
37 Quoted by P. Bourdieu and A. Sayad, *Le Déracinement* (Paris, Minuit, 1964), p. 16.
38 Quoted in Charles A. Ageron, *Histoire de l'Algérie contemporaine* (Paris, PUF, 1964), pp. 37-8.
39 Quoted in M. C. Sahli, *Décoloniser l'histoire* (Paris, Maspero, 1965), p. 44.
40 E. Wolf, *Peasant Wars of the Twentieth Century* (New York, Harper & Row, 1969), p. 213.
41 Le Capitaine Vassière, *Les Ould Rechaich* (Alger, N. A., 1863), p. 90.
42 Quoted in A. Nouschi, *Enquête sur le niveau de vie des populations rurales constantinoises de la conquête jusqu'en 1919* (Paris, PUF, 1968), p. 97.
43 Ch. A. Ageron, *Les Algériens musulmans et la France: 1871-1919* (Paris, PUF, 1968), vol. 1, p. 97.
44 Hermassi, *Leadership and National Development*, p. 22.
45 Ageron, *Les Algériens musulmans*, vol. 1, pp. 87, 90.
46 Ibid., p. 94.

Notes to pages 46–71

47 *El Montekheb* (A French language newspaper published in Constantine) (2 May 1882).
48 Ageron, *Les Algériens musulmans*, vol. 2, p. 740.
49 Ibid., p. 740.
50 Sahli, *Décoloniser l'histoire*, pp. 121–2.
51 Benachenhou, *Formation du sous-développement*, p. 194.
52 T. Tidafi, *L'Agriculture algérienne et ses perspectives de développement* (Paris, Maspero, 1969), p. 26.
53 Ageron, *Politiques coloniales au Maghreb* (Paris, PUF, 1972), p. 235.

3 Colonial development, population and manpower

1 L. Vignon, *La France dans l'Algérie* (Paris, Hachette et Cie, 1887), pp. 98–9.
2 P. Gaffarel, *L'Algérie: Histoire, conquête et colonisation* (Paris, 1933), p. 48.
3 Quoted in Ageron, *Les Algériens musulmans*, vol. 1, p. 548.
4 Ibid., p. 548.
5 C. Clark, 'Economic and social implications of population control', in *Population Control*, ed. A. Allison (New York, Penguin, 1970), p. 225.
6 H. Coontz, *Population and the Economic Interpretation* (London, Routledge & Kegan Paul, 1957), p. 192.
7 Ibid., p. 192.
8 *ANF* 80 443.
9 Ibid., 443.
10 Ibid., 443.
11 Ibid., 443.
12 Ibid., 443.
13 Ibid., 443.
14 Quoted in Ruedy, *Land Policy*, pp. 88–9.
15 Ageron, *Les Algériens musulmans*, p. 31.
16 G. Tillion, *Algeria* (New York, A. Knopf, 1958), p. 33.

4 Socio-economic consequences of colonial development

1 Ageron, *Histoire de l'Algérie*, p. 80.
2 Benachenhou, *Formation du sous-développement*, p. 305.
3 Berque, 'La Bourgeoisie algérienne', 12.
4 Massignon, 'Enquête', 184.
5 M. M. Chabbi, *La Turaja bal khatwat il al-mam* (Beirut, Al-Mussa il al arabiyah, Dirassat oua Nashr, 1971), p. 17.
6 R. Lespen, *Alger* (Paris, Alcan, 1930), pp. 754–5.
7 *Tableaux de l'économie algérienne* (Algiers, 1960), pp. 22, 31.
8 Guy Perville, 'Le Sentiment national des étudiants Algériens de langue française de 1912 a 1962', *Relations Internationales* (1974, no. 2), 234.
9 *Tableaux de l'économie Algérienne*, p. 31.
10 A. Nouschi, *La Naissance du nationalisme Algérien* (Paris, Minuit, 1962), p. 102.
11 Quoted ibid.

Notes to pages 73–92

12 *Rapport général du Plan de Constantine*, p. 29.
13 Robert Descoitres et al., *L'Algérie des Bidonvilles* (Paris, Mouton, 1961), pp. 86, 112.
14 Ageron, *Les Algériens musulmans*, vol. 2, p. 848.
15 V. Demontes, *L'Algérie économique*, (1930), vol. 5, p. 387.
16 St Germes, 'L'Industrialisation de l'Algérie', in *Industrialisation de l'Afrique du Nord* (1952), p. 39.
17 Gouvernement Général, *Perspectives décennales du developpement en Algérie* (March 1958), p. 55.
18 M. Trebous, *Migration and Development: The Case of Algeria* (Paris, Development Centre of the OELD, 1970), pp. 56, 154.
19 Le Chao-King, *Les Travailleurs coloniaux en France* (Paris, PUF, 1939), p. 29.
20 Ibid., p. 29.
21 British Naval Intelligence, *Handbook Area Guide: Algeria* (1944), p. 45.
22 J. Augarde, 'La Migration Algeriénne', *Hommes et Migrations*, no. 116 (1970), 15.
23 André Michel, *Les Travailleurs algériens en France* (Paris, CNRS, 1956), p. 219.
24 R. Benattig, *Politique économique de l'état et évolution de la situation de l'emploi et des revenus en milieu rural (L'Algérie, 1962–1979)*, Thèse du 3e Cycle (Paris VII, November 1980).
25 Michael K. Clark, *Algeria in Turmoil* (New York, Praeger, 1959), pp. 20–1.

5 The aftermath of the war of national liberation

1 It is worth noting that of the innumerable, if not all the urban women and teenage girls who occupied the streets, without asking men's permission, on this memorable day, none bothered to shroud herself in the customary *haik* or veil.
2 This official figure may be too high; according to some unofficial estimates, the number of dead may run to between 400,000 and 700,000.
3 *Statistiques officielles*, published in the Charter of Algiers by the post-war FLN party (Algiers, 1964); quoted by M. Dahmani, *L'Algérie: Légitimité historique et continuité politique* (Paris, Le Sycomore, 1979), p. 23.
4 Europa Publications, 'Algeria', in *The Middle East and North Africa* (London, 1971–2), p. 152.
5 Samir Amin, *The Maghreb in the Modern World: Algeria, Tunisia, Morocco*, trans. from the French by M. Perl (London, Penguin, 1970), pp. 60–87.
6 *L'Agriculture algérienne*, Special Issue entitled *Le Développement africain* (Paris, October 1961), p. 143.
7 Gouvernement Général, *Rapport général du Plan de Constantine* (Algiers, 1960), p. 25.
8 *Statistiques générales de l'Algérie, Tableaux de L'économie algérienne* (1960), pp. 61.
9 Délégation Générale du Gouvernement en Algérie, Direction du plan et des études économiques, *Plan de Constantine 1959–63*, Rapport Général, p. 71.
10 *Tableaux de l'économie algérienne* (1960), pp. 142, 144.
11 Externally orientated and determined.

Notes to pages 93-188

12 P. Bourdieu and A. Said, *Le Déracinement* (Paris, Minuit, 1964), pp. 21-2.
13 I. Clegg, *Workers' Self-Management in Algeria* (New York, Monthly Review Press, 1969), p. 110.
14 André Tiano, *Le Maghreb entre les mythes* (Paris, PUF, 1967), p. 601.
15 Secretariat d'Etat au Plan, *Comptes économiques 1963-1973* (Algiers).
16 Ministère du Travail et des Affaires Sociales, *Evolution des problèmes de l'emploi en Algérie* (Algiers, May 1976).
17 J. Chnetzler, *Le Développement algérien* (Paris, Masson, 1981), p. 79.

6 Industrialisation as the motor of development

1 UNIDO, *World Industry since 1960: Progress and Prospects* (New York, 1979), E 70, 11B3.
2 Source not cited.
3 S. Amin, *Unequal Development* (New York, Monthly Review Press, 1976), pp. 59-60.
4 O. Cox, *Capitalism as a System* (New York Monthly Review Press, 1964), p. 18.
5 Ibid.
6 Quoted by G. Glezerman, *Socialist Society: Scientific Principles of Development* (Moscow, Progress Publishers, 1971), p. 17.
7 For a comprehensive treatment of this topic, see P. Sweezy, *The Theory of Capitalist Development* (New York, Monthly Review Press, 1968), pp. 25-95, 152-69; and P. C. Gregory and R. C. Stuart, *Soviet Economic Structure and Performance* (New York, Harper and Row, 1981), pp. 68-9.
8 Gregory and Stuart, *Soviet Economic Structure*, p. 73.
9 Quoted in A. Erlich, *The Soviet Industrialization Debate 1924-1928* (Cambridge, Mass., Harvard University Press, 1960), p. 35.
10 Quoted by Gregory and Stuart, *Soviet Economic Structure*, p. 72.
11 Ibid., p. 75.
12 Ibid., p. 75.
13 Ibid., p. 83.
14 See Dahmani, *L'Algérie*, p. 40.
15 A. Benachenhou, *Planification et développement en Algérie: 1962-80* (Algiers, 1980).
16 Dahmani, *L'Algérie*.

8 Agriculture: the stagnation of production and its consequences

1 Ministère de l'Agriculture et de la Révolution Agraire (MARA), *Recensement général de l'agriculture*, 1972/73.
2 Hamid M. Temmar, *Stratégie de développement independant: Le cas de l'Algérie: un bilan* (Paris, Publisud, 1983), pp. 68-9.
3 MARA, *Evolution de l'agriculture de 1967 à 1978*, September 1979.
4 Secretariat d'Etat au Plan, *Directives pour les études socio-economiques par zone sur l'agriculture*, Annexe III, 'A l'enquête socio-economique sur le Oued Rhir', tome IV; and AARDES, *Systèmes de production et Révolution Agraire*, Algiers,

December 1974); and AARDES, *Etude sur le secteur privé agricole, Wilaya de Tlemcen.*
5 MARA, *Résultats de l'analyse de l'enquête main-d'oeuvre dans le secteur privé* (1968), p. 17.
6 *Charte de la Révolution agraire*, Présidence du Conseil (undated), Imprimerie Officiel, p. 24.
7 MPAT, *Synthèse du bilan* (Roneotype), Annexe 1–4, p. 10.
8 MARA, *L'Evolution de l'agriculture* (Roneotype), p. 11, Tableau 2.
9 MARA, *Statistique agricole*, Series A and B (several issues).
10 MPAT, *Synthèse du bilan.*
11 This study was entitled 'Bilan et perspectives à propos des acquisitions de terrains pour l'implantation des projets industriels relevant de l'ensemble du secteur industrie et enérgie pour la periode 1962–1980'; it was completed in December 1978.
12 MARA, *Statistique agricole*, Series B, several issues.
13 Temmar, *Stratégie de développement indépendant*, p. 84.
14 MARA, *Plan quadriennal, 1970–73, Rapport sur le secteur agricole* (1970), p. 89.
15 Slimane Bedrani, *L'Agriculture algérienne depuis 1966* (Algiers, Office des Publications Universitaires, 1981).
16 MARA, *Statistique agricole*, Series A and B, several issues covering this period. These figures were utilised to justify official expenditures. Therefore this did not imply that all the 155,000 hectares were actually completed.
17 Claudine Chaulet, *La Mitidja autogérée* (Algiers, SNED, 1971), p. 206.
18 *Statistique agricole*, no. 20 (1978), 133.
19 *Projet du Premier Plan du Développement*, Livre IV, fascicule III, vol. I (February 1967).
20 Vera Benslah, *La Productivité des cadres agricoles: Le Rôle joué par la formation professionnelle* (CREA, 1983).
21 Bedrani, *L'Agriculture algérienne*, p. 139.

9 Education and development

1 Marx, *Theses of Feuerbach.*

Conclusion

1 A. El-Kenz, 'La Fin du populisme', paper delivered at the conference 'The social impact and responses to the economic crisis in Africa', organised by the CODESIRA, Dakar, 21–3 July 1986.
2 G. Lukacs, *History and Class Consciousness* (Cambridge, Mass., MIT Press, 1968), p. 50.

Index

Arabic names with the prefixes Ben and Ibn have been indexed under these prefixes.

AARDES (Association Algérienne de Recherches Démographiques, Economiques et Sociales), 239, 240, 241, 257, 318, 319
Abbas, Ferhat, 98
Abdelkader, El Emir, 38, 39
Abdesslam, Belaid, 121, 122, 124
Ageron, Charles Robert, 47, 60, 61, 67, 315, 316, 317
Agrarian revolution, 105, 176, 178, 179, 185, 188, 193, 198, 201, 206, 212, 237, 242, 282, 307
Agricultural co-operatives (CAPRA, CAPCS), 95, 107, 176, 185, 191, 192, 193, 200, 282, 283
Agriculture, 6, 7, 58, 63, 64–6, 70, 73, 91, 95, 99, 100, 103, 105, 107, 110, 112, 117–20, 122, 124–6, 129, 130, 137, 145, 154, 159, 160, 172, 176, 177–9, 181–3, 187, 189, 193–5, 197, 198, 200, 205, 206, 208–11, 217, 241–3, 252–7, 266, 271, 277–9, 282, 283, 286, 287, 291, 292, 297–9, 301, 306–9, 318
Ait Ahmed, Hocine, 84
Ait Amara, Hamid, 259
Algerian Board of Cereal Imports (OAIC), 100, 107
Algerian Board of Fruit and Vegetables (OFLA), 183, 184, 185, 193
Algerian Communist Party (PCA), 82, 85, 190

Algerian National Assembly, 98, 99, 110, 111
Algerian Popular Party (PPA), 4, 7, 73, 80, 81, 121, 130, 135, 303
Amin, Samir, 2, 3, 62, 70, 312, 317, 318
Army, French, 2, 3, 21, 39, 40, 43, 56, 77, 84, 85, 95, 120, 310
Association of the Algerian Ulamah, 81–2, 85, 96, 236, 307, 310

Barber, Elinor, 16, 312
Bedrani, Slimane, 197, 319
Benachenhou, Abdelatif, 2, 48, 49, 64, 66, 71, 78, 312, 315, 316, 318
Ben Bella, Ahmed, 5, 84, 95, 97, 98, 99, 102, 108, 109, 110, 111, 164, 249, 306
Ben Boulaid, Mustapha, 83, 84
Ben Chérif, Ahmed, 138, 205
Benjadid, Chadli, 81, 97, 137, 150, 158, 175, 205, 250, 251, 261, 262, 265, 273, 276, 277, 283, 284, 285, 298, 299, 301, 303, 310
Ben M'Hidi, Larbi, 84
Bentobal, Lakhdar, 84, 96
Ben Yahia, Mohammed, 125
Bitat, Rabah, 83, 84
Boudiaf, Mohammed, 83
Boudin, J. Ch., 42, 43, 315
Boumedienne, Houari, 5, 7–9, 97, 98, 103, 121, 122–4, 127–9, 131–6, 138, 147, 153, 159, 160, 166, 180,

320

Index

188, 190, 204, 211, 234, 236, 237, 243, 249, 250, 260, 262, 263, 271, 273, 277, 284, 300, 303, 304, 306, 307, 309
Bourdieu, Pierre, 93, 315, 318
Boussouf, Abdelhafid, 84, 96
Bouteflika, Abdelaziz, 262
Brahimi, Abdelhamid, 160, 277
Bugeaud, Marshall, 40, 41, 57
Bukharin, Nikolai, 117

Capitalism, 3, 4, 7, 15, 116, 118, 271, 305, 312
CCE (executive committee of coordination and implementation), 84
Central committee, FLN Party, 111, 267
Central committee MTLD, 80–3
CNRA (National Council of the Algerian Revolution), 84, 95
Colonialism, French, 2, 36, 39, 56, 58, 76, 77, 89, 90, 94, 95
Colonisation, French, 2, 4, 28, 29, 35, 39, 40, 42, 46, 48, 50–3, 55–9, 61, 69, 77, 82, 91, 92, 114, 163, 180, 185, 305
Compradorisation of the economy and society, 160, 250, 261, 284, 301, 310
Compradors, 96, 121, 122, 125–33, 142, 160, 162, 163, 175, 190, 205, 239, 268, 270, 273, 283, 304, 309, 310
Cultural revolution, 235, 236, 307

Democratic Union of the Algerian Manifesto (UDMA), 82, 85, 91
Didouche, Mourad, 83, 84

Education, 28, 66–8, 76, 79, 99, 130, 139, 189, 218–36, 278, 287, 289–92, 301, 306, 319
Expropriation of land, 24, 39, 43, 47–9, 52, 58, 60, 94, 176, 190, 242, 283

Factories, 71, 77, 90, 97, 98, 100, 102, 111, 143, 145, 147, 153, 157

Gallissot, René, 2, 50, 313
Gaulle, Charles de, 73, 91
Gellner, Ernest, 20, 313
General Union of Algerian Workers (UGTA), 97, 102, 104, 107, 123, 139, 140, 142, 306, 307
Ghozali, Ahmed, 137
Gunder-Frank, André, 1, 312

Hamel, Benaouda, 7, 312
Hermassi, Elbaki, 19, 20, 23, 45, 313, 315
Hydrocarbons, 72, 91, 98–101, 103, 111, 121–3, 125–7, 129, 131, 135–8, 142, 143, 145, 151, 152, 154, 160, 172, 203, 205, 228, 253, 278, 279, 281, 282, 294, 298, 299

Ibn Khaldun, Abdul Rahman, 22, 241, 313
Imperialism, 114, 132
Industrial complexes, 122, 135, 145, 150, 153, 156, 157, 302
Industrial revolution, 114, 189, 309
Industrialisation, 6, 8–10, 15, 69–74, 79, 91, 95, 109, 111–23, 125–35, 137, 140–2, 145, 147, 149, 154, 159–62, 164–6, 172, 174, 189, 197, 202, 209, 211–12, 217, 218, 224, 229, 231, 232, 236, 237, 243, 262–4, 266, 270, 272–7, 285–7, 291, 298, 299, 301, 302, 304, 307, 310, 318
Industry, 6, 9, 15, 36, 70–3, 77, 91, 103, 111, 117–22, 124–32, 138, 142–4, 147, 154, 156, 157, 159, 160, 164, 166, 167, 172, 173, 178, 181, 189, 197, 203, 205, 208, 212, 231–4, 239, 242, 253, 256, 266, 267, 269, 271, 272, 275, 277–9, 281, 286, 287, 291, 292, 299, 301, 302, 307

Khider, Mohammed, 84
Krim, Belkacem, 83, 84, 96

Index

Lacheraf, Mustapha, 314, 315
Lacoste, Robert, 92, 104
Land tenure (Pre-colonial), 24-6
Lenin, V. I., 116, 117

Marx, K., 22, 117, 312, 319
Mechanisation, 61, 65, 66, 69, 181, 188, 195, 198, 297
Messali, Hadj, 83
Ministry of Agriculture and Agrarian Reform (MARA), 105, 106, 130, 180, 181, 183-6, 192, 194-6, 198-204, 206-10, 217, 232, 318, 319
Ministry of Finance, 128, 129, 131, 185
Ministry of Industry and Energy (MIE), 122-5, 127-35, 147, 204, 232, 233, 272
Ministry of Planning and Territorial Reorganisation (MPAT), 132, 135, 142, 143, 146, 148, 152, 194, 200, 212, 213, 215-17, 225, 226, 233, 248, 253, 255, 256, 258, 263-5, 277, 279-83, 285-7, 292, 319
Movement for the Triumph of Democratic Liberties (MTLD), 4, 7, 73, 80-3, 125, 130, 135, 303

National Board of Agrarian Reform (ONRA), 105-7, 183
National charter, 252
Nationalisation, 6, 8, 79, 95, 100, 102, 104, 110, 112, 122, 124-8, 103-34, 151, 172, 191, 303, 306
Nationalism, 4, 7
National Liberation Army (ALN), 4, 5, 7, 73, 81, 83-5, 89, 91, 95-7, 108, 109, 121, 228, 310
National Liberation Front (FLN), 4, 5, 7, 81-2, 83, 84, 85, 89, 94-7, 109, 159, 221, 228, 303
National steel company (SNS), 101, 148, 150, 154-7
North African Star (ENA), 4, 7, 78, 79, 80, 81, 82, 261, 303
Nouschi, André, 61, 70, 313, 315, 316

Party of National Liberation, 94, 95, 102, 111, 122, 139, 140, 142, 160, 169, 188, 243, 263, 267, 284, 293, 294, 299, 304
Peasants, 3, 24, 25, 27, 40, 44, 46, 47, 49, 52, 55, 57, 58, 60, 63, 81, 89, 92, 94, 112, 176, 178, 179, 185, 188, 190, 200, 201, 242, 252, 271
Planning, 95, 99, 124, 125, 128, 129, 131, 132, 151, 157, 159, 160, 178, 187, 194, 200, 218, 219, 232, 233, 238, 242, 243, 250, 254, 262, 263, 268, 269, 278, 279, 294, 298, 299
Populism, 81, 304, 306, 307
Preobrazhensky, 117, 118
Proletarianisation, 3, 4, 36, 57, 59, 60
Provisional government of the Algerian Republic (GPRA), 5, 84, 96-8, 108, 109

Rinn, Louis, 17, 18

Said, Abdelmalik, 93, 315, 318
Schorger, William, 20, 313
Sénatus-consulte (Law of 1863), 44, 45, 47
Settlers' paramilitary organisation (OAS), 90
Shaller, William, 17
Socialism, Algerian, 85, 116, 119, 138, 140, 166, 252, 271, 304, 306, 307
Socialist management of enterprises (GSE), 123, 138, 139-41
SONACOME (Algerian mechanical company), 148, 157, 158
SONAREM (mining company), 148, 149, 150
SONATRACH (Algerian oil company), 100, 101, 110, 122, 123, 126, 127, 130, 131, 136, 138, 148-54, 281, 282, 300
Special organisation (OS), 80-3

Technology, 102, 114, 115, 117, 118,

121, 145, 156, 173, 199, 223, 229, 230, 236, 250, 270, 272, 274, 275, 289, 298
Temmar, Hamid, 203, 207, 318
Tractors, 71, 102, 105, 157, 184, 187, 195, 198–200, 283
Tribes, 18–23, 25, 44, 46, 315

Wolf, Eric, 44, 315
Worker's self-management, 5, 97, 99, 100, 102–8, 110, 123, 124, 176, 182–4, 190, 193, 197–201, 203, 206, 212, 242, 282, 306, 309, 318

Yahiaoui, Mohammed, 262

For EU product safety concerns, contact us at Calle de José Abascal, 56–1°,
28003 Madrid, Spain or eugpsr@cambridge.org.

www.ingramcontent.com/pod-product-compliance
Lightning Source LLC
LaVergne TN
LVHW040732250326
834688LV00031B/260